2018

D0216335

DISCARDED
From the Nashville Public
Library

Property of
The Public Library of Nashville and Davidson County
225 Polk Ave., Nashville, Tn. 37203

Imitation of Life

Rutgers Films in Print

Charles Affron, Mirella Jona Affron, and Robert Lyons, editors

My Darling Clementine, John Ford, director
edited by Robert Lyons

The Last Metro, François Truffaut, director
edited by Mirella Jona Affron and E. Rubinstein

Touch of Evil, Orson Welles, director
edited by Terry Comito

The Marriage of Maria Braun, Rainer Werner Fassbinder, director
edited by Joyce Rheuban

Letter from an Unknown Woman, Max Ophuls, director
edited by Virginia Wright Wexman with Karen Hollinger

Rashomon, Akira Kurosawa, director
edited by Donald Richie

8 1/2, Federico Fellini, director
edited by Charles Affron

La Strada, Federico Fellini, director
edited by Peter Bondanella and Manuela Gieri

Breathless, Jean-Luc Godard, director
edited by Dudley Andrew

Bringing Up Baby, Howard Hawks, director
edited by Gerald Mast

Chimes at Midnight, Orson Welles, director
edited by Bridget Gellert Lyons

L'avventura, Michelangelo Antonioni, director
edited by Seymour Chatman and Guido Fink

Meet John Doe, Frank Capra, director
edited by Charles Wolfe

Invasion of the Body Snatchers, Don Siegel, director
edited by Al LaValley

Memories of Underdevelopment, Tomás Gutiérrez Alea, director
introduction by Michael Chanan

Imitation of Life, Douglas Sirk, director
edited by Lucy Fischer

Imitation of Life

Douglas Sirk

director

Lucy Fischer, editor

Rutgers University Press

New Brunswick, New Jersey

Imitation of Life is volume 16 in the Rutgers Films in Print series

Copyright © 1991 by Rutgers, The State University
All Rights Reserved
Manufactured in the United States of America

Library of Congress Cataloging-in-Publication Data

Imitation of life / Douglas Sirk, director ; Lucy Fischer, editor.

    p.   cm. — (Rutgers films in print ; v. 16)

    Includes bibliographical references (p.

    Filmography: p.

    ISBN 0-8135-1644-7 (cloth)

    ISBN 0-8135-1645-5 (pbk.)

1. Imitation of life (Motion picture) 2. Sirk, Douglas, 1900–1987. 3. Hurst, Fannie, 1889–1968—Film and video adaptations. I. Sirk, Douglas, 1900–1987. II. Fischer, Lucy. III. Imitation of life (Motion picture)

PN1997.I4553145   1991

791.43′72—dc20   90-8979

                                  CIP

British Cataloging-in-Publication information available

The continuity script is based on the film, *Imitation of Life,* copyright © 1959 by Universal Pictures, a division of Universal City Studios, Inc. Courtesy of MCA Publishing Rights, a division of MCA Inc.

Stills on pages 33, 55, 70, 71, 74, 78, 85, 99, 115, 131, 135, 137 courtesy of the Museum of Modern Art/Film Stills Archive.

Excerpts from Fannie Hurst's *Imitation of Life* (New York: Collier & Son, 1933) reprinted by permission of Brandeis University and Washington University. Fannie Hurst, "Zora Neale Hurston: A Personality Sketch," *Yale University Library Gazette* 35 (1961), reprinted by permission of the *Yale University Library Gazette.* Zora Neale Hurston, "Two Women in Particular," from *Dust Tracks on the Road* (Philadelphia: J.B. Lippincott, 1942), copyright © 1942 by Zora Neale Hurston; reprinted by permission of Harper & Row, Publishers, Inc.

"Imitation of Life: Production Notes," copyright © 1959 by Universal Pictures, a division of Universal City Studios, Inc. Courtesy of MCA Publishing Rights, a division of MCA Inc. Richard Dyer, "Four Films of Lana Turner," *Movie* 25 (Winter 1977–78), reprinted by permission of the author. Charles Affron, "Performing Performing: Irony and Affect," *Cinema Journal* 20, no. 1 (Fall 1980), copyright © 1980 by the Board of Trustees of the University of Illinois, reprinted by permission. "The Bad and the Beautiful," *Time* 71 (21 April 1958), copyright © 1958 by Time, Inc., reprinted by permission.

James Harvey, "Sirkumstantial Evidence," *Film Comment* 14 (July/August 1978), reprinted by permission of the author. Jon Halliday, excerpts from *Sirk on Sirk* (New York: Viking, 1972), reprinted by permission of Martin Secker & Warburg Limited.

"New Films," *Cue* (18 April 1959), copyright © 1988 by *Cue* Magazine, reprinted by permission of *New York* Magazine. Paul V. Beckley, "Imitation of Life," *New York Herald Tribune* (18 April 1959), reprinted by permission of the I.H.T. Corporation. Bosley Crowther, "Screen: Sob Story Back," *New York Times* (18 April 1959), copyright © 1959 by The New York Times Company, reprinted by permission. "Imitation of Life," *Time* (11 May 1959), copyright © 1959 by Time, Inc., reprinted by permission. Rainer Werner Fassbinder, "Imitation of Life" from "Six Films by Douglas Sirk," trans. Thomas Elsaesser, in *Douglas Sirk,* ed. Laura Mulvey and Jon Halliday (Edinburgh: Edinburgh Film Festival, 1972). Translation copyright © 1972 by Thomas Elsaesser, reprinted by permission.

Fred Camper, "The Films of Douglas Sirk," *Screen* 12, no. 2 (Summer 1971), copyright © 1971 by Fred Camper. Paul Willemen, "Distanciation and Douglas Sirk," *Screen* 12, no. 2 (1971), copyright © 1971 by Paul Willemen. Paul Willemen, "Towards an Analysis of the Sirkian System," *Screen* 13, no. 4 (1972–73), copyright © 1972 by Paul Willemen. Michael Stern, "Imitation of Life," in *Douglas Sirk* (Boston: Twayne, 1979), copyright © 1979 by Michael Stern, reprinted by permission of Twayne Publishers, a division of G. K. Hall & Co., Boston. Jeremy G. Butler, "*Imitation of Life* (1934 and 1959): Style and the Domestic Melodrama," *Jump Cut* no. 32 (April 1986), reprinted by permission of *Jump Cut* and the author. Marina Heung, "What's the Matter with Sara Jane?: Daughters and Mothers in Douglas Sirk's *Imitation of Life,*" *Cinema Journal* 26, no. 3 (Spring 1987), copyright © 1987 by the Board of Trustees of the University of Illinois, reprinted by permission. Sandy Flitterman-Lewis, "Imitation(s) of Life: The Black Woman's Double Determination as Troubling 'Other,'" *Literature and Psychology* 35, no. 4 (1988), reprinted by permission.

FOR MARK, WHO MAKES THIS IMITATION
OF LIFE DECIDEDLY REAL

Acknowledgments

There are many individuals I wish to thank for their assistance on this project. As always, I have found great support from my colleagues at the University of Pittsburgh. Marcia Landy graciously read several drafts of the introductory essay and made many useful suggestions for revision. Dana Polan was a fund of information on relevant texts to consult for my research, and generously read a version of the introduction. Jim Knapp and Robert Hinman (as directors of graduate study in the Department of English) granted me research assistance in the form of several highly capable graduate students: Cynthia Guise, Leasa Burton, Bethany Ogdon, and Mary Savanick. I am indebted to them as well as to John Champagne, who helped check my continuity script. I was also assisted by several University of Pittsburgh Faculty Research Grants, which helped absorb the cost of permissions and frame enlargements. For the latter, I would also like to credit Jeff Cepull of the University Center for Instructional Resources. Support from the chair of the English Department, Phil Smith, allowed me time for work on the book.

I would like to thank the editor of this series, Leslie Mitchener, for her supreme patience in seeing this project to completion. I would also like to thank the Doheny Library of the University of Southern California, The Museum of Modern Art Film Study Center (and Charles Silver), and the Museum of Modern Art Film Stills Archive (and Mary Corliss).

If truth be told, work on a book always takes a toll on one's personal life. I would like to express my gratitude to my husband, Mark, and to my son, David, for understanding that, and understanding me, and understanding how I need to do it all.

Contents

Introduction

    Three-Way Mirror: *Imitation of Life* / 3
    Lucy Fischer

    Douglas Sirk: A Biographical Sketch / 29

Imitation of Life

    Credits and Cast / 41

    The Continuity Script / 43

Contexts

Source

    Excerpts from *Imitation of Life* / 161
    Fannie Hurst

    Zora Hurston: A Personality Sketch / 173
    Fannie Hurst

    Two Women in Particular / 177
    Zora Neale Hurston

The Production/ The Star

    Imitation of Life: Production Notes / 183

Four Films of Lana Turner / 186
Richard Dyer

Performing Performing: Irony and Affect / 207
Charles Affron

The Bad & the Beautiful / 216

The Director: Interviews

    Sirkumstantial Evidence / 221
    James Harvey

    Sirk on Sirk / 226
    Jon Halliday

Reviews and Commentaries

Reviews

    Cue / 237

    New York Herald Tribune / 239
    Paul V. Beckley

    New York Times / 241
    Bosley Crowther

    Time / 243

    Six Films by Douglas Sirk / 244
    Rainer Werner Fassbinder

Commentaries

    The Films of Douglas Sirk / 251
    Fred Camper

Distanciation and Douglas
Sirk / 268
Paul Willemen

Towards an Analysis of the Sirkian
System / 273
Paul Willemen

Imitation of Life / 279
Michael Stern

Imitation of Life (1934 and 1959):
Style and the Domestic
Melodrama / 289
Jeremy G. Butler

"What's the Matter with Sarah
Jane?": Daughters and Mothers in
Douglas Sirk's *Imitation of
Life* / 302
Marina Heung

Imitation(s) *of Life:* The Black
Woman's Double Determination as
Troubling "Other" / 325
Sandy Flitterman-Lewis

Filmography and Bibliography

Sirk Filmography, 1934–
1959 / 339

Selected Bibliography / 343

Introduction

Imitation of Life *is more than just a good title, it is a wonderful title. I would have made the picture just for the title, because it is all there."*

—Douglas Sirk

Three-Way Mirror: *Imitation of Life*

Lucy Fischer

Introduction: Magnificent Obsession

*The most important tool of my trade was a mirror. I always had a three-way
full-length mirror placed outside my trailer door so that I could check my
appearance before I went on the set.*

—Lana Turner

*The mirror is the imitation of life. What is interesting about a mirror is that it
does not show yourself as you are, it shows you your own opposite.*

—Douglas Sirk

It seems safe to say (some thirty years after its release), that *Imitation of
Life* (1959) is a text that fascinates us—that constitutes a Magnificent Obsession. Although Sirk scholarship of the seventies failed to privilege the film,
the eighties addressed it with compensatory preoccupation.[1] Thus, analyses of

1. *Magnificent Obsession* (1954) is a film directed by Douglas Sirk. The following describes some of
the work on Sirk in the 1970s that impinged on *Imitation*. In 1972, Mike Prokosh published "*Imitation of Life*" in the volume *Douglas Sirk*, edited by Laura Mulvey and Jon Halliday (Edinburgh:
Edinburgh Film Festival, 1972), pp. 89–93. In that same volume, Rainer Werner Fassbinder ("Six
Films by Douglas Sirk," pp. 95–107) and Paul Willemen ("Distanciation and Douglas Sirk," pp. 23–
29) described the "Sirkian system," noting *Imitation* in passing. Halliday also transcribed an extended interview with the director that situated *Imitation* within his career. Various journal articles
appeared that cited *Imitation:* Fred Camper, "The Films of Douglas Sirk," *Screen* 12, no. 2 (Summer
1971): 44–62; James McCourt, "Douglas Sirk: Melo Maestro," *Film Comment* 11 (November–
December 1975): 18–21; Steve Neale, "Douglas Sirk," *Framework,* no. 5 (Winter 1977): 16–18;
Laura Mulvey, "Notes on Sirk and Melodrama," *Movie* 25 (Winter 1977/78), rpt. in *Home Is Where
the Heart Is: Studies in Melodrama and the Woman's Film,* ed. Christine Gledhill (London: British
Film Institute, 1987). In 1979, Michael Stern published a second study of the cinéaste with a section
on *Imitation* (*Douglas Sirk* [Boston: Twayne]).

Imitation appeared by Charles Affron (1980), Eithne Bourget (1980), T. Pulleine (1981), V. Amiel (1982), Jacqueline Nacache (1982), Jacques Valot (1982), Peter Ruedi (1983), Jackie Byars (1983), Jean-Loup Bourget (1984), Yann Tobin (1984), Jeremy Butler (1986), Marina Heung (1987), Michael Selig (1988), Sandy Flitterman-Lewis (1988), and Lauren Berlant (1989).[2] Several are included in the Commentaries section of this volume.

Given such collective captivation, we are urged to fathom the critical phenomenon. Why has *Imitation* haunted us? Why has it resurfaced like an academic *idée fixe?* Put simply, *Imitation* compels us because it marks the intersection of numerous powerful cultural forces that define the postwar era and the place of cinema within it.

Some of these factors involve the history of the film. *Imitation* was released during the decline of the classical cinema and the birth of the modernist movement. On the American scene, the era saw the creation of such radical works as Orson Welles's *Touch of Evil* (1958) that pushed traditional film to its limits. (Sirk recalls its being shot on a contiguous sound stage to *Tarnished Angels.*)[3] On the international front, 1959 heralded the inception of the French New Wave— the debut of Jean-Luc Godard's *Breathless,* François Truffaut's *The Four Hundred Blows,* and Alain Resnais's *Hiroshima Mon Amour. Imitation,* with its exaggerated generic codes, embraced the art film's ironic stance toward transparent style. As Sirk's last Hollywood work, it assumed iconic status.

Imitation was also a star vehicle—a "comeback" for Lana Turner, a glamour queen whose personal and professional life was in crisis. The film was a box-office smash, investing it with the imprimatur of commercial success. Furthermore, it gained referential resonance as a Hollywood remake of a film shot by John Stahl in 1934.

The appeal of *Imitation* is also linked to the trajectory of film scholarship. The

2. Charles Affron, "Performing Performing: Irony and Affect," *Cinema Journal* 20, no. 1 (Fall 1980): 42–52; Eithne Bourget, "Une surface de verre," *Positif,* no. 229 (April 1980): 54–55; T. Pulleine, "*Imitation of Life*," *Monthly Film Bulletin* 48, no. 574 (November 1981); V. Amiel, "Quelques leçons à faire pleurer (sur *Mirage de la vie,*)" *Positif,* no. 259 (September 1982): 19–20; Jacqueline Nacache, "Le mirage de la vie," *Cinéma,* no. 282 (June 1982): 96–97; Jacques Valot, "Mirage de la vie," *La Revue du Cinéma,* no. 373 (June 1982): 63–64; Peter Ruedi, "*Imitation of Life*," *Theater Heute* (June 1983): 2–7; Jackie Louise Byars, "Gender Representation in American Family Melodramas of the Nineteen-Fifties" (Ph.D. diss., University of Texas, Austin 1983); Jean-Loup Bourget, *Douglas Sirk* (Paris: Edilig, 1984); Yann Tobin, "Une sequence pour l'éternité," *Positif,* no. 281–282 (July–August 1984): 62–65; Jeremy Butler, "*Imitation of Life:* Style and the Domestic Melodrama," *Jump Cut,* no. 32 (April 1986): 25–28; Marina Heung, "What's the Matter with Sara Jane?" *Cinema Journal* 26, no. 3 (Spring 1987): 21–43; Michael Selig, "Contradiction and Reading: Social Class and Sex Class in *Imitation of Life*," *Wide Angle* 10, no. 4 (1988): 13–23; Sandy Flitterman-Lewis, "Imitation(s) of Life: The Black Woman's Double Determination as Troubling 'Other,'" *Literature and Psychology* 35, no. 4 (1988): 44–57; Lauren Berlant, "The National Body: *Imitation of Life*," in "Comparative American Identities: Race, Sex and Nationality in the Modern Text," *Selected Papers from the English Institute* (New York: Routledge, Chapman and Hall, 1991).

3. Jon Halliday, *Sirk on Sirk* (New York: Viking, 1972), p. 114.

sixties saw the continued ascendancy of French auteurist theory—and Sirk was an early inductee into the artistic pantheon. His self-reflexive bent marked *Imitation* (a work set in the theater) an exemplary text within his canon. With the emergence of genre studies, melodrama captured center stage. Sirk's films were viewed as both typical and unique—taking pedestrian sentimentality to its sublime extreme.

Imitation also profited from the currency of ideological criticism. Its inclusion of dominant black characters in a period of heightened racial awareness attracted writers concerned with color and class. Its status as a "woman's picture" (focusing on the struggles of two single working mothers) made it ripe for feminist investigation. That it was based on a popular Fannie Hurst novel assured its relevance to the field. The book was even republished in 1990, disjunctively illustrated with stills from the Sirk film depicting characters "mismatched" with the printed narrative.[4]

Thus, *Imitation* is a cinematic prism (like the transparent, faceted beads that fall during its credits)—one capable of breaking a social/intellectual "spectrum" into its component parts. Some of these elements have been thoroughly examined: the film's status as remake, its inscription of authorial style, its parodic self-consciousness, its melodramatic imagination, its psycho-dramatic patterning, its ideological thrust. I will table these for fear of imitation of (the discourse on) *Imitation of Life*.

But while the film has been assiduously studied, its treatment has displayed a certain hermeticism, one, perhaps, indicative of a genre with its heart in the home.[5] (As Thomas Elsaesser has noted: "Melodrama is iconographically fixed by the claustrophobic atmosphere of the bourgeois household.")[6] *Imitation*'s formal and narrative structures have been favored at the expense of its links to the social terrain. I will seek to expand the "interior monologue" that has explained it by conjoining the lessons of textual and cultural inquiry to overcome a certain critical "agoraphobia."

In particular, I will highlight three aspects of the Sirkian drama that most emphatically evoke the film's contemporaneous public scene: (1) the question of women and work, (2) the issue of race, (3) the matter of star biography. By executing a cultural analysis (which intercuts diegetic and extradiegetic space), I

---

4. Fannie Hurst, *Imitation of Life* (1933; rpt. New York: Harper & Row, 1990). In the novel the heroine's name is Bea Pullman, for example, and in Sirk's film it is Lora Meredith. In the novel, her daughter's name is Jessie, while in the film it is Susie.

5. Jackie Louise Byars ("Gender Representation") examines women and work in her excellent dissertation chapter on *Imitation,* but does not include much concrete social history. Marina Heung ("What's the Matter?") brings to bear crucial information on the circumstances of black domestics in her work on the film.

6. Thomas Elsaesser, "Tales of Sound and Fury: Observations on the Family Melodrama," in *Home Is Where the Heart Is: Studies in Melodrama and the Woman's Film,* ed. Christine Gledhill (London: British Film Institute, 1987), p. 62.

will cast *Imitation* not only as a vibrant fiction but as a cinematic "afterimage" of personal and collective consciousness. (As Marcia Landy writes, "the seemingly escapist aspects of melodrama are intimately tied to pressing social concerns.")[7]

Lana Turner's most valuable professional aid was a three-way mirror used to scrutinize her appearance. In a sense, it will be my tool as well—shifted from the realm of ego to that of history—utilized to monitor a tripaneled vision of *Imitation*'s political milieu. A looking glass, however, does not return an unmediated picture. Rather, as Sirk notes, its imagery can bend, deflect, invert, or oppose.

Panel One: Working Girls

The economically and rhetorically enforced allocation and division of
productive and reproductive roles according to gender reached the peak of its
social installation in the United States between the end of World War Two and
the beginning of the American Women's Movement.

—Janet Walker[8]

Imitation of Life recounts a decade in the life of Lora Meredith (Lana Turner), a young widow struggling to raise her child, Susie. Though, in the early years, Lora holds a variety of odd jobs, she eventually becomes an actress, achieving fame as a Broadway star. Her success is made possible by her association with Annie Johnson (Juanita Moore), a black single mother whom Lora encounters on a New York City beach. Annie moves into the Meredith apartment (with her daughter, Sarah Jane), and assumes the roles of nanny and housekeeper. While Annie has no suitors, Lora is courted by a photographer, Steve Archer (John Gavin), who wants her to marry and settle down. During the years of the women's liaison, both endure parental conflicts, and maternal *angst* is at the core of the melodrama: Sarah Jane attempts to "pass" (which causes Annie to die of heartache); Susie falls in love with her mother's beau. Though Lora initially rejects Steve's proposal in favor of her career, her emotional world seems vacant. By the end of the drama, she wonders if she has been living an imitation of life.

The film was released in 1959, but that is not its only historical marker. Rather, we must take a cue from the time-line of the narrative, and consider the late 1940s when the tale begins. The chronology hits us forcefully in the opening sequence, set at Coney Island. As Lora frantically searches for her lost daughter, she passes a boardwalk sign advertising the 1947 Mardi Gras. Thus, the story is situated in the immediate postwar era, a period of drastic change for American

7. Marcia Landy, Introd., in *Imitations of Life: A Reader on Film and Television Melodrama* (Detroit: Wayne State University Press, 1991), p. 21.
8. Janet Walker, "Hollywood, Freud and the Representation of Women: Regulation and Contradiction, 1945–Early 60s," in *Home Is Where the Heart Is,* ed. Gledhill, p. 197.

women. A later montage (chronicling Lora's success as an actress) takes us explicitly from 1948 to 1958. This decade witnessed shifts in female employment and its relation to domestic responsibilities. For Lora (a single parent, the sole support of her child), this career-family tension constitutes the crux of the drama.

William Chafe charts how the war years saw female employment grow by over 50 percent—the largest gains coming for older married women.[9] While such developments were salutory, others were troubling: women's wages trailed men's; females were discouraged from joining unions; inadequate child care plagued parent-workers; delinquency and teenage marriage rose. Upon the end of the war there was a sharp decrease in the ranks of women workers, as returning soldiers were given priority. Contrary to clichés, most women seeking jobs were eventually rehired.[10] By 1955, the proportion of women employed exceeded the highest levels of wartime. By 1956, 22 million worked—and half were wives.[11] Two documents of the era testify to this metamorphosis. In 1957, the National Manpower Council published *Womanpower,* a study of female employment. In 1958, *Work in the Lives of Married Women,* its domestic companion piece, was released.[12]

Though females made professional strides, their advancements were qualified by restrictive attitudes. The feminist movement suffered a period of public eclipse in the fifties.[13] Furthermore, retrograde views surfaced about women and work. When the men were in combat, female employees were seen as patriotic; when the soldiers returned, women were viewed as competitive. When wartime quotas were paramount, use of day care was encouraged; it was criticized when the emergency was lifted.

Though this ideological shift could not deter lower-class women (in dire need of jobs), it did discourage middle-class wives for whom employment was economically "optional." They came to need a new excuse to work—and rising inflation provided them one. As Chafe observes, these women "sought jobs, not careers—an extra pay check for the family." Working was sanctioned primarily for women over thirty-five, whose child-care duties were generally completed.[14]

Clearly, women in the fifties were given mixed signals: "More women than

9. William Henry Chafe, *The American Woman: Her Changing Social, Economic, and Political Roles, 1920–1970* (New York: Oxford University Press, 1972), pp. 135, 144; Eugenia Kaledin, *Mothers and More: American Women in the 1950s* (Boston: Twayne, 1984), p. 67.

10. Chafe, *American Woman*, pp. 150, 179–180.

11. "Women Hold Third of Jobs," *Life,* 24 December 1956, p. 31.

12. *Womanpower* (New York: Columbia University Press, 1957); *Work in the Lives of Married Women* (New York: Columbia University Press, 1958).

13. David A. Schulz, *The Changing Family: Its Function and Future,* 2nd ed. (Englewood Cliffs, N.J.: Prentice-Hall, 1976), p. 286; in *Survival in the Doldrums: The American Women's Rights Movement, 1945 to the 1960s,* Leila J. Rupp and Verta Taylor describe a continuity between the women's movement of the 1950s and the feminist movement of the 1960s (New York: Oxford University Press, 1987), pp. 3–11.

14. Chafe, *American Woman*, pp. 194, 192; Kaledin, p. 66.

ever were working outside the home in a society which continued to endorse the traditional . . . roles of wife, mother and homemaker."[15] By mid-decade, a strain was apparent in society's conception of the female: in December 1956, *Life* magazine dedicated a double-issue to "The American Woman: Her Achievements and Troubles."

In that magazine issue, Robert Coughlan blamed the female in *all* her varied incarnations. He critiqued the erotic woman who "demands and needs sexual gratification from" a man—a posture which denied her "full release."[16] He was also suspicious of the "New York Career Woman": a "bright, well-educated, ambitious" wife in her mid-thirties who abandoned feminine tasks to pursue outside work. In his stance he evoked Ferdinand Lundberg and Marynia Farnham's *Modern Woman: The Lost Sex* (1947), which lambasted the equal rights movement for leading woman astray.[17] While *Life* acknowledged an increased number of working women, it regarded careers as secondary. Mrs. Peter Marshall remarked: "Ask any thoughtful, honest woman what the most satisfying moments of her life have been and she will never mention the day she got her first job."[18]

Coughlan also chastized the housewife who succumbed to the "suburban syndrome"—becoming "morbidly depressed."[19] It is this woman who Betty Friedan later described sympathetically in *The Feminine Mystique* (1963) as experiencing "The Problem That Has No Name": "Each suburban wife struggled with it alone. . . . She was afraid to ask even of herself the silent question—'Is this all?' "[20]

The era was also rife with ambivalence toward the mother. Coughlan attacked her for embracing her role "with a vengeance," becoming an "overwhelming" parent. Here, he echoed Philip Wylie's *Generation of Vipers* (1942) which configured mom as a predatory leech weakening her children's will to maturation and separation: "The spectacle of the female devouring her young in the firm belief that it is for their own good is too old in man's legends to be overlooked."[21]

Lora Meredith's saga begins in 1947, the year *Modern Woman* was published. It ends in 1958, the release date of *Work in the Lives of Married Women*. Both volumes cast their intertextual shadows upon the screen in a wash of contradiction: the former as a caution to the working mother, the latter as a tribute to the professional woman.

---

15. Barbara McGowan, "Postwar Attitudes Toward Women and Work," in *New Research on Women and Sex Roles,* ed. Dorothy G. McGuigan (Ann Arbor: University of Michigan Press, 1974), p. 144.
16. Robert Coughlan, "Modern Marriage," *Life,* 24 December 1956, p. 115.
17. Ferdinand Lundberg and Marynia Farnham, *Modern Woman: The Lost Sex* (New York: Harper & Bros., 1947).
18. Mrs. Peter Marshall, "An Introduction," *Life,* 24 December 1956, p. 2.
19. Coughlan, "Modern Marriage," p. 111.
20. Betty Friedan, *The Feminine Mystique* (New York: Dell, 1963), p. 11.
21. Philip Wylie, *Generation of Vipers* (New York: Rinehart & Co., 1942), p. 185.

Upstairs/Downstairs

*There are two kinds of females in this country—colored women and white
ladies. Colored women are maids, cooks . . . crossing guards . . . welfare
recipients . . . and the only time they become ladies is when they are cleaning
ladies.*

—Louise Stone[22]

Louise Stone describes the difference in America between "colored women"
and "white ladies." The above discussion of female employment has presumed
the latter—the category favored by traditional research. As one reads *Womanpower* or *Work in the Lives of Married Women,* few sections pertain to the
"Negro"; the baseline is Caucasian. Given the prominence of black working
women in *Imitation* (Annie and Sarah Jane), it is imperative to investigate their
status in the forties and fifties.[23]

One finds that black women were more likely to be employed than white, due
to their marginal economic situations. A greater number of black female workers
were married, given "the heavy responsibility . . . Negro women . . . carry for
the support of children and other dependents."[24] Most black women were engaged in the service sector, predominantly as private household help.
Traditionally, the "ideal" female domestic was configured as single and between
the ages of twenty and twenty-five:

Married women take away food for the support of their families; married
women have so many responsibilities and problems in their own home they
oftener than not go out to work with a weary body and a disturbed mind;
married women find it difficult to live and sleep on employers' premises.[25]

The percentage of black women engaged in private service steadily decreased
from 1890 on as opportunities arose in factories, laundries, offices, and stores.[26]
Work in the Lives of Married Women reports that "Negro women . . . [were]
increasingly able to move up and out of the lowest paid jobs."[27] Thus, scholars
speak of the profession's "passing," its "disappearance," its "decline."[28] The
occupation also experienced progressively higher rates of turnover.

22. Louise Stone, "What It's Like to Be a Colored Woman," *Washington Post,* 13 November 1966,
as quoted in Gerda Lerner, *Black Women in White America: A Documentary History* (New York:
Pantheon, 1972), p. 217.
23. See Heung, "What's the Matter?"
24. National Manpower Council, *Womanpower,* pp. 77, 139.
25. Elizabeth Ross Haynes, "Negroes in Domestic Service in the United States," *Journal of Negro
History* 8, no. 4 (October 1923): 391.
26. National Manpower Council, *Womanpower,* pp. 139–40.
27. National Manpower Council, *Work in the Lives,* p. 87.
28. David Chaplin, "Domestic Service and the Negro," in *Blue-Collar World: Studies of the American Worker,* eds. Arthur B. Shostak and Willam Gomberg (Englewood Cliffs, N.J.: Prentice-Hall,
1964), p. 527.

World War II saw a shortage of household help as women of color found jobs in shipyards, aircraft plants, arsenals, and foundries. In *Black Metropolis* (1945), St. Clair Drake and Horace R. Cayton note that "middle-class white housewives . . . began to complain about 'the servant problem' as Negro women . . . headed for the war plants."[29] *Newsweek* of 1949 claimed that domestic workers decreased by 500,000 while the female work force increased by 4,500,000.[30] Though the international conflict temporarily expanded opportunities for blacks, Gunnar Myrdal found the long-term gains less dramatic than during World War I; by 1947, many advances had entirely evaporated.[31] Significantly, *Newsweek* reported the revival of urban, cornerside "slave markets" in 1949, where white housewives bartered for black household help.[32]

At the turn of the century, many maids "lived in"; by the forties and fifties this arrangement was exceptional. In 1949, *Newsweek* noted that: "Almost universally, houseworkers do not want to 'sleep in.' They want work by the day or hour that will leave them masters of their own time in the evenings and on the weekends."[33] Drake and Cayton saw this as creating a greater distance between employer and employee:

> Most Negro domestic servants work for ordinary middle-class white families and do not have the intimate personal ties which characterize the few situations where the white family can afford a permanent retainer who lives on the premises and is almost a member of the family.[34]

While maids tended white children, their progeny were watched by sitters, relatives, or friends—part of what Hariette Pipes McAdoo called the black "kin-help exchange network."[35]

Throughout its history, domestic service has been riddled with discontent. "[It] is almost universally defined as a problem, but generally from the employer's perspective."[36] The oppressed, however, are the workers, plagued by monotony, low pay, long hours, isolation, vague standards, inadequate equipment, invasion of privacy, the stress of deference, the absence of unionization.[37] In particular,

29. St. Clair Drake and Horace R. Cayton, *Black Metropolis: A Study of Negro Life in a Northern City* (New York: Harcourt, Brace and Co., 1945), p. 246.

30. "The Servant Problem," *Newsweek,* 19 September 1949, p. 48.

31. Gunnar Myrdal, *An American Dilemma: The Negro Problem and Modern Democracy* (New York: Harper & Row, 1944), p. 409; Davis McEntire and Julia Turnpol, "Postwar Status of Negro Workers in San Francisco Area," *Monthly Labor Review* 70 (Jan.–June 1950): 612.

32. "The Servant Problem," p. 48.

33. Ibid.

34. Drake and Cayton, *Black Metropolis,* pp. 244–245.

35. Harriette Pipes McAdoo, "Black Mothers and the Extended Family Support Network," in *The Black Woman,* ed. La Frances Rodgers-Rose (Beverly Hills: Sage Publications, 1980), p. 141.

36. Chaplin, "Domestic Service," p. 529.

37. Isabel Eaton, "Special Report on Negro Domestic Service in the Seventh Ward, Philadelphia," in *The Philadelphia Negro,* ed. W. E. B. Du Bois (New York: Benjamin Blom, 1899; rpt. 1967), pp.

employees experience difficulties separating the professional from the personal, a byproduct of work in a private home. Often, maids suffer an "over-identification with management," especially when they care for the family's children.[38]

For these reasons, black women have generally considered domestic service the least desirable occupation, a "social stigma."[39] Drake and Cayton found that servants hoped their offspring would locate other employment. This is not to deny the potentially redemptive aspects of domestic service: friendship with one's employer; economic and political fringe benefits; middle- or upper-class role models.

The sense of housework as a disgrace (as an occupational "scar of shame") was exacerbated, however, in the forties and fifties by the false promise of the war years and the hopes of the burgeoning civil rights movement. Rhoda Lois Blumberg noted the following revolutionary events occurring between 1953 and 1958, years which overlap the time-line of *Imitation Of Life*. In June 1953, a successful bus boycott took place in Baton Rouge, Louisiana. In May 1954, the United States Supreme Court (in *Brown* vs. *the Board of Education*) found segregation in public schools to be inherently unequal. In 1955, *Brown II* mandated desegregation "with all deliberate speed." In the same year, the Interstate Commerce Commission outlawed segregated buses and waiting rooms for passengers crossing state lines. Emmett Till was lynched in Mississippi. After Rosa Parks was arrested in Alabama for violating bus segregation, a boycott was launched and Reverend Martin Luther King, Jr., was elected president of the Montgomery Improvement Association. On 21 December, the buses were integrated. In January of 1956, the Southern Christian Leadership Conference was founded. Later that year, the Supreme Court ordered the University of Alabama to admit a black woman for graduate study. Congress passed the first Civil Rights Act in eighty-two years. Arkansas governor Orval Faubus called out the National Guard to prevent nine black students from entering a Little Rock high school; a court order required the militia to be withdrawn. In July, blacks in Tuskegee, Alabama, organized a boycott against white merchants in order to protest a redistricting move to exclude black voters. The year 1958 witnessed a successful voter registration drive in Tennessee which led to severe economic reprisals.[40]

463–467; Drake and Cayton, *Black Metropolis,* p. 247; Chaplin, "Domestic Service," pp. 531–532; Myrdal, *American Dilemma* p. 1086; Jean Collier Brown, U.S. Dept. of Labor, Bulletin 165 of the Women's Bureau, *The Negro Woman Worker* (Washington D.C.: GPO, 1938), rpt. in *Black Workers: A Documentary History from Colonial Times to the Present,* eds. Philip S. Foner and Ronald L. Lewis (Philadelphia: Temple University Press, 1989), p. 467.

38. Chaplin "Domestic Service," p. 528; Bonnie Thornton Dill, "The Means to Put My Children Through: Child-Rearing Goals and Strategies Among Black Female Domestic Servants," in *The Black Woman,* ed. La Frances Rodgers-Rose (Beverly Hills: Sage Publications, 1980), p. 109.

39. Eaton, "Special Report," p. 467.

40. Rhoda Lois Blumberg, *Civil Rights: The 1960s Freedom Struggle* (Boston: Twayne, 1984), pp. xvii–xix.

Blacks' rejection of domestic service might also have been spurred by the feminist movement, which reconfigured homemaking as drudgery. (As early as 1949, Edith Stern had deemed women "household slaves" who led the "kind of life that theoretically became passé with the Emancipation Proclamation.")[41] In 1970, for the first time, domestic labor failed to represent the largest segment of the female African American occupational force.[42] Carolyn Reed, a maid interviewed for Robert Hamburger's oral history, recalled:

> . . . the sixties . . . was . . . [the] point that I began to be politically aware. It was during the time of the civil rights movement, and then you knew exactly where you stood. . . . One of my biggest educations was when [my employer] planned a party on the day of the March on Washington. . . . I was just grouchy, really grouchy all day long, because I knew that I was supposed to be in Washington.[43]

It is within this cultural context that Annie Johnson performs domestic labor for Lora Meredith. We wonder how she remains so content with her imitation of life.

Annie's forbearance leads us to her status as *literary* creation—her roots in the imagination of Fannie Hurst. For while Sirk's film alters the context of the novel (where the maid concocts a pancake recipe that hurtles her employer to success as a restaurateur), the women's relationship is largely the same. They are configured as friends, and racial and class tensions are minimized.

It is intriguing to juxtapose the portrayal of Annie with an aspect of Hurst's biography.[44] On 1 May, 1925, she met author Zora Neale Hurston at an awards dinner for *Opportunity: A Journal of Negro Life*. The magazine had published Hurston's story, "Spunk," which garnered second prize; Hurst was one of the judges. Known for her sympathy to black causes, she had spoken on race relations to the Circle for Negro Belief, the New York Urban League, and the City-Wide Citizens' Committee on Harlem.

Hurston had been born to a large Florida family and had worked as a maid for white people, "failing more often than not because she not only refused to act humble but also refused the sexual advances of her male employers. Too, she was more interested in reading than in dusting and dishwashing."[45] She had attended Howard University and Barnard College and had authored several literary works.

41. Edith Stern, "Women Are Household Slaves," *American Mercury* 68, no. 301 (1949): 71.
42. Judith Rollins, *Between Women: Domestics and Their Employers* (Philadelphia: Temple University Press, 1985), p. 56.
43. Robert Hamburger, *A Stranger in the House* (New York: Collier, 1978), p. 159.
44. I am indebted to Peter Wollen who first mentioned to me that Zora Neale Hurston had worked for Fannie Hurst.
45. Lillie P. Howard, *Zora Neale Hurston* (Boston: Twayne, 1980) p. 16.

Impressed by Hurston, Hurst hired her as a live-in assistant:

[Zora] walked into my study one day by telephone appointment, carelessly, a big-boned, good-boned young woman, handsome and light yellow, with no show of desire for the position of secretary for which she was applying. . . . As Zora expressed it, we "took a shine" to one another and I engaged her on the spot as my live-in secretary.

But the very independence that attracted Hurst made Hurston unsuited to office work:

Her shorthand was short on legibility, her typing hit or miss, mostly the latter, her filing, a game of find-the-thimble. Her mind ran ahead of my thoughts and she would interject with an impatient suggestion or clarification of what I wanted to say. If dictation bored her she would interrupt, stretch wide her arms and yawn: "Let's get out the car . . ."

Exasperated, Hurst released Hurston from clerical chores, and asked her to stay on as "companion and chauffeur."[46]

Despite their hierarchal positioning, the women became confidantes and Hurston regarded Hurst as a friend and ally. In Hurston's autobiography, *Dust Tracks on a Road,* she selects Hurst as one of "Two Women in Particular" that most influenced her life (the other being Ethel Waters). The two writers often discussed their respective projects while tooling around in Hurst's car.[47]

Given Hurston's status as an ex-maid, as Hurst's cherished live-in secretary/companion/chauffeur, one wonders if the author formulated the beloved figure of Delilah (in *Imitation*) with Hurston partially in mind. To some degree this might explain Hurst's focus on intimacy versus work. Though Hurst's memoirs of Hurston reveal no passive, idealized employee/saint, they configure her as somewhat stoical.

Hurst felt that Hurston had "very little indignation for the imposed status of her race."[48] In the women's journeys together, they often encountered "the ogre of discrimination":

At hotels, Zora was either assigned to servants' quarters or informed that they were full up. When I also refused accommodations, Zora's attitude was swift and adamant: "If you are going to take that stand, it will be impossible for us to travel together. This is the way it is and I can take care of myself as I have all my life."[49]

46. Fannie Hurst, "Zora Hurston: A Personality Sketch" *Yale University Library Gazette* 35 (1961): 17–18.
47. Zora Neale Hurston, *Dust Tracks on a Road* 1942; rpt. New York: J. B. Lippincott, 1971), pp. 238–243.
48. Howard, *Hurston,* p. 167.
49. Hurst, "Zora Hurston," p. 20.

Hurston's own words in 1942 attest to her apparent tolerance: "I have no race prejudice of any kind. . . . So I give you all my right hand of fellowship and love, and hope for the same from you."[50] Hurston's generosity extended to Hurst's novel. In a 1940 letter to Hurst (from North Carolina), she wrote: "You have a grand set of admirers in this part of the world because of *Imitation of Life*."[51] Clearly, Hurston was among them.

Panel Two: Simulation of Strife

I want to be honest with you, darling. I want more—everything! Maybe too much.

—Lora Meredith to Steve Archer

Seems to me, Miss Meredith, I'm just right for you. You wouldn't have to pay no wages. Just let me come and do *for you.*

—Annie Johnson to Lora Meredith

Having sketched the social scene faced by the postwar working woman, how does this off-screen space inflect the melodramatic tableau?

Given the specter of world combat, it seems significant that Lora Meredith has no husband—as though the narrative must replay the situation of men away. (At one point, Steve even mentions his military service.) David Rodowick finds male absence common in films of the period, where the father "functioned solely to throw the system into turmoil by his . . . death or desertion."[52] The patriarchal void allows Lora to work without conflict: "When [my husband] died," she tells Steve, "I *had* to make a living doing something." Thus, originally, her professional orientation is justified and contained.

But Lora harbors grandiose yearnings (like Friedan's housewives who sought more than "husband . . . children and . . . home").[53] She reveals she wants nothing "but the stage," hastily adding "except Susie" (as though reminded that maternal concern *should* be paramount). Lora further undercuts her aspirations with the taint of libidinal excess—wondering whether she is after "too much." Her theatrical ambitions are partly rationalized by her deceased spouse's occupation as director; thus, she is dutifully following in his footsteps. Nowhere in her agony is there any sense that achievement might make her a *superior* parent. Yet, *Work in the Lives of Married Women* had stated that: "Women . . . often find in

50. Howard, *Hurston*, p. 168.
51. Cynthia Ann Brandimarte, "Fannie Hurst and Her Fiction: Prescriptions for America's Working Women" (Ph.D. diss., University of Texas, Austin, 1980), pp. 90–91.
52. David Rodowick, "Madness, Authority and Ideology: The Domestic Melodrama of the 1950s," in *Home Is Where the Heart Is*, ed. Gledhill, p. 278.
53. Friedan, *Feminine Mystique*, p. 27.

at least part-time work release from tension so that their maternal energy is re-
newed." Many employed mothers are gratified to provide a higher standard of
living. "*We* are the good [parents]," they declare.[54]

When Lora transcends poverty and becomes an established performer, professional tensions surface. (Her "success montage" blazons her face on the cover of
a 1953 *Newsweek*—one of many magazines then documenting the problem of
working mothers.) Lora earns enough to quit: the economic rationale for employment is eliminated. Her occupational ambivalence is complicated by her affair
with Steve, who prods her toward domesticity. When he proposes marriage, he
claims that he wants to "give her a home" and "take care" of her. When a famous
playwright wishes to audition her, Steve pressures Lora to refuse. "I'm not asking you . . . I'm telling you," he shouts, arguing that his love should be
"enough." In his posture, we are reminded of *Life*'s dramatization of an average
husband evaluating a career-woman partner:

> He admires her as a person but does not think she is much of a wife. She
> dislikes housework, she never learned how to cook, she turned the children
> over to nurses as soon as she could. She gives them presents but doesn't give
> much of herself to them. She never gives much of herself to *him*. He wishes
> she would do more of the things that women are supposed to do. He wishes
> she were more of a *woman*.

Significantly, this *Life* article is illustrated by a photograph of Mrs. Martha
Robinson, an actress "who gave up a promising future to be full-time mother and
wife." Captioned "At Hearthside," it shows her reviewing old theater clippings
with her daughters, while her husband reads in a corner. "When wives work,"
she says, "somebody gets neglected along the line." She assures us that she has
"never regretted her decision."[55]

In this respect, Sirk's film offers no imitation of *Life*. For Lora would find little
consolation in skimming antique stage reviews. This vignette also signals that
there is more than an accidental linkage of Lora's status as a working mother and
her role as an actress. For the ideology of the fifties cast *all* working mothers as
performers, dissembling their maternal functions.[56]

In Lora's assertion of career and artistry she rivals male ambition. While she
has lofty goals, Steve compromises—placing him in a subordinate stance. Early
on, he confesses that he wants his photographs hung in the Museum of Modern
Art, claiming that he "believe[s] in chasing rainbows." When he later sells a
photo for a beer advertisement, Lora mocks his "idea of achieving something."
As though to counter him, she retorts: "I'm going up and up—and nobody's

---

54. National Manpower Council, *Work in the Lives*, pp. 113, 137.
55. Coughlan, "Modern Marriage," pp. 110, 118.
56. Lucy Fischer, *Shot/Countershot: Film Tradition and Women's Cinema* (Princeton, N.J.: Princeton University Press, 1989), pp. 63–88.

going to pull me down!" Thus, she assumes the site of power, and he the locus of passivity: she remain true to herself while *he* leads the imitation of life. Peter Biskind notes a "feminization of men and . . . masculinization of women" in films of the fifties.[57] Significantly, an illustration in the 1956 *Life* shows male and female faces blended—like the macabre feminine visages in Ingmar Bergman's *Persona* (1966).[58]

The more Lora scales the ladder of success, the more she displaces her traditional role of homemaker/mother; the more a chasm opens within her domestic space. This lack is aggravated by the absence of a husband who might share household responsibilities. *Work in the Lives of Married Women* argued that female employment did *not* always mean familial deprivation: "The father who takes the laundry to the laundromat, or dries the dishes in the evening . . . is just a good father and a decent partner doing his share . . . [and] may often represent an asset for children."[59]

Instead, Lora's domestic gap is filled by Annie Johnson—the second heroine of the drama. Clearly, she does not have the luxury to ponder the propriety of employment: her color, her poverty, her parenthood, her educational level dictate her occupational fate. On one level, Annie represents Lora's other psychic *half*— the conventional lobe that she must stifle to reach her goal. Annie seems the good mother to Lora's bad, the nurturant woman to her egotistical, the natural female to her synthetic, the "janitorial" self to her professional. This depiction is mediated by the discourse of race, which configures the Negro madonna as "mammy." Annie Johnson was not alone in this media portrayal; the stereotype had been revived in the television show *Beulah* (1950–1953) as well as in the film *The Member of the Wedding* (1952).[60]

In a 1947 "feminist" article, Della Cyrus justified the professional woman's exodus from home by asserting the maternal *superiority* of the lower-caste caretaker: "Could it be that the much maligned, 'dumb' nursemaid had her points after all, when she was easygoing, relaxed, unambitious, foolishly contented, and childlike with her young charges?"[61] Thus, the dichotomy Annie/Lora is both symbolically and literally black and white.[62] Annie's maternal depiction also draws on the experience of actual domestics. Bonnie Thornton Dill reported

57. Peter Biskind, *Seeing Is Believing: How Hollywood Taught Us to Stop Worrying and Love the Fifties* (New York: Pantheon, 1983), p. 274.
58. Coughlan, "Modern Marriage," p. 108.
59. National Manpower Council, *Work in the Lives*, p. 142.
60. Sybil DelGaudio, "The Mammy in Hollywood Film: I'd Walk a Million Miles for One o' Her Smiles," *Jump Cut*, no. 28 (April 1983): 23–25.
61. Della D. Cyrus, "Why Mothers Fail," *Atlantic Monthly*, March 1947, p. 60.
62. For previous discussions of the issue of race, see Butler, "*Imitation of Life*," Byars "Gender Representation," Flitterman-Lewis "Imitation(s) of Life," Heung, "What's the Matter?". Heung, especially, raises issues of social history related to questions of race—in particular, the status of domestic labor. I see my work in this section as building upon and extending her excellent insights.

that "the women . . . who had child care responsibilities talked about themselves as being 'like a mother' to their employer's children."[63]

As a composite whole, Annie/Lora represents postwar woman in her unseemly disjunction, in her attempts to have and do it all. (As Friedan observes, "the image of American woman . . . suffered a schizophrenic split" in this era.)[64] That *Imitation* surfaces the rift serves a progressive purpose, for as Fredric Jameson writes, "we cannot fully do justice to the ideological function of works . . . unless we are willing to concede the presence within them of a more positive function . . . their utopian or transcendent potential."[65]

But, ultimately, *Imitation* settles tensions by means of a conservative denouement—resolving what Friedan has called "the new feminine morality story" by "exorcising of the forbidden career dream . . . of independence."[66] Read from this perspective, *Imitation* is a drama of cleft female consciousness in which the regressive triumphs over the revolutionary self. By the end of the narrative, Lora doubts her theatrical success and is haunted by her lapses as a parent. Any pride in her work emerges only by default—as a defense against Susie's accusations. "Why, you give me credit for *nothing,*" Lora screams, countering her daughter's charges of neglect. "Yes, I'm ambitious—perhaps too ambitious—but it's been for your sake as well as mine!" While Lora is chastened, Annie is dead, leading us to wonder whether *any* vision of womanhood survives this cultural bifurcation. The women's equalization seems figured in the choreography of the mise-en-scène. In shots of Lora framed in a mirror, she is frequently joined or supplanted by Annie.[67] This underscores Sirk's notion that the looking glass both reveals one's self and "[one's] own opposite."[68]

While many aspects of *Imitation* seem to reflect the surrounding societal scene, others warp the view. Annie is not only a symbolic *part* of Lora but her practical *supplement*—the duplicate underclass clone a "New York Career Woman" needs to survive. From this vantage point, the film provides white females a wish fulfillment fantasy of a double who appears at the door, offering, *gratis,* the custodial services they require. Moreover, Annie performs them with a sense of contentment unknown to postwar black women, for whom domestic work was a "last resort."[69] (Equally apocryphal is Lora's hiring additional servants to tend the ailing Annie, keeping her on as a costly member of the family.)

Ironically, though middle-class housewives could afford maids in the 1950s, a struggling single parent (like the early Lora Meredith) was unlikely to do so.

63. Dill, "Means," p. 121.
64. Friedan, *Feminine Mystique*, p. 40.
65. Fredric Jameson, "Reification and Utopia in Mass Culture," *Social Text*, no. 1 (1979): 144.
66. Friedan, *Feminine Mystique*, p. 40.
67. Lauren Berlant first mentioned this dynamic to me. It occurs, for example, in shots 174 and 339 of the continuity.
68. Halliday, *Sirk on Sirk*, p. 48.
69. Lerner, *Black Women*, p. 230.

That Annie would live in violates the era's statistical patterns. And *nowhere* in the literature is there mention of maids residing on premises with a child. Furthermore, Annie's accidental encounter with Lora (at a public beach), seems a sanitized version of the street corner "slave markets," reappearing in urban centers around 1947. It was far likelier that the homeless Annie would be taken in by the black "kin-help exchange network," than by a poor white stranger like Lora Meredith.[70] The erasure of Annie's communal world is foregrounded near the end of the film when Annie makes her plans for an elaborate mass funeral. "It never occurred to me that you had many friends," Lora blankly remarks.

While Lora's need of child care is blamed on her job, many middle-class, stay-at-home moms of the era had equal assistance. *Life* described a housewife ("home manager, mother, hostess and useful civic worker") who has full-time help.[71] Similarly, the 1958 Manpower report noted a *conventional* homemaker with the following schedule:

> [The family's] early breakfast was prepared by the housekeeper, who saw the children off to school while the mother prepared for her day's activities. Active in PTA and civic and women's groups . . . she returned home too 'exhausted to dine with three bickering girls,' who were fed by the housekeeper.[72]

Thus a false opposition is established in the film between *salaried* work and adequate mothering—volunteerism being sanctioned.

Despite Annie's remedial presence, anxieties surface within the Meredith/ Johnson household, and circulate around the women's offspring. As though to replicate wartime concerns with juvenile delinquency and teenage marriage, Sarah Jane (Susan Kohner) plans to runaway and elope, and Susie (Sandra Dee) falls for Steve. Postwar consciousness hovers at the cinematic borders: while direct reference to the civil rights movement is avoided, its spirit materializes at certain narrative junctures. Sarah Jane's attempt to "pass" at school reminds us of the struggles around *Brown* vs. *the Board of Education;* her rejection of a black doll invokes research on children's racial identification; her anger with her mother bespeaks her generation's rejection of domestic work; her affair with a white man reminds us of loosening prohibitions against screen miscegenation;[73]

---

70. McAdoo, "Black Mothers," p. 141.
71. "Busy Wife's Achievements," *Life,* 24 December 1956, p. 41.
72. National Manpower Council, *Work in the Lives,* p. 111.
73. Heung, "What's the Matter?" pp. 39–40; Kenneth B. Clark, *Prejudice and Your Child* (Boston: Beacon, 1955), pp. 44–46; Mary Ellen Goodman, *Race Awareness in Young Children* (New York: Collier, 1952), pp. 55, 256; Biskind, *Seeing Is Believing,* p. 291; According to Peter Biskind, 1956 marked the year that prohibitions against miscegenation were removed from the Hollywood Production Code. Other films in the era that deal with interracial sexual relationships are *Pinky* (1949), *Island in the Sun* (1957), and *Night of the Quarter Moon* (1959). Donald Bogle (*Blacks in American Films and Television: An Encyclopedia* [New York: Garland, 1988]), however, makes the point that often the threat of this issue was defused by having one of the couple a light-skinned black, played by

Mahalia Jackson's presence at Annie's funeral sparks associations to the singer's participation in civil rights demonstrations, and her role in mainstreaming of black gospel music.[74]

Ultimately, *Imitation* offers woman little way out—leaves her caught within a conundrum. Lora, the careerist (who abdicates home) is a female manquée. Annie, the traditional woman (whose *job* is domesticity), is similarly condemned. To the extent that she is configured as a black *working woman*, she fails at raising her daughter. (This crisis is crystallized in Sarah Jane's mockery of her mother's role: a parody of slave servility performed for Lora's company.) To the degree that Annie is seen as a *devoted parent*, she is penalized for her dedication. Ultimately, she is cast as an overbearing mother who demands racial bonding from her daughter, suffocating the resistant Sarah Jane. (Rainer Werner Fassbinder even calls her "terroristic" and "brutal.")[75] On her deathbed, Annie indulges in self-reproach: "I know I was selfish and . . . loved . . . too much."

Both Annie and Lora are variations on Lundberg and Farnham's *lost* sex—a theme that is woven through the film. It is significant that *Imitation* opens with a scene of Susie *lost* at the beach, and immediately presents Lora as a confused (or "*lost*") parent. When, in the tumult, she meets Steve, he plays the role of her irate husband. He tells an onlooker: "she not only spoils" the children—but "goes around *losing* them." Susie is, of course, *found* by Annie, who, initially, seems an ideal caretaker, refusing to be separated from her own child. By the narrative's end, however, Sarah Jane is as *lost* as Susie—having shunned her mother's influence and affection. Thus, the drama articulates a discourse of the *lost and found* as relayed between mothers and daughters.

The women's sole escape is toward theater—the realm of Luce Irigaray's female mimicry—where they can "play with mimesis . . . to try to recover the place of exploitation by discourse, without allowing [themselves] to be simply reduced to it."[76] This motif emerges at the film's opening, with its reference to the Coney Island Mardi Gras.

Lora is literally an actress who finds her salvation on stage, and her maternal activities seem contaminated by her dramatic role. (Susie even tells her: "Please don't play the martyr.") Susie, however, is Lora's Electral understudy, standing in for her in a romance with Steve. (She even considers borrowing her mother's coat to meet him—investing it with an aura of costume.) Sarah Jane pretends to be white and works as a showgirl; she mimics a slave when serving Lora and her

a white performer (e.g., Jeanne Crain, Julie London, and Joan Collins respectively). Clearly, this also obtains for Susan Kohner in Sirk's *Imitation of Life*.

74. Mahalia Jackson with Evan McLeod Wylie, *Movin' On Up* (New York: Hawthorn, 1966), pp. 118–131.

75. Fassbinder, "Six Films," p. 106.

76. Luce Irigaray, "The Power of Discourse and the Subordination of the Feminine" in *This Sex Which is Not One*, trans. Catherine Porter (Ithaca, N.Y.: Cornell University Press, 1985), p. 76.

guests; Annie pretends to be Sarah Jane's "mammy"; but in her real domestic site, masks her employment in a charade of "friendship," a fact that replicates servants' over-identification with management.[77] Finally, she scripts her demise in the mise-en-scène of a funereal production number.

While the women seem marked by theatrical blame, male characters dissemble as well—but their lapses are comical or opaque. David Edwards fakes burning the only copy of his new play when Lora refuses to star in it. Lora's agent, Allen Loomis (Robert Alda), modulates his support for her, depending on how her career is going. Steve champions artistic integrity, but settles for hack work in an ad agency. He nonetheless assumes the right to judge Lora, continually reminding "her (and the audience) of the falseness of her success."[78]

On one level the ubiquity of illusion in *Imitation* supports Elizabeth Burns's claim that:

> ordinary social conduct at its most routine or informal . . . is composed and contrived. Each person tries to produce himself in his own drama, to hand out parts to others, and to make sure that some of them act the part of spectators.[79]

On the other hand, the fact that the drama positions theatricality as a greater problem for women modifies its progressive, "universal" thrust.

While the women are plagued by "the discrepancy of seeming and being," a similar charge might be aimed at the film—whose dissonant blend of mawkishness and satire elaborates a thematic masquerade.[80] (As Annie lies dying, she utters [in maudlin tones], words whose sardonic implications are clear: "Our weddin' day—and the day we die—are the great events of life.") Brandon French sees duplicity in numerous works of the period:

> On the surface, fifties films promoted women's domesticity and inequality and sought easy, optimistic conclusions to any problems their fictions treated. But a significant number of movies simultaneously reflected, unconsciously or otherwise, the malaise of domesticity and untenably narrow boundaries of the female role.[81]

Thus, while the term "passing" attaches to Sarah Jane's racial identification, it also applies to the film, which postures (alternately) as a recuperative melodrama and subversive parody. The word is also metaphoric for the position of women in postwar society, who, having achieved freedoms in the forties, later suffer a

77. Heung, "What's the Matter?" pp. 26–32.
78. Stern, *"Imitation of Life,"* p. 186.
79. Elizabeth Burns, *Theatricality: A Study of Convention in the Theatre and in Social Life* (London: Longman, 1972), p. 139.
80. Elsaesser, "Tales of Sound and Fury," p. 67.
81. Brandon French, *On the Verge of Revolt: Women in American Films of the Fifties* (New York: Ungar, 1978), p. xxi.

"give-back," and are asked to remain content with the sacrifice. Black women must "pass" for satisfied domestics and white ladies for happy housewives. (Ironically, Loomis [in evaluating Lora's appearance] tells her: "Your face will pass.") Even Coughlan acknowledges a contradiction: "Between the ideal [of womanhood] and reality something is urgently wrong."[82]

In *The Feminine Mystique,* Friedan noted a *McCall's* piece, published in the mid-fifties, that encapsulated the *Zeitgeist* of the times:

> the bored editors . . . ran a little article called "The Mother Who Ran Away." To their amazement, it brought the highest readership of any article they had ever run. "It was our moment of truth," said a former editor. "We suddenly realized that all those women at home with their three and a half children were miserably unhappy."[83]

In other words, they had been acting, role-playing as much as Sirk's protagonists. While *McCall's* heroine fled into the night ("lost" herself in a way that Lundberg and Farnham failed to imagine) *McCall's* readers escaped into fantasy—into literary and celluloid imitations of life.

Panel Three: Hollywood Mythos/Imitation of Hype

The one "career woman" who was always welcome in the pages of women's magazines was the actress. . . . you wrote about her as a housewife. You never showed her doing or enjoying her work . . . unless she eventually paid for it by losing her husband or her child, or otherwise admitting failure as a woman.

—Betty Friedan

Annie Johnson and Lora Meredith are both working women, enacted by two female screen professionals: Juanita Moore and Lana Turner. Though the former delivered an inspiring performance (simultaneously wrenching and restrained), her career subsequently faltered. After receiving the Oscar nomination for Best Supporting Actress in 1959, she found only minor roles in films like *Walk on the Wild Side* (1962), and *The Singing Nun* (1966). In an era when the black film scene was dominated by Sidney Poitier, few significant parts were conceived for women. Those available were offered to light-skinned beauties like Dorothy Dandridge or (in a mode of racial inversion) to white actresses passing for black or mulatto (Julie London in *Night of the Quarter Moon* [1959], Susan Kohner in *Imitation of Life*.)[84] The audience of 1959 preferred more mythic racial

82. Coughlan, "Modern Marriage," p. 109.
83. Friedan, *Feminine Mystique,* p. 44.
84. In the 1934 version of *Imitation of Life* by John Stahl, Fredi Washington, a light-skinned black woman, played Peola, the character who is the equivalent of Sirk's Sarah Jane. Born in 1903, Washington was regarded as the "mulatto ideal" who became typecast as a woman trying "to cross the

characterizations: *Black Orpheus* received the Academy Award for Best Foreign Film, and Dandridge starred in *Porgy and Bess*. Juanita Moore's career seemed as limited as Annie Johnson's.

The situation was different for Lana Turner, a Hollywood star with a high public profile. In addition to playing a working parent, she was one: an actress/mother like the *persona* she inhabits. Furthermore, her string of unstable marriages left her a single parent. Thus, Turner's life revealed numerous parallels to *Imitation,* illustrating Richard Dyer's point that celebrity images "correspond to novelistic notions of character."[85] Like the ghost of postwar social history, the specter of Turner's legend stalks the text—which seems a "remake" of the conditions that sustained it.

If the maternal dyad is central to *Imitation,* it is the linchpin of Turner's private narrative; she dedicates her autobiography to her "beloved mother". She was raised by Mildred Turner after her father deserted them when she was a young child. Mildred was poor, and toiled as a beautician to support the family. On several occasions, Lana was sent to live with virtual strangers, and "longed to be with [her] mother." Lana retrospectively admires Mildred's accomplishments, and describes her situation in histrionic terms: "My mother did her best to insulate me from the anxieties that must have tormented her in those lean times . . . *a woman alone, with a child to support* (my italics).[86] After Lana was "discovered" in Hollywood at fifteen, Mildred played an important supervisory role in her daughter's career, joining the ranks of Hollywood "stage mothers."

The maternal drama occupied the foreground as Turner's life developed. After wedding Stephen Crane in 1942, she learned that his first marriage was still binding; the Turner/Crane nuptials were annulled. Lana soon found herself pregnant: "Here I was expecting the child of a man who wasn't my husband."[87] Crane and Turner wed again in 1943, but their reunion was short-lived.

The birth of their daughter, Cheryl, was the stuff of tear-jerkers, since mother and child had incompatible Rh factors. (Mildred's mother had died in childbirth from a similar medical syndrome.) As Turner mused: "It's one of life's bitter ironies that I, who wanted a big family, could bear only one child. Eventually I lost three babies . . . [and] it took a miracle just to save [Cheryl's] life." Extending maternal pathos, Lana confessed that she had already aborted a child by her first husband, Artie Shaw, and would terminate a pregnancy by a lover, Tyrone Power.[88]

color line" (Bogle, *Blacks in American Films,* p. 478). In truth, she refused to "pass" even though theater colleagues urged her to do so to enjoy a more successful stage career. Ironically, she ran into problems as an openly black actress. Playing opposite Paul Robeson in *The Emperor Jones* (1933), she had her skin darkened with pancake make-up in order to make it clear that she was Negro, and that miscegenation was not involved (Ibid., p. 80).

85. Richard Dyer, *Stars* (London: British Film Institute, 1982), p. 110.
86. Lana Turner, *Lana: The Lady, the Legend, the Truth* (New York: Dutton, 1982), p. 24.
87. Ibid., p. 84.
88. Ibid.. pp. 90, 64, 119.

As Cheryl grew, Turner experienced radical conflicts about parenthood—which was counterposed to her job as an actress. "I adored [the child] but because I worked so often and late, she usually saw more of my mother and Nana than she did of me." Turner was also aware of the disparity between fan magazine coverage and pallid reality:

I [can] remember well the first time I gave Cheryl a bath. She must have been close to a year old. . . . It was . . . Nana's day off. The house was empty, and it was the first time I had been absolutely alone with my baby. So I was surprised to read the romanticized account that appeared in *Photoplay* in December 1943, many months before I actually bathed Cheryl: '. . . My name is Cheryl Christina Crane. . . . There's my grandmother, and Daddy and Mother, and two maids, and my nurse and me. Only sometimes I wonder what the nurse is for—because Mother likes to do everything for me.'

Throughout this period, Turner tried to "maintain the image of a woman who had combined a satisfying marriage with a successful film career."[89] Her deception was assisted by the discourse of journalism which negated cinema as labor. Dyer cites news features that depict "Stars off the Set," or "Hollywood at Play": "what is suppressed . . . in these articles is that making films is work." Production interviews were frequently illustrated with stills of the leads' sumptuous dressing rooms: "Even on the shop-floor, stars [were] not shown . . . making films."[90] Thus, the audience might well have believed that Turner could be both exemplary movie queen and superior parent.

Crane's recollections of childhood support the picture of maternal absence, of a stark contrast between publicity hype and daily life:

What I cannot bring back from the mist of those first postwar years is memory of Mother herself. I have seen all the posed press photos from that era . . . but they inspire in me no sense of memory whatsoever, no recollection of the warmth of a cuddle or the softness of a kiss. Most of the time Mother was off somewhere making movies or on holiday.

Despite her pain, Crane was aware of her mother's position, and comprehended that Turner's behavior was "standard [Hollywood] operating procedure":

There was nothing unusual about a star mother being uninvolved with her children. Until the 1950s . . . cinema goddesses kept murderous work schedules, often making as many as three pictures a year. Most stars had little time and less inclination to take on the extra job of raising children. The task was usually turned over to hired help.[91]

89. Ibid., pp. 143–145, 157.
90. Dyer, *Stars*, pp. 44–45.
91. Cheryl Crane with Cliff Jahr, *Detour: A Hollywood Story* (New York: William Morrow, 1988), pp. 76, 73.

In Cheryl's case, the surrogate caregivers were her grandmother and myriad nurses. Following Hollywood custom, Turner hired European women; there is no indication that Cheryl's nannies were ever black.

When Lana was home, her daughter found her unavailable, a "perfect dream of golden beauty, unattainable, beyond reach." The child quickly learned the alienating rules of the game: "As I was handed up [to Mother] for a careful hug and peck, lips never touched lips, skin hardly touched skin. It was for show." Ironically, a fan sent Cheryl a three-foot Turner replica, which she deemed her "Mommy doll." Because it was so precious, she was forbidden to play with it— just as she was with her parent. In recent years, Crane has come to empathize with her mother's plight. Life had simply "miscast her in the role."[92]

In this characterization of Turner's drama, we find echoes of *Imitation*: the sentimental tone, the struggle of women alone, the focus on mothers and daughters, the conflict between work and family, the question of theatrical role-playing, the reliance on surrogate caregivers, the charges of abuse and neglect. Some of these themes were perennials in Turner's media coverage. (As Dyer remarks, the star system relishes a sense of the "dream soured.")[93] The press had chronicled Turner's numerous truncated marriages—envisioning her as unlucky in love. Her daughter had experienced a series of publicized problems: trouble in school, runaway episodes. But there was one occurrence, prior to *Imitation*'s release, that entirely structured its reading and reception: Cheryl Crane's stabbing of Turner's lover, Johnny Stompanato. (As David Rodowick has noted: "The melodramatic text forces the equation of sexuality and violence.")[94]

The event took place on 4 April 1958—Good Friday—when the three principals were alone in the house. Crane, then fifteen (the age her mother was "discovered"), overheard a fight between Turner and Stompanato, and was alarmed when he threatened physical violence. Crane obtained a knife from the kitchen and stood outside the entrance to her mother's pink bedroom. When Turner opened the door, Crane thought she saw Stompanato lunging and jabbed him in the chest. During the ensuing weeks, the scandal received constant media focus. The world followed the inquest and Turner's testimony. Eventually, the court ruled justifiable homicide, but Crane was removed from her parents' custody and placed in her grandmother's charge. Thus, in the lurid lifestyle of the rich and famous, Turner's status as an "unfit mother" was broadcast, and her battles with gigolos and recalcitrant children were charted. Rumors circulated that exacerbated the situation: Lana had murdered her lover and blamed Cheryl; the girl had been sexually involved with Stompanato.

It was within this context that *Imitation* was made and released. Clearly, its narrative of mother/daughter tension, of the failures of the professional woman,

92. Ibid., pp. 77–78.
93. Dyer, *Stars*, p. 50.
94. Rodowick, "Madness, Authority and Ideology," p. 272.

had particular resonance for the movie-viewing public of 1959—steeped in the Feminine Mystique and the Turner Mythos. Even the news reports of the crime made snide connections between the actress's personal and cinematic incarnations. A *Time* column was entitled "The Bad & the Beautiful," a reference to a 1952 film in which Turner appeared. Its opening line mockingly compared her life to soap opera: "Can a simple girl from a mining town in Idaho find happiness as a glamorous movie queen?" Later, in the essay's description of the hearing, it called Turner's deposition a "performance" which "rang true." The piece also described the proceedings in theatrical terms: "At the Los Angeles Hall of Records, onlookers crowded the corridors to get a glimpse of the drama, ohed and ahed as the principles threaded into the courtroom."[95]

In a similar vein, *Life* counterposed pictures of Turner on the stand with stills from her cinematic courtroom scenes: *The Postman Always Rings Twice* (1947), *Cass Timberlane* (1948), and *Peyton Place* (1957). It also implied that her testimony was contrived: "Lana had been nominated for an Academy Award . . . but this was a dramatic, personal triumph far beyond anything she had achieved as an actress."[96] *Peyton Place* experienced a 20 percent box-office surge: Turner was cast there as a witness at the homicide trial of her daughter's friend.[97]

It is a common belief that the production of *Imitation* capitalized on the Stompanato scandal. Though the narrative skirts the subject of murder, it concerns the life of a performer and invokes maternal neglect, mother/daughter strife, and incestuous rivalry over a man. Turner herself recognized the association between life and art. In discussing the offer to do the film, she remarked:

One element of the story spooked me. It was the relationship of the actress and her teenage daughter, to whom she had given every advantage but love and attention, the only important ones. I knew that painful comparisons would inevitably be made. "No, I can't do it," I said. "I'm frightened."

Later, she rationalized her affirmative decision by finding "the role . . . the perfect way to show people that [she] could rise above the tragedy."[98]

The parallels between fact and fiction were not lost on Cheryl Crane, who suspected that Turner had always "liked to play real life scenes . . . that showed special maternal concern." (Crane called these occasions "nice cinematic moment[s].") At the premiere of *Peyton Place,* she watched Turner and her screen daughter, concluding that "the techniques Mother used to intimidate and control me came not from a well of feeling but from her bag of actress tricks."[99]

Given the circumstances of April 1958, Crane's reaction to *Imitation* was more severe. She vividly recalls visiting the set and being appalled to find the crew

95. "The Bad and the Beautiful," *Time,* 21 April 1958, pp. 17–18.
96. "Lana's Plea for Daughter Is Real-Life Drama Triumph," *Life,* 21 April 1958, p. 21.
97. "Cheryl—If . . . If . . . If," *Newsweek,* 21 April 1958, p. 34.
98. Turner, *Lana,* p. 256.
99. Crane, *Detour,* pp. 4, 111, 210.

shooting at a school she had attended: "I sensed I would never be part of any graduation ceremony, mock or real, but there I stood getting my diploma in the person of actress Sandra Dee."[100] Crane (who regretted not resembling her mother) found that Dee ("pert, pretty and blond"), looked "more like Mother's daughter" than she.

When Crane finally viewed *Imitation,* she was shocked more profoundly: "When I saw . . . how much it borrowed from our lives—the amorous star who spoils and ignores her daughter, the pink bedroom, my actual junior high school, the graduation present of a horse—well, it all made me feel used."[101] In particular, Crane felt "a shiver of recognition" as Sandra Dee spoke the lines: "Oh, Mama, stop *acting,*" or complained of receiving love only "by telephone, by postcard, by magazine interview."

Crane later acknowledged the pressures on Turner to accept the role, given her financial debt and career slump. Furthermore, Lana was thirty-nine, a difficult age for a Hollywood glamour queen forced to negotiate the role shift from ingenue to matron. As Christian Viviani notes, "any star worth her salt gave in at least once in her career to the ritual of maternal suffering . . . it assured her that the public was ready to accept her ageing."[102] Again, this situation is doubled in *Imitation.* Though more middle-aged women than ever were working, much is made of Lora's advanced years. When Steve first learns of her career ambitions, he inquires: "Aren't you a little late getting started?" Allen Loomis tells her that "time isn't on your side."

While Crane saw ties between her own life and the Merediths, Turner also identified with the Johnsons. The hardest scene for her to shoot was Annie's funeral:

> I most dreaded the part when Annie's repentant daughter would throw herself on the casket, reminding the star of her troubled relationship with her own daughter. . . . When I heard the first strains of that [funeral] song in my rehearsal, I simply broke down. Images of my own life, my own dark fears flooded my mind.[103]

She recalled that she "dissolved in tears," and "fled"—perhaps like *McCall's* Mother Who Ran Away.

A poster for *Imitation* underscores the links between its promotional address and the Stompanato affair. In tying the film to its literary source (written in 1932), the ad mentions "Fannie Hurst's best selling novel of *today's* tormented generation" (my italics).[104] This temporal move displaces the distanced setting of

100. Ibid., p. 261.
101. Ibid., pp. 272–273.
102. Christian Viviani, "Who Is Without Sin?: The Maternal Melodrama in American Film, 1930–39," in *Home Is Where the Heart Is,* ed. Gledhill, p. 84.
103. Turner, *Lana,* p. 257.
104. Joe Morella, Edward Epstein, Eleanor Clark, *Those Great Movie Ads* (New Rochelle, N.Y.: Arlington House, 1972), p. 198.

the 1930s in favor of the sensational scene of the 1950s. Similarly, the film trailers highlight themes relevant to Turner's romantic and parental struggles. On-screen graphics announce: "What a mother says to a daughter" and "What a daughter says to a mother." Clips reiterate the damning lines (spoken by Sandra Dee) that Crane most dreads. A narrator's voice promises that Turner will play a "great stage star," with countless "men in her life."[105] (During the scandal, *Time* ran a Hedda Hopper quote which read: "To [Turner] men are like new dresses, to be . . . doffed at her pleasure.")[106]

Clearly, Turner's personal tragedy was utilized to sell *Imitation,* and contributed to its commercial success. Just as Steve aestheticized Lora's Coney Island trauma (in a photograph he entitled "Mother in Distress"), so Universal narrativized Turner's tabloid scandal. *Imitation* proved one of the studio's largest box-office hits and (despite the ethics of her complicity), Turner grew rich on the deal: having forfeited a large fee, she earned a major share of the work's profits.[107] Thus, while Hollywood used her, she manipulated it—in a reciprocal orgy of public and private exploitation. If the newspapers taunted her, she got the better of them, laughing all the way to the bank.

Epilogue: Fatal Attraction

Obsession: Compulsive preoccupation with a fixed idea or unwanted feeling or emotion, often with symptoms of anxiety.

I began by querying our collective enchantment with *Imitation of Life* and configured it a chiasma for myriad compelling cultural forces. In particular, I conjured three social scenes—women and work, race relations, star mythology— and envisioned the text a tripaneled "mirror" that constituted, transposed, and reflected these worlds.

In the stories of Lora Meredith and Annie Johnson, we found a veiled saga of the postwar American woman: her unresolved tensions between job, family, and romance; her struggles with upward mobility; her conflicts between employment and motherhood; her need for social services; her status as an older worker. In Lora, the film initially imagines a resistant heroine who avoids the Happy Housewife Syndrome, rejecting the comforts of bourgeois marriage for a risky career. Eventually, she is bridled—united with her daughter and lover in a instant of defeat and regret. (Sirk admits that, in melodrama, "there is no real solution to the predicament . . . just the *deus ex machina* which is . . . called 'the happy end.'")[108] In Annie, the movie conceives a transcendent madonna and domestic

---

105. "Script for Trailer #1/North to IMITATION OF LIFE," 4 March 1959 (Doheny Library, University of Southern California).
106. "Death on the Pink Carpet," *Time,* 14 April 1958, p. 21.
107. "All Time Rentals," *Variety,* 6 May 1987; Crane, *Detour,* p. 275.
108. Halliday, *Sirk on Sirk,* p. 132.

servant. Although at first she is favored over the rebellious woman, the two heroines are leveled: both are failed parents and disillusioned workers who question their choices and fate.

While the film vocalizes the growing aspirations of women (their discontent with the sexual and racial status quo), it creates an ambivalent discourse around this topic. Through the alter egos Annie/Lora, it splits female consciousness into shifting, incompatible halves—good mother and bad, natural woman and perverse, black and white, lower- and upper-caste, housewife and professional—rather than imagining their potential merging. And it fabricates a suspect solution to the dilemma of the middle-class professional woman: a deferent black double who assumes the position she vacates.

Superimposed upon *Imitation*'s collective tale is the story of an individual—Lana Turner—a notorious woman, plagued by conflicts of personal life and career. Like Lora Meredith, she is a gorgeous, single, working mother dependent on surrogate care, raising a troubled daughter who is resentful of her achievement. Though Sirk undercuts a conservative thrust (with strategies of distanciation and hyperbole), some have seen in his irony a "misogynist edge."[109] Sirk himself admits that he could not always "conquer [his] material," that he both "loved" and "hated" it.[110]

While we have found ourselves drawn to the film (its plush style, its cult aura, its comic amplification of generic codes, its skewering of bourgeois existence), we have, at times, felt this pull a fatal attraction: pained as we are by the text's program for black and white working women; by its inability (like Sarah Jane in her final meeting with Annie) to utter proudly the word "mama." These are the uneasy emotions that accompany cinematic obsession: such "unwanted feelings" and "symptoms of anxiety" keep *Imitation* perennially under our critical skins.

109. Christine Gledhill, "Introduction—The Melodramatic Field: An Investigation," in *Home Is Where the Heart Is: Studies in Melodrama and the Woman's Film*, ed. Gledhill (London: British Film Institute, 1987), p. 12.
110. Halliday, *Sirk on Sirk*, pp. 95–96.

Douglas Sirk: A Biographical Sketch

Douglas Sirk (named Claus Detler Sierck) was born to Danish parents in Hamburg, Germany, on 26 April 1900.[1] Sirk's family returned to Denmark for a period of time, and he spent his childhood in Skagen, where he received a classical education. His family went back to Germany after World War I—a period of great cultural and political upheaval—and Sirk attended various schools and universities. Sources mention his studying at the Naval Academy in Murwik in 1918, his pursuing law at Munich university, and philosophy at Jena in 1919, and his studying painting and art history (under Erwin Panofsky) at the University of Hamburg from 1920 to 1922. While in Hamburg, Sirk attended Albert Einstein's famous lectures on relativity, and was moved by the "dark and mighty breath of the new century."

Sirk's first occupational interest was journalism, his father's profession. In 1920 (as a break from university work), he began to write for the *Neue Hamburger Zeitung*. Then, in 1921, he became involved in the theater, and was hired as an assistant dramaturg at the Deutches Schauspielhaus in Hamburg. He tired soon of recommending plays to stage, and finally got an opportunity to direct one: *Stationmaster Death* by Hermann Bossdorf. "From there on," he admits, he "was lost to theater."

In 1921, Sirk was appointed director of the Kleines Theater in Chemnitz, which was run as a collective. He was soon frustrated by its penchant for producing crowd-pleasers: melodramas and comedies. In 1923, he moved to the Schauspielhaus in Bremen, a superior theater in a more sophisticated town. En route, he stopped in Berlin and worked as a set designer for a film—building on

---

This biographical sketch attempts to integrate previously published information on Sirk's life. Various sources offer contradictory information and such variances have been noted. The sources consulted are listed at the end of the sketch.

1. Some sources spell his name "Sierk." Some assert that his birthplace was Skagen, Denmark. See Bawden, Katz, Sadoul, and Smith and Cawkwell.

his early interest in art. Over the next six years, Sirk struggled in his theatrical work to transcend the ubiquity of expressionist influence. In so doing, he staged August Strindberg's *Dream Play,* Friedrich von Schiller's *The Robbers,* Bertolt Brecht's *The Threepenny Opera,* William Shakespeare's *Othello, Antony and Cleopatra,* and *Cymbeline,* and Arnolt Bronnen's *Rheinische Rebellen.* He also presented works by Heinrich von Kleist, J. W. von Goethe, Henrik Ibsen, George Bernard Shaw, and Luigi Pirandello. Sirk did some acting (in Euripides' *Medea* and in Strindberg's *Easter*), but considers it of no professional import. While in Bremen, Sirk met his wife, Hilde Jary, an actress in the theater company. In 1927, he "Germanized" his name to Hans Detlef Sierck.

In 1929, during the onslaught of the Depression, he was named the manager of the Altes Theater in Leipzig—where Goethe had attended dramas. It was a diffi-cult time for the arts and Sirk bemoaned the fact that only the wealthy could afford theater tickets. He would work in Leipzig actively until 1933 and hold a title until 1936. While there, he also taught at a local drama school. At the Altes Theater, Sirk oversaw adaptations of works by Shakespeare, Ibsen, Schiller, Shaw, Brecht, Pedro Calderón, Strindberg, and Sophocles. The fascists were gaining power and he began to acquire a leftist, avant-garde reputation. In 1930, he angered Nazi critics with his production of Bernhard Blume's play about Sacco and Vanzetti, *Im Namen Des Volkes!* In 1933, he staged Georg Kaiser and Kurt Weill's *The Silver Lake,* and the official Nazi newspaper, *Volkischer Beobachter,* called the authors "salon bolshevists" and threatened that the drama stood to "cost [them] very dear." Between 1929 and 1936 he presented some one hundred productions in the classical, modern, and experimental repertory. Dur-ing this period, Sirk was approached to be head of the Berliner Staatstheater—an offer that was withdrawn when it was learned that his wife was Jewish.

Sirk became involved with the cinema in 1934 when he was hired by Ger-many's major studio, UFA, to make three short films—among them, *Der Eingebildete Kranke* (Molière's *The Imaginary Invalid*), and *Dreimal Liebe* (*Three Times Love*). He made the move to cinema hoping that Nazi censorship would be less severe than in the theater. (UFA was privately owned at the time, and Sirk claims that no fascists were yet a part of it.) In 1935, he was given his first feature assignment, a comic, semi-musical (rife with mistaken identity) which (following early sound film practice) was made both in German (*April, April*) and in Dutch (*'T was één April*). (The latter was co-directed by Jacques van Pol.) He also made *Das Mädchen vom Moorhof* (*The Girl from the Marsh Croft*), based on a love story by Selma Lagerlöf; and *Stützen der Gesellschaft* (*Pillars of Society*), based on a work of social commentary by Ibsen. In 1936, Sirk directed *Schlussakkord* (*Final Accord*), a maternal melodrama, and, for the first time "went off the literary thing" to make "a complete break with [his] theatrical past." He also directed *Das Hofkonzert* (*The Court Concert*)—a musi-cal romance set in the nineteenth century, which Sirk has deemed a "piece of Viennese pastry." UFA gave him responsibility for building the career of its new acting discovery, Zarah Leander. In 1937, he directed her in *Zu Neuen Ufern* (*Life Begins Anew/To New Shores*)—a dark romance with a crime subplot. The same year, they worked together on *La Habanera*—a drama of doomed lovers, set in Puerto Rico. Sirk considers both films to be works of social criticism. He also coscripted Hans Hinrich's *Liebling der Matrosen* and collaborated on a screenplay for *Dreiklang*—based on two Russian stories (*The Shot* by Aleksandr Pushkin and *First Love* by Ivan Turgenev). Other unrealized projects in Germany were screen versions of Anton Chekhov's *The Shooting Party* and of William Faulkner's *Pylon* (both later filmed in Hollywood). Sirk also attempted to make a film about the medieval Children's Crusade—but never found financial backing for it. He ultimately completed nine features between 1935 and 1937, mastering his craft, picture by picture. As he has stated: "I learned to trust my eyes rather more than the windiness of words."

In December 1937, Sirk traveled to Italy with his wife under the guise of "scouting locations" for *Wiltons Zoo*. (He had thought of leaving Germany earlier, but did not have a passport.) In Rome, he feigned illness while he made arrangements to go to Zurich and Paris. Sirk rejected an appeal by Josef Goebbels to return to Germany, and UFA filed a lawsuit against him for breach of contract.

In 1938, Sirk was asked to expand Jean Renoir's short film, *Une Partie de Campagne* (made in 1936, released in 1946) into a feature, but the project was abandoned. Sirk was interested because Renoir had influenced him in both his cinematic and theatrical work: "This Mozartian touch . . . an eye like a painter." In 1939, Sirk directed *Accord Final* in Paris—a love story set in the world of music—and *Boefje* in Holland—a film that enacts a struggle between an adolescent criminal and a priest. Sirk then received an invitation from Warner Brothers to direct a version of *Zu Neuen Ufern* in the United States, and he decided to emigrate. He would work there for two decades.

Once in American (in 1940), the remake project was scratched and his contract with Warner Brothers terminated. (The studio realized that it would be commercial suicide to revise a German picture at that time.) For a while, Sirk worked the script stages around Hollywood on numerous unconsummated projects. Disgusted with the film industry, he raised chickens in the San Fernando Valley and farmed alfalfa in Pomona County. Though "completely broke," he recalls that "it was maybe [his] happiest time in America." In 1941, he made a short color film about a monastery/winery. He was, then, invited to head a San Francisco light opera company, but plans were aborted with America's entrance into the war. Sirk temporarily returned to agriculture.

In 1942, Sirk signed a seven-year contract with Columbia Pictures as a writer, but directed an independent film (his American debut), *Hitler's Madman* (released in 1943), a low-budget feature, distributed by MGM. It was the first film he signed as "Douglas Sirk." He was asked by Maria Matray to do a remake of *The Cabinet of Dr. Caligari* (1919), but the project was abandoned after several months of work. In 1944, he completed a second picture, *Summer Storm* (distributed by United Artists), an adaptation of the Chekhov piece Sirk had wanted to film in Germany. A tale of murder and seduction, set in pre-revolutionary Russia, it was both a critical and a commercial success. In 1944, he prepared a production of *Cagliostro* (based on Alexandre Dumas's *Memoirs of a Physician*), but the project was never realized. In 1945, he directed *A Scandal in Paris* (released in 1946), a drama about the life of French criminal Eugène Vidocq. And in 1946, he made *Lured* (released in 1947), a story of the British vice squad, set in turn-of-the-century London. He also worked uncredited on Edgar Ulmer's *The Strange Woman* (1946). In 1947, he made *Sleep, My Love* (released in 1948), a film about a man who seeks to murder his wife. He also worked uncredited on *Siren of Atlantis* (directed by Gregg Tallas). In 1948, he shot *Slightly French* (about relations between a film director and his stars) and *Shockproof* (released in 1949), a tale of love and homicide. He also worked uncredited on *Lulu Belle*, directed by Leslie Fenton.

In 1949, his contract with Columbia was terminated. Sirk was "sick of the whole business" and fed up with Harry Cohn, head of the studio. He journeyed to Germany, where he spent a year—finding the film world in shambles and the political climate hostile to returning émigrés. Back in Hollywood in 1950, he scripted a remake of Fritz Lang's *M,* which was later directed by Joseph Losey. He also produced and directed *The First Legion,* based on a play by Emmet Lavery, set in a Jesuit seminary.

In 1950, he signed a seven-year contract with Universal (where he would make his best-known films). His first projects were *Mystery Submarine* (about an American undercover agent who infiltrates a German ship) and *Thunder on the Hill* (released in 1951), about a woman mistakenly charged with murder. In 1951 he worked on *The Lady Pays Off* (about a female teacher), *Weekend with Father* (a romance about a widow and a widower), and *Has Anybody Seen My Gal?* (released in 1952), about an eccentric millionaire investigating his heirs. The last was his first color feature and his initial encounter with Rock Hudson, who would appear in seven other Sirk films. In 1952 he shot *No Room for the Groom* (about a Korean veteran), *Meet Me at the Fair* (about an orphan befriended by showpeople), *Take Me to Town* (about a preacher's liaison with a woman "with a past"), and *All I Desire* (about a wife's return to the Wisconsin town she has long abandoned). (The latter three were all released the following year.) *Take Me to Town* marked the beginning of two important collaborations for Sirk—with cinematographer Russell Metty, and with producer Ross Hunter. He would work with both of them, intermittently, for the duration of his career.

In 1953, Sirk shot a 3D western, *Taza, Son of Cochise* (released in 1954), and a historical spectacle about Attila the Hun, *Sign of the Pagan* (released in 1954), his first Cinemascope film. He also directed *Magnificent Obsession* (released in 1954)—a remake of a 1935 John Stahl work. In 1954 he shot *Captain Lightfoot* (released in 1955), a work set in the Irish Revolution of the nineteenth century,

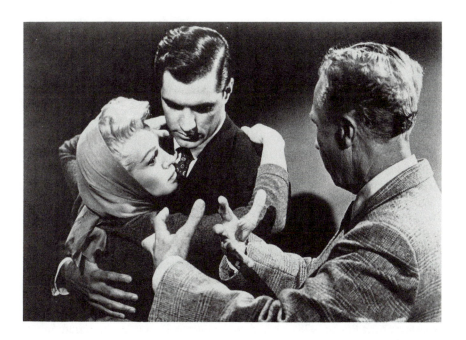

and in 1955 a series of his most famous melodramas. *All That Heaven Allows* concerns a love affair between a widow and a younger man; *There's Always Tomorrow* (1956) deals with a married man's interest in an ex-lover; and *Written on the Wind* (1956) charts the dissolution of a Texas oil family. Sirk also worked uncredited on *Never Say Goodbye.* In 1956, he directed *Battle Hymn* (released in 1957), the story of an American airman, and *Interlude,* a film which brought him back to Europe (Bavaria and Austria). In 1956–57, he made *The Tarnished Angels,* an adaptation of Faulkner's *Pylon* (which he had wanted to film in Germany). In 1957, he directed *A Time to Live and a Time to Die* (released in 1958)—based on an Erich Maria Remarque novel about two lovers in war-torn Europe—a film which he shot in Germany. In 1958, he made *Imitation of Life* (released in 1959)—one of Universal's greatest box office successes of all time.

Ultimately, Sirk made twenty-one films for Universal, between 1950 and 1959. Working with producers Albert Zugsmith and Ross Hunter, he had been quite content there—finding that the studio granted him more freedom (on script development, camerawork, and editing) than had Columbia. He also enjoyed the opportunity of working with the era's major stars, not only Rock Hudson but Lana Turner, Jane Wyman, Jeff Chandler, Claudette Colbert, Ann Blyth, Linda Darnell, Van Heflin, Patricia Neal, Piper Laurie, Tony Curtis, Dan Dailey, Ann Sheridan, Sterling Hayden, Barbara Stanwyck, Agnes Moorhead, John Gavin, Jack Palance, Joan Bennett, Lauren Bacall, Robert Stack, Dan Duryea, June Allyson, Rossano Brazzi, and Dorothy Malone.

In 1959, Sirk ended his association with Universal. Few understood why he would leave when he had reached the peak of his career. Later, he recalled: "I had outgrown this kind of picture-making which . . . was typical of Hollywood in the fifties and of American society, too, which tolerated only the play that pleases, not the thing that disturbs the mind." He worked on a screenplay for an independent production of *The Streets of Montmartre,* a biography of Utrillo (co-scripted by Eugène Ionesco), but the project was dropped when Sirk became ill. He settled in Ruvigliana, a village near Lugano, Switzerland, and became involved again with European theater. In the sixties, he periodically staged works with the Residenz Theater in Munich and with other companies in Hamburg. Among the works he presented were Edmond Rostand's *Cyrano de Bergerac,* Eugène Ionesco's *Le Roi Se Meurt,* Shakespeare's *The Tempest,* Schiller's *The Parasite,* and Molière's *The Miser.* The last play he staged was Tennessee William's *The Seven Descents of Myrtle*—done in Hamburg in 1969. He resumed use of the name Detlef Sierck.

During the mid- to late-1970s, Sirk taught at the Munich Acadamy of Film and Television and supervised the making of three dramatic shorts: *Sprich zu Mir Wie die Regen* (*Talk to Me Like the Rain,* 1975), which was based on a Williams work; *Silvesternacht* (1977)—adapted from a play by Arthur Schnitzler, and *Bourbon Street Blues* (1978)—based on Williams's *The Lady of Larkspur Street.* The latter work was credited to Sirk.

In 1979, Sirk returned to the United States for a three-week visit to San Francisco and New York, receiving the adulation of a fresh generation of film viewers and scholars, and serving as an advocate for the New German Cinema. He died on 14 January 1987, in Lugano, Switzerland—reportedly, of cancer. In 1972, to close his interview with Jon Halliday, he referred to his life as "A long day's journey. . . . The end of a circle." To quell the note of pessimism in that characterization, he added: "Don't take this as resignation. There's still a lot that heaven allows."

Sources

Bawden, Liz-Anne, ed. *Oxford Companion to Film.* New York and London: Oxford, 1976.

Coursodon, Jean-Pierre and Pierre Sauvage. *American Directors, Volume 1.* New York: McGraw-Hill, 1983.

"Douglas Sirk, Made *Magnificent Obsession.*" *New York Times* (16 January 1987): D 19.

Halliday, Jon. *Sirk on Sirk.* New York: Viking, 1972.

Horrigan, James. "An Analysis of the Construction of an Author: Douglas Sirk." Ph.D. dissertation, Northwestern University, 1980.

Katz, Ephram. *The Film Encyclopedia.* New York: Thomas Y. Crowell, 1979.

Manvell, Roger, ed. *International Encyclopedia of Film.* New York: Crown
    Publishers, 1972.

"Melodrama Master Douglas Sirk Succumbs in Switzerland at 86." *Variety* (21
    January 1987): 6, 237.

Mulvey, Laura and Jon Halliday, eds. *Douglas Sirk.* Edinburgh: Edinburgh
    Film Festival, 1972.

Quinlan, David, ed. *Illustrated Guide to Film Directors.* Totowa, N.J.: Barnes
    and Noble Books, 1983.

Sadoul, Georges. *Dictionary of Film Makers.* Berkeley and Los Angeles:
    University of California Press, 1972.

Smith, John and Tim Cawkwell, eds. *World Encyclopedia of Film.* New York:
    World Publishing, 1972.

Stern, Michael, *Douglas Sirk.* Boston: Twayne, 1979.

Wakeman, John, ed. *World Film Directors.* New York: The H. W. Wilson Co.,
    1987.

Imitation of Life

Imitation of Life

Executing a shot-by-shot analysis of *Imitation of Life* is a challenge because of the ubiquity of camera and character movement and the failure of any shot to be static. Though one may identify a shot as beginning at a certain codified distance, the camera moves throughout, sliding from close-up to medium shot to long shot in a single take. Sirk's thoughts on this issue seem relevant: "the camera is the main thing . . . because there is *emotion* in the motion pictures. Motion is emotion, in a way it can never be in the theatre" (Halliday, *Sirk on Sirk,* p. 43).

In preparing the continuity script, I have used the 35mm print on file at the Library of Congress, and the current videotape release print. I have also consulted Universal's own "Continuity and Dialogue" for *Imitation,* which is housed at the Doheny Library of the University of Southern California.

Costumes have been noted where they seem relevant (particularly in relation to the character of Lora Meredith). The "Imitation of Life" musical theme has been noted in the continuity, but not the other more incidental music.

Camera distance, placement, and movement will be indicated by the following abbreviations:

ELS   extreme long shot (landscape or other spatial entity; human figures are subordinate to the total field).

LS   long shot (ranging from the totality of a unified, room-sized decor to the whole human figure).

MS   medium shot (human figure from the knees or waist up).

MCU   medium close-up (head and shoulders/chest).

CU   close-up (the whole of a face, other part of body, or object).

ECU   extreme close-up (section of face, other part of body or object).

When characters are described as moving "right" or "left," this means *screen*-right and *screen*-left (that is, as viewed from the perspective of the spectator).

I have maintained the "dialect" indicated in the original script for the dialogue of the character of Annie.

Credits and Cast

Director
Douglas Sirk

Producer
Ross Hunter

Production Company
Universal-International

Screenplay
Eleanore Griffin and Allan Scott,
  based on the novel by Fannie Hurst

Director of Photography
Russell Metty

Art Directors
Alexander Golitzen
Richard H. Riedel

Costumes
Bill Thomas
Gowns for Lana Turner by Jean Louis
Jewels for Lana Turner by Laykin
  et Cie

Editor
Milton Carruth

Sound
Leslie I. Carey
Joe Lapis

Music
Frank Skinner
Joseph Gershenson
"Imitation of Life": Music by Sammy
  Fain; lyrics by Paul Francis
  Webster; sung by Earl Grant
"Trouble of the World": Traditional;
  sung by Mahalia Jackson
"Empty Arms": Music by Arnold
  Hughes; lyrics by Frederick
  Herbert; sung by Susan Kohner

Set Design
Russell A. Gausman
Julia Heron

Make-up
Bud Westmore

Hair Stylist
Larry Germain

Assistant Director
Frank Shaw

Special Photography
Clifford Stine

Process
Eastmancolor by Pathé

U.S. Release Date
April 17, 1959 (New York premiere)

Length
125 minutes

Cast

Lora Meredith
Lana Turner

Steve Archer
John Gavin

Susie Meredith (age 16)
Sandra Dee

Sarah Jane Johnson (age 18)
Susan Kohner

Allen Loomis
Robert Alda

David Edwards
Dan O'Herlihy

Annie Johnson
Juanita Moore

Choir Soloist
Mahalia Jackson

Sarah Jane (age 8)
Karin Dicker

Susie (age 6)
Terry Burnham

Young Man
John Vivyan

Photographer
Lee Goodman

Showgirl
Ann Robinson

Frankie
Troy Donahue

Receptionist
Sandra Gould

Early Man
David Tomack

Minister
Joel Fluellen

Stage Manager
Jack Weston

Fat Man
Billy House

Teacher
Maida Severn

Romano
Than Wyenn

Fay
Peg Shirley

The Continuity Script

Credits

The credits unroll (in a series of dissolves), against a fuchsia background. Clear glass, faceted, jewel-like beads slowly fall from the top of the screen to the bottom—collecting at lower frame level. They gradually fill the frame like a container until it is entirely packed. The beads shift in space ever so slightly. During the credits, the following theme song ("Imitation of Life"), is sung by Earl Grant:

What is love without the giving?
Without love you're only living
An imitation, an imitation of life.

Skies above in flaming color,
Without love, they're so much duller,
A false creation, an imitation of life.

Would the song of the lark sound just as sweet?
Would the moon be as bright above?
Everyday would be gray and incomplete
Without the one you love.

Lips that kiss can tell you clearly
Without this, our lives are merely
An imitation, an imitation of life.

Coney Island, exterior, day

1. ELS: *Coney Island beach, with bathers in the foreground water. A ferris wheel and roller coaster are visible on the horizon. From off-screen, we hear the sound of "The Blue Danube Waltz" being played in hurdy-gurdy style.*

2. *High* ELS: *people milling on the beach.*

3. *High* ELS: *as in 2, but seen from another direction.*

4. ELS: *beach with boardwalk in the background. Crowds of people mill around.*
   Dissolve.

5. MS: *railing of the boardwalk, with people passing behind; only their legs are visible. Lora Meredith comes in from screen-right toward the railing until her legs are seen behind it. She stops and leans over it. She is wearing a light blue, scoop-neck shirtwaist dress, with a black belt. She wears sandals and an apricot scarf.*
   LORA: Susie! Susie!
   The camera pulls back and cranes left to follow her as she moves left. It frames her in MLS *as she stands behind a boardwalk sign that reads: "Coming—The 1947 Coney Island Mardi Gras. Sept. 8th Thru 14th." The camera cranes left and pulls back to frame Lora in a more extreme* LS. *She bends over the railing.*
   LORA: Susie!
   The camera cranes left and pulls back as Lora runs left toward the stairs to the beach. The camera cranes down to the bottom of the flight, keeping her in LS. *As she descends the stairs, she passes Steve Archer, a photographer who is taking pictures.*
   LORA: Susie!
   The camera leaves Steve and passes further left, toward the foreground— as Lora speaks to an older man. The camera stops and frames them in MS.
   LORA: Pardon me! Have you seen a little girl in a blue sunsuit?
   The man walks away, annoyed.
   LORA: Oh!
   Lora turns right and walks toward Steve. The camera pans to follow.

6. MCU: *Lora bumps into Steve as he is taking photographs.*
   LORA: Oh, I'm awfully sorry!
   STEVE: No harm done.
   LORA: I'm looking for my daughter! Have you seen a little girl—all by herself?

STEVE: No, but if you'll—

LORA (*turning away*): Well, she's lost and I—Susie!

STEVE (*grabbing her and turning her around*): Relax, lady! Take it easy!

LORA: Susie!

STEVE: The easiest way to find Susie is to go to the police.

LORA: Well, where are the police?

Steve looks up at the boardwalk and pushes Lora toward the stairs. The camera cranes to follow them.

STEVE: Right there. (*He points up the stairs.*)

The camera moves with them and tilts up to frame a policeman and Annie Johnson. Lora ascends the stairs as Annie descends.

POLICEMAN (*to Annie*): Right where?

ANNIE (*pointing*): Right down there—under the pier.

Annie walks down the stairs as the camera follows. She passes Steve, who is still taking pictures. The shot ends with Steve taking snapshots, framed in MS.

7. MLS: *Sarah Jane Johnson and Susie Meredith, amidst other children, playing under the pier. Sarah Jane chases Susie. The children are squealing and laughing. Annie enters left and walks into the depth of the frame.*

ANNIE: Come, children! Do you hear me, Sarah Jane?

The children continue to run.

ANNIE: Hot dogs!

SUSIE: Hot dogs! Come on! Boy!

8. MS: *Annie, Susie, and Sarah Jane under the pier. The children eat their hot dogs.*

ANNIE (*taking off her shoes*): It might be the noise of that old ocean, but it seems to me I didn't hear any "thank yous" for those hot dogs.

SUSIE: I was too hungry! Thank you.

SARAH JANE: Thank you!

ANNIE (*putting her arm around Susie*): Honey, you're gonna be all right. I reported you.

SUSIE (*grabbing Sarah Jane's arm and pulling her up*): Come on, Sarah Jane!

ANNIE (*stopping them*): No, you're gonna stay right here.

SUSIE and SARAH JANE: Oh!

The girls sit down.

ANNIE: Else how your mama gonna find you, huh?

LORA (*off*): Susie!

9. MLS: *people under the pier, Lora and a policeman run into frame from the left. The camera pans right and moves in as the camera finds Annie, Susie, and Sarah Jane. Lora takes Susie in her arms.*

LORA: Oh, Susie! Oh, my baby! Oh, I thought you were lost! (*Turning toward the policeman.*) Thank you, officer! Thank you very much!
The officer salutes and walks away. Lora turns toward Annie. The camera frames the two women and their children in MS.

LORA: And thank you for being so kind, Mrs. ——?

ANNIE: Johnson.

LORA: Oh–I'm Lora Meredith. Oh, I've never been so frightened in my life! One moment I had her and the next moment she was gone! (*Turning toward Susie and pushing her toward Annie.*) Well, thank Mrs. Johnson for being so nice.

SUSIE: Thank you.

LORA: And say good-bye to the little girl.

SUSIE: Good-bye? Now?

LORA: But, darling, we have to go back to the city.

SUSIE: But we wanna play!

SARAH JANE: Please!

SUSIE: Please, Mommie, please!

LORA: Oh, all right, but only for a little while.

SUSIE: Come on, Sarah Jane! You're it!
The girls run off as Lora and Annie watch.

10. MCU: *beach umbrella. Sarah Jane and Susie run into the frame (from the left) and knock it over to reveal a couple embracing.*

11. MCU: *Annie and Lora, sitting and talking under the pier. Annie faces the camera; Lora is seen from the rear.*

LORA: Susie doesn't have many children to play with where we live.

ANNIE: I guess Sarah Jane's kinda lonesome, too. They got along fine, right off.

12. MCU, *reverse angle of 11: Lora and Annie. Lora faces the camera; Annie is seen from the rear.*

LORA (*taking off her sunglasses*): Sarah Jane's a lovely child. How long have you taken care of her?

ANNIE: All her life.

LORA: Oh, I wish I had someone to look after Susie.

ANNIE: A maid to live in?
Lora nods.

13. MCU: *Annie and Lora. Annie faces the camera; Lora is seen from the rear (as in 11).*

ANNIE: Someone to take care of your little girl? A strong, healthy, settled-down woman who eats like a bird—and doesn't care if she gets no time off—and will work real cheap?

14. MCU: *Lora and Annie, as in 12.*

LORA (*laughing*): Oh, well, yes, if one exists. Ah—some day—

15. MCU: *Annie and Lora, as in 11.*

ANNIE: Why not today? I'm available.

LORA: You?

ANNIE: Me—Annie Johnson.

16. MCU: *Lora and Annie, as in 12.*

LORA: You mean you'd consider leaving that lovely little girl?

17. CU: *Annie.*

ANNIE (*glancing off*): Oh, I wouldn't be leavin' her. My baby goes where I go.

18. CU: *Lora.*

LORA: Sarah Jane is your child?

19. CU: *Annie.*

ANNIE (*looking off*): Yes ma'am. It surprises most people. Sarah Jane favors her daddy. He was practically white. He left before she was born.

20. MCU: *Lora and Annie. Lora faces the camera; Annie is seen from the rear. Lora looks off, then glances at Annie.*

ANNIE: Seems to me, Miss Meredith, I'm just right for you.

21. CU: *Annie.*

ANNIE: You wouldn't have to pay no wages. Just let me come and do for you.

22. CU: *Lora and Annie. Lora is facing the camera; Annie is seen from the rear.*

LORA: I couldn't do that. I'd have to pay you and I—can't now.

23. MS: *Susie and Sarah Jane on the beach. Susie is in the foreground and Sarah Jane in the background. The girls kneel on either side of a sleeping fat man. Sarah Jane deposits a beer can on his stomach.*

24. MCU: *Lora and Annie, as in 20. Lora stares off-screen, reacts, rises quickly, and exits.*

LORA: Susie!

25. MS: *fat man sleeping on the beach, with Sarah Jane beside him. Steve kneels down to take a picture of the man.*

26. MS: *Susie and Sarah Jane laughing as the beer can rises and falls on the fat man's stomach. The man wakes up, looks at Susie, then throws the beer can off to the right. He sits up and looks from one child to the other.*

MAN (*to children*): I oughta knock your blocks off!

27. MS: *Steve. He speaks as he turns the knob of his camera.*

STEVE: I'll take care of it, Mister. I'll wham the hides off both of them.

LORA (*coming up behind Steve*): Susie!

28. MS: *Susie, Sarah Jane, and the fat man.*

LORA (*off*): What are you doing?

Susie runs toward Lora.

MAN: About time you showed up!

29. MS: *Steve and Lora. Susie runs to Lora, who hugs her.*

MAN: Your husband can't keep these brats in line—

STEVE: No use talking to her—she not only spoils them, she goes around losing them!

LORA: I don't know what this is all about!

30. MCU: *Susie, who turns from Lora's embrace.*

SUSIE: Mommie, look at his stomach! It went up and down! It was so funny.

The camera pulls back as Sarah Jane comes toward Lora.

SARAH JANE (*pointing to Steve*): He took our picture!

The camera pans left as the two girls cross to Steve, who squats down.

SUSIE: Will you send me one?

SARAH JANE: Me, too?

STEVE: Sure. Where? (*Looking toward Lora.*)

31. MCU: *Lora, rolling her eyes.*

SUSIE (*off*): Send it to Susan Meredith, 450 Prescott Place, Apartment Thirty-two.

LORA (*grabbing Susie, as the camera pulls back and left, to include Steve, Sarah Jane, and Susie*): Never mind, dear.

SUSIE: See? I remembered.

Annie walks into the background with her suitcase and Lora's pocketbook. Lora takes her handbag.

SUSIE: And send her one, too (*indicating Sarah Jane*). Where do you live, Sarah Jane?

32. MCU: *Sarah Jane and Susie.*

SARAH JANE: Where do I—(*Looking at Annie.*) No place.

33. MS: *Annie, Lora, Susie (facing camera), and Sarah Jane (her back to the camera).*

ANNIE: We'll find a place come night, honey. (*She pulls Sarah Jane toward her as the camera moves in closer.*)

LORA (*grabbing Susie*): Come on, darling, we have to go. Say good-bye to Sarah Jane and Mrs. Johnson.

SUSIE: Good-bye.

LORA: It was very nice meeting you.

Lora and Susie walk away past the camera. The camera moves in to Annie and Sarah Jane and frames them in MS.

ANNIE: Same here. And good luck, Mrs. Meredith.

SARAH JANE: Mommie, I'm tired.

ANNIE: I know, baby.

34. MS: *Lora and Susie. They move away from the camera, stop, and turn back (in Annie and Sarah Jane's direction).*

ANNIE (*off*): I know.

SARAH JANE (*off*): I wanna go home, too!

35. MS: *Steve, watching, as Annie holds Sarah Jane and tries to comfort her. Annie and Sarah Jane begin to leave.*

ANNIE: Come on, honey.
Annie reaches for her suitcase; Steve picks it up and hands it to her.
ANNIE: Thank you.
LORA (*off*): Mrs. Johnson!
Annie stops and turns toward the camera.

36. MS: *Lora and Susie. Lora smiles and motions (to Annie and Sarah Jane) with her head.*

37. MS: *Steve, Annie, and Sarah Jane.*
ANNIE: Oh—oh—come on—
Annie and Sarah Jane link hands and run toward the camera and out of frame. Steve watches, and the camera holds on him in MS.
Dissolve.

Street of Brownstone Houses, exterior, evening

38. *Diagonal* LS: *street. Susie and Sarah Jane run forward and across the street toward the camera. Lora and Annie follow. Susie and Sarah Jane are laughing.*

39. LS, *reverse angle: brownstone building façade. Sarah Jane and Susie (backs toward camera) run across the street toward the building. Lora and Annie follow.*
Dissolve.

Hallway, interior, evening

40. LS: *Susie and Sarah Jane run into the hall from the stairs. The camera pans left around a corner toward the door of Lora's apartment, framing them in* MS.
SUSIE: I win!

41. MS: *top of stairs, as Lora and Annie ascend. The camera tilts up and pulls back as Lora moves down the hall and Annie follows. Lora searches for her keys. The camera frames them in* LS.
LORA: I don't like to mention it again, but you must understand that this arrangement can only be for tonight.
ANNIE: Oh, I understand, Miss Lora.
LORA: There must be plenty of jobs for a woman like you.
ANNIE: But people just won't take in a woman with a child. And, no matter what, I won't be separated from my baby.
SUSIE: Hurry up, mother. I want to show Sarah Jane my dolls.
Susie pushes Lora to the door. The camera pans left.
LORA (*unlocking door*): Well, all right.

Lora's Apartment, interior, evening

42. CU: *Lora entering the dark apartment, as seen from inside. As she turns on the light, the camera pans left and angles back. Sarah Jane and Susie enter and run down the hall to the bedroom at the end of the corridor. Annie enters. Lora continues across the living room and turns on the overhead fan. The camera cranes back up and pans right. It cranes forward as she goes toward the kitchen, stopping outside the door frame.*

LORA: There's a little place off the kitchen—(*She opens the door and turns on the light.*) but you could uh—hardly call it a room.

43. LS: *Annie and Lora in the doorway to the back room (as seen from inside). Lora stands outside the door and Annie comes past her, stops, and looks the room over.*

44. MLS: *Annie and Lora in the doorway to the back room. Annie turns to Lora.*

ANNIE: Oh, it'll do for Sarah Jane and me. (*She walks toward the kitchen, and the camera follows her.*) And the kitchen! We can make use of that, too!

LORA: Well, I'll get you some pillows and blankets.

ANNIE: Thank you.

The camera pans right and dollies in as Lora walks into Susie's room. She exits the frame right, and the camera holds on Susie and Sarah Jane in MS, who are on the bed with dolls. As Susie talks, Lora crosses left, in the background, and walks into a closet.

SUSIE: Here, Sarah Jane (*holding out the black doll*). You can have Nancy.

45. MCU: *Sarah Jane, facing the camera and Susie, her back to the camera. Sarah Jane shakes her head.*

SUSIE: It's a present. Mommie just got it for me.
SARAH JANE (*pointing to a white doll*): I want that . . .
46. MCU, *reverse angle of 45: Susie (facing the camera) and Sarah Jane (her back to the camera).*
SARAH JANE: . . . one!
SUSIE: Frieda's my friend! I've had her all my life! Mommie! Mommie!
The camera pans right to follow Susie as she crawls across the bed to Lora, who emerges from the closet with bed linen.
LORA: Yes?
SUSIE: She took my doll!
LORA: Oh.
ANNIE (*off*): Sarah Jane!
47. MS: *Annie in the doorway to the bedroom.*
ANNIE: Where are your manners? Now give it back!
Annie takes the doll away and gives it to Susie. Annie gives the black doll to Sarah Jane.
SARAH JANE: I don't want the black one!
ANNIE (*to Lora*): I'll take those. (*She takes the blankets.*)
LORA: It's been a long day and they're both tired and cranky.
ANNIE: Yes, Miss Lora. Everything will be all right.
Annie ushers Sarah Jane away as the camera pans left.
ANNIE: Now, come on, come on.
48. MS: *Annie and Sarah Jane walking forward toward their room. Sarah Jane is sobbing as she holds the black doll. The camera pans left and tilts down as they pass.*
ANNIE: Come on.
49. CU: *Annie entering the doorway to the back room. She almost exits in the foreground. Sarah Jane stops.*
SARAH JANE: I don't want to live in the back!
50. CU: *Annie and Sarah Jane (seen from behind) in the doorway to the back room.*
SARAH JANE: Why do we always have to live in the back?
ANNIE: Shhh, honey!
Annie pulls Sarah Jane into the room. Sarah Jane drops the doll on the floor and the camera tilts down to frame it. The door closes.
Fade out.
Lora's Apartment, interior, day
51. *Fade in.* MS: *kitchen, as seen through the doorway. Annie is ironing and the milkman, Mr. McKinney, puts down the dairy order.*
ANNIE (*whispering*): Thank you, Mr. McKinney. Shhh! (*She points.*)
He touches his cap and moves to the door.
ANNIE: Good-bye.
The camera pulls back through the doorway; it pans right and dollies to follow him across the living room. He looks off to the right.

52. MLS: *Susie and Sarah Jane in the living room trying to silence their laughter.*
    SARAH JANE: Shhh!
    Susie giggles.
53. MCU: *hall, as McKinney, smiling as he turns, mouths "Good-bye" to the girls. He opens the door and exits. The camera pans left to Lora who emerges from a back bedroom. She is wearing a beige/off-white print robe. The camera pulls back and pans left as she comes forward into the living room. She hesitates at the entrance, then crosses and kneels by Susie, as the camera pans left to follow.*
    LORA: Good morning, darling (*kissing Susie*). (*To Sarah Jane*) Good morning, Sarah Jane.
    SARAH JANE (*rising and coming forward from a sofa in the background*): I want a kiss, too.
54. MCU: *Lora, Susie, and Sarah Jane.*
    LORA (*hesitatingly*): Well, of course. (*She kisses Sarah Jane on the cheek*).
    SUSIE: Annie said we had to be quiet until you got up.
55. MCU: *Susie, Sarah Jane, and Lora (back to the camera).*
    SUSIE: Now we can talk out loud! Now we can even scream!
    Susie and Sarah Jane scream. Lora covers her ears.
56. MS: *Annie opens the door from the kitchen. Susie and Sarah Jane scream, off.*
    ANNIE: Children!
57. MS: *Sarah Jane, Susie, and Lora (as in 55).*
    ANNIE (*off*): Children!
58. MS: *Annie in kitchen doorway.*
    ANNIE: What? Oh, good morning, Miss Lora.
    LORA (*off*): Morning.
    ANNIE: How are you this morning?
    LORA (*off*): I'm just fine.
    Lora walks toward the kitchen and into the shot in MCU. The camera pans right to follow her.
    LORA: I'd love some coffee. (*Noticing her clothes hanging in the kitchen.*) Annie, you shouldn't have done my laundry!
    ANNIE: I like takin' care of pretty things.
    LORA: Thank you. (*She turns away and walks further into the kitchen. The camera follows behind.*) Eggs! Where did they come from?
59. MCU: *Lora, back to the camera and Annie, facing camera.*
    ANNIE: The milkman was here a minute ago, and—I just told him to leave your regular order.
60. Low MS: *Lora, facing the camera and Annie, back to camera by the stove.*
    LORA: Oh, no. (*Lifting coffeepot.*) He didn't come to leave my order. He

stopped doing that two weeks ago. (*She walks toward the table and the camera pans left to follow.*)

ANNIE (*taking the coffeepot from her*): May I?

LORA (*sitting at the table as Annie pours*): Thank you. He wanted to collect something on his bill.

ANNIE (*pouring coffee*): Didn't say anything about a bill to me. He was very polite. (*Handing a cup to Lora.*) Just gave me the order and said it looked like things were pickin' up for Miss Meredith.

61. MCU: *Lora putting sugar in her coffee.*

LORA: He thought you were my maid. Now he thinks I'm prosperous.

62. MS: *Annie and Lora (both seen from behind). Annie turns toward the camera (from the refrigerator), holding the cream pitcher.*

ANNIE: No sin in lookin' prosperous. It's just a way of showin' your trust in the Lord—tellin' Him you're ready whenever He is.

63. MCU: *Lora, at the table. A phone rings (off) and she turns left. The camera pans left and tilts up as Annie crosses the foreground to the phone, which is on a table in the living room.*

ANNIE: I'll get it, Miss Lora. (*Framed in* MS *as she answers the phone.*) Miss Meredith's residence. (*Annie walks back into the kitchen, carrying the phone. The camera pans right to follow her, eventually framing her and Lora in* MS.) Well, well—I'll see if it's convenient for Miss Meredith to come to the phone. (*Annie covers the mouthpiece.*)

LORA: Is it the landlord—Mr. Barrett?

ANNIE: Pretty sure he said the Ac—Acme Model Agency.

Lora takes the phone and Annie moves away into the foreground.

LORA: Hello. Yes this is uh—Miss Meredith.

The camera pans right, then left to follow Annie moving in the kitchen as Lora talks.

LORA: Yes, yes, I can be there by then. Fine. Thank you! (*Hanging up the phone.*) Oh, Annie, I've got a job modelling.

64. MCU: *Annie, turning from the stove.*

ANNIE: A job!

65. MS: *Lora, facing the camera and Annie, her back to the camera.*

LORA: I've registered everywhere, but this is the first call.

66. MCU: *Annie.*

ANNIE: Now, isn't that fine!

67. MS: *Lora and Annie (as in 65). The camera tilts down and moves right to Lora as she sits at the far side of the table. Annie moves right, across the foreground. Lora bites her fingernails and looks at Annie.*

LORA: Um—Annie . . .

68. CU: *Annie.*

LORA (*off*): . . . if you have no other plans, will you stay with Susie until I come back?

ANNIE: Why, certainly.

69. MCU: *Lora at the table (looking off right, toward Annie).*

    LORA: Do you know, this will be the first money I've earned since I
    came to New York—except for those envelopes?

70. CU: *Annie.*

    ANNIE (*turning to look at the boxes on top of the refrigerator*): Why, I
    was wondering what they were.

    LORA (*off*): I address them for a mail-order house . . .

71. MCU: *Lora.*

    LORA: . . . by hand. Gives them a personal touch. And I can do them at
    home. They should've been finished yesterday. Well, it can't be helped.
    If I get a job modelling, at least I'll be seen!

    Dissolve.

Photography Studio, interior, day

72. CU: *flea powder can, held in Lora's hand. The camera pulls back to re-
    veal Lora posed with a St. Bernard dog, as a man adjusts her position.
    She is wearing a blue checked shirtwaist dress with white trim and a belt.*

    PHOTOGRAPHER (*petting dog*): Good boy! (*To Lora and dog.*) Yes,
    that's fine! Now that's what I want! Now hold it! Beautiful! (*Walking
    right toward his camera and putting the cloth over his head to shoot.*)
    Just a minute! Hold it!

73. MLS: *Lora and the dog. She sneezes.*

74. MS: *photographer at his camera.*

    PHOTOGRAPHER: How could you sneeze? I had it.

    LORA (*off*): I'm sorry, but it must be this flea powder.

    *The photographer approaches her and the camera pans left with him. He
    repositions her.*

    PHOTOGRAPHER: No—no—no! Don't move! You'll unfocus me!
    (*Walking right as the camera follows him. He addresses his assistant*):
    Art they want, and I get sneezes! (*To Lora.*) Now don't move a hair!
    Not one hair!

75. MS: *Lora posing, and the photographer's assistant in the background.*

    ASSISTANT: Hold it! Hold it! (*Walking forward and taking out a hand-
    kerchief to wipe the dog's mouth and eyes. The camera follows him and
    frames him in* MCU. *He moves back to sit down.*) Okay.

    Lora holds back another sneeze.

76. MLS: *photographer taking picture.*

    PHOTOGRAPHER: Got it. Perfect. (*Walking left, over to Lora, the
    camera following; she sneezes. He addresses the dog.*) You were won-
    derful, Henry. (*He hugs the dog.*)

    LORA: I never sneeze, really, I can't imagine . . .

    PHOTOGRAPHER (*talking over her*): Your check will be in the mail.

    LORA: Oh, but it would be so much more convenient if I could . . .

    He walks right and the camera pans to follow him.

PHOTOGRAPHER: Checks are mailed out on Thursday. We don't want to confuse the bookkeeper. (*Taking flea powder from Lora.*) Don't forget to leave the wardrobe.

He walks away with his assistant toward the right. The camera moves left to focus on Lora. She sighs, walks left past the dog (making a face and growling at him), then out of frame. The camera moves right to frame the dog as he barks.

Dissolve.

Lora's Apartment, interior, night

77. MCU: *pan shot of Annie walking left into the kitchen. Lora is inside, taking a box of envelopes off the refrigerator and putting it on the table. She is wearing a blue suit, with a white, sleeveless, V-necked blouse.*

ANNIE: But wouldn't you like to have a bite to eat? (*She helps Lora off with her jacket.*)

LORA: Later, thanks.

Annie begins to close the rear door.

78. MS: *Annie closing the rear door. The camera tilts down and moves right as she sits at the table and prepares to address envelopes. Annie is facing the camera in* MCU; *Lora is seen from the back.*

LORA: You can keep the money from this batch, Annie. It'll pay you for staying today and cooking and . . .

ANNIE: Uh-uh. That money goes into our kitty.

79. MCU, *reverse angle of 78: Lora (facing the camera) and Annie (seen from behind).*
    LORA: "Our"? Seems as if you intend staying.
80. MCU, *reverse angle of 79.*
    ANNIE: Seems like I do, if—if you want it.
81. CU, *reverse angle of 80.*
    LORA: You know I do, but you can see how bad things are.
82. CU, *reverse angle of 81.*
    ANNIE: Miss Lora, we just come from a place where—where my color deviled by baby. Now anything happens here has gotta be better.
83. CU, *reverse angle of 82.*
    LORA (*smiling*): Oh, Annie!
84. CU, *reverse angle of 83.*
    ANNIE (*embarrassed*): Oh . . . oh.
    Fade out.
    Lora's Apartment, interior, night (some days later)
85. *Fade in.* MS: *interior of living room as Lora returns home. The camera follows her to the left as she walks in. She wears the same blue suit and white blouse as in the previous scene.*
    LORA: Susie! Susie! (*Walking toward the rear bedrooms.*) I'm home!
    Susie runs out, followed by Sarah Jane. Lora stoops, kissing and embracing Susie.
    LORA: Oh, baby! (*Touching Sarah Jane's cheek.*) Hi, there . . .
    ANNIE (*entering, drying her hands*): Hello, Miss Lora.
    LORA: Hello, Annie.
    SUSIE: Mommie—
86. CU: *Susie, Sarah Jane, and Lora.*
    SUSIE: We had such fun today! Annie took us to the park and we caught a squirrel!
    SARAH JANE: No, we didn't.
    SUSIE: Well, we nearly did!
    LORA: Well, tomorrow I'll take you both to the park . . .
87. MS: *Lora, Sarah Jane, Susie, and Annie.*
    LORA: . . . and we'll really catch one!
    Susie and Sarah Jane squeal and hug Lora.
    ANNIE: How did it go?
    LORA (*rising from a kneeling position*): Oh, Annie . . . (*Shaking her head and walking toward Annie, the camera following behind.*) . . . it didn't. (*Turning so that she and Annie are framed in* MCU.) I'm exhausted. Walked my feet off, trying to see every agent on Broadway—and some off-Broadway. Way off.
    A bell rings.
    LORA (*smiling bravely*): I'll get it.

Lora walks forward out of frame. The camera remains on Annie.

ANNIE: The children have eaten.

88. MS: *Lora at the intercom by the front door to her apartment.*

LORA: Yes?

STEVE (*off*): Hello, this is Steve Archer.

LORA: Steve Archer?

Lobby of Lora's Apartment Building, interior, night

89. MS: *Steve, talking into the intercom.*

STEVE: I brought the pictures.

LORA (*off*): You brought the pictures?

STEVE: The ones of the children on the beach.

Lora's apartment, interior, night

90. MS: *Lora at intercom as in 88.*

LORA: Oh, the man on the beach!

SARAH JANE (*off*): ·The man on the beach?

91. MS: *Annie, Sarah Jane, and Susie as the children run forward into closer view.*

SUSIE: The man on the beach!

SARAH JANE: It's our picture with the fat man!

92. MS: *Lora at intercom as in 90.*

SUSIE (*off*): Mommie, tell him to come up!

SARAH JANE (*off*): Yes, please!

LORA: Oh, all right, (*Into the intercom.*) Will you come up, Mr. Archer? *Susie and Sarah Jane shriek and run to the door. The camera pans right as Lora turns on the lights to the living room.*

Hallway, interior, night

93. LS: *Susie and Sarah Jane run to meet Steve.*

SUSIE: You have our picture!

Steve laughs and picks Susie up in his arms. They all walk toward the camera and the apartment door.

STEVE: Oh-ho! Hi, Susie! Hi, Sarah Jane!

SUSIE: Hurry! Hurry!

SARAH JANE: Where is it?

STEVE: Aren't you kids supposed to be in bed?

SARAH JANE: No, we're waiting for you!

Lora's Apartment, interior, night

94. High MLS: (*from inside Lora's apartment*) *as Steve and the children enter. Lora is opening the door. Annie is seen in the background.*

STEVE: Hello!

Steve puts Susie down and gives the girls the picture.

LORA: Good evening!

The girls run off (left and forward), to the sofa where they sit down and pull out the picture. The camera follows them (craning and panning).

Susie looks at the picture and falls on the floor laughing. The camera tilts down and right to frame her.

95. LS: *Lora and Steve by the front door; Annie is in the background closing it. Lora and Steve walk into the living room, she ahead of him. The camera pans left and tilts down as Lora takes the photo from Susie on the floor.*

LORA (*walking*): Well, if it's that funny, let me see it!

She takes the photo and the camera tilts up as she and Sarah Jane look at it. Susie leaps up and Annie walks into the frame from the right.

SUSIE: Don't you think it's funny, Annie?

96. CU: *black-and-white insert of the photograph (held in Annie's hand). It depicts the girls on the beach with the fat man. The girls giggle (off).*

LORA (*off*): I don't know who's funnier, you or that . . .

97. MS: *Lora, Susie, Sarah Jane, and Annie.*

LORA: . . . man!

ANNIE (*looking sternly at Sarah Jane*): All I gotta say, it's lucky I didn't catch Sarah Jane playin' such pranks. It just ain't seemly, Miss Lora. Now—off to bed.

Lora kisses Susie on the cheek.

LORA (*to Sarah Jane*): 'Night.

Annie picks up Susie and walks toward the bedroom, Sarah Jane follows. They move right and back and the camera cranes to follow. We catch sight of Steve on the right.

ANNIE (*to Steve*): Good night, Mr. Archer.

STEVE: Good night, ladies.

Lora walks into the frame from the left and moves toward Steve.

LORA: Won't you sit down?

Steve nods and they walk left to sit down. The camera pans and tilts to follow.

LORA (*still walking and sitting down*): It was very nice of you to remember the children.

98. MS: *Steve sits down on a chair, the camera tilting down.*

STEVE: I like what you did—for Sarah Jane and Annie.

99. MS: *Lora on the sofa (facing the camera) and Steve on a chair (his back to the camera).*

LORA: Well, they—they didn't have a place, and—since I live here alone. . . . I'm a widow.

STEVE: Oh, you . . . are.

Lora nods. Steve rises and moves to sit beside her on the sofa. The camera pans left to follow him. He pulls a picture out of an envelope and hands it it her.

STEVE: What do you think of this?

100. CU: *black-and-white insert of a photograph, held in Lora's hand. It de-*

picts her leaning over the railing at Coney Island on the day that she lost Susie and met Steve, Annie, and Sarah Jane (as shot 5).

STEVE (*off*): "Mother in Distress."

101. CU: *Lora (facing the camera) and Steve (seen from the rear).*
LORA: Well, it's good—very good! Who are you, anyway? Well—you don't look like a photographer.

102. CU, *reverse angle of 101.*
STEVE: Apparently the Army thought I did! Anyway, they made me one. Now all I want to do is get pictures like this—in The Museum of Modern Art.

103. CU, *reverse angle of 102.*
LORA: Oh, you're aiming high!
STEVE: Why not? It doesn't cost any more. Don't you believe in chasing rainbows?
LORA: Hm, well, if I didn't I—I wouldn't be here. I'm an actress.

104. CU, *reverse angle of 103. Steve looks at Lora very closely.*

105. CU, *reverse angle of 104.*
LORA: What's the matter?

106. CU, *reverse angle of 105.*
STEVE: Your bones.

107. CU, *reverse angle of 106.*
LORA: What about my bones?
STEVE (*touching her face*): They're perfect.

108. CU, *reverse angle of 107.*
STEVE: My camera could easily have a love affair with you.
The film's theme music begins.

109. CU, *reverse angle of 108.*
LORA: Don't you think it's getting a little late?
She rises.

110. MS: *Lora and Steve rising from the sofa.*
STEVE: I don't suppose you'd like to have dinner with me.
LORA: Maybe—sometime.
She starts to walk toward the door and Steve follows. The camera moves ahead of them. They pause and are framed in MS.
STEVE: I don't mean right away. How about tomorrow?
LORA: I'm sorry, but I don't like to miss having dinner with the children two nights in a row.

111. MCU: *Steve (facing camera) and Lora (back to the camera).*
STEVE: I can understand that. How about lunch?

112. MS: *Lora (facing camera) and Steve (back to camera).*
LORA: Lunch—would you mind taking me to Rodney's? It's a little place on Forty-fifth and Eighth. Unemployed actors can afford it. Sort of a poor man's "21."

STEVE (*laughing*): All right. I'll meet you there at noon. (*He turns toward the camera and walks out of frame, past the camera.*)

113. MS: *Steve, seen from behind reaching for the front door knob. He opens it, then turns toward the camera (and Lora). The theme music ends.*
STEVE: By the way, the name's Steve.
Dissolve.

Rodney's Restaurant, interior, day

114. *High* MLS: *Lora and Steve sitting at a table in Rodney's Restaurant. He looks around at the other patrons.*
STEVE: Everybody in here an actor?
LORA: Just about.
STEVE: So far, you're the only one I really believe.

115. *High* MS: *Steve and Lora seated at their table.*
LORA: Thank you. Only, so far, you're the only one in New York who does. But someday, I'm going to make them *all* feel that way. (*She dabs her mouth with a napkin.*)
STEVE: Aren't you—aren't you a little late getting started? I mean, it's—
LORA (*cutting him off*): Yes—five years late. That's why every day counts.
STEVE: Why the five-year lapse?
LORA: My husband was in the theater, too—a director—a good director. Everything I know, I owe to him. It was a small town, and a little theater—but professional. When he died, I—had to make a living doing something else. I never really wanted anything but the stage. Oh, except Susie. So, it took me five years to save enough money to come to New York.
STEVE: But you did it!
Lora nods. The camera tilts up as a waiter approaches their table.
LORA: And I'm going to be an actress . . .
FAY (*a friend, calling from off-screen*): Lora?
LORA: . . . an important . . .
Steve and Lora turn to look at the woman who has called Lora.
FAY (*stepping into the frame*): Lora?
LORA (*to Steve*): Oh, excuse me.
Lora rises and walks toward Fay. The camera dollies to follow her, first left and then right. It holds on the two women in MS.
FAY: Nothing in it for me, honey, but they're beginning to cast a new Tennessee Williams play.
LORA: Oh—what agent?
FAY: Allen Loomis—today—so put on your roller skates.
LORA: Oh, thanks, Fay!
Lora goes back to her table. The camera dollies right to follow her, stopping when it frames Steve, Lora, and the waiter in MS.

WAITER: Coffee?

Lora moves left and the camera dollies to follow her.

LORA (*picking up her purse*): Sorry, but I've got to go.

STEVE (*grabbing her arm*): You haven't eaten!

LORA: Well, you go ahead. Good-bye!

STEVE: How about dinner? Tonight—we'll take Susie.

LORA: Uh—uh—fine.

STEVE: Where?

LORA: Why don't you come and have dinner with us?

STEVE (*off*): All right.

Lora exits left and the camera pans to follow her.

FAY (*as Lora passes*): Good luck!

LORA: Thanks, Fay.

Dissolve.

Loomis's Office Building, interior, day

116. LS: *Lora walks down the hall of an office building, moving into the diagonal depth of the frame. She is wearing the same blue suit and white blouse as in earlier scenes, accessorized by black patent leather shoes and purse, and white gloves. She stops at a door.*

117. MCU: *Lora before the door (which reads: "Allen Loomis/Theatrical Agency"). She adjusts her posture and begins to open it.*

118. LS (*on a match cut*): *Lora opening the door into Loomis's outer office. She walks toward the desk of the secretary (who is speaking to another woman), leans on the railing, and turns toward the camera.*

ACTRESS (*to the secretary, Annette*): Well, when can I have an appointment?

ANNETTE: How about a week from today? Thursday.

119. MS: *Lora, Annette (both facing the camera), and the actress (back to the camera).*

ACTRESS: Put me down. It's Iris Dawn. Don't forget it.

The actress leaves and the secretary turns toward Lora and then looks down again to her papers. Lora turns toward the desk.

120. MS: *Lora (facing the camera) and Annette (back to camera). Lora is leaning on the railing of Annette's desk.*

LORA: Well, I'm sorry to add to your troubles, but—uh—I'm afraid I'm a little late for my appointment.

ANNETTE: Name, please? (*She consults her book.*)

LORA: Miss Meredith.

ANNETTE: Mere—Meredith (*Looking in her book.*) Well, I don't seem to have you down.

LORA: Oh, well, never mind. Just tell Mr. Loomis that Robert Hayes sent me.

121. MCU: *Annette.*

ANNETTE: Robert Hayes?

LORA (*off*): From International Studio.

122. MCU: *Lora.*

LORA: It's probably just a slip-up from the Coast, but uh—Mr. Hayes won't like it at all.

123. MCU: *Annette.*

LORA (*off*): I hope you didn't slip up.

ANNETTE: Me?

124. MS: *Lora and Annette, as in 120.*

LORA: Well, if you say there's no appointment—uh—good bye. (*She turns to go.*)

ANNETTE: Oh—well, uh—just a second! Why don't you sit down and—uh—I'll see if I can straighten this whole thing out.

LORA: Thank you.

Lora walks away. Annette slides her chair right, moving toward her intercom. The camera pans to follow her and frames her in a low CU.

ANNETTE (*speaking into the intercom*): Mr. Loomis?

LOOMIS (*off/over intercom*): Yes?

ANNETTE: There's a Miss Meredith here from Hollywood.

125. MS: *Lora, seated in an office chair, listening.*

LOOMIS (*off, mumbles*).

ANNETTE: Yes, quite lovely!

126. CU: *Annette, poised over intercom (as at the end of 120).*

LOOMIS (*off*): Think we should send her away?

ANNETTE: No, no, I think you ought to see her.

LOOMIS: Fine.

Annette slides her chair left and the camera pans to follow. She looks at Lora, who is seated in the background.

ANNETTE: Okay, Miss—Miss Meredith. You can go in now.

Lora rises in the background and walks past Annette's desk.

127. MLS (*over Annette's desk): private door to Loomis's office. A woman is walking out (toward the camera). The door opens to reveal Allen Loomis in the far background. Lora walks in and Annette follows her.*

ANNETTE: Uh—this way. (*She closes the door and turns toward the camera, smiling.*)

128. MS: *Loomis behind his desk (facing the camera) and Lora seated before the desk (on the left). The camera moves in closer to her as he walks to the far left corner of his desk and unwraps a cigar.*

LORA: Robert sends his warmest greetings.

LOOMIS: Well, thanks. And how is he?

LORA: Marvelous. He's lost fifteen pounds and you know what an effort that is for him.

LOOMIS: And—uh—what can I do for you? (*He moves right and the camera pans to follow him, eventually framing him alone in* MS.)

LORA: Well, Robert thought that I shouldn't do any more pictures before I get a show on Broadway.

LOOMIS: Very sensible.

LORA (*off*): Oh, I'm glad you think so, too.

129. MS: *Lora, seated.*

LORA: That's why Robert sent me to you. He thought that I'd get more uh-uh-personal attention from you.

130. MCU: *Loomis.*

LOOMIS: He could be right, there. (*Looking toward Lora and indicating his cigar.*) Do you mind?

LORA (*off*): No.

Loomis sits down, lighting his cigar; the camera tilts down to follow him.

131. MS: *Lora seated before his desk.*

LORA: Incidentally, how's the new Tennessee Williams play?

132. MS: *Loomis at his desk.*

LOOMIS: Bound to be a blockbuster—but all cast.

A buzzer sounds. Loomis wheels his chair right and the camera pans to follow. He picks up the phone.

LOOMIS: Oh, Lillian. What?

133. MS: *Lora, listening.*

LOOMIS (*off*): Oh, well—can't you break it? Oh. No, I don't mind.

134. MS: *Loomis, talking on the phone.*

LOOMIS: I don't mind your standing me up. I'm fine! I'll just kill my-self! Yeah. (*He hangs up the phone.*)

135. MS: *Lora.*

LOOMIS (*off*): Never be a bachelor. There's no security!

LORA (*laughing*): I know how you feel.

136. MS: *Loomis.*

LOOMIS: Yeah? Say, how'd you like to go with me tonight?

137. MS: *Lora.*

LORA: Oh, I'm afraid I can't.

138. MS: *Loomis.*

LOOMIS: Big party. Lots of important people.

139. MS: *Lora.*

LORA: Well, I—I—could see if I could break a couple of engagements. I'll call my place. (*She leans forward to reach the phone.*)

140. MS: *Loomis (raising his hand, as though to stop her).*

LOOMIS: I'll call. What's the number?

141. MS: *Lora.*

LORA: Montgomery—

LOOMIS (*off*): Montgomery—

LORA: —seven—six—one—two—oh.

142. MS: *Loomis dialing phone.*

LOOMIS: one—two—oh. (*He looks toward the camera.*)

Lora's Apartment, interior, day

143. MLS: *kitchen of Lora's apartment, seen from outside the kitchen door-way, in the living room. Susie and Sarah Jane are seated at a table in the foreground, left. Annie is on the right by the stove. As the phone rings, Annie moves through the door frame into the living room to answer it and the camera frames her in* MS.

ANNIE: Miss Meredith's residence.

Loomis's Office, interior, day

144. MS: *Loomis on the telephone, seated at his desk.*

LOOMIS: Oh, this *is* Miss Meredith's residence?

145. MS: *Lora, smiling.*

LORA: That'll be Annie, my maid. (*She holds out her hand toward the telephone.*) I'll talk to her.

146. MS: *Loomis. He covers the phone mouthpiece and hands the receiver to Lora, who is on the left. The camera pans, slightly, to follow him.*

147. MS: *Lora and Loomis, seen from over his desk. She is on the left (facing camera) and he is partially visible on the right (with his back toward the camera). He continues to hand her the telephone.*

LORA: Annie? Uh—call the Waldorf and tell—um—uh—you-know-who I cannot have cocktails and dinner with him.

Lora's Apartment, interior, day

148. MS: *Annie in the living room, on the telephone and Sarah Jane and Susie in the kitchen, as at the end of 143.*

ANNIE: Uh—"I know who"? Oh—oh, yes, Miss Lora! I'll do that?

Loomis's Office, interior, day

149. MS: *Lora and Loomis, as in 147. He crosses in front of the camera, to-ward the left as Lora reaches to hang up the telephone. He stands by her in front of the desk and the camera moves in to frame them in* MCU (*he on the left and she on the right*).

LORA: Thank you. Well, Mr. Loomis, it looks like I'm free.

LOOMIS: Well, that'll be just fine! Should be an interesting evening for me. Hollywood actress and—oh, that reminds me. Excuse me. (*He leans forward toward the intercom on his desk. The camera tilts down.*)

ANNETTE (*off/over intercom*): Yes, Mr. Loomis?

LOOMIS: Annette, get me Hollywood—Mr. Robert Hayes. (*To Lora.*) International Studios, right? (*Into intercom.*) International—

LORA (*upset*): Uh—maybe you—better not go through with that call. *He stands up and the camera tilts up slightly.*

LOOMIS: You don't think so? Why not?

LORA: Because Robert Hayes doesn't exist.

LOOMIS: I understand. (*Bending down toward the intercom.*) Annette, cancel the call.

ANNETTE (*off*): Yes, Mr. Loomis.

LORA: I was desperate.

Loomis walks into the background, then turns around to face the camera.

LOOMIS: You were pretty good. You lied. All actresses lie, I know that. But I believed you.

Lora crosses in front of the camera toward the left, blocking Loomis. The camera pans left to follow her.

LORA: I'm sorry.

Loomis stands behind her, looking over her shoulder (he is on the right and she on the left). They are framed in MCU.

LOOMIS: Don't leave. You took me in. For all of twenty seconds, you took me in—but I don't mind. It was a good acting job—and you're very pretty. Now about tonight—shall I pick you up?

LORA: Uh-no. It'll be easier for me to meet you here.

LOOMIS: Eight o'clock?

LORA: You'll find me very prompt, Mr. Loomis.

She exits left and he moves a bit in her direction, with the camera panning slightly to follow. The shot ends with Loomis, framed in MCU, *looking off-screen left, watching her leave.*

Dissolve.

Loomis's Office Reception Room, interior, night

150. *Low* LS: *Lora entering the darkened reception area through the door from the outside hallway. She wears a scoop-neck cocktail sheath accompanied by pearl earrings, a necklace, and short, white gloves. She crosses the office right (with the camera panning to follow) and walks into the depth of the frame, toward the door to his office, passing through a swinging gate. As the gate makes a noise, she looks back, reacting. She knocks on Loomis's door and we see his shadow on the other side. He opens the door.*

LOOMIS: Come on in.

Lora begins to walk through the doorway.

151. MS (*match cut*): *Lora and Loomis in his office as she continues through the door. They cross his office to the right and the camera pans to follow.*

LOOMIS: Sit down. I just had a few letters to sign.

Lora sits down.

LOOMIS: Oh, a drink?

LORA: No, thank you. But aren't we going to be late to the party?

Loomis walks toward the background right, with the camera panning to follow him. He opens a cabinet.

LOOMIS: Plenty of time! Plenty. And I need a drink. So relax. (*He takes out a bottle of liquor and begins to pour a drink.*)

152. MS: *Lora seated.*

LOOMIS (*off*): Say—you're not allergic to mink, are you?

LORA: Mink? No, I don't think so.

LOOMIS (*off*): Good!

153. MS: *Loomis at his bar, his back to the camera. He moves right and the camera pans with him to a closet. He opens it and takes out a full-length mink coat. He walks left and the camera pans to follow.*

LOOMIS: Try this on for size.

He crosses left to Lora (as the camera pans) and she rises. He holds the coat out to her.

LORA: Whose is it?

LOOMIS: Mine. And I only loan it to very special clients. I want you to wear it tonight.

LORA: You want *me* to wear—

LOOMIS: Please. Got to think of my reputation.

154. MCU: *Loomis (facing the camera) and Lora (her back to the camera). He is still holding up the mink coat.*

LOOMIS: I haven't been seen with a girl without a mink since the heat wave of '39. (*Gesturing with the coat.*) Come on!

Lora turns toward the camera as he slips the coat on her shoulders.

LOOMIS (*touching Lora's shoulders*): We should spend a little time talk-

ing about our future. You can act—well, that's of no importance at the
moment. The main thing is, you're a beaut. (*He kisses her neck and
she pulls away, turning around to face the camera.*)

155. MCU (*match cut*): *Lora turning to face the camera and Loomis (his back
to the camera).*

    LORA: Please don't!

    LOOMIS: Oh, and you're decent, too! No doubt possess some fine
    principles.

156. MCU, *reverse angle of 155.*

    LOOMIS: Well, me—I'm a man of very few principles, and they're all
    open to revision.

    *He turns around and moves into background and right, moving to the bar.
    The camera pans with him, losing Lora. He turns around and points to
    the camera (and Lora).*

    LOOMIS: But, I'm in a position to do something for you.

157. MS: *Lora.*

    LORA: You'll get ten percent of everything I make. Isn't that enough?

158. MCU: *Loomis.*

    LOOMIS: No. Now sit down and listen.

159. MCU: *Lora sitting down, the camera tilting.*

160. MS: *Loomis sitting on the edge of his desk, putting his drink down.*

    LOOMIS: Here it is—short and clear. You're not a chicken. You're no
    high-hearted kid out of some drama school, wanting to do or die for
    dear old Thespis.

161. *High* MS: *Lora seated.*

    LOOMIS (*off*): And you're beginning under a handicap.

    LORA: Well, I know I'm starting late.

    LOOMIS: So time isn't on your side.

162. MS: *Loomis, seated on his desk. He rises and walks left toward Lora; the
camera pans to follow.*

    LOOMIS: But you do have some qualifications. Your face will pass, and
    you have good, nice, long, silky legs. (*Sitting down beside Lora.*) I like
    them. You have a chest full of quality and quantity—I like it.

163. CU: *Lora (facing the camera) and Loomis (his back to the cameras).*

    LORA: Aren't you taking a few things for granted? After all—

    LOOMIS: Me? I don't count. But there are certain people who do, and
    you're going to meet all of them. That is, if you're really serious about
    your career.

    LORA: I am, but—

    LOOMIS: Good. Then you're going everyplace with me.

164. MCU, *reverse angle of 163.*

    LOOMIS: Every party, every opening night, every saloon in town. With a
    complete new wardrobe, at my expense. Oh, it's—it's tax deductible.

But this is a tough, competitive racket. And, although it's a lot more than any agent is supposed to do, I'd do it.

Loomis pats Lora's leg. She stands (as the camera tilts up) and moves away, right. Loomis stands and moves with her. The camera pulls back and pans right, framing them in MS.

LORA: What's this got to do with acting?

LOOMIS: Nothing. But I'll show you how to realize your ambitions. If you do as I say. If the Dramatists' Club wants to eat and sleep with you . . .

Lora turns toward him suddenly (her back to the camera).

LOOMIS: . . . you will eat and sleep with them. If some producer with a hand as cold as a toad wants to do a painting of you in the nude, you'll accommodate him, for a very small part.

165. CMU: *Lora (facing the camera) and Loomis (back to the camera).*

LORA: It's disgusting!

LOOMIS: It pays off.

LORA: You're disgusting!

LOOMIS: Maybe I am.

166. MCU: *Lora (back to the camera) and Loomis (facing the camera).*

LOOMIS: But let me assure you, once you got it made (*walking toward Lora*), you can be idealistic all of ten seconds before you die.

167. MCU: *Lora (facing the camera) and Loomis (back to the camera). The door to Loomis's reception room is visible in the background.*

LORA: You're trying to cheapen me. But you won't. Not me. Oh, I'll make it, Mr. Loomis, but it'll be *my* way!

She turns her back to the camera and walks toward the door; the camera pans slightly left. She stops, remembers the mink coat, takes it off, faces the camera, and throws it to Loomis. She turns her back to him, opens the door and disappears into the outer office. Loomis catches the coat, looks surprised, and turns toward the door, his back to the camera. Dissolve.

Lora's Apartment, interior, night

168. MS (*from the living room, through the kitchen doorway): Annie and Steve sitting at the kitchen table, addressing envelopes.*

STEVE: You have a wonderful handwriting, Annie.

ANNIE: Oh, thank you, Mr. Steve. But my spellin' wouldn't take no prizes.

STEVE: I don't think Lora has anything to worry about, as long as you're with her.

ANNIE: Oh, we'll get by. I made an agreement with the landlord. He's really a nice person.

STEVE: Oh?

ANNIE: Just for doin' the staircases twice a week, we get . . .

169. MCU: *Steve and Annie at the table (he is on the left and she on the right).*
    ANNIE: . . . ten dollars off our rent.
    STEVE: Is that a fact?
    ANNIE: I also answered an ad in the paper and got myself a job while the kids are at school.
    STEVE: Doing what?
    ANNIE: Doing shirts for a gentleman. He's real persnickety about his shirts.
    They smile and look off-screen when they hear the sound of the front door opening.

170. MS: *Lora (seen from inside the living room) entering the apartment. As she comes in, she leans against the door, wearily. The camera pans left and angles in as she crosses forward, stops, and turns on the lights. She moves further left, passing the kitchen doorway (through which we see Annie and Steve); the camera pans left with her. Lora turns to face the kitchen and Annie and Steve rise to greet her.*
    LORA: Oh—Steve—uh—
    STEVE: Hello.
    Lora moves left into the living room (losing Annie and Steve); the camera pans with her.
    LORA: I'm sorry, It's just that I got so involved.

171. MS: *Annie and Steve (through the kitchen doorway) as they begin to move out of the kitchen.*
    STEVE: We're having a wonderful time.
    Annie walks into the living room, while Steve stands in the doorway. The camera follows Annie.
    ANNIE: How'd everything go, Miss Lora?

172. MS: *Annie and Lora (both seen from behind). Lora stands before a mirror.*
    LORA: Oh, just fine. I went to the "21" with Mr. Loomis. (*Turning to face Annie and the camera.*) And, oh, everybody there was somebody exciting and important. And for the first time, I felt that I was somebody, too.

173. MS: *Annie and Steve (Annie is in the living room and Steve, in the kitchen door frame).*
    ANNIE: Is Mr. Loomis gonna find you a job?

174. MS: *Lora (facing the camera, with the mirror in the background) and Annie (facing Lora, her back to the camera). Lora moves forward and left as she talks (losing Annie, who is now reflected in the mirror). The camera pans to follow.*
    LORA: Oh, well—he—uh—he wanted to represent me but—

175. MS: *Annie (in the living room) and Steve (in the kitchen doorway, as in 173). They smile, anticipating her words.*

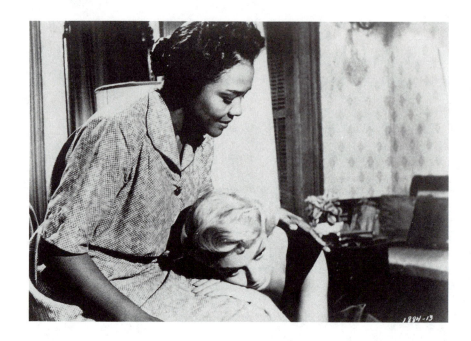

176. MS: *Lora by the mirror (in which Annie is reflected). Lora looks upset and starts to cry. The camera tilts down as she turns suddenly and drops onto the edge of a chair.*

LORA: But I—Oh, Annie! (*She sobs.*)

Annie rushes toward her, crossing in front of the chair and left.

ANNIE (*putting her arm on Lora's back*): What's wrong, Miss Lora?

Annie sits down and Lora rests her head on Annie's lap.

LORA (*crying*): Everything! Everything!

ANNIE: Now, you just rest. Everything'll work out. I'll get you a glass of hot milk, huh?

Annie rises and starts forward (the camera adjusts its framing slightly). Lora cries into a handkerchief.

177. MS: *Steve, standing, as Annie walks into the frame from the left. She passes him and exits into the kitchen. He walks left and bends down by Lora. The camera pans and tilts to follow him framing the couple in a* MS.

STEVE: Can I help in any way?

LORA (*crying*): No. No one can. Oh, I'm so ashamed. It was—horrible! He tried to make me feel so cheap!

STEVE: You could never be cheap.

LORA (*turning her back to him and to the camera*): You don't know what I mean!

STEVE (*moving around to face her, taking her arms*): Yes, I do. It hap-
   pens all the time. Not just in the theater. Please—
Lora stands and turns around; the camera tilts up.
LORA: But, I love the theater! It's what I want, and—
Steve stands and grabs her. She turns toward him, her back to camera.
STEVE: Then hold on to your dreams. Forget tonight.
LORA: But, they seem so stale after tonight. (*Sobbing.*) So stale I can't
   believe in them anymore!
*She turns away from him, facing the camera, and exits right, crossing in
front of him. The camera pans slightly right.*
LORA: Maybe I'm a fool.
178. MCU: *Lora (seen from the rear) walking toward the wall by the kitchen
   doorway.*
   LORA: Maybe I should see things as they really are (*turning toward the
   camera*) and not as I want them to be.
*The camera tilts up and pans left a bit as Steve enters on the left and
leans over her, against the wall.*
STEVE: If I know you, they'll have to be the way you want them.
The theme music begins.
LORA (*smiling*): Thanks, Steve. You're so—so good for what ails me.
STEVE: It's all part of the Archer service. Day or night.

*Annie becomes visible in the background through the kitchen doorway.
She and Steve exchange glances as the camera pans left to frame them.
The camera pans right as Steve crosses right and pauses by the curtained
hallway.*

STEVE: I'll call you soon, Lora. Tomorrow.

LORA: Yes, please. Tomorrow.

*He exits right and the camera pans slightly left and tilts down toward
Lora. The theme music ends.
Dissolve.*

179. MS: *Lora entering Susie's darkened bedroom (shot from inside the room).
The camera pans right and tilts down as she crosses and sits on the edge
of the bed. She looks down at Susie (sleeping with her white doll) and
reaches to pull the covers down.*

180. CU: *Susie asleep, as Lora (in a match cut) pulls the covers down to reveal a bandage on the child's left wrist.*

181. MCU: *Lora, sitting on the bed. She looks upset, examines the bandage,
and covers Susie. She turns toward the doorway, then rises and exits (her
back to the camera) into the rear of the frame, moving into the hall.*

182. MCU: *Annie, in the kitchen, seen in profile, pouring hot milk from a pan
into a glass. She turns toward the camera as Lora enters the frame from
behind the camera, on the right (her back to the camera).*

LORA: Annie, what's happened to Susie's wrist?

ANNIE (*moving forward as she speaks, the camera readjusting its framing*): Oh, nothing serious. Just a little experiment.

183. CU: *Lora (facing the camera) and Annie (back to the camera).*

LORA: Experiment?

ANNIE: Sarah Jane's fault.

184. CU: *Lora (back to the camera) and Annie (facing the camera).*

ANNIE: After class, one of the kids said that—Negro blood was different. So, later this evenin', Sarah Jane wanted to compare her blood
with Susie's. Well, I spanked . . .

185. CU: *Lora (facing the camera) and Annie (Back to the camera).*

ANNIE: . . . her good.

186. MS: *Lora (on the right) and Annie (on the left). Lora crosses left and the
camera pans to follow. As Lora sits, the camera tilts down.*

LORA: Oh, well—you know how children are. They—they were only
playing.

187. CU: *Annie (looking disturbed).*

ANNIE: I hope so, Miss Lora. I hope so.

Fade out.

Façade of School Building, exterior, day

188. *Fade in. Low MS: school exterior. Snow and rain are falling as Annie is*

seen crossing the sidewalk and ascending the steps toward the doors of the building. The camera tilts up to follow her, framing the words "Public School."

Classroom, interior, day

189. LS: *teacher at the blackboard, seen from the rear corner of the classroom, looking over the students' heads.*

    TEACHER: Santa Claus has many names in many different countries. *(Pointing to the blackboard.)* In Holland, he is called Sinter Klaas . . .

190. MS: *Sarah Jane, seated at a desk, listening.*

    TEACHER *(off)*: . . . in France, Saint Nicolas, in Sweden . . .

191. *Low* MLS: *teacher at the blackboard, seen on the diagonal. The students are seen from the rear, sitting at their desks.*

    TEACHER: . . . he is known as Yule Tomte; in Germany, he is . . .
    A knock is heard at the door and the teacher turns right. She puts down her pointer and walks right, the camera panning to follow. She opens the door and Annie walks in, carrying boots.

    TEACHER: Can I . . .

192. MS: *Sarah Jane at her seat, slinking down, embarrassed. As the teacher and Annie talk, she hides her face in a book.*

    TEACHER *(off)*: . . . do something for you?

    ANNIE *(off)*: Sorry to trouble you, Miss, but I brought these for my little girl.

193. CU: *Annie (facing the camera) and the teacher (her back to the camera).*

    TEACHER: I'm afraid you've made a mistake. I don't have any little colored girl in my class. *(Annie peers over her shoulder.)*

    ANNIE: But they said, 3B. This is 3B *(she turns to look at the door)*, isn't . . .

194. MS: *Sarah Jane, peering out from behind her book.*

195. CU: *Annie (facing the camera) and the teacher (back to the camera).*

    ANNIE *(smiling)*: Why, there's Sarah Jane.
    The teacher turns toward the camera, looking toward Sarah Jane.

196. MS: *Sarah Jane, hiding behind her book.*

197. CU: *teacher and Annie facing the camera. Annie begins to walk into the classroom. The camera pulls back and pans left to follow her.*

    ANNIE: There's my baby!

    TEACHER *(startled)*: You mean Sarah Jane Johnson?

    ANNIE: Yes, ma'am. I'm Mrs. Johnson. *(She walks off, left.)*

198. MLS: *Annie, holding boots, walking into the classroom. The camera dollies left as Annie walks down the aisle between rows of desks. It moves close to Sarah Jane as Annie stops by her desk, framing the child in CU, as she hides behind her book.*

    ANNIE *(off)*: Sarah Jane. Baby, I brought you your . . .

Sarah Jane rises, upset, and runs off right. The camera pans and tilts to
follow her as she runs into the depth of the frame toward the front door.
Annie follows behind her.

TEACHER (*standing at the door*): We didn't know . . .

School Coat Room, interior, day

199. MLS: *Sarah Jane searching for her coat.*

ANNIE (*off*): Sarah Jane! Wait! Sarah Jane!

Sarah Jane exits right, and Annie runs into the frame left.

ANNIE: Baby, wait! (*She exits on the right.*)

School Façade, exterior, day

200. LS: *school façade, as seen through the rain and snow. The camera tilts
down slightly as Sarah Jane and Annie (following her) run toward the
camera.*

201. LS: *school as seen from a Christmas tree lot across the street. Annie and
Sarah Jane run forward along a path between some trees.*

ANNIE: Sarah Jane! Wait! Wait!

*As Annie overtakes Sarah Jane, they stop by a sign in the foreground
which reads "Xmas Trees/Special Orders." Annie kneels down by Sarah
Jane and the camera tilts down, framing them in* MS.

ANNIE (*tying Sarah Jane's scarf*): Now, let me do it. Now, put your coat
  on. What do you want to do, catch pneumonia?

SARAH JANE: I hope I do!

202. MCU: *Annie (her back to the camera) and Sarah Jane (facing the camera), as Annie adjusts Sarah Jane's coat.*

    SARAH JANE: I hope I die!

    ANNIE: Honey, nothin's hurt. You shouldn't have let them think . . .

    SARAH JANE: They didn't ask me! Why should I tell them?

    ANNIE: Because . . .

203. MCU: *Annie (facing the camera) and Sarah Jane (back to the camera).*

    ANNIE: . . . that's what you are, and it's nothin' to be ashamed of.

204. MCU: *Annie (her back to the camera) and Sarah Jane (facing the camera).*

    SARAH JANE: Why do you have to be my mother? Why?

    Sarah Jane pulls away and crosses in front of the camera and exits right (as the camera pans right, slightly). Annie rises to follow.

    Dissolve.

    Lora's Apartment, interior, day

205. MS: *Lora and Susie in the latter's bedroom. Lora wears a straight blue skirt with a matching blue sweater. Susie is in bed on the right and Lora sits on the bed, left. Lora removes a thermometer from Susie's mouth and looks at it.*

    LORA: Why, you're practically normal.

    Susie giggles.

    Through a doorway in Susie's room that connects with the hall, Annie and Sarah Jane are seen to enter the apartment. They exit the frame, right. Lora looks distressed and rises to greet them, exiting the frame. Susie stands by the doorway of her bedroom, looking toward the hall.

206. MLS: *Annie, Sarah Jane, Lora in the kitchen. Sarah Jane is sitting on the table as Annie bends over and removes her daughter's boots. Lora enters the room.*

    LORA: Why, you two are soaking wet! (*Crossing behind the table toward the right to get to a cabinet.*) Get out of those things and I'll make some tea.

    ANNIE: I'll be fine. You better get ready. Mr. Steve's comin'.

    As Annie talks, Lora moves behind the table toward the left, moving to the stove to prepare the tea.

    LORA: It'll serve him right to wait. He was due here over an hour ago.

    Susie enters the kitchen.

    LORA: I just don't want everybody having colds. Cups and . . .

207. CU: *Lora looking off-screen at Annie and Sarah Jane.*

    LORA: What's wrong?

208. CU: *Sarah Jane (on the left, in profile) and Annie (facing the camera).*

    ANNIE: Sarah Jane's been "passin'" at school . . . pretending she's white.

Sarah Jane turns toward the camera and looks slightly toward the left; the camera pans to follow.

SARAH JANE: But, I am white! I'm as white as Susie!

209. MCU: *Lora, staring off toward the right. The camera pans right and pulls back as she crosses to Sarah Jane and puts her arm around her.*

LORA: Why, honey, don't you see it . . . it doesn't make any difference to us . . . because we all love you. I'll take you back to school myself.

SARAH JANE (*angrily turning toward her*): I'm never going back to that school! (*She hops off the table and runs screen-right toward the door, as the camera pans and pulls back to follow.*) Never, as long as I live!

The camera pans left again, slightly, to frame Annie in CU, *looking after Sarah Jane, upset.*

210. MS: *Susie. She runs right as the camera pans and pulls back to follow her.*

SUSIE: Sarah Jane!

The camera rests on a CU *of Lora (on the left) and Annie (on the right).*

SUSIE (*off*): Don't cry!

Annie looks toward Lora.

LORA: Annie, don't be upset. Children are always pretending.

211. CU: *Annie (facing the camera, eyes lowered) and Lora (back to the camera).*

LORA: You know that.

ANNIE: No. It's a sin to be ashamed of what you are. (*Raising her eyes.*) And it's even worse to pretend . . . to lie. Sarah Jane has to learn that the lord must've had his reasons . . .

212. MCU: *Lora (facing the camera) and Annie (back to the camera).*

ANNIE: . . . for making some of us white . . .

213. CU: *Annie (facing the camera) and Lora (seen, peripherally, her back to the camera).*

ANNIE: . . . and some of us black.

As Annie talks, Susie opens the door behind Annie and enters the kitchen, moving right. The camera pans right to follow her.

SUSIE: Sarah Jane doesn't want me with her.

Susie crosses in front of Annie and walks left toward Lora; the camera pans to follow. The camera frames the three in a CU.

SUSIE: She says I'm not her friend. She says nobody's her friend.

LORA: Oh, darling, she's upset right now, but she'll be better soon. So will you, if you get back in bed. Come on.

Lora rises and exits with Susie, on the right. The camera moves up and in, framing Annie alone in CU.

214. CU: *Lora, turning around toward the camera (and Annie).*

LORA: Don't worry, Annie. I'm sure you'll be able to explain things to her.

215. CU: *Annie.*

> ANNIE: I don't know. How do you explain to your child, she was born to be hurt?

216. CU: *Lora, reacting.*

217. MS: *Lora and Annie. Annie rises, turns her back to the camera and walks out of the kitchen, closing the door behind her. The camera dollies into the depth of the frame to follow her.*
Dissolve.

Hallway of Lora's Apartment House, interior, day

218. MLS: *Steve Archer coming forward in the hallway, a magazine in his hand. The camera pans left to follow him to the door of Lora's apartment in the foreground. He rings the buzzer.*

Lora's Apartment, interior, day

219. MS: *Lora, her camelhair coat in hand, turning her back to the camera in response to the doorbell. She puts down her coat and walks toward the door in the background, and lets Steve in.*

> LORA: Hello. (*She turns toward the camera and begins reentering the room, putting on her light blue scarf.*)
>
> STEVE: Hi. Sorry I'm late.
>
> LORA: That's all right, I'm . . . I'm ready. I . . . I thought you'd never get here.

As Lora ties her scarf, Steve stands behind her. He opens a magazine and holds it in front of her. She looks at it and gasps.

220. CU *(insert): magazine held in Steve's hand. It shows an advertisement which incorporates Steve's photograph of Susie and Sarah Jane on the beach with the fat man, a can of beer on his stomach. The page reads: "P-E Beer/The lager that doubles holiday pleasure." Lora's hand comes into frame and clutches the magazine.*

221. MS: *Lora (holding the magazine) and Steve; she turns toward him (so that she is seen in profile).*

> LORA: Why, Steve . . . you sold it!
>
> STEVE: More than that (*throwing the magazine down and grabbing Lora*). They gave me a job . . . a steady one . . . on the advertising staff.
>
> LORA: Oh, that's wonderful! But, darling . . . is it really what you want?
>
> STEVE (*turning, and getting Lora's coat*): Well, it's not The Museum of Modern Art . . . but they pay you in the nicest-looking green folding money. (*Helping Lora on with her coat and embracing her.*) Which reminds me . . . this is the season for spending it. Let's go. (*He picks up his hat and they walk to the door in the background.*) We have to get a tree . . . and I have a list of gifts for . . . (*exiting into the corridor*) . . . the kids and Annie.

Hallway of Lora's Apartment House, interior, day

222. MCU: *Steve (on the left) and Lora (on the right). They move toward the right, down the corridor. The camera pans to follow.*

 STEVE (*crossing in front of Lora*): And I hope you like what I picked out for you.

 Lora pauses; they are now framed in MS *with Lora on the left and Steve on the right.*

 LORA: Oh, Steve, you . . . but . . .

 STEVE: You have to have something to put under a tree, don't you?

 LORA: Well, I know, but . . .

 STEVE (*signalling with his head*): This way, ma'am.

 Lora crosses behind him and the two begin walking toward the right. The camera dollies right and angles behind them as they move down the hall into the background.

 LORA: Uh, I feel awful. (*Stopping.*) I haven't been able to buy you anything really nice. You know . . . it's been five months without a job and . . .

223. CU: *Steve (facing the camera) and Lora (back to the camera).*

 STEVE: Then I guess you'll have to marry me.

224. CU: *Lora (facing the camera) looking shocked, and Steve (seen peripherally, back to the camera).*

 STEVE: It's the least you can do for me for Christmas.

225. CU: *Steve (facing the camera) and Lora (back to the camera).*
STEVE: I love you.
226. MS: *Lora (on left, facing the camera) and Steve (on right, back to the camera).*
LORA: But, darling you . . . you're just getting started and . . . It would be foolish.
STEVE: At least we'd be foolish together.
LORA: But marriage is such a big step.
STEVE: I want us to be together.
LORA: But we are! Most of the time.
STEVE (*shaking his head*): Most of the time, you're out fighting to get somewhere. Breaking your heart trying to do for yourself and Susie what . . . what I want to do for you . . . what I finally can do for you now.
As Steve talks a man appears in the background, carrying Christmas presents, and pushes past Steve and Lora.
MAN: Pardon me. I'm sorry.
LORA: Oh.
As the man walks forward, Lora is pushed forward and the camera dollies ahead of her.
MAN: Pardon me.
LORA: Wait a minute!
Lora stops and wedges herself against a wall. She turns left toward Steve, who has followed her.
227. CU: *Steve (on the left, facing the camera) and Lora (on the right, back to the camera).*
STEVE: I want to give you a home . . . (*the theme music begins*) . . . take care of you . . . love you.
228. CU: *Lora (on right, facing the camera) and Steve (on left, back to the camera).*
LORA: Oh, Steve . . . you don't know me at all. I still love the theater.
229. CU: *Steve (on the left, facing the camera) and Lora (on the right, her back to the camera).*
STEVE: You've tried it and it's only hurt you. Realize that and you'll get over it.
230. CU: *Steve (on the left, his back to the camera) and Lora (on the right, facing the camera).*
LORA: I want to be honest with you, darling. I want more . . . everything . . . (*embracing Steve*) . . . maybe too much!
231. CU: *Steve (on left, facing the camera) and Lora (on right, in profile).*
STEVE: Well, don't think I want any less. So let's settle something right now. Do you love me?
232. CU: *Steve (in periphery on left) and Lora (on right).*

LORA: I think I do.

As they embrace, Lora's looks off, right.

233. MS: *Lora and Steve. She pulls away from him, moving left toward a wall. The camera pans and dollies to follow her. She pauses.*

STEVE: I want to kiss you so badly.

234. CU: *Lora and Steve, about to kiss.*

LORA: Oh, but if you did, the way things are right now, I . . . I might say something I wouldn't really mean.

STEVE: That's why I want to kiss you.

The theme music ends. As they begin to kiss, a phone rings off-screen. Lora pulls away and looks off.

LORA: Oh, that's my phone. (*She exits left.*)

235. CU: *Lora moving left toward her front door. The camera pans to follow her. As she opens the door, Annie can be seen on the phone inside, in the background.*

ANNIE: Hello . . .

Steve's hand reaches into the frame from the right and pulls Lora around to embrace her. The camera pans right to follow.

ANNIE (*off*): . . . Miss Meredith's residence.

236. CU: *Annie, talking on the phone.*

ANNIE: Who? Mr. Loomis?

237. CU: *Lora and Steve kissing. Lora glances off left, toward her apartment. Steve breaks their kiss.*

STEVE: She's not in. (*He kisses her again.*)

238. CU: *Annie, smiling, talking on the telephone.*

ANNIE: She isn't in, Mr. Loomis. No, not even if it's important.

239. CU: *Lora and Steve, kissing. Lora glances off left, toward her apartment. They stop kissing.*

ANNIE (*off*): What? A job?

LORA: I . . . I have to find out! It . . . it could be something.

She pulls free, turns left and hurries into the apartment and takes the receiver from Annie. The camera pans left to follow her, remaining outside the door. Steve walks to the door frame and waits in the corridor, looking in.

LORA: Yes, Mr. Loomis?

LOOMIS (*off*): You . . .

240. MCU: *Lora (on the phone) and Annie (standing beside her, listening).*

LOOMIS (*off*): . . . look good with the Saint Bernard dog.

LORA: The Saint Bernard dog?

David Edwards's Apartment, interior, day

241. *Low* MS: *Allen Loomis on the telephone.*

LOOMIS: Yes, uh-huh.

He walks forward and left, as the camera dollies back ahead of him. We see a butler at a bar in the background arranging Christmas packages.

LOOMIS: Well, that's you in the picture, isn't it? (*Reaching down and grasping a magazine.*) Sprinkling flea powder? (*Responding to something she says that we cannot hear.*) All right. Well, I'm here with David Edwards.

Lora's Apartment, interior, day

242. MCU: *Lora on the telephone, on the left; Annie is listening, on the right.*

LORA: David . . .

LOOMIS (*off*): . . . Edwards. Yes.

David Edwards's Apartment, interior, day

243. MS: *Loomis in apartment, with butler in the background. Loomis sits down and talks on the phone.*

LOOMIS: You know . . . the prize-winning playwright. (*He chuckles.*) He saw that picture in the magazine.

David Edwards walks into the frame from the background/right. He sits down near Loomis and lights a cigarette.

LOOMIS: It seems he's looking for a girl with that certain *je ne sais quoi* for his new play . . . that certain something you managed to get with the dog.

244. CU: *Lora (on the phone) and Annie (listening).*

LOOMIS (*off*): Now, it's not a very big part, I know, but . . .

LORA: If this is one of your jokes, Mr. Loomis . . .

245. CU: *Loomis on the telephone (in foreground), Edwards (in midground), and the butler (in the background).*

LOOMIS: Jokes? Well, so help me, I'm only thinking percentage-wise. The part calls for about . . .

EDWARDS: Two and a half.

LOOMIS: Two-fifty a week.

Lora's Apartment, interior, day

246. MCU: *Lora (on the phone) and Annie (listening). Lora looks startled.*

LOOMIS (*off*): Look, I've left the script with my secretary. Can you pick it up immediately?

LORA: Uh . . . yes!

247. MCU: *Steve, in the doorway, looking up.*

LORA (*off*): Yes, Mr. Loomis.

248. MLS: *Steve (in the doorway, seen from behind). Lora and Annie are seen through the door frame, in the background.*

LORA (*finishing her phone conversation*): Yes.

Lora excitedly hangs up the phone. She walks into the hall, moving right, and the camera pans her as she approaches Steve.

LORA: He wants me to come right over and pick up a script. I'm to audition tomorrow.

She begins to move past him, and he blocks her. The camera pans slightly left to follow them.

STEVE: And you're going down there?

LORA: Yes, of course.

STEVE: Even after what happened last time?

LORA: Oh, this has nothing to do with Loomis. I'm to audition for David Edwards.

STEVE: How do you know that?

LORA: Well, I know.

She begins to walk away behind him, moving right. He turns around to follow her, and the camera pans right. They are framed in MS, *Steve on the left and Lora on the right.*

LORA: I just know.

STEVE (*grabbing her arm*): All right. But do you know if he's gonna be any different from Loomis?

LORA (*pulling away*): No, I don't.

STEVE: Then I don't want you to go.

LORA: Do you know what you're asking? Don't you realize what this could mean to me?

STEVE: I'm not asking you not to go down there, Lora. I'm telling you.

LORA: And what makes you think you have that right?

STEVE: Because I love you. Isn't that enough?

LORA: No, Steve, I'm sorry. (*Turning away.*) Good night.

She turns right and walks down the hall. The camera pans and dollies right, keeping her within view, as she moves into the background, back to the camera. Steve enters the frame in the foreground, following her.

STEVE: Lora, wait!

They both disappear down the stairs in the background, right, their backs to the camera.

249. *Low* MLS: *Lora and Steve on the stairs, he pursuing her, both of them facing the camera.*

STEVE: I didn't mean to sound dictatorial or to try to run your life, but . . .

They pause at the foot of the stairs, framed in MCU, *he on the left and she on the right.*

STEVE: . . . you have to understand how I feel.

LORA: And what about me? What about the way I feel?

STEVE: Oh, stop acting!

LORA (*stepping down a stair*): I'm not acting! I want to achieve something . . .

250. MCU: *Steve (facing the camera, on the left) and Lora (back to the camera, on the right).*

LORA: . . . something you'll never understand.

STEVE: What you're after isn't real. What you're after is just a . . .

LORA: At least I'm after something!

251. MCU: *Steve (on the left) and Lora (on the right), both seen in profile.*

LORA: What's a snapshot of a disgusting old man with a beer can on his belly? Is that your idea of achieving something? Is a beer can real? Going up and down and up and down! Well, I'm going up and up and up—and nobody's going to pull me down!

She turns right and flees down the stairs. The camera pans right, losing Steve.

STEVE (*off*): Lora, listen.

He reenters the frame, grabs her and stops her. He is on the right and she on the left.

STEVE: You know how hard I've been try . . .

252. MCU: *Steve (facing the camera, on the right) and Lora (back to the camera, on the left).*

STEVE: . . . ing to do something with my pictures. It's meant everything to me, too. Every minute for a long time now.

253. MCU: *Lora (facing the camera, on the left) and Steve (back to the camera, on the right).*

LORA: No, it hasn't. Or you wouldn't give it up . . . to sell beer.

She turns away and walks left and back, down the stairs, her back to the camera.

254. Low MLS: *Lora and Steve coming down the stairs, as seen from below. As they talk, the camera cranes down and right to follow them.*

STEVE: I gave it up for something much better . . . something right now . . . you.

LORA: But you're asking me to give up something I've wanted all my life . . . ever since I was a child! (*Turning around toward him and pausing.*) And I can't do it!

They continue to walk down the stairs.

STEVE: If you grew up, you could!

Lora stops and turns around to look at him.

LORA: What do you mean?

STEVE (*stepping down a stair*): You're not a child anymore . . . and I might not be around to pick up the pieces this time.

255. MCU: *Lora (facing the camera, on the right) and Steve (back to the camera, on the left). She glares at him.*

LORA: Good! I'd like it that way! Forever!

She turns around, her back to the camera.

256. LS: *Lora and Steve are seen through the glass front door to the apartment building. The camera is positioned outside. Lora continues turning on a match cut. She runs forward, swinging the door open wide, hurries into the snow, and exits past the camera on the left. Steve comes forward slowly, closes the door behind him, puts on his hat and exits right of the camera.*

Dissolve.

Lora's Apartment, interior, night

257. MS: *Annie, Susie, Sarah Jane, in Lora's living room. Annie sits on a chair, with Susie on her lap. Sarah Jane leans over the back of the chair. As Annie talks Lora comes into the background/left, holding a script.*

ANNIE: And Joseph and Mary couldn't find no place at the inn—so they had to go to the stable, among the animals.

SARAH JANE: The animals?

ANNIE: Uh-huh. And in the manger, Jesus was born. And the . . .

The camera tilts up, past the others, and pans to follow Lora, who moves right. She crosses to a mirror on the wall (which reflects her image), stops, and smiles into it as she silently reads her lines.

ANNIE (*off*): . . . Heavenly Hosts sang hallelujah! There was a shining bright star in the sky.

Lora walks forward and the camera pulls back to include Annie, Sarah Jane, and Susie, on the left.

ANNIE: . . . and it was a beautiful time. (*The phone rings and Annie stands up and approaches Lora.*) That'll be Mr. Steve again. (*She exits, crossing in front of Lora and moving right.*)

258. MS: *Annie moving (back to camera) to the phone. She picks up the phone receiver, smiles, and speaks. The theme music comes on.*

ANNIE: Hello.

STEVE (*off*): Hello, Annie.

ANNIE: Oh, hello, Mr. Steve.

Steve's Apartment, interior, night

259. *Low* MLS: *Steve on the telephone, seated at a table. Snow falls outside his window.*

STEVE: Has she come in yet?

ANNIE (*off*): I'm sorry.

STEVE: I see. Well, Merry Christmas, Annie.

Lora's Apartment, interior, night

260. MS: *Annie on the telephone.*

ANNIE: Merry Christmas to you, Mr. Steve.

261. MS: *Susie, Sarah Jane, and Lora in the living room. The girls stand by a chair, on the left; Lora stands on the right.*

SUSIE: Mommie, isn't Steve coming here tonight?

Lora crosses in the foreground and moves left toward the girls. The camera pans to follow.

LORA: I think you'd better go to bed, both of you.

SUSIE: But Annie was telling us a story.

LORA: Oh, all right, Annie can finish it.

ANNIE (*entering the frame on the right*): Now, where were we?

The camera moves in slightly as Annie sits down and Lora moves around the chair, toward the background.

SUSIE: Jesus was almost borned!

262. MCU: *Annie (on the right, facing the camera) and Susie (on the left, back to camera).*
    ANNIE: That's right! As soon as the Holy Infant was born, the Three Wise Men saw a beautiful bright star in the sky . . .

263. MCU: *Annie, Susie, Sarah Jane, and Lora. Annie is in the foreground/right, her back to the camera. Susie and Sarah Jane stand by the chair, on the left, facing her. Lora stands behind the chair, holding her script.*
    ANNIE: . . . the Star of Bethlehem . . .
    SARAH JANE: Was Jesus white or black?
    LORA (*looking up from her script*): Well . . . it doesn't matter. He's the way you imagine Him.
    SUSIE: But Annie said He was a real man.

264. MCU: *Annie (on the right, facing the camera) and Susie (on the left, back to camera).*
    SUSIE: He's not a pretend man.
    ANNIE: He was real . . . He is real.

265. MCU: *Susie, Sarah Jane, and Annie. Annie is on the right, her back to the camera. The two girls are on the left and face the camera.*
    SUSIE: Then what color was He?
    SARAH JANE: He was like me . . . white.
    Dissolve.

Theater, interior, day

266. *High* LS: *theater stage, as seen from the wings and facing an empty auditorium. Edwards and Loomis are sitting in aisle seats near the front of the theater. Several others are seated there as well. On stage, a man explains the scene to Lora—pointing to various blocking positions. She wears the same blue suit seen earlier, but this time with a navy, V-necked blouse.*

STAGE MANAGER: Now, the closet door is over here. The clothes closet door is over there. The door to your bedroom is over here. And you trip over the vacuum cleaner over there. (*He walks to the wings and turns toward her.*) All right! Come on . . . come on! Let's have your off-stage line.

Lora begins to run off-stage in his direction.

267. MS: *Lora, running off-stage. The camera pans and dollies left to follow her. As she approaches the stage manager, he moves forward and left and she remains in the background. The camera moves down and close to him. He closes his eyes and shakes his head.*

268. *High* MS (*from stage*): *Edwards and Loomis in their seats, looking at the stage. Edwards leans forward on the seat ahead of him.*

LORA (*off*): Is anybody home?

269. MS: *Lora walking on stage, toward the camera. The camera dollies back ahead of her.*

LORA: Marjorie! Oh, Marjorie! (*She mimes opening a door.*) Colonel! What are you doing in there? (*She mimes shutting that door and walking to another and opening it. The camera dollies right and pivots around a bit.*) Why, Mr. Overmeyer! Why aren't you in Duluth?

270. *High* MS (*from stage*): *Edwards and Loomis in their seats. The men bow their heads, disgusted with Lora's acting.*

271. MS: *Lora continuing the scene. She lunges forward, pretending to open another door.*

LORA: Oh, Herbert! You, too?

EDWARDS (*off*): No, no, . . .

Lora spins around and the camera pans left to reveal Loomis and Edwards, in the background, rushing to the stage.

EDWARDS: . . . No, Miss Meredith!

272. *High* MS: *Loomis and Edwards (as seen from the stage) as they approach the footlights.*

LOOMIS: David! David! She can do it, David! I guarantee it. She's just a little nervous.

EDWARDS (*gesturing toward Lora*): Miss Meredith!

273. CU: *Loomis and Edwards, backs toward the camera, standing in the foreground. Lora squats down on the stage before them.*

LORA: Yes, sir?

274. MCU: *Loomis, Edwards, and Lora. Loomis and Edwards are facing the*

*camera, positioned at the footlights. Lora is on stage, her back to the
camera.*

EDWARDS: This scene is supposed to be played for high comedy . . .
with delicate reactions . . . not loud, goggle-eyed "takes"!

275. MS: *Lora and Loomis. She faces the camera, squatting on the stage; he
has his back to the camera, and is standing before the stage.*

LORA: I'm sorry, Mr. Edwards . . . (*She rises.*)

276. MS: *Lora, continuing to stand.*

LORA: . . . but, I'm an actress . . . and a good one. But I couldn't play
this part . . . for high comedy. Nobody could.

277. MCU: *Loomis and Edwards, facing the stage, from below.*

LORA (*off*): Nobody.

LOOMIS (*turning away from her*): I think that's all, Miss Meredith.
The camera tilts up a bit as Edwards walks down the theater aisle.

LORA (*off*): And if you'll forgive me for saying it . . .
Loomis and Edwards stop and turn toward the stage.

278. Low LS: *Lora and stage manager on stage.*

LORA: . . . you're too good a writer to have such a scene in your play.

STAGE MANAGER (*approaching her from the left, moving right*): Okay,
sister! This way out!
*He points left (the direction from which he came) and she hands him the
script and walks left, toward the wings.*

279. MS: *Loomis and Edwards at the footlights.*

LOOMIS: I might as well confess, David. She's not really my client.

EDWARDS: Tell her to wait a minute.

LOOMIS: Wha . . . ? (*He crosses in front of Edwards and exits toward
the right, pursuing Lora. The camera pans right slightly to follow him.*)

280. LS: *Lora and the stage manager on stage, seen from the stage facing the
auditorium. Loomis and Edwards run up on the stage, in the background,
as Lora disappears in the foreground.*

LOOMIS: Lora! (*The camera tilts down and pans right as Loomis comes
into the extreme foreground and goes down a small flight of stairs in
pursuit of Lora, who is again seen on screen.*) Lora, wait a minute! I
think we've still got a chance. Mr. Edwards . . .

LORA: No, I don't . . .

EDWARDS (*walking into the frame in the foreground/left*): Miss Meredith . . . it's been a long time since anyone told me off.

281. MCU: *Lora (on the right, facing the camera) and Edwards (on the left,
back to camera).*

EDWARDS: Tell me . . . what would you do with that scene?

LORA: I'd cut it.

282. CU: *Edwards (facing the camera, on the left) and Lora (back on camera,
on the right).*

LORA: Drop it entirely.

EDWARDS: That's not a bad idea. Let me think. Yes . . . but the scene has a couple of lines that are important.

283. MCU: *Lora (on the right, facing the camera) and Edwards (on the left, back to camera).*

LORA: Give them to Amy.

284. CU: *Edwards (facing the camera, on the left) and Lora (back to camera, on the right).*

EDWARDS: Yes . . . it would work. Huh! Think you could play Amy?

285. MCU: *Lora (on the right, facing the camera) and Edwards (on the left, back to camera).*

LORA: Amy?

286. *High* MS: *Loomis, Edwards, Lora.*

EDWARDS: Of course, we'll have to work very hard together, Miss Meredith. (*He takes her arm and they begin to walk left. Loomis follows. The camera tilts up, pulls back, and pans right.*)

LORA: Oh, I'd love it.

EDWARDS: So would I. (*He and Lora walk forward and turn left; the camera pivots around to follow them.*) Tom!

STAGE MANAGER (*off*): Yes, Mr. Edwards.

As the camera continues to move left, following Edwards and Lora, the stage manager is seen on stage.

EDWARDS: Call off auditions for the day. I'm busy.

Edwards and Lora exit left. The stage manager whistles. Loomis approaches him from behind. The manager turns toward Loomis and the two are framed in MS.

LOOMIS: You know, I always believed in that girl.

Dissolve.

Theater, exterior, night

287. *Low* CU: *theater marquee. it reads: "STOPOVER by David Edwards." From off-screen, we hear the sound of an audience clapping. Dissolve.*

Theater, interior, night

288. *High* LS: *stage and audience. The cast is taking its bows and the audience is clapping.*

289. MS: *three audience members (two men and a woman) clapping, facing the stage.*

290. MCU: *leading man, on stage. He walks left to give a bouquet to the leading lady. The camera pans and dollies left, which brings Lora into frame. She wears a camel-colored sheath dress with a matching coat, trimmed in leopard skin. She also wears a small black hat. As the leading lady steps forward, the camera holds on Lora, smiling.*

291. LS: *cast on stage as the audience stands, claps, and shouts. The camera is situated in the audience. The curtains close.*

292. MLS: *Lora amidst actors backstage. Lora comes forward to Edwards and the camera pans a bit left. Both smile.*

293. MLS: *stage (with curtains drawn), seen from the audience's perspective as they continue to clap. The curtains open to reveal the stars on stage. They take their bows. Someone in the audience shouts for Lora Meredith.*

294. Low MCU: *man in the audience clapping. Other audience members shout for Lora Meredith.*

295. MS: *leading man (on right) and leading lady (on left) taking bows. The leading man gestures, left, toward the wings.*

296. MS: *Lora, stage manager, and Edwards, backstage. They push Lora toward the stage and she begins to exit toward the background.*

297. Low LS: *Lora walking on stage from the wings (on the left side of the stage). The camera pans right ever so slightly.*

298. MCU: *Steve in audience, clapping.*

299. LS: *Lora on stage, taking bows. The leading man walks into the frame from the right and takes her hand. The camera pans right as he leads her to the leading lady at the center of the stage.*

300. MCU: *Steve in the audience, rising from his seat. The camera tilts up. He turns away from the stage, toward the left, and the camera pans to follow.*

301. High LS: *audience continuing to clap as the curtains close. The shot is taken from the audience's perspective, facing toward the stage.*

302. MS: *Lora hurrying backstage toward Edwards, the stage manager, and others. Her dresser removes her coat.*
    LORA: Thank you, David! They applauded me! Did you hear them?
    EDWARDS: Why not? You were great!
    AUDIENCE (*off*): Author, author!
    STAGE MANAGER (*gesturing to Edwards*): It's your turn, Mr. Edwards.
    Edwards kisses Lora and exits right.
    LORA (*turning to stage manager*): Tom, may I borrow a dime?
    STAGE MANAGER (*digging in his pockets*): Sure.
    LORA: I'll pay you back!
    STAGE MANAGER: Don't rush. You'll be around a long time.
    Lora exits left, passing Loomis, half embracing him. The camera pans left to follow as she goes to the phone on the wall in the background.

303. MS: *Edwards, taking bows on stage. He is seen from the audience's perspective, through clapping hands.*

304. MCU: *Lora, dialing the phone. Her back is to the camera, but we see her face reflected in a mirror that hangs to the left of the wall phone.*

Lora's Apartment, interior, night

305. MS: *phone on a table, ringing. Annie enters in the background/left from behind a curtained doorway. She answers the phone.*
    ANNIE: Yes?
    A door opens in the background and Susie pokes her head out.

ANNIE: Oh, Miss Lora!

Annie gestures to Susie who runs forward, toward the telephone.

Theater, interior, night

306. MCU: *Lora, on the phone. She stands in partial profile and we also see her reflected in the mirror.*

LORA: And they liked me, too!

Lora's Apartment, interior, night

307. MLS: *Annie and Susie. Annie speaks on the phone, as Susie climbs up on the telephone table.*

ANNIE: They did?

Sarah Jane runs into the room and stands on the right, then in front of Annie.

ANNIE: Oh, now isn't that wonderful!

Theater, interior, night

308. MCU: *Lora, on the phone. She is in partial profile and we also see her reflected in the mirror.*

ANNIE (*off*): Here . . . you want Susie?

LORA: Yes. Yes, let me speak to her, please!

Lora's Apartment, interior, night

309. MCU: *Susie (on left), and Sarah Jane (in foreground/middle) and Annie (on the right).*

ANNIE (*handing Susie the phone and whispering*): "Congratulations, Mommie."

SUSIE: Congratulations, Mommie. Did you remember your lines?

Theater, interior, night

310. MCU: *Lora, on the phone. She is in partial profile and we also see her reflected in the mirror.*

LORA: Yes, I remembered all my lines.

SUSIE (*off*): Did they clap for you?

LORA: Yes, they did clap for me, too.

Lora's Apartment, interior, night

311. MCU: *Susie (on the phone on the right) and Annie (embracing Sarah Jane).*

LORA (*off*): I'll be home very soon. I'll only stay a little while and . . .

Theater, interior, night

312. MCU: *Lora, on the phone. She is in partial profile and we also see her reflected in the mirror.*

LORA: . . . and then I'll come right home.

SUSIE (*off*): Here's a kiss, Mommie.

LORA: Oh! And here's one for you, too. (*She makes a kissing sound and chuckles.*)

The camera pulls back and moves right as Edwards approaches Lora from behind. He hangs up the phone.

EDWARDS: Let's go, let's go. The papers will be out soon and the party's waiting.

They exit past the camera, on the right.

Dissolve.

Edwards's Apartment, interior, night

313. CU: *newspaper, held in Edwards's hands, as he turns the page and we see his face behind it. He moves back into the depth of the frame toward his guests as the camera pulls back toward the foreground, framing him in* LS.

EDWARDS: "This should be a prize play for David Edwards, for tonight we saw the ranking comedy of the season, marvelously performed by Geraldine Moore and Preston Mitchell."

The party guests shout in response and Loomis approaches Edwards from the right.

LOOMIS: Listen to the *Times.*

Loomis walks into the background and right, toward Lora, who is seated on a chair. The camera pans to follow.

LOOMIS: Atkinson says: "A new star was born. Lora Meredith, an actress who heretofore has been hiding her light under a bushel . . ."

314. MS: *Loomis standing on the left, reading newspaper, and Lora seated on the right. She wears a floor-length, light blue evening gown with a chiffon train. She wears a matching blue necklace and earring set, as well as a bracelet and a ring.*

LOOMIS: ". . . somewhere in the hinterlands, gave a great performance in a small part last night."

The guests clap in response.

LOOMIS (*bending down to kiss her, as the camera tilts down*): Congratulations, baby!

LORA: Thank you, Allen.

Loomis sits down on Lora's right and Edwards enters the frame on the left and stands behind Lora.

LOOMIS: Lora, this is a great night for us.

EDWARDS: For us?

315. MS: *Edwards, Lora, Loomis, and another man. Edwards is on the left, hovering over Lora, looking at the newspaper. Another man stands behind her. Loomis sits on the right.*

LOOMIS: Oh. Ohh! (*Rising.*) Well, I, for one, can't keep my beady eyes open any more. I'm going home. (*The camera tilts up a bit and Loomis and the other man exit, on the left.*)

MAN: Well, good night, David.

EDWARDS: Good night, all you lucky people.

Lora stands and starts to move away. Edwards restrains her, then exits in the foreground/left.

316. MLS: *Geraldine Moore and Preston Mitchell rise from the sofa and walk toward the background, as the camera tilts up and moves in behind them. Edwards appears in the background right, kissing people and saying good-bye. The camera dollies behind the stars as they approach Edwards.*
MOORE: Good night, David.
EDWARDS: Good night, Gerry.
Others say good night. Edwards walks left to the door as he ushers his guests out.
EDWARDS: See you tomorrow. Good night, all.
Lora appears in the foreground/right. Her back is to the camera as she looks toward the apartment door. Loomis approaches her, his coat in hand, from the background.
LOOMIS: Well, congratulations again, baby. We did it, all right. I'll see you first thing in the morning . . .
LORA: Yes, Allen.
Edwards approaches the two from behind.
LOOMIS: . . . in my office.
Loomis exits left and Edwards looks after him.
EDWARDS (*turning to Lora*): Agents!
Lora and Edwards laugh. Edwards walks forward and takes Lora's hand and they walk right, the camera panning slightly.
EDWARDS: By morning, it'll be all over town that he wrote your part, directed you personally, and was your lover before you met me.
LORA: Oh!
Lora laughs and David moves right (as the camera pans to follow) toward the window. He begins sliding it open.
317. MS (*from outside the window*): *Edwards and Lora at the window, looking out. He puts his arm around her.*
EDWARDS: Well, lady, there's your new empire.
318. LS: *buildings in Manhattan, outside the window, as seen from Edwards's apartment.*
EDWARDS (*off*): Not big . . . just stretches from Forty-second to Fifty-second Street.
319. MCU: *Edwards and Lora looking out the window, as seen through the window.*
EDWARDS: But it's the heart of the world. You happy?
LORA: Oh, yes! Yes! I can't thank you . . . I . . . I can't begin to thank you for . . . for giving me the chance.
EDWARDS: No thanks. (*He moves away from the window, into the background/right. The camera pans slightly to follow him.*) It's something we did together.
LORA (*still looking out the window*): Yes.
EDWARDS (*walking forward toward the window to stand behind*

Lora): We'll have more evenings like this . . . more plays. I promise that.

LORA: Please . . . and with you. David! Always with you! You are good for me.

EDWARDS (*turning Lora towards him, away from the window*): You mean that?

320. MCU: *Edwards (back to the camera, on the left) and Lora (facing the camera, on the right).*

LORA: Well, you must be, because I . . . I've never felt this way before . . . never so . . . so complete and . . .

321. MCU: *Edwards (on left, facing the camera) and Lora (on right, back to camera).*

LORA: . . . so happy.

EDWARDS: I don't think I could be happier with anyone else, either. I'm in love with you, Lora. But, I must hasten to add, I always fall in love with my leading ladies.

322. CU: *Edwards (back to camera, on the left) and Lora (facing camera, on the right).*

LORA: Maybe that's all it is . . . but I don't care . . . because I'm loving you now. You and . . . tonight. Thank you.

They kiss and the theme music comes in briefly.

323. MS: *Lora and Edwards embracing. Edwards faces the camera and Lora has her back to the camera. They pull apart.*

324. MCU: *Lora and Edwards kissing, seen more in profile. The camera cranes up and right, framing a view of Manhattan through the window. Dissolve.*

325. *Montage sequence, indicating Lora's rise to stardom in the theater (in Edwards's plays). The first shot depicts a lighted sign on the theater exterior which reads: "SUMMER MADNESS starring Lora Meredith." Dissolve.*

326. *The sign superimposed over a background shot of applauding theater audiences. The number "1948" comes on in the background and exits past the camera. The theme music comes up at a faster tempo. Dissolve.*

327. MS: *Annie clapping backstage. We also see a sign on a building which reads "Music Box," and cars going by. The number "1949" comes forward and exits past the camera. Dissolve.*

328. *Two theater marquees which read: "Morosco/Lora Meredith in SWEET SURRENDER." A CU of Lora's face comes forward along with the number "1950." The number eventually exits past the camera. Dissolve.*

329. *Exterior of Imperial theater with lighted sign. Lora's face remains on*

screen as the number "1951" comes forward and exits past the camera. Dissolve.

330. *Composite image of John Drew Theater sign, audiences clapping, cars going by. The number "1952" comes forward, and exits past the camera. Dissolve.*

331. *High* CU *of various magazines, spread out on a surface, as the number "1953" comes forward. The camera rests on an issue of* Newsweek *that has Lora's photo on the cover. Dissolve.*

332. *The cover of* Newsweek, *which remains in view as a high-angle image of audiences clapping is superimposed; we notice Steve and a young woman. Images of theater lights (captured in a pan shot) are also superimposed. The number "1954" comes forward and exits past the camera. Dissolve.*

333. *Another high shot of the theater audience, as lights move over the background. A theater poster is superimposed, which reads: "Lora Meredith in David Edwards' Brilliant Comedy HAPPINESS. Produced by Cheryl Vaughn, Staged by Robert Larkin, Broadway Playhouse, Now Playing." The number "1955" comes forward and exits past the camera. Dissolve.*

334. *Image of theater audience clapping in the background, upon which is superimposed a theater marquee for the Plymouth theater and a sign which reads: "Lora Meredith, ALWAYS LAUGHTER by David Edwards." The number "1956" comes forward and exits past the camera. The number "1957" also comes forward over the background and exits past the camera.*
Dissolve.

335. *Clinton Theater marquee, which reads: "Lora Meredith In BORN TO LAUGH." The number "1958" comes forward and exits behind the camera. (With this image the montage ends).*
Theater, interior, night

336. *High* MS: *people in a theater audience clapping.*

337. MS: *Annie in theater wings, looking off toward the stage, smiling and clapping.*

338. MLS: *Lora taking a bow on stage, holding bouquets. Annie is seen in the opposite wing, clapping. The curtains begin to close.*
Dissolve.

339. MLS: *Lora in her dressing room. She sits with her back to camera, at a mirror, in which she is reflected. Annie approaches her (back to camera) from behind. Annie is also reflected in the mirror. Lora is wearing a light blue, floor-length, sheath evening gown. A knock is heard. Annie turns left and moves into the foreground, opening the dressing room door. In the mirror, we see her admit Edwards. He approaches Lora, and embraces her shoulders from behind. He is also reflected in the mirror.*
EDWARDS: Marvelous performance, darling! Just as fresh as it was seven months ago. (*He leans over to kiss her on the cheek.*)
LORA: Ha!
EDWARDS: Now, hurry up and get ready.
He turns and begins to move into the foreground, still reflected in the mirror. Lora takes his hand to stop him. He moves toward her, right, and the camera pivots to follow as Edwards sits on her dressing table. Annie is seen in the background, hanging up clothes.
LORA: David . . . Can't I beg off tonight? I am so . . .
EDWARDS: Beg off? Impossible, darling. There's some nice, untouched money out there from Cincinnati. Hardware, I believe. They want to meet you, to invest in your success . . . and my next play.
ANNIE: She ought to go to bed right now.
EDWARDS (*standing, pivoting around left and taking Annie's arm*): Annie, you're much too pretty to be a watchdog.
ANNIE: And I can bite sometimes.
EDWARDS (*bending over Lora, as the camera reframes slightly to the right*): Five minutes, darling . . . (*He exits through the door on the left, and the camera pans to follow.*)

340. MS: *Lora (seen from the rear) sitting before her dressing table. She is reflected in the mirror, as is Annie.*

   ANNIE (*off*): Doesn't he ever stop? (*Annie walks over to Lora, disappearing from the mirror view, and entering the frame, foreground/right. She bends over to put on Lora's shoes. The camera tilts a bit down.*)

   LORA: He can't, Annie. If he did, he'd be sure to find out how sad he really is.

   Annie rises, walks left to behind Lora and helps her put on her necklace. Both are reflected in the mirror. Lora is also seen in the foreground; Annie is not.

   LORA: And I know that feeling. Funny, isn't it? After all this time . . . the struggling and heartache . . . and you make it . . . then you find out it doesn't seem worth it . . . something's missing.

   The theme music begins. Annie walks into the frame, left, and sits on Lora's dressing table.

   LORA: Now David wants to marry me. I don't know.

   ANNIE: Do you love him?

   LORA: No. But he's good for me in many ways. At least, I'm trying to make myself think he is. And of course, it . . . it would be better for Susie.

   ANNIE (*bending down, touching Lora's shoulder*): This ain't no time to make decisions. You're tired and you don't know what you want.

   LORA: Maybe I don't want so much anymore.

   ANNIE (*walking to the closet on the left*): But what would you do if you gave it all up?

   Lora stands as Annie brings her her jacket (which is blue, like her dress, and fur-trimmed).

   LORA: Well, I could spend more time with Susie. (*Lora walks left to Annie and the camera pans left as Annie puts on Lora's coat. She pauses.*) And you could stay at home with Sarah Jane. Do you know, I . . . I haven't been up to see my baby at school in weeks?

   ANNIE: Susie knows you love her. (*Walking around to stand in front of Lora, in the foreground.*) And you need show business as much as it needs you.

   The theme music ends.

   LORA: Oh . . . Annie . . . what would I do without you?

   A noise is heard. The women look off left.

341. LS: *Edwards (entering the door, left) and Annie, and Lora.*

   EDWARDS (*looking Lora over*): Well, beautiful!

   LORA: Do you really like it?

   Annie adjusts Lora's clothes and gets her gloves and bag for her from her dressing table.

   EDWARDS: You're more beautiful than I could ever possibly remember. (*Looking at his watch.*) And we're late!

Annie hands Lora her gloves and bag.

LORA: Good night, Annie.

ANNIE (*walking with Lora and Edwards to the door, left, and shaking her finger at him*): You see she gets home at a decent hour!

Edwards turns toward Annie and closes the door. She shakes her head and walks toward the foreground.

Dissolve.

Lora's Connecticut House, exterior, day

342. ELS: *driveway of the house with a moving van parked; men carry furniture inside the house.*

Lora's Connecticut House, interior, day

343. MLS: *Annie and Lora in the living room, their backs to the camera, standing before a console, and picking up small decorative objects. Lora wears orange toreador pants with a matching print top and over-skirt. She turns toward the camera and begins to walk toward the foreground.*

LORA: Annie, I think we'll try these uh . . . over here.

Lora walks right, Annie trailing behind, and the camera pans and dollies to follow them. As they move to the other side of the room we see Lora's butler, Kenneth, and some moving men by the door in the background.

ANNIE: Miss Lora, we been spendin' an awful lot of money up here. Do you think we can really afford to have this place?

The women place the objects on a console at the other end of the room.

LORA: Well, we can't afford not to.

Lora walks left and the camera pans to follow. Kenneth appears in the foreground/left.

KENNETH: (*off*): Ma'am! (*On-screen*) Ma'am.

He indicates moving men with a large piece of furniture, whom we now see on the left, by the front door.

LORA (*pointing*): Oh, uh . . . uh . . . would you put it over there, please?

KENNETH (*mumbling to men*): Right in front of the window.

Lora puts down an object on the console, on the left, and walks into the background, toward the men and the furniture; the camera dollies behind her.

LORA (*muttering*): Oh, that's fine.

MOVER: Will you sign this, Ma'am?

LORA: Uh-huh.

344. MS: *Lora, Kenneth, and the mover as she signs the form.*

MOVER (*giving her the receipt*): Thank you very much. (*To other moving man.*) Come on, let's go, Joe.

The men cross in front of Lora and go off, right. The camera moves in as Annie enters the frame from the foreground, right, her back to the camera.

ANNIE: Did you see the bills from Susie's new school?

LORA (*arranging papers*): Uh-huh . . . and it doesn't matter.

ANNIE: But, Miss Lora . . .

LORA: No matter what it costs. Susie's going to have everything that I missed. (*She lights a cigarette.*)

ANNIE: From her letters, she misses you, more'n she'd ever miss Latin. She just wrote and told me . . .

LORA (*turning to Annie*): Annie . . . you still haven't told me what the doctor said about those spells you've been getting.

ANNIE: Oh, what do doctors always say when they can't find nothin' wrong? "Take it easy."

LORA: Well, do . . . and I mean it.

ANNIE (*turning away to the right*): Oh, Miss Lora . . .

LORA (*moving toward Annie right, the camera following*): You know you can have anyone you want in here to help you.

ANNIE: Oh, be more work gettin' 'em outta' my way.

A doorbell rings and the women turn right.

SARAH JANE (*off*): I'll get it!

Annie walks off right and the camera pivots around to follow, revealing Sarah Jane (now eighteen years old) walking down the stairs in the background. Sarah Jane walks to the door, moving right, and begins to open it.

345. MS: *Sarah Jane opening the front door.*

SARAH JANE: Hello, Mr. Edwards.

Edwards walks in and the camera pans a bit left.

EDWARDS: Hello, Sarah Jane. How are you? (*He walks off-screen left.*)

SARAH JANE: Fine, thanks. (*Moving forward and shouting toward the foreground and toward Annie, who is off-screen.*) I'm going to the village. I'll be back by three. (*She walks back and right toward the door and exits. The camera pans to follow.*)

346. LS: *Edwards (back to the camera) walking into the living room, dropping his coat on a ledge. The camera pans to follow him left, past the fireplace, bringing Annie and Lora into frame, on the left.*

EDWARDS: Annie, that daughter of yours gets prettier every day . . . and so sophisticated. (*To Lora.*) Darling!

347. MS: *Edwards (back to camera) approaching Lora (facing the camera).*

LORA: Hello, dear.

EDWARDS (*looking at the new piece of furniture*): Oh, nice!

LORA (*turning around to the furniture*): Yes, it's new.

EDWARDS (*crossing right to a cigarette box on a table*): Didn't you get my messages yesterday? Or have you given up telephones?

LORA (*looking toward him on the right and walking forward*): Oh . . . well, we've been so busy, David, getting the house in order. Uh . . . (*She gestures left and walks in that direction as the camera pans with them. She sits.*) . . . come sit down. Would you like a drink?

EDWARDS (*sitting down*): A long one. It's quite a trek from Manhattan.
Annie enters from the foreground/right and crosses in front of them.
ANNIE: Your usual?
EDWARDS: Uh-hum.
ANNIE: I'll get it. (*She exits, left*).
EDWARDS: All right, enough chitchat. Have you read my new play?
348. MCU: *Lora (facing the camera, on the left) and Edwards (back to the camera, in the right corner of the frame).*
EDWARDS: Great, isn't it?
LORA: Yes, it's very good, but . . . David . . . darling, I don't think I should do another comedy.
He leans forward, as though to get up. She restrains him.
LORA: No . . . no . . . wait a minute. I've decided to do the new Stewart . . .
349. MCU: *Edwards (facing the camera, on the right) and Lora (back to camera, on the left).*
LORA: . . . play.
EDWARDS: That? What part? Not the dull social worker with the high dreams and low heels!
LORA: Yes.
EDWARDS: It's drama! No clothes . . . no sex!

350. MS: *Lora and Edwards on the couch, he on the right and she the left.*
     EDWARDS: No fun!
     LORA (*standing and moving left, the camera following her*): I know, but it's a great chance for . . . for good acting.
     EDWARDS (*off*): . . . And that "colored" . . . (*He comes on screen, rising up in the lower right corner of the frame.*) . . . angle in it. It's . . .

351. MS: *Annie behind the bar, fixing Edwards's drink. She looks off, toward the camera.*
     EDWARDS (*off*): . . . absolutely controversial! What do you know about contro . . .

352. MLS: *Lora (facing the camera) and Edwards (back to camera) standing, facing one another.*
     EDWARDS: . . . versy?
     LORA: Nothing! (*She turns, left, and walks away, the camera panning to follow, losing Edwards.*) And I don't want to know. (*Turning towards Edwards and pausing.*) I only know it's a good script, and they're not easy to find. (*Moving left, the camera panning her.*) Besides, I . . . I feel I need something different . . . a new experience.
     Lora pauses and we see Annie, behind the bar, in the background.
     EDWARDS (*off*): All right . . . if you want a flop, have it on your own time. (*He enters the frame from the foreground/right, his back to the camera; He approaches Lora.*) I wrote my play for you . . . I tailored it to you every mood. (*Walking into the depth of the frame, toward Annie and the bar.*) I never wrote better laughs in my life. And you tell me . . . you want controversy! Hah!
     LORA (*walking forward, the camera pulling back*): It may sound ungrateful. (*Turning her back to the camera, looking at Edwards.*) After all you've done for me . . .
     EDWARDS (*walking forward toward Lora*): You're right! It is ungrateful. But, then, I never expected gratitude. May I have my property back?
     LORA (*turning and exiting the frame.*): Of course.
     The camera holds on Edwards in MS.

353. MLS: *Lora, her back to the camera, walking over to a desk in the background. She takes the script from a drawer and the camera pans right as she comes forward to Edwards, and he comes on from the right/foreground and moves towards her.*
     LORA (*handing script to Edwards*): Good luck, David. I know it will be a hit.
     EDWARDS (*leafing through it*): You know without you . . . it will never be done. (*He begins to walk toward the fire and the camera pans right.*) Under the circumstances . . . I think it's best if I destroy it. (*He walks further right, as the camera pans and tosses it into the fire.*)
     ANNIE (*off*): What? Why, Mr. Edwards!

Lora (on the left) and Annie (on the right) are seen on the peripheries of the frame.

EDWARDS: There goes my pride . . . up in ashes! Well . . . good-bye!
Edwards exits right and Annie walks into the frame, toward the fireplace, turning to Lora.

354. MS: *Lora, in front of a window.*

LORA: Just a theatrical gesture. He never makes less than six copies.
(*She turns and walks away, toward the window.*)
Dissolve.

Façade of Imperial Theater, exterior, night

355. LS: *lighted sign of Imperial Theater, with an illuminated picture of Lora Meredith in NO GREATER GLORY.*
Dissolve.

Imperial Theater, interior, night

356. LS: *theater stage, as seen from the perspective of the audience. The camera is positioned so as to include the backs of the spectators. They clap for the cast, which bows.*

357. High MS: *Edwards and Loomis in the first row of the audience, clapping. Other members of the audience are seen behind them.*

358. LS: *Lora on stage, as seen from the audience's perspective. She bows alone and the curtains close.*

359. High MS: *Loomis and Edwards in the first row of the audience. Loomis turns to Edwards.*

LOOMIS: Wasn't she great? You're going to join us, aren't you?

EDWARDS: No. (*He removes his glasses.*) Just wish her all the luck in the world for me. Tell her I was wrong. (*He rises, crosses in front of Loomis and exits left.*)

360. Low LS: *Lora on stage, alone, taking another bow.*

361. Low MS: *theater box, where Annie, Sarah Jane, and Susie (now sixteen years old) sit and clap. Susie and Sarah Jane are now teenagers.*

SUSIE (*rising and approaching Annie*): Oh, Annie, wasn't Mother just wonderful? (*She moves toward the door at the rear of the box.*)

ANNIE: Susie! Susie! Wait!

SUSIE: We've gotta hurry. Remember Mama's bringing them all home. (*Pulling Sarah Jane.*) Sarah Jane!

The two girls move toward the door of the box.

362. High MS: *Steve and a woman companion in the audience clapping.*

363. Low LS: *Lora on stage as the curtains close again.*
Dissolve.

364. LS: *Lora's dressing room. Guests are in the foreground and background while she receives them in the midground. Lora wears a white, sequined, strapless, street-length cocktail dress.*

LORA (*to some guests*): Thank you! Oh, that's very sweet!

From a door in the rear, Loomis walks in and greets and embraces her.

LOOMIS: Darling, you were wonderful!

From the rear door, Steve and his friend walk into the dressing room. Pulling away from Loomis, Lora notices them.

LORA: Steve!

The Theme music begins.

365. MS: *Lora (on the right, her back to the camera), Steve (on the left, facing the camera) and his friend, Louise (facing the camera) in the middle.* Lora takes his hand.

STEVE: Hello, Lora . . . and congratulations.

366. CU: *Lora (facing the camera) and Steve (back to camera) with Loomis seen over Lora's shoulder in the background.*

LORA: Oh, Steve . . . I can't believe it.

367. MS: *Lora (back to camera, on the right), Steve (on the left, facing the camera) and Louise (facing the camera) in the middle.*

STEVE (*turning toward Louise*): Oh, Lora, I'd . . . I'd like you to know Louise Morton.

LORA: How do you do?

LOUISE (*stepping forward toward Lora*): How do you do, Miss Meredith. I loved your performance.

LORA: Thank you very much. (*Turning around toward her other guests and the camera.*) Uh . . . Steve Archer . . . everybody. (*People greet him from off-screen. Lora takes his hand and looks at him.*) A very old and dear friend. (*Ushering Louise forward.*) Oh, and uh—Miss Morton.

Lora turns toward Steve again and grasps his arm. Louise looks at them as she stands in the foreground, her back to the camera.

LORA: Oh, Steve, it's been so long! Ten years! And you haven't changed a bit!

STEVE: How are Annie and the kids?

LORA: Oh, Annie's fine. You'd never knew the children . . . they're so grown up and lovely. (*Turning around.*) Look . . . we're all going to my house to wait for the reviews. (*Turning toward Steve again.*) Why don't you join us?

368. MS: *Loomis and a woman.*

LOOMIS: Well, let's get going!

The camera pulls back as Lora enters the frame in the foreground, her back to the screen. She adjusts her make-up in a mirror as Loomis puts on her stole. They turn and exit in the foreground, past the camera, along with other guests. The theme music fades.

Dissolve.

Lora's House, interior, night

369. MS: *Lora's kitchen, where Annie and Kenneth are preparing the hors d'oeuvres tray. Kenneth exits the frame in the foreground/right. Annie*

moves left to the sink and the camera pans to follow, picking up Susie, who is sitting at the counter. Susie wears a white, off-the-shoulder, street-length cocktail dress, with a blue chiffon scarf-like train.

SUSIE: Hm. I'm glad the opening's over. Now I hope Mother will have some time for me before my graduation. You know, I have a lot of subjects I want to discuss with her and I don't want to forget any of them. (*To Annie, who has walked to the sink counter, holding a bowl.*) Annie . . . do you want to hear them?

ANNIE: Sure, honey. Sure do.

Annie exits the frame on the right. Susie gets up and moves into the foreground/right as the camera pans to follow. As she does so, the camera picks up Annie, working at the counter.

SUSIE (*with a list in hand*): Well, the most important is Jane Bealer's party. There are gonna be boys. And under that I have an "A" and a "B" I want to discuss with Mother. "A" . . . how do I make a boy like me? And "B" (*giggling*) . . . should I let him kiss me?

ANNIE: Isn't that subject comin' up a little soon?

SUSIE: Well, but the girls at school discuss it all the time.

A doorbell is heard and Susie runs off right. The camera holds on Annie, who looks after her.

370. MCU: *Susie, who runs past camera to the kitchen door. Guests can be seen arriving in the background. We spot Loomis.*

SUSIE: My goodness. They're here already! (*She runs past the camera in the foreground.*)

371. MS: *Susie and Annie in the kitchen. Susie runs left past the counter and the camera pans to follow her. She adjusts her hair in a wall mirror by the sink. Annie approaches her.*

ANNIE: Honey, will you run upstairs and get Sarah Jane?

SUSIE: All right.

Susie runs left toward the back kitchen stairs and disappears from the frame. The camera holds on Annie, working at the counter.

372. MS: *Dining room as seen from the kitchen. Lora and Kenneth are reflected in a fireplace mirror as they enter the room from the living room. The two then enter the frame as Lora inspects the table. We can also see Steve and Louise reflected in the background mirror.*

KENNETH: All right, ma'am?

LORA: Oh, yes . . . it's wonderful.

KENNETH: Thank you.

Lora beckons to Steve, who is off-screen. She walks right and then into the foreground, as the camera pans right and pulls back. Kenneth adjusts things on the table. Lora looks off-screen, behind the camera. The theme music comes in.

LORA: Annie!

373. MS: *Annie at the end of the serving counter, in the background. She looks up.*

LORA (*off*): Are you ready for a surprise? (*She walks into the foreground, her back to the camera.*) Wait till you see who's here!

374. MS: *Steve (as seen through the kitchen door), entering the kitchen from the dining room. In the background, Kenneth is busy at the table.*

375. MS: *Annie and Lora in the kitchen. Lora turns around to Annie as Steve (seen from behind), walks in past the camera, toward Annie at the counter in the background.*

STEVE: Hello, Annie.

ANNIE (*walking toward Steve and the foreground, taking his hand*): Why, Mr. Steve. My goodness.

LORA (*to Steve*): I'll get you a drink. (*She walks off screen-right.*)

ANNIE: You certainly look fine!

376. MCU: *Steve (on the left, facing the camera) and Annie (on the right, seen from the rear).*

STEVE: You, too, Annie. How's everything been?

ANNIE: Oh, each day, I count my blessings!

STEVE: You call doing this at one o'clock in the morning a blessing?

377. MCU: *Steve (left) and Annie (right) in profile, favoring her slightly.*

ANNIE: Yes, sir. I can remember when plenty of ham and eggs was more'n a blessin' . . . it was a miracle!

The two turn right and Lora enters the frame in the foreground/right, handing Steve a drink. As Lora talks, Annie walks into the background, turns to face them, and works at the counter, observing the couple's conversation.

LORA: Here you are! Scotch and water. I remembered.

STEVE: Thanks. But I'd better get back to Louise.

LORA: Oh, she wouldn't even know you're there. She's being mesmerized by Allen Loomis. Oh, Steve . . . it's good to have you here. I mean it. And now that we finally have you back (*turning to Annie*), we will not let you go.

ANNIE: No, sir. You're gonna stay with us.

Lora puts her arm around Steve as he crosses in front of her. The camera pans right with them, and Annie moves toward the sink in the background.

LORA: Listen . . . I have this Sunday off . . . the first Sunday I've had in weeks, and we're going to drive into the country for a picnic . . . Susie, Sarah Jane, and Annie.

378. MCU: *Steve (facing the camera, on the right) and Lora (seen from the rear, on the left).*

LORA: How does that sound?

STEVE: Wonderful.

SUSIE (*off*): Steve!

Steve looks up.

379. LS: *Susie running down the back kitchen stairs, toward the camera.*

SUSIE (*laughing*): I heard your voice!

Steve (his back to the camera) comes in from the foreground, picks Susie up, and whirls her around. He pauses. Lora comes into the frame in the foreground, her back to the camera. Annie is seen in the background.

STEVE (*looking forward, toward Lora*): This can't be Susie! So pretty . . . and not little any more.

SUSIE: Little! Why, I'm graduating in two weeks! Oh, you'll come, won't you, Steve?

As Susie speaks Sarah Jane comes down the kitchen stairs in the background. She is wearing an orange, strapless, sheath dress.

STEVE: I wouldn't miss it for the world.

SUSIE (*turning to Sarah Jane*): Sarah Jane, look who's here!

STEVE (*walking toward Sarah Jane, as the camera moves in behind him*): Sarah Jane?

SARAH JANE: Hello, Steve. (*The camera continues to move in toward her.*)

STEVE: It can't be. Why, you were all legs!

SARAH JANE: I still have them.

STEVE: Yes . . . but they came up to here (*indicates waist*).

They laugh and embrace. Susie comes back into full view on the left.

SUSIE: Oh Steve! Don't ever go away from us again. Will you promise?

LOOMIS (*Off*): Well, are we holding the party in . . .

Susie, Sarah Jane, and Steve look off-screen right, toward the kitchen door.

380. MS: *Loomis, leaning in the kitchen doorway, facing the camera.*

LOOMIS: . . . here? Hi, Annie. Sarah Jane.

381. MCU: *Lora (with Annie seen in the background).*

LORA: No, Allen. We're coming right out.

The camera pans a bit left as she moves to Susie and takes her arm. Steve comes forward, and the three exit past the camera, which pans right slightly. Sarah Jane moves forward and pauses by the counter. Her smile fades as she watches the others exit.

382. MLS: *Steve and Lora (seen from the rear and through the kitchen doorway), walking into the dining room. Susie is visible walking with them, and Kenneth is seen working in the dining room.*

LORA: What a surprise to see you.

STEVE: What a surprise to see you again.

383. MS: *Sarah Jane in the kitchen, with Annie seen in the background. The camera pans left a bit as she turns and walks into the background.*

384. LS: *living room. A man plays the theme music on a piano in the foreground as Loomis, Lora, and Steve cross in the background. Susie catches up with them, running in from frame-right.*

LORA: You have an open invitation to come here any time you can get away from Madison Avenue.

SUSIE: Oh, yes, do, Steve! Not just any time, but all the time!

Lora looks off-screen left, then pulls Susie, who pulls Steve.

LORA: Come on (*laughing*).

SUSIE (*to Steve*); Even though it is a long drive.

STEVE: You forget, young . . .

385. MLS: *Steve, Lora, Susie, coming through a terrace door toward the camera, which dollies left to frame them.*

STEVE: . . . lady, I used to walk up three flights of stairs to see you in the old days!

SUSIE (*running forward and left, the camera following her*): Oh, Mama, look! A falling star!

Steve and Lora (and other guests) run into the frame and gaze up. Susie shuts her eyes.

386. LS: *Annie walking across the living room, as seen through the terrace doorway. Kenneth is also seen in a rear corridor, carrying a tray of food.*

ANNIE: Food's on!

The theme music ends.

387. MCU: *Lora, Susie, Steve on the terrace. Susie has her eyes closed, her head raised toward the sky. Lora has turned around.*

STEVE: Excuse me.

LORA (*turning to Susie and to the camera*): Did you wish on it?

SUSIE: Uh-hum. I wish it could always be like tonight. All of us to-gether. Don't you?

LORA: Yes, my darling. And I'm going to do something about it! I will not do another play for a long, long time!

SUSIE (*hugging Lora*): Oh, Mama!

LORA (*ushering Susie inside*): Come on.

Fade out.

Driveway of Lora's House, exterior, day

388. *Fade in.* MS (*through station wagon window*): *Lora and Susie emerging from the house in the background, and walking toward the car, as Steve and Kenneth load picnic gear. Lora wears a beige suit with a white blouse. Susie wears a yellow sport shirt and khaki pants, and a yellow sweater tied around her shoulders. Lora and Susie walk right and disappear from the frame.*

Lora's House, interior, day

389. MS: *Annie and Sarah Jane in the latter's bedroom. Sarah Jane is in bed, looking ill, and Annie holds a compress to her forehead.*

ANNIE: We're goin' now, honey. Now if that headache ain't gone in an hour's time, you take another aspirin. Do you hear?

SARAH JANE: Yes, Mama. Have a good time.

Annie rises and moves right. The camera pulls back and pans right a bit.

SARAH JANE: Mama?

ANNIE (*turning left, and approaching Sarah Jane*): Yes, baby?

SARAH JANE: Tell them I'm . . . I'm sorry I had to miss the picnic.

ANNIE: Okay. Okay.

Annie walks out of the room, disappearing behind a screen. Sarah Jane throws the compress from her head and gets up. She walks to a closet in the background/right and the camera pans to follow, pausing as she takes out some clothes. She moves forward and right toward a window as the camera pulls back and pans right. She pulls the curtain back, smiles, and walks away, disappearing on the left.

Dissolve.

Country Meadow, exterior, day

390. LS: *Susie and Annie by a campfire. Annie sits on a folding chair, on the left, and Susie sits on the grass, on the right. Picnic things are strewn on the ground and a pond is seen in the background. Annie knits.*

SUSIE: By the time I find Steve, the fire'll be just perfect.

ANNIE: Now, you let them alone. Maybe they got things to talk about.

391. MLS: *as in 390.*

SUSIE: This is a fine picnic. Sarah Jane suddenly announces she's getting the flu, and Mama and Steve just go off. Oh, well . . . if this is the way it's going to be, I guess I might as well get on with my list.

Now . . . (*taking a pad in hand*) . . . I can cross off "pink sweater for Elizabeth" and "yellow sweater for Sarah Jane." Then we skip ahead to . . . algebra. Do you think another year of that stuff is a good idea?

ANNIE: I sure do! It's gonna come in mighty handy with prices always goin' up.

SUSIE: Which brings us back to the subject of boys. What do you think about kissin', Annie? (*She giggles.*)

ANNIE: Well, there's kissin' . . . and kissin' . . .

392. MS: *Steve and Lora walking down a dirt road. The camera pans left and pulls back before them as they walk along. The theme music plays.*

STEVE: Oh, I still take pictures every chance I get. Still trying to get 'em exhibited.

LORA: Oh, stop hedging. What is your job, really?

STEVE: I'm vice-president in charge of advertising for P. C. Beer. Don't tell anybody.

LORA: Why not? I think it's wonderful!

STEVE: Because I'm quitting . . . just as soon as I can wind things up.

LORA (*pausing momentarily*): But why?

STEVE (*walking again*): Didn't you ever get the feeling that you're tired of what you're doing? And did you ever get the urge not to do what you don't want to do? To . . . let yourself go and follow the wind . . . or a star . . . (*pausing*) . . . maybe even a dusty old rainbow?

LORA: Yes . . .

STEVE: Well, that's why I'm going.

LORA: Where to?

STEVE: I don't know. Around the world, I guess, for a start.

LORA: You going alone?

STEVE: (*walking left as the camera pans, dropping Lora from the frame*): I'm afraid so. I . . . I went through my entire little black book.

393. MCU: *Lora, walking left toward Steve, as the camera pans. As she moves, Steve comes into frame on the left.*

LORA: Well, you shouldn't have skipped my name. (*She pauses and he turns to her.*) I . . . I don't know why I said that, Steve . . . except that I haven't been this happy with anyone for years!

STEVE: You know I still have you in my blood, don't you?

LORA: Oh, Steve . . . do you really?

STEVE: I never got over you, Lora. No matter how hard I tried . . . I couldn't.

They kiss and the theme music ends.

394. MLS: *Annie (sitting in a chair on the right, knitting) and Susie, squatting in the foreground/left.*

ANNIE: Now, there's a kind of kissin' that's not careless and doesn't lead to harm . . . when the two people kissin' are nice and right. Kissin' is part of fallin' in love and the Lord wants His children to fall in love . . . when they're old enough and got sense enough. Then kissin' is like yeast is to bread. If people never got around to kissin' . . .

SUSIE: Pardon me, Annie, but I'm starving to death. Can't I please find Steve?

ANNIE (*looking off, screen-left*): Don't think you'll have to.

SUSIE (*rising, turning and moving left. The camera pans with her and picks up Lora and Steve*): Oh, Steve! It's time to cook the steaks. Even Annie says so.

Dissolve.

Lora's House, interior, evening

395. *Low* LS: *Lora and Steve walk into the entrance hall. The camera pans left and tilts down as they descend the steps into the living room.*

LORA: Telling them will be wonderful! But Loomis. Oh!

STEVE: Why tell him at all?

They walk around a room divider, and the camera pivots and pans right.

LORA: Why, he has a lot of commitments he'll have to get me out of.

ANNIE (*off*): Susie . . .

Lora walks right, the camera following her, dropping Steve from the frame. In the background, it picks up Annie and Susie, entering the house, unloading picnic gear. Lora and Susie are momentarily framed through a circular-patterned, wrought-iron, room divider.

SUSIE: Yeah?

ANNIE: . . . will you go upstairs and see how Sarah Jane is? Tell her I'll be right up.

SUSIE (*walking to the stairs*): Okay. (*She pauses and looks back at a suitcase.*) Wait a minute, Annie. Let me help you with that.

ANNIE: Thank you, honey.

Kenneth walks into the hall with an additional suitcase and the camera pivots left as Lora sits on the sofa and picks up the phone. She is seen through the room divider.

LORA (*into phone*): Hello, Allen? I . . . Oh . . . Oh, you've been trying to call me? Well, I'm sorry. We've been out all day.

396. *Low* MCU: *Steve looking down at this pipe, then off.*

LORA (*off*): When?

397. MCU: *Lora on phone (no longer framed by the room divider).*

LORA: Oh, . . . well, it sounds simply marvelous! But . . . no. No, not for dinner. I'm having guests. Why don't you bring him for cocktails? Yes! All right! (*She hangs up the phone and looks up, off-screen.*) Steve! Amerigo Felluci!

398. *Low* MCU: *Steve, as in 396.*

STEVE: The Italian movie director?

LORA (*off*): Yes.

399. MCU: *Lora, as in 397.*
   LORA: Oh, he wants me for the part of Rena in . . . in *No More Laughter.*
400. *Low* MS: *Steve, lighting his pipe.*
   LORA (*off*): His agent is in New York now to talk to me about it.
   STEVE: I see. That means you'd have to go to Italy.
401. MS: *Steve (seen from the rear, in the left corner of the frame) and Lora (seen frontally, right, seated on the couch).*
   LORA: Mmm. Of course. Oh! (*She stands [as the camera tilts up], pauses, and takes a cigarette from the coffee table.*) Well, I'll . . . have to give a two-week notice to the play. (*Moving right, around coffee table [as the camera follows and drops Steve from the frame] and then left, toward Steve, the camera following, and picking him up again.*) Yes. (*To Steve.*) Well, don't be so calm. They want me for Rena!
   STEVE: Well, who is she?
   LORA: Only the best part since Scarlett O'Hara!
   He lights her cigarette.
402. *Low* MS: *Susie at the top of the steps, knocking on Sarah Jane's bedroom door, seen through the stair railing.*
   SUSIE: (*poking her head in the door and entering*): Sarah Jane?
403. MS: *Annie (her back to the camera) at the kitchen sink, a window in the background. She moves to a cupboard on the right and the camera pans with her, as we see Sarah Jane passing by the window and hiding at its right border. Annie moves back, left, toward the sink but does not see Sarah Jane. Annie moves out of frame, left, while the window and Sarah Jane remain in view. Sarah Jane runs past the window, screen-right, and the camera pans right, past the cupboards to pick her up again, entering the kitchen door, in the rear. She runs right and up the stairs, the camera panning to frame her. She wears an orange shirtwaist dress, with a full skirt.*
404. *Low* MS: *Susie coming out of Sarah Jane's bedroom door and moving right, down the stairs, the camera panning. She stops and turns as Sarah Jane comes up another flight, in the rear. The camera tilts up and pans left as Susie moves to meet Sarah Jane at the bedroom door.*
   SUSIE: Sarah Jane! Where've you been? I've been looking all over for you! You know you're supposed to be in bed.
   SARAH JANE (*opening her door and putting her hand over Susie's mouth*): Shhh!
   Sarah Jane ushers Susie into her room, looks down the stairway to see if all is clear, and enters, shutting the door.
405. LS: *Susie and Sarah Jane entering the latter's room, seen from the inside. Sarah Jane overtakes Susie, grabs her arm, and directs her left, the camera dollying to follow. She shoves Susie down on the side of the bed.*

SARAH JANE: Come on! Sit down! (*She begins to undress.*) Cross your heart . . . (*Susie does.*) . . . you won't tell my Mama?

SUSIE: No, no, I won't tell Annie.

406. MS: *Sarah Jane (facing the camera on the left) and Susie (seen from the rear on the right) as Sarah Jane continues to undress.*

SUSIE: Well, what is it?

SARAH JANE: I've been out . . . (*she flings her skirt aside and pauses dramatically.*) . . . with my boyfriend. (*She turns around, her back to the camera, and walks into the background.*)

407. MS: *Susie, sitting on the bed. She rises and the camera angles around, left, and dollies and pans as she rushes across to lean against the bathroom doorway.*

SUSIE: Boyfriend! I didn't know you had a boyfriend! Where's he from?

408. CU: *Sarah Jane, in the bathroom, turning around to Susie as she slips on a nightgown.*

SARAH JANE: The village.

409. CU: *Susie, leaning against the bathroom doorway.*

SUSIE: Oh. Did you meet him in school?

SARAH JANE (*off*): School? (*She comes into frame in CU, her back to the camera, and stands in front of Susie.*) No! There's an ice cream parlor in the village with a jukebox. (*She moves right and Susie follows; the camera pans with them. Sarah Jane turns and sits down on the bed facing us, while Susie is seen on the left, her back to the camera.*)

SUSIE: Yeah?

SARAH JANE: And he used to stand outside . . . and every time I'd walk by . . . he'd whistle.

SUSIE: No kidding!

Sarah Jane gets under the covers and Susie runs toward the bed; the camera pans right to follow her.

410. CU: *Susie (on the right, seen from the rear, sitting down on the bed) and Sarah Jane (on the left, facing the camera and Susie).*

SARAH JANE: At first, I pretended he wasn't on earth.

SUSIE: Yeah? (*She giggles.*)

SARAH JANE: But finally, I had to laugh. And he followed me . . .

411. CU, *reverse angle of 410: Susie (right, facing camera) and Sarah Jane (left, seen from the rear) on the bed.*

SARAH JANE: . . . and we started to talk. He's cute. Really cute.

SUSIE: Is he a colored boy?

SARAH JANE: Why did you ask that?

SUSIE: I don't know.

412. CU: *Susie and Sarah Jane, as in 410.*

SUSIE: It just slipped out.

SARAH JANE: It was the first thing you thought of.

SUSIE: I told you . . . it just slipped out!

SARAH JANE: Well, he's white! And if he every finds out about me . . .
I'll kill myself!

SUSIE: But, why?

SARAH JANE: Because I'm white, too! And if I have to be colored, then
I want to die!

SUSIE: Sarah Jane! What are you saying?

SARAH JANE: I want to have a chance in life. I don't want to have to
come . . . through back doors, or feel lower than other people, . . . or
apologize for my mother's color.

SUSIE: Don't say that!

SARAH JANE: She can't help her color . . . but I can . . . and I will!

413. CU: *Susie and Sarah Jane on the bed (as in 411).*

SUSIE: But we've always talked things over, and . . . well, you never
told me this before.

414. CU: *Susie and Sarah Jane on the bed, as in 412. Sarah Jane leans on the
pillow and Susie moves a bit left. The camera pans right toward Sarah
Jane. She lifts her head as she talks.*

SARAH JANE: Because I never had a boyfriend before. Because he
wants to marry me some day. (*She raises her head.*) A white boy! Me!
But how do you think he'd feel, or his folks, with a black in-law? What
do you think people would say where we'd live, if they knew my
mother? They'd spit at me! (*She lies down.*) And my children!

SUSIE: (*reaching for her*): Sarah . . .

415. CU: *Susie, as she leans forward to comfort Sarah Jane.*

SUSIE: . . . Jane, you know that's not true!

*As Sarah Jane lifts her head, it becomes visible in the right corner of the
frame.*

SARAH JANE: It is. That's why he mustn't know her. I don't want anybody to know her.

SUSIE: But what if he comes here?

416. CU: *Susie (left, seen in a rear/profile view) and Sarah Jane (right, facing
the camera) on the bed.*

SARAH JANE: He doesn't even know where I live. I pretend I'm a . . .
I'm a rich girl with strict parents.

SUSIE: But he's bound to find out.

SARAH JANE: How? I'm going to be everything he thinks I am. I look
it. And that's all that matters.

417. CU: *Susie (on the left, facing the camera) and Sarah Jane (on the right,
rear-profile view) on bed.*

SARAH JANE: And you're not to say anything, either!

SUSIE: I won't! You know I won't! I never did! But . . . Sarah Jane, if
Mama every found out, why she'd never stand for it.

418. MS: *Sarah Jane (on the right, facing the camera) and Susie (on the left, seen from the rear) on bed.*
     SARAH JANE: I don't care! Your mother doesn't . . .
419. MCU: *Susie (on the left, in profile) and Sarah Jane (on the right, in profile).*
     SARAH JANE: . . . own me!
     Susie pulls away.
420. *Low* LS: *front hall, as seen from the living room. Steve comes into frame as he approaches the front door, followed by Lora.*
     STEVE: I guess I won't be seeing you before you leave, so . . . (*turning and opening the front door*) . . . good luck in Italy.
     LORA: Why, you make that sound like good-bye.
421. MCU: *Lora (on the left, in profile) and Steve (on the right, in profile) at the door.*
     LORA: Why couldn't we meet in Italy?
     STEVE: What for? You'll have the film. You won't need me. (*He turns to leave but Lora stops him.*)
     LORA: But, Steve, wait!
     STEVE: You tell Susie I'll be at her graduation. Good-bye, Lora. (*He exits.*)
     Lora's House, exterior, day
422. MLS: *Steve (seen from the rear) exiting Lora's house, crossing the street to where his car is parked in the background.*
423. MCU: *Lora, looking out the front door (as seen from outside). She lowers her eyes, turns around, and begins to shut the door. Fade out.*
     Lora's House, interior, night
424. *Fade in. Low* LS (*from the living room*): *Lora, in a white floor-length evening gown (decorated with a blue sash and train), walking right, on the balcony landing toward the stairs. She also wears a diamond neck-lace. The camera pans right and tilts down, losing Lora, and picking up Kenneth downstairs. She reappears on the left, coming down a flight of stairs. On the balcony landing, Sarah Jane (wearing a yellow shirtwaist dress, with floral embroidery on the bodice) emerges from her room. Lora stops and turns to her. Kenneth exits in the foreground/right.*
     LORA: Oh, Sarah Jane!
     SARAH JANE: Yes, Miss Lora?
     LORA: I'm having some people come for a business meeting, and later the dinner guests . . .
425. *Low* MS: *Sarah Jane on the balcony landing, as seen from Lora's perspective below.*
     LORA (*off*): . . . will arrive. I wonder if you could help your mother a bit.
     SARAH JANE: Well, Miss Lora, I'd . . . well, I . . . I'd like to, but . . .

426. *High* MCU: *Lora, seen from Sarah Jane's perspective, above. Lora looks up over a railing.*

 SARAH JANE (*off*): . . . I have a . . .

 LORA: A date? Is it the Hawkins boy?

427. *Low* MCU: *Sarah Jane, as in 425.*

 SARAH JANE: Hawkins?

 LORA (*off*): Well, the Miller's chauffeur, down the road.

 SARAH JANE: Why do you say that?

428. *High* MCU: *Lora, as in 426.*

 LORA: Well, I met him at the station the other day and he asked about you.

429. *Low* MS: *Lora (on the lower landing, seen from the rear) and Sarah Jane (facing the camera, on the upstairs landing).*

 SARAH JANE: No! It's with someone else.

 LORA: Oh. Well, all right . . . you run along. I'll try to manage here. (*She turns and responds to an off-screen doorbell ringing.*) Oh, there they are!

 Lora exits down the stairs, right. The camera pans a bit, then holds on Sarah Jane, who turns and exits down a back stairs across the landing. The camera pans right to follow her.

430. *High* LS: *kitchen, as Sarah Jane descends the back stairs. Annie (wearing a blue, shirtwaist dress, with a white apron) is busy in the background, putting plates on the counter. Sarah Jane pulls herself up, then sits on the counter, her back to her mother. Annie approaches Sarah Jane, from behind.*

431. MS: *Annie and Sarah Jane (as in end of 430).*

 ANNIE: Look, honey, why don't you go over to the party at the church?

 SARAH JANE: They bore me!

 ANNIE: You're makin' a big mistake. You're young. You shouldn't be sittin' around. Miss Lora feels the same way. She'll lend you her car.

 SARAH JANE: Oh, she will? How nice of her!

 ANNIE: I'd be happy knowin' you're meetin' nice young folks.

 SARAH JANE (*turning to Annie, suddenly*): Busboys, cooks, chauffeurs! Hmph! (*Turning to face the camera again.*) Like Hawkins! No, thank you. I've seen your nice young folks!

 ANNIE: I don't want to fight with you, honey. (*She walks left and the camera pans, losing Sarah Jane.*) Not tonight. I don't feel too good. (*She picks up a tray and moves right to Sarah Jane, who comes into view again.*) While I get started on the anchovies, will you take this tray in to Miss Lora and her friends? (*She walks into the background, her back to camera.*)

 SARAH JANE: Why, certainly! Anything at all for Miss Lora and her friends.

*Sarah Jane hops down from the counter, turns to Annie in the back-
ground, picks up the tray, and exits right. Annie looks after her.*

432. MS: *living room. Loomis and Lora sit on a sofa in the background and
Romano, the Italian film representative, sits on the right.*

LOOMIS: But, Signor Romano, why should she need rehearsals?

ROMANO: [*Says something in Italian*].

LOOMIS: You know her work! Her last play was a fantastic success. I'm
sure . . .

ROMANO (*standing, as the camera tilts up*): But Felluci always insists
on two weeks rehearsal!

433. *Low* MCU: *Romano.*

ROMANO: Pictures are a different medium than the stage. She will need
the rehearsal! She will . . . (*He pauses, as he looks off screen-left.*)

434. MCU: *Lora, reacting to Romano, then looking off, left.*

435. MCU: *Loomis, turning left, the camera panning. Sarah Jane emerges
from the background, a tray balanced on her head. The camera pans left
and tilts up as she comes forward, then tilts down as she serves.*

SARAH JANE: Fetched you-all a mess o' crawdads. Miss Lora, for you
an' your friends!

436. MCU: *Lora.*

LORA: Well, that's quite a trick . . .(*She sets her glass down on the
coffee table.*) . . . Sarah Jane! Where did you learn it?

437. CU: *Sarah Jane.*
> SARAH JANE: Oh, no trick to totin', Miss Lora. Ah l'arned it from my mammy . . . and she l'arned it from old Massa . . . 'fo she belonged to you! (*She looks up and smiles at Romano.*)

438. *Low* MS: *Romano (still standing), smiling back at Sarah Jane and bowing, slightly.*

439. LS: *Sarah Jane, Loomis, Lora, Romano in living room, as seen through the wrought-iron, geometric-patterned room divider in the foreground. Sarah Jane exits into the background.*
> LOOMIS: Well!
>
> LORA (*rising, walking screen-left, and into the background*): Excuse me.
>
> LOOMIS (*to Romano*): Another drink, Signor Romano?

440. MLS: *Lora entering the kitchen (as seen from inside the room). The camera pulls back and pans left slightly as she comes forward and stops by the far end of the counter. She speaks to Sarah Jane who is in the foreground, also facing the camera.*
> LORA: Sarah Jane, why did you do that? What's the matter with you? (*Turning to Annie.*) Annie, did you see what she did?
>
> ANNIE (*off*): I heard her.

SARAH JANE: You and my mother are so anxious for me to be colored . . . I was going to show you I could be.

LORA (*walking toward Sarah Jane, the camera panning right, until her back is to the camera*): You weren't being colored! You were being childish!

441. CU: *Lora (on the right, facing the camera) and Sarah Jane (on the left, her back to the camera).*

LORA: I don't understand why you would want to hurt your mother . . .

442. MCU: *Annie, looking off, at Lora and Sarah Jane.*

LORA (*off*): . . . or me.

ANNIE (*moving forward and right, with the camera panning, until it picks up Sarah Jane*): I told her she has to be patient. Things'll work out.

SARAH JANE: How? (*Looking off.*) Miss Lora . . . you don't know what it means to be . . . different.

443. CU: *Lora and Sarah Jane (as in 441).*

LORA: Have I ever treated you as if you were different? Has Susie? Has anyone here?

444. CU: *Sarah Jane, looking down.*

SARAH JANE: No. (*Looking up and off.*) You've been wonderful . . .

445. CU: *Lora and Sarah Jane (as in 443).*

SARAH JANE: . . . but . . .

LORA: Then don't ever do this to us again! Or to yourself. It won't solve anything, Sarah Jane. (*She begins to exit, left.*)

446. MLS: *Annie, Sarah Jane, and Lora in the kitchen. Lora exits (her back to the camera) and Annie and Sarah Jane stand facing the camera in the foreground. Annie, wearily, moves left and forward, as the camera pans, and sits at a table in the foreground. As Sarah Jane approaches her and bends down, the camera moves in and tilts down, framing the two in CU.*

SARAH JANE: Oh, Mama . . . oh, please! . . . Try to understand. I didn't mean to hurt you. (*She embraces Annie.*) I love you. (*She sobs.*)

ANNIE (*crying*): Oh, I know, baby. You're just like a puppy that's been cooped up too much. That's why I wanted you to go to the party.

SARAH JANE (*breaking away from Annie*): Oh, Mama . . . don't you see that won't help? (*She exits right as Annie looks off and then down.*) *Dissolve.*

447. *Low* MLS: *Sarah Jane coming down the back kitchen stairs later that night, carrying her shoes. The camera pans right, tilts down and then pans left as she comes forward and stops to put on her shoes. She looks off.*

448. LS: *Kenneth lighting candles in the dining room, as seen through the kitchen door frame.*

449. CU: *Sarah Jane. She turns left (toward the kitchen window) and the camera pans to follow.*

LOOMIS (*Off*): Lora, wait a minute.
Sarah Jane hesitates and looks forward. She then heads into the background/right and the camera pans as she exits the rear door.
LORA (*off*): I didn't mean the whole thing. I . . .
LOOMIS (*off*): Signor Romano . . .
Dissolve.

Street Corner, exterior, night

450. MLS: *Sarah Jane walking forward along the sidewalk of a deserted street in town, as a mellow jazz theme plays in the background. She stops before an empty store window. In the background, through the store window, we see a young man (Frankie) coming around the corner. Sarah Jane turns right and the camera dollies with her as she hurries to the corner and down the side street toward Frankie, as he crosses the street diagonally toward her.*
SARAH JANE: Frankie! You're late! I thought you'd never get here. Well, let's walk down by the river. I want to talk to you.
FRANKIE: We can talk here.

451. MCU: *Frankie (on the left, in near-profile) and Sarah Jane (on the right, in near-profile).*
SARAH JANE: Frankie . . . I'm . . . I'm having trouble at home.

FRANKIE: Your mother?

SARAH JANE: Yes. (*Moving toward him.*) Frankie . . . you said you wanted to take a job in Jersey. Couldn't we run away? I'd do anything to be with you. Anything!

FRANKIE: (*leaning back and left, on the storefront window, the camera panning with him, losing Sarah Jane, then picking her up again in reflection*): That's not a bad idea. That's not a bad idea at all. Just tell me one thing . . .

SARAH JANE (*off-screen, but reflected*): Yes?

FRANKIE: Is it true?

SARAH JANE (*off*): Is what true?

FRANKIE (*moving right, the camera panning with him, picking up Sarah Jane so that they are shown again in a two-shot,* MCU): Is your mother a nigger? Tell me! TELL ME! (*The background jazz theme becomes loud, discordant, and abrasive.*)

SARAH JANE: What difference does it make? You love me . . .

FRANKIE: All the kids talking behind my back! Is it true?

452. MCU: *Sarah Jane (on the right, facing the camera) and Frankie (on the left, seen from behind).*

SARAH JANE: No!

FRANKIE: Are you black?

SARAH JANE: No, I'm as white as you!

FRANKIE (*slapping her*): You're lying!

453. MS: *Frankie (on the left) and Sarah Jane (on the right) as he continues to slap her. She reels back, right, from the impact. The camera pans left, losing them, but picking them up as reflected in the window of the vacant store. She retreats backward across the street, toward a wall, and he pursues her.*

SARAH JANE (*off*): No, I'm not.

FRANKIE (*off, but reflected in the glass*): You're lying.

SARAH JANE (*off, but reflected in the glass*): I'm not!

FRANKIE (*off, but reflected in the glass*): You are! (*He gives her another blow to the face.*)

454. MS: *Frankie (back to the camera) hitting Sarah Jane, as she crouches next to a building wall, amidst packing boxes. He pulls her upright to face him as he slaps her again, the camera tilting up and panning right. Sarah Jane screams.*

455. MS: *Frankie (in the background, facing the camera) and Sarah Jane (seen from the rear, in the foreground) as he slaps her again. Sarah Jane screams.*

456. MS: *Frankie hitting Sarah Jane (as in 454). She sinks down, leaning on the packing boxes, and the camera tilts down. He exits left. She falls into a puddle of water. Sarah Jane screams.*

457. *High* MS: *Sarah Jane lying on the street, against the boxes, as Frankie (whose legs are visible) walks away, left. The camera tilts up and pans a bit left, to frame him in* LS, *as he moves into the depth of the frame. He looks back over his shoulder.*

458. *High* MS: *Sarah Jane lying in the puddle.*

459. LS: *Frankie walking away into the depth of the frame, as at the end of 457.*

460. *High* MS: *Sarah Jane. She pulls herself up and looks off left, as the camera tilts up. Then she falls back down, the camera tilting down. The jazz theme comes to a crashing climax.*

Lora's House, interior, night

461. MLS: *Lora and Annie in Lora's bedroom. Lora sits on a sofa, wearing a luxurious, peach-colored, gray/fur-trimmed lounging robe. Annie (in a nightgown and a simple navy robe) sits at her feet, massaging them.*
    LORA: Mm! O that felt so good! (*Sitting up.*) And I'm glad the guests have gone!
    ANNIE: And I'm glad you're not goin' to Italy!
    LORA: So am I! Felluci wanted me in Rome in one week. But I won't miss Susie's graduation . . . not for anything! (*She puts on her shoe.*) You know, I can't believe it. Susie and Sarah Jane all grown up. You and I have gone through a lot together, haven't we?

462. MCU: *Annie (facing the camera, on the right) and Lora (back to camera, on the left).*
    ANNIE: The years are flyin'. I'm gettin' old.
    LORA: You never sounded so solemn before. Don't you feel well, Annie?
    ANNIE: Oh, just a little tired.
    LORA: Do you need anything? Any money?
    ANNIE: No, Miss Lora. Thanks to you, I'm well fixed.

463. MLS: *Annie and Lora on the sofa.*
    ANNIE: I've plenty to send Sarah Jane to college (*rising and moving left, the camera panning with her*), and something to set aside for her, and enough for my funeral. (*She walks into the depth of the frame, her back to the camera.*)
    LORA: Oh, Annie, that funeral again! (*Lora gets up, moves right, to the other end of the sofa. She sits again and lights a cigarette. The camera pans right with her.*)
    ANNIE (*facing the camera and walking toward the foreground and fluffing pillows on the sofa*): Well, I'm gettin' on . . . and that's the one thing I've always wanted to splurge on. I really want it elegant. Got it all written down the way I want it to be and all the friends I'd like to have there.
    LORA (*rising and crossing, foreground/left and moving into the back-*

ground, near Annie): It never occurred to me that you had many
friends. You never have any visit you.

ANNIE: I know lots of people! Oh, hundreds!

464. *Low* MS: *Lora (on the left) and Annie (on the right) facing one another.*

LORA: Really?

ANNIE: I belong to the Baptist church, and I belong to several lodges,
too.

LORA: I didn't know.

465. MS: *Annie (seen from the front, on the right) and Lora (seen semi-rear, on the left periphery of the frame; she is also reflected in a mirror on the rear wall).*

ANNIE: Miss Lora, you never asked.

A door opens in the background, and Susie rushes in. The women turn around.

SUSIE: Mama! Annie! Quick! Quick! It's Sarah Jane.

ANNIE: Oh!

The women rush toward the door and the camera pans right.

466. *Low* LS: *Annie, Susie, and Lora rushing into the upper hall as seen through the balustrade of the staircase landing. The camera cranes back, down, and right as Annie rushes down the stairs and sits on the stairs below Sarah Jane (who is slumped over), embracing her.*

ANNIE: Sarah Jane! Oh, my baby.

LORA (*to Susie*): Get some water and towels!

Susie exits.

ANNIE: What happened, baby? What happened?

SARAH JANE: Leave me alone!

ANNIE: Honey, who did this to you? Tell me!

SARAH JANE: Leave me alone! (*She covers her face with her hands.*)

ANNIE: Sarah Jane, you've got to tell me!

LORA: Who was it?!

467. CU *crane shot: Susie, hurrying down the stairs, with towels and a bowl of water, moving to the right. As she crouches down at the bottom of the stairs, Lora comes into view.*

SUSIE: It was her boyfriend.

LORA: Boyfriend?

Susie hands the towels down to Annie and the camera pans right, picking up Sarah Jane in a frontal CU, *and Annie in a rear* CU.

SARAH JANE: Yes. He found out I'm not white . . . (*As Annie lifts a towel to Sarah Jane's face, the latter pushes it away.*) . . . because you keep telling the world I'm your daughter. Anything you can spoil you spoil.

Sarah Jane stands up and begins to move left. The camera pans and picks up Lora.

LORA: Stop that! Stop it! (*She rises and the camera tilts up.*) Don't you talk to your mother like that!

468. *High* MCU: *Annie rising from a sitting position on the stairs as the camera tilts up. She faces Sarah Jane in the foreground.*

ANNIE: I told you! Lies don't help none!

469. *Low* MLS: *Annie (seen from behind) and Lora, Susie and Sarah Jane on the stairs (facing the camera).*

ANNIE: This always happens when you lie!

SARAH JANE: It wouldn't if you weren't always around!

Susie rises. Sarah Jane runs up the stairs onto the landing and slams the door to her bedroom. The others look on, distressed. Lora turns toward Annie. Fade out.

Lawn of Girls' School, exterior, day

470. *Fade in.* MS: *Lora and Susie standing before a tea table on the lawn of Susie's school on graduation day. Susie is wearing a white chiffon and taffeta dress with white gloves. Lora wears a gray sleeveless dress with a black scarf/train, a black hat, and sunglasses. Susie looks about nervously; a woman in the background gets some tea.*

WOMAN: (*to person serving tea*): Thank you.

SUSIE: Are you . . . are you sure Annie'll make it in time?

LORA (*sipping tea*): Honey, you know Annie. If she says she will, she will.

They walk forward and the camera pulls back and pans left.

SUSIE: Oh, Mama, I'm so happy. Gee, you know I . . . I never really believed you'd be here.

Lora laughs.

SUSIE (*pausing*): Are you sorry about the picture?

LORA (*turning to face Susie*): I'm only sorry I couldn't bring your present with me . . . (*She sets the cup down.*) . . . but he's a little too big!

471. MS: *Susie (on the right, facing the camera) and Lora (in rear-profile, on the left).*

SUSIE: He? Who . . . who's he? Who's too big?

LORA: That thoroughbred you told me about?

SUSIE: Uh-huh! Yeah!

LORA: The one you loved so? Well, he's waiting for you at home!

SUSIE: You got him! You mean he's mine?

LORA: Yes! (*She laughs.*).

SUSIE: (*hugging Lora*): Oh, Mama, thank you!

LORA: Happy graduation, angel!

A car horn beeps. Susie looks off toward the camera and begins to exit.

472. MS: *Susie (seen from the rear, running left) and Lora (looking left); the camera pans a bit left to follow. As the women pause, we see, in the background, a red convertible car pulling up.*

473. MLS: *Susie and Lora, seen frontally. Susie turns around to address Lora, behind her.*

    SUSIE: Oh, Mama, look! (*Turning toward camera.*) It's Annie . . .

474. MS: *exterior of Steve's convertible, parked in the driveway. The camera pans left as Steve walks around behind the car and begins to open the door for Annie, who is seated on the passenger side.*

    SUSIE (*off*): . . . and Steve!

475. MS: *Susie, facing the camera, looking off.*

    SUSIE: Steve!

    She runs past the camera and we see Lora in MLS *standing behind.*

476. MLS: *Annie (wearing a gray coat and matching hat, over a black and white dress) and Steve standing beside the car, both smiling and looking off-right. The camera pans right slightly as they come forward and Susie rushes into frame from the right, embracing Steve.*

    SUSIE (*laughing, to Steve*): Hi!

    STEVE: Susie! (*He laughs.*)

    SUSIE (*leaving Steve and running to hug Annie*): Oh, and Annie . . . I'm so glad you made it! (*Taking Steve's hands.*) And Steve, you're such a darling to come!

    STEVE: I meant it when I said I wouldn't miss it for the . . . (*He looks off, right.*) Lora!

    The camera pans right as he walks right to Lora. Lora, Steve, and Susie are framed in MS *when the camera stops.*

    LORA: Hello, Steve.

    STEVE: I thought you were in Italy. (*He looks off, left.*) Annie, why didn't you tell me?

    ANNIE (*off*): Slipped my mind, I'm afraid. (*She walks into the frame from the left, holding something out to Lora. The camera moves in a bit.*) This came for you this mornin'.

    LORA: Oh.

    ANNIE (*looking left, toward Susie, as the camera pans left, losing Lora and Steve, framing Annie and Susie in* MCU): Honey . . .

    SUSIE: Yeah?

    ANNIE: Sarah Jane's much better.

    SUSIE: Oh, I'm glad!

    ANNIE: She's sorry she couldn't come, but she sends her love.

    SUSIE: Oh, I think I'm going to faint! You know, this is the most exciting day of my entire life! I never expected you'd all be here!

477. MCU: *Lora (on the right, facing the camera) and Steve on the left (seen in profile). She is holding a telegram.*

    LORA: Oh, it . . . it's from Felluci! Oh, he still wants me for the part! And he'll wait after all!

478. MCU: *Susie (on the left) and Annie (on the right) looking off and reacting; Susie is disappointed.*

LORA (*off*): Imagine! He's even made my plane reservations. I'm to leave in two weeks.

SUSIE (*upset*): Two weeks? Oh, Mama.

479. MCU: *Lora and Steve. The camera dollies left as she moves toward Susie and Annie, leaving Steve. The three women are framed in* MCU: *Susie, left; Annie, center; Lora, right.*

LORA: Oh . . . at least that time will be ours together. Oh, don't look like that, Susie. Felluci agreed to my terms. I can't turn him down now!

SUSIE: I know, Mother, I know. (*She turns away from Lora.*)

ANNIE (*grabbing Susie by the shoulders and turning her around*): Look, honey . . . your mama feels worse than you.

In the background, on a school building porch, a teacher claps her hands and calls people. Annie, Susie, and Lora turn around and the camera tilts up a bit.

TEACHER: Girls! The exercises are beginning! Come on!

Susie begins moving, right, and Lora grabs her.

LORA (*hugging Susie*): Darling . . .

Susie walks off right and Annie walks into frame on the left. The camera pans right, picking up Steve (seen from the rear), then holds on Annie and Susie walking into the background.

LORA (*turning to Steve*): When do you leave, Steve?

STEVE: I don't know when I'll be able to get away now.

LORA: Oh, would you do me a favor? Will you look after my child for me while I'm gone? Please!

STEVE: I can think of nothing I'd like better.

LORA: Oh.

He takes Lora's arm and they begin to walk across the lawn into the background, where people are taking their seats. The camera pans a bit right as they go.

Lora's House, interior, day

480. MLS: *Sarah Jane, sitting on her bedroom floor, near the side of her bed. Records are scattered on the floor and she is listening to one on a small record player. She rises and the camera tilts up and pans right as she runs across the room to a window in the background and looks out.*

Lora's House, exterior, day

481. *High* LS (*from Sarah Jane's point of view*): *Steve and Susie, with two horses, by the barn. He helps her mount her horse and moves to his.*

STEVE: All right?

SUSIE: Fine! Let's ride down to the river.

482. *Low* MS: *Sarah Jane looking out the window, as seen from the exterior of the house. She looks jealous and sullen.*

483. MLS: *Steve, Susie, and a stable groom by the side of the barn. Steve mounts his horse.*

HOLD

EP

30
ORIG: Main   P

791.4372 I315

AUTH:
TITLE: imitation of life

i30331560
PAGED: 08/08/2016
LCKIN: 07-10-10 09:36AM

Green Hills

.P1304719X

Fri
Aug
19

D   H A R O B E D
                         2284
        N O S W A D

2284

2284

STEVE (*to groom*): Thank you.
They ride off, left, as the groom looks on.
Lora's House, interior, day
484. MLS: *Sarah Jane flipping the curtains and walking left away from the window as music plays on the record player. The camera pans left as she dances forward; it tilts down to frame her feet as she executes steps among the strewn records, and kicks a toy stuffed animal out of the frame.*
Meadow, exterior, day
485. LS: *pan left with Steve and Susie riding in the meadow. The camera leaves Steve and focuses on Susie as her horse gallops left and jumps a low wall. Steve's horse follows into the frame and they both exit left.*
486. LS: *Susie and Steve riding, galloping forward in the meadow, the camera panning left slightly. Susie turns her horse around to face Steve's.*
SUSIE: Isn't this fun? I wrote Mother last week and told her . . .
487. MS: *Steve (on the right, facing the camera) and Susie (on the left, seen from the rear) mounted, facing one another.*
SUSIE: . . . you were riding like Audie Murphy.
STEVE: I'll wear my six-shooters tomorrow morning.
SUSIE: And your black tie tomorrow night at Bocce's.
STEVE: Did we make it definitely to . . .
488. MS: *Susie (on the left, facing camera) and Steve (on right, seen from the rear) mounted.*
STEVE: . . . morrow?
SUSIE: Well, you said Monday night.
STEVE: Well, I hope you won't be disappointed. It's nothing glamorous.
SUSIE: Disappointed? With you, Steve? Never! Come on! I'll race you back to the old mill! (*They begin to move off screen-right.*)
489. MS: *Steve and Susie, mounted, turning their horses around. They ride off, right and into the background, as the camera pans.*
Dissolve.
Bocce's Restaurant, interior, night
490. LS: *Steve and Susie entering the foyer of the restaurant and moving right, the camera panning. Susie wears a white fur cape, under which is a modest cocktail dress with a white, embroidered bodice, a cummerbund, and a black skirt. She wears a string of pearls and matching earrings. Steve leaves his hat with the coatcheck woman and moves right with Susie, the camera dollying and panning in front of a room divider. They move into the main dining room as the headwaiter greets them, the camera following.*
STEVE: I hope you won't be disappointed.
SUSIE: Oh, no! I think it's romantic!
HEADWAITER: Good evening. A table for two?
STEVE: Please.
They walk off right, following the headwaiter. The camera pans right and pivots around to follow them.

491. *High* MS: *Steve and Susie being seated at a booth (Susie on the left and Steve on the right); the headwaiter pulls away the table. He then walks into the background to get the menus.*

     SUSIE: Oh, Steve! What a wonderful place to end a perfect evening!

     STEVE (*to waiter*): I'll have cognac and . . .

     SUSIE: Oh, could I have one, too? Just once?

     STEVE (*indicating "no"*): Uh-uh.

492. MCU: *Susie and Steve at the booth, Susie on the left and Steve on the right.*

     SUSIE: Maybe a little wine?

     STEVE: No. (*To waiter.*) coke. (*To Susie.*) You don't want 'em to lose their license, do you?

     SUSIE: No . . . of course not, but . . .

     STEVE: Shall we dance?

     SUSIE: Dance? (*Rising.*) Oh, I'd love to.

493. MS: *Steve and Susie rising from the table. The camera cranes back and up slightly, then pans right as the couple crosses to the dance floor; they begin to dance.*

     SUSIE: Steve. You know, you're about the only one that I can talk seriously with.

     STEVE: What about Annie? I thought she was everybody's Rock of Gibraltar.

     They turn on the dance floor and the camera dollies left as they do.

     SUSIE: She still treats me like I was a child! As if I were just out of rompers! And you don't.

     STEVE: Well . . . you're almost a woman.

494. MCU: *Susie (on left) and Steve (on right) dancing. The camera moves with them as they dance, turn, and move slowly to the right.*

     SUSIE: Almost?!

     STEVE: But any time you have anything serious on your mind, you try it out on me.

     SUSIE: Well, I . . . I do have a problem that's been bothering me.

     STEVE: Let's have it.

     SUSIE: Oh . . . no, maybe I shouldn't.

     STEVE: I'll bet I know what it's about.

     SUSIE: You do?

     STEVE: Boys.

     SUSIE: Oh, no! You were teasing me.

     STEVE: Yes.

     SUSIE: Steve . . . what's the proper age for people to . . . well, to get married?

     STEVE: That is a problem. I'm no authority.

     SUSIE: Isn't being in love enough?

STEVE: As long as it's on both sides. And at your age, there's always the possibility of uh . . . being in love with love.
SUSIE: Oh, no! No, it's real. I am!
STEVE: In love?
SUSIE: Uh-hum.
STEVE: Want to talk about it?
SUSIE: Well, I . . . No . . . not yet.
The band stops playing and Susie and Steve stop dancing and walk forward and left. The camera pulls back and pans left as they leave the dance floor.
SUSIE: Sometimes, though, I . . . I feel awfully lonely.
STEVE: Love is always a little lonely in the beginning. (*They pass the headwaiter and sit down at the booth, Susie on the left and Steve on the right.*). Especially, when you're not sure the other party feels as you do.
495. MCU: *Susie (left, facing the camera) and Steve (right, seen in rear/profile), sitting at the booth.*
SUSIE: But, it's heavenly, though. Don't you agree?
STEVE: I do! Marvelous! (*Holding up his glass.*) No substitute for it!
They drink.
Dissolve.

Lora's House, interior, night

496. *Low* LS: *Annie and Susie in Susie's bedroom, standing next to her dresser. Susie whirls around to face Annie. Susie wears a full skirted, blue-gray suit. Annie wears a blue shirtwaist dress.*

SUSIE: Oh, I'm so glad I'm alive! I've never been so glad before! (*She runs into the foreground, sits on a chair and kicks off her slippers and puts on her shoes.*) Every time we've been together it's been just perfect!

ANNIE: I think you ought to go out more with friends your own age.

SUSIE: When I can go out with Steve? Oh, Annie, you can't believe how much we have in common! (*A car horn sounds and she gets up and runs left across the room and looks out the window.*) Oh, it's Steve! (*She begins to run right to leave.*)

ANNIE (*grabbing her*): Now you're not goin' out without a coat!

SUSIE: Oh, I was going to borrow one of Mother's. Steve's seen all of mine.

ANNIE: Sarah Jane bought herself a new one. (*Walking off screen-right.*) You can wear hers.

The car horn honks again and Susie primps at the mirror. She runs left to the window and leans out.

SUSIE: Oh . . . I'll be right down! (*She runs across the room, right, and exits.*)

497. MLS: *Annie in Sarah Jane's room, getting a coat from her closet. Susie rushes in from the left, and the camera pans right slightly.*

SUSIE: Annie, I haven't seen Sarah Jane in weeks. (*Sitting on a chair.*) Does she like that new job in New York?

ANNIE: Oh, yes! (*Taking things out of the coat pockets and handing Susie the coat.*)

SUSIE: Thanks. (*She walks off-screen, behind the camera.*)

ANNIE: The head librarian thinks she's so good, why, she even gave her a raise.

SUSIE (*off*): Oh, that's wonderful!

Annie walks forward and right, holding a piece of paper, the camera panning with her, until it loses her and picks up Susie fixing her hair in the mirror; Annie's image is reflected in the mirror, as she puzzles over the paper.

ANNIE: Why, she just wrote me the other day and she said that . . .

A car horn is heard. Susie leaves the mirror and moves forward toward Annie; the camera pans left and moves in to Annie as Susie kisses her cheek.

SUSIE: Oh, don't wait up for me, Annie! I'm going to be terribly late. Good night, sweet!

Susie runs off, left, and the camera holds on Annie in MS, *reading the sheet of paper in her hands, looking disturbed.*

ANNIE: Harry's Club?

She moves left, the camera panning to follow, toward a nightstand, and takes out a telephone book and opens it on the bed.

Lora's House, exterior, night

498. LS: *Susie crossing the front terrace and lawn to meet Steve, who stands by his car in the background. He opens the door for her as she approaches.*

SUSIE: Hope I didn't keep you waiting too long, Steve.

Lora's House, interior, night

499. MS: *Annie on the telephone in Sarah Jane's bedroom, facing the camera, looking troubled.*

ANNIE: Hello . . . is this the Manhattan Public Library?

MAN'S VOICE (*off, over telephone*): Yes, it is.

ANNIE: Well, may I speak to Miss Sarah Jane Johnson, please?

MAN'S VOICE: Well, I'm sorry, the library is closed.

ANNIE: Yes, I know, but she's on a late shift . . . reclassifyin' books after hours, she said.

MAN'S VOICE: Well, there's no one here by that name.

ANNIE: You have no one there by that name?

MAN'S VOICE: No.

ANNIE: Are you sure? Absolutely sure?

MAN'S VOICE: Yes, I'm sure. No one.

ANNIE: I see. Well, thank you very much. Thank you.

Dissolve.

New York City Street, exterior, night

500. LS: *taxi arriving at "Harry's Club." The car moves left and the camera pans with it.*

501. CU: *Annie in the taxi, as seen through the rear window. She peers out the window, right, as the cab driver exits on the right and opens the door for her. She exits the cab and the camera pans right and tilts up, as she enters the front door of the club. She is wearing a blue coat and a matching beret-style hat.*

Harry's Club, interior, night

502. *Low* MLS: *Annie walking down the stairs into Harry's Club. She pauses and looks into the main room. As she moves right the camera pans right and moves in slightly, as the host confronts her.*

HOST: May I help you, lady?

ANNIE: Is there a girl named Sarah Jane Johnson workin' here?

HOST: Never heard of her!

Two other guests come down the stairs from the left and the host confronts them.

HOST: Two?

He and they walk off right. Annie comes forward (as the camera pulls back and pans right), and moves past a louvered screen. She stops and looks off through the smoke-filled room into the background. Patrons are seated at tables watching Sarah Jane start her number. Sarah Jane is dressed in an abbreviated, black, sequined, corset-like costume, with a short, feather-ruffled skirt.

503. CU: *Annie, looking off (at Sarah Jane), through louvered screen.*
504. MS: *Sarah Jane, performing, as seen over the table of a man who sits near the stage. The camera pans left as she dances and sings, then right as she approaches the man at the table, and strokes his face. As she moves left again, the camera pans with her, as she sits on the table, next to another man.*

> SARAH JANE (*singing*): The loneliest word I've heard of is "empty."
> Anything empty is sad.
> An empty purse can make a good girl bad—
> You hear me, dad?
> The loneliest word . . .

505. CU: *Annie, looking through louvered screen, her face shadowed by the slats.*

> SARAH JANE (*singing, off*): . . . I've heard of is "empty."

506. MS: *Sarah Jane, singing, near table with the second male customer. The camera pans right as she leans in that direction, bringing the first male customer back into view. The camera pulls back a bit as she walks into the background (away from the table) and begins to dance again.*

> SARAH JANE (*singing*): Empty things make me so sad,
> So fill me up with what I formerly had.

As she dances she moves left and the camera pans with her, picking up the first customer in the foreground, laughing crudely.

507. MS: *Sarah Jane, reclining on a table, next to a third male customer, continuing her number; the camera tilts down and moves slightly to the right.*

> SARAH JANE (*singing*): Now Venus, you know, was loaded with charms
> And look at what happened to her . . .

As she stands up from the table, the camera moves left and pulls back as she continues to dance and sing.

> SARAH JANE (*singing*): Waitin' around, she's minus two arms—
> Could happen to me, no, sir!

508. CU: *Annie looking off (at Sarah Jane) through the louvered screen, her face in the shadows.*
509. MLS: *Sarah Jane, in front of a table, continuing to perform.*

> SARAH JANE (*singing*): Now is the time to fill what is empty.
> Fill my life brim full of charms.
> Help me refill these empty, empty, empty arms.

When she finishes her number, the audience applauds and she exits the stage through an archway in the background.

510. CU: *Annie, looking through the louvered screen. She moves left and the camera pans with her.*

511. LS: *Club floor as the host seats a couple in the foreground. Annie is seen in the background, beside the louvered screen. She sneaks across the floor in the background, moving left, and the camera pans with her. It loses her in the background and picks up the host in the foreground, also moving left in* CU. *He exits the frame left, and we hold on Sarah Jane and another man talking, seen through the louvered screen in* MS. *The camera moves in as they talk.*

MAN: I thought you were great tonight! Really great!

SARAH JANE: Thank you. (*She giggles.*)

MAN: Where do you go when you run out of here every night? You got a boyfriend?

Annie moves into frame in the right background, by a wall, looking at Sarah Jane and the man.

SARAH JANE: Could be.

MAN (*beginning to embrace her*): Ha . . . if you weren't such a cute little . . .

ANNIE: Sarah Jane Johnson! You put your clothes on and get out of this place!

Sarah Jane and the man look right, toward Annie.

512. CU: *Sarah Jane and the man (he is seen, on the left, through the louvered screen). They look off at Annie.*
     MAN: Say, honey, who is this character?
     SARAH JANE: I don't know. I've never seen her before in my life!
513. MS: *Annie.*
     ANNIE: Now, quit lyin'! To tell me you had a respectable job in the library . . .
514. CU: *the host and another restaurant employee talking. The camera pans right with the host as he moves toward the group, crossing in front of them in the foreground, his back to the camera.*
     HOST: Hey! What's goin' on here?
     SARAH JANE: Oh, she must be crazy! Tell her my name's Judy Brand. Make her go away!
     Sarah Jane exits left and the man moves toward Annie in the back- ground/right. The camera dollies in and moves right slightly, framing them in MS.
     HOST: Look, lady, why don't you blow?
     ANNIE: You'd better keep out of this, mister! This girl here is my daughter . . .
     The man turns left.
     ANNIE: . . . and if you don't tell her to go home with me, her mother . . .
515. MCU: *Sarah Jane and the man with whom she had been flirting, standing to the side of the louvered screen.*
     ANNIE (*off*): . . . I'll have the law on you!
     MAN (*to Sarah Jane*): Your mother Well, I'll be . . .
     The camera pans right as Sarah Jane hurries out of frame in the back- ground; it picks up the host and Annie in the foreground. Annie begins to walk into the background and the host stops her.
     HOST: Go on, beat it! She's through, anyway.
     Annie exits right, and the camera holds on the host.
     Dissolve.
     Alley at the Rear of Harry's Club, exterior, night
516. MLS: *Sarah Jane, exiting with her valises, wearing a khaki shirtwaist dress. The camera pans left a bit and tilts down as she rests her suitcases on the ground. She then picks them up and begins to move right, the camera panning and moving in with her to frame her in* MS. *She stops when she sees Annie by a storefront in the background.*
     ANNIE: Sarah Jane!
517. MS: *Sarah Jane (on the left, facing the camera) and Annie (on the right, her back to the camera). Sarah Jane walks forward, ignoring Annie, who follows behind her. The camera pulls back and pans right ahead of them.*
     ANNIE: What did you expect me to do when I find you dancing in that

low-down dive? Honey, think! If it ever got back to the Teachers' College that you were mixed up in such a place . . . (*Stopping Sarah Jane and turning her around.*) . . . they would never let you in!

SARAH JANE: I wouldn't be found dead in a colored teachers' college! (*She begins to pull away.*).

518. LS: *Sarah Jane and Annie on the street, seen from across the street. Sarah Jane starts forward, and Annie hurries after her. A taxi passes in front of them in the foreground, honking. The camera pulls back and pans right as they continue forward, to the other side of the street.*

ANNIE: Please, come home! We'll have some coffee and we'll talk about this. Honey! (*She stops Sarah Jane and turns her around; both are framed facing one another in* MS.) Nobody's all right about anything. And nobody's all wrong. Now, if you don't want to be a teacher, all right. We'll talk about what you want to be.

Sarah Jane turns away from Annie and faces the camera, moving forward, as the camera pulls back and Annie follows her.

ANNIE: Honey . . . Miss Lora gets home from Italy in the mornin' and I'm sure . . .

Sarah Jane moves out of frame past the camera, and Annie pauses.

ANNIE: Sarah Jane! (*She moves right as the camera pans her.*) Sarah Jane! (*She moans and sinks down on some steps, leaning on the railing. The camera tilts down*). Sarah Jane . . .

519. LS: *street as Sarah Jane walks into the background, her back to the camera. She exits from view around a corner.*

520. MS: *Annie, leaning on railing and looking through it, crying. Dissolve.*

Lora's House, exterior, day

521. LS: *limousine pulling up in front of the house. Dissolve.*

Lora's House, interior, day

522. ELS: *Lora's living room as Lora and Susie hurry in from the entrance hall in the background. Susie is wearing an apricot, double-breasted suit with short, white gloves. Lora wears a fur-trimmed taupe suit with matching hat and gloves.*

LORA: Oh, Susie darling! (*looking around.*) Oh, all the flowers! (*Spinning around.*) Oh, it's wonderful. (*She crosses left to the window, the camera panning left.*) Oh, I was never so glad to be home!

SUSIE (*laughing*): Annie was up at the crack of dawn.

523. *Low* LS: *Lora at the window and Susie at her right, seen on the diagonal.*

LORA (*turning from the window*): Where is she?

SUSIE: Well . . . I don't know.

LORA (*walking across the room, right, the camera panning*): Annie! Annie!

SUSIE (*following Lora out of the living room, into the dining room*): That's funny. You know she was so anxious to see you.
As they move, the camera continues to pan right, picking up Kenneth taking luggage upstairs.

524. MS (*inside kitchen*): *Lora and Susie (facing camera) running into the room. The camera pans right with Lora as she moves along, picking up Annie (in a blue print dress), sitting at the kitchen table.*
LORA: Annie! Annie . . . what's the matter?
SUSIE (*moving into the frame*): What happened?
LORA: Is it Sarah Jane?
Annie looks up and hands Lora a piece of paper.
LORA (*reading*): "Mama, if you really want to be kind . . . really a mother . . . don't try to find me. Just pretend that I . . . died, or was never born. This is my life and I'm going to live it my way. Sarah Jane."

525. MCU: *Lora (on the left, facing the camera) and Annie (on the right, seen from the rear).*
LORA: Oh, darling, I'm sorry. (*She bends down a bit and the camera tilts down.*) We'll find her and bring her back.

526. MS: *Lora (left), Susie (center), and Annie (right) around the table.*
ANNIE: No, Miss Lora. It's her life and I'm done with interfering. All I'd like to know, somehow, is where she is . . .
As Annie talks, Lora straightens up.

527. MCU: *Lora and Annie (as in 525).*
ANNIE: . . . so if she should ever need anything, I can kinda help her.
LORA: Do you have any idea where she might have gone?

528. MS: *Susie (behind the table) and Annie (seated).*
ANNIE: No, ma'am.
SUSIE: I'll bet Steve will know what to do. I'll call him.
LORA (*coming into frame left, speaking to Susie*): All right. (*To Annie.*) You lie down for a while.
Annie rises from the table and the camera tilts up.
LORA: We're going to take care of you for a change.
Annie walks into the background, up the stairs; Lora exits left.

529. MLS: *Susie sitting on the top of a chair in the living room, speaking on the telephone. A fire blazes in the fireplace.*
SUSIE: Hello, Steve? (*Giggling.*) Yes. Susie!
Lora enters right, crossing in front of the fireplace. She takes the phone from Susie.
LORA (*whispering*): Let me have it. (*Aloud.*) Hello. No, this isn't Susie. That's right!

530. MS: *Lora (on the right) and Susie (on the left). Lora talks and Susie looks at her from behind the chair.*

LORA: Oh, a few moments ago. Oh, it was wonderful! Yes. And thank
you for taking such good care of my child. Yes, she is! (*Laughing.*)

SUSIE (*whispering*): What's he saying about me?

LORA (*covering the mouthpiece of the phone*): He thinks you're as cute
as a button. And you are. (*Into phone.*) Only, Steve, something dread-
ful has happened.

Steve's Office, interior, day

531. MS: *Steve seated behind his desk, holding the phone.*

STEVE: When? No. I'll put a detective agency on it and I'll report the
moment I hear anything. Good-bye. (*He breaks the connection and
dials.*)

Dissolve.

Lora's House, interior, day

532. *High* MLS: *Steve, Lora (facing the camera), and Annie (back to camera)
seated, as Kenneth serves them drinks. Lora is wearing a floor-length,
wrap-around, off-white dressing gown, with an orange chiffon sash. Annie
wears a blue shirtwaist dress.*

STEVE: Then under the name of—Linda Carroll, she got herself a job in
the chorus line at the Moulin Rouge in Hollywood.

ANNIE: Where's she living?

STEVE: At a motel—nearby.

ANNIE (*rising*): Thanks, Mr. Steve. I'm going out there. (*The camera
    cranes up and left as she starts forward. She stops and turns around as
    Lora begins to speak.*)

LORA: No, Annie—you can't. You're not well enough! (*Rising.*) I'll go
    get her myself.

ANNIE: No, Miss Lora. I have to go. (*Turning forward and moving left
    in the foreground as the camera cranes back and follows.*) I've just got
    to see my baby once more. (*She mounts the steps to the entrance hall
    and stops as Steve begins to speak.*)

STEVE: All right, Annie—I'll have my office make your train
    reservations.

ANNIE (*crossing the entrance hall, left, as the camera follows, losing
    Lora and Steve*): Thanks, but I'm not goin' by train. I'm goin' to fly.
    I'm in a hurry. (*She mounts the stairs up to the second floor.*)

Los Angeles Airport, exterior, day

533. LS: *airplane landing on the runway, flying toward the camera. The
    camera pans left to follow it as it lands, then stops, as the plane moves
    into the background.*
    Dissolve.

Moulin Rouge Nightclub, interior, night

534. MCU: *bronze statue of a woman in the lobby. On either side of it is the
    neon sign: "Moulin Rouge." The camera pans left and tilts down to show
    patrons entering from the foreground and background. Annie moves for-
    ward, up the foyer steps, and exits past the camera as the headwaiter
    greets patrons. She wears her blue coat and hat over a blue and white
    print dress.*

535. LS: *stage show as seen from the runway as men and women (in scanty at-
    tire and massive headdresses) dance.*

536. High MS: *club audience as seen from the stage, over the orchestra pit.*

537. MLS: *stage (as seen from the runway) as male and female specialty
    dancers perform amidst the chorus. Chorus girls prance by across the
    runway in the foreground.*

538. Low MS: *Annie in the foyer, moving away from the camera. The camera
    tilts down to show patrons and waiters moving about. Annie hesitates and
    looks around, as though uncertain.*

539. MS: *Male and female specialty dancers on stage. Legs of chorus girls are
    seen dancing and passing by in the foreground. The camera pans slightly
    left to follow the dancing couple.*

540. LS: *Annie moving right through the lobby, in the midground. The camera
    pans to follow her.*

541. MLS: *club stage, from the rear of the theater. Annie's back is visible in
    the foreground, left, as she moves into the frame and positions herself by*

the runway, looking up at the showgirls passing by. In the background, we
see a new set of showgirls come on stage in rocking chairs, from the
right; they hold bottles of champagne and glasses.

542. *Low* MLS: *one of the showgirls, posed on a rocking chair. She moves out
of view, left, as the moving set rotates and Sarah Jane comes into view.
The set stops and the camera holds on Sarah Jane, going through the
number. She is wearing a gold, strapless costume, with a skirt/train positioned between her legs. She also wears long blue gloves.*

543. *Low* MS: *Annie, looking up at the stage, distressed.*

544. CU: *Sarah Jane, performing her stage routine. She shakes her shoulders
provocatively and stares off, right, and winks.*

545. *High* MS: *club audience, as seen from the stage. Male patrons smile at
her.*

546. *Low* MS *(from stage left): Sarah Jane going through her sexy routine.*

547. *High* MS: *Annie looking up at the stage. The camera tilts up as a waiter
approaches her, from the rear.*

548. MS: *Sarah Jane on stage, going through her routine, as showgirls pass in
front of her in the foreground.*

549. *High* MS: *Annie, turning around to the waiter behind her, then walking
right across the room. The camera pans her. She stops and looks toward
the stage again.*

550. *Low* MLS: *Sarah Jane getting up from the rocking chair and continuing her routine. She looks off left and seems upset.*

551. *High* MLS: *Annie turning around and exiting the room.*

552. MS: *Sarah Jane, on stage, doing her routine (as seen from stage left). The camera is mounted on a moving platform that takes Sarah Jane and the other chorus girls off-stage. As the curtain closes, the platform stops moving and Sarah Jane stands up; the camera tilts up and pans right as showgirls pass her. Her friend approaches her from the right.*

   SHOWGIRL: Well, what's up, honey?

   Annie appears at a doorway in the background, between the two women.

   SARAH JANE: Well, I—I don't know. Just a funny feeling. (*She walks right and Annie disappears from view.*)

   SHOWGIRL: Well, don't forget the guys are pickin' us up at twelve thirty.

   SARAH JANE: (*stopping and turning around to her friend*): Well, I'll rush back to the motel and change. See you then.

   Sarah Jane exits right and the camera holds on the showgirl. Annie reappears in the background doorway. The showgirl exits right and Annie moves into the backstage area, then turns around and exits into the background.

   Dissolve.

   Motel, interior, night

553. *Low* MS: *Sarah Jane (seen from the rear) dressing in her motel room. A chair is in the foreground. A knock is heard at the door. She is wearing a black and slate gray, sheath-style cocktail dress.*

   SARAH JANE (*sitting down on a second chair in the midground and facing the camera, as seen through the back of the foreground chair*): Door's open!

   Annie walks in from the background/right.

   SARAH JANE (*not seeing Annie*): I'll be ready in a minute! (*Turning to the door.*) I hope they're not here—(*She begins to stand.*)

   ANNIE: Now, don't be mad, honey, Nobody saw me.

   The camera pans left and tilts up as Sarah Jane comes forward and sits on the foreground chair, facing the camera, which frames her in a low MCU.

   SARAH JANE: It *was* you! (*She slams her shoe on the dresser.*) You *were* there tonight! Oh, why can't you leave me alone?!

554. MS: *Annie, by the door.*

   ANNIE: I tried, Sarah Jane. You'll never know how hard I tried.

555. CU: *Sarah Jane, seated.*

   SARAH JANE: Well, I might as well pack.

   She stands and swirls around and walks across the room into the depth of the frame. The camera tilts up and follows her. Annie crosses left as Sarah Jane brings forward her suitcase and opens it on the bed.

ANNIE: Look, baby—

SARAH JANE: I suppose you've been to the boss! (*Throwing clothes from her bureau drawer into her suitcase.*) Lost me my job—my friends! (*She turns toward Annie.*)

ANNIE: I've been no place! I didn't come to bother you—

SARAH JANE: Well, you won't. Not ever again. Spoil things for me here and I'll just go somewhere else.

556. MCU: *Annie (facing the camera, on the left) and Sarah Jane (seen from the rear, on the right).*

SARAH JANE: And I'll keep on going until you're so tired and so—

ANNIE: Baby—I am tired. I'm as tired as I ever want to be. (*Looking off, left.*) You mind if I sit down? (*She begins to walk left.*)

557. MLS: *Annie and Sarah Jane, moving left toward a chair. Sarah Jane rushes ahead and blocks the chair.*

SARAH JANE: Yes, I do. Somebody's coming. That's why the door was unlocked.

ANNIE (*moving forward*): I'll only stay a minute. I just want to look at you. That's why I came. Are you happy here, honey? Are you findin' what you really want?

SARAH JANE (*turning around and moving forward*): I'm somebody else! (*She moves to look in a mirror and the camera pans to follow. The mirror frames both her and Annie.*) I'm white! White! WHITE! (*She *sobs and turns around to face Annie, the camera panning right to frame them both, in a low* MS.) Does that answer you?

ANNIE: I guess so.

558. MCU: *Sarah Jane (on the left, facing the camera) and Annie (on the right, seen from the rear).*

SARAH JANE: Then please, Mama, will you go? And never do this again! And if—by accident—we should ever pass on the street, please don't recognize me!

559. MCU, *reverse angle of 558: Annie (facing the camera) and Sarah Jane (seen from the rear).*

ANNIE: I won't, Sarah Jane. I promise, I settled all that in my mind.

560. CU: *Sarah Jane (on the left, facing the camera) and Annie (on the right, seen from the rear).*

ANNIE: There's just one thing I wish from you.

SARAH JANE: What?

561. CU, *reverse angle of 560: Annie (on the right, facing the camera) and Sarah Jane (on the left, seen from the rear).*

ANNIE: If you're ever in trouble—if you ever need anything at all—if you ever want to come home, and you shouldn't be able to—get in touch with me—

562. CU: *Sarah Jane (facing the camera) and Annie (as seen from rear). (As in 560).*

ANNIE: —will you let Miss Lora know?

SARAH JANE: Yes! Yes—anything! Now, will you go?!

563. CU, *reverse angle of 562.*

ANNIE: That wasn't all I wanted, honey. That was only part of it.

SARAH JANE: What's the rest?

ANNIE: I'd like to hold you in my arms once more—like you were still my baby.

564. CU, *reverse angle of 563: Sarah Jane (facing the camera) and Annie (seen from the rear).*

SARAH JANE: All right, Mama. All right!

ANNIE *(hugging Sarah Jane)*: Oh, Sarah Jane!

565. ECU: *Annie (on the left, facing the camera) and Sarah Jane (on the right, seen from the rear) embracing.*

ANNIE *(sobbing)*: Oh, my baby! My beautiful, beautiful baby!

566. ECU: *Sarah Jane (on the left, facing the camera) and Annie (on the right, seen from the rear) embracing. Sarah Jane's face is full of pained emotion. Annie continues to cry.*

567. ECU: *Annie (on the left, facing the camera) and Sarah Jane (on the right, seen from the rear) embracing.*

ANNIE: I love you so much. Nothin' you ever do can stop that.

568. ECU: *Sarah Jane (on the left, facing the camera) and Annie (on the right, seen from the rear) embracing.*

SARAH JANE (*grabbing Annie closer and crying*): Oh, Mama! Oh, Mama—Mama!

569. ECU: *Annie (on the right, facing the camera) and Sarah Jane (on the left, rear to camera) embracing.*
ANNIE (*with tears streaming down her cheeks*): Oh, my baby!
Both react to an off-screen knock and look right. Sarah Jane starts to move in that direction across the room.

570. MCU, *pan: Sarah Jane as she moves right across the room. The camera pauses as we see Sarah Jane's showgirl friend enter the door in the background.*
SHOWGIRL: Come on, Linda—they're waiting! (*She looks left and crosses behind Sarah Jane, approaching Annie. The camera pans her and loses Sarah Jane.*) Say, listen—if you're the new maid, I want to report that my shower is full of ants!
ANNIE: Oh, I'm sorry, Miss. That must be very uncomfortable. But I just happened to be in town and I—dropped in to see Miss Linda. I used to take care of her. (*She moves forward and right to Sarah Jane and the camera pans her, losing the showgirl. It frames her with Sarah Jane in* MCU.) Well—I guess I'll be running along. My plane's leaving in a little while—Miss Linda. Good-bye honey. You take good care of yourself.
SARAH JANE: Good-bye (*She mouths the word "Mama."*)
Annie turns around, walks into the depth of the frame and right, toward the door; the camera pans her. Sarah Jane turns around as the showgirl enters frame-left. Annie exits. The camera pans left and moves in as the showgirl talks, framing her with Sarah Jane.
SHOWGIRL (*to Sarah Jane*): Well—get you! So, honey child, you had a Mammy!
The camera pans right as Sarah Jane moves toward the door, eventually framing her in MCU.
SARAH JANE (*leaning on door, sadly and sobbing*): Yes—all my life. (*The door shuts. Fade out.*)

Lora's House, interior, day

571. *Fade in.* MS: *Lora emerging from her upstairs room into the hall (as seen from the hall). She is wearing an orange sleeveless top and pants, cinched at the waist with an orange scarf. The camera pans left as she comes forward and looks down over the railing into the living room below. We see Steve and Susie at the bar.*
LORA: Hello, Steve!
STEVE: Hello, Lora!
Lora crosses in front of the camera and exits left, as we hold on a high shot of Steve and Susie.

572. MS: *Steve (on the left, seated at the bar) and Susie (on the right, standing behind the counter). She is wearing a white and black print dress.*

SUSIE (*fixing him a drink*): You know, some of my girlfriends get embarrassed when their mothers wear shorts or pants and things like that, but—I don't really mind.

STEVE: Well, that's very big of you.

SUSIE (*giggling*): Here, I mixed you a highball, but you only get one before lunch!

STEVE: Yes, ma'am!

Steve gets up and walks forward, meeting Lora who comes in from behind the camera. The camera pans right, losing Susie.

LORA: I just had a call from Loomis.

STEVE: Don't say a word. He's got a new role for you.

LORA (*turning and walking into the frame, back to the camera, which pans slightly left, picking up Susie again*): No, no!

SUSIE (*to Lora*): Highball?

LORA: Yes. No, they've flown over a print of the Italian picture.

573. MS: *Lora, Susie, and Steve. Susie is behind the bar, facing the camera, on the left; Lora sits on a stool before it, in the middle, also facing the camera. Steve is looking at Lora and is seen from the rear, on the left.*

LORA: And he's arranged a special showing tonight, and a party afterward. (*Turning around to Susie.*) Oh, darling, I'd like you to see it, too, but—I'm worried about Annie. (*Turning forward.*) Ever since she came back from Los Angeles she's changed. And Doctor Miller's quite concerned about her condition. (*Turning around toward Susie.*) I think someone should stay in the house with her tonight. Do you mind?

SUSIE: No, of course not, Mama. (*To Steve.*) I'll see you tomorrow, Steve!

STEVE: Sure.

Susie exits left.

LORA: What can we do to help Annie, Steve?

STEVE: There's no answer, Lora—never has been—not for a broken heart.

Dissolve.

574. MLS: *Annie's bedroom. Annie is in bed in the background, left, and Susie sits on a chair in the foreground, right, eating from a tray. She wears a gray, V-necked sweater with a white blouse and matching gray pants.*

SUSIE: Um—and I know Mother didn't understand! Oh, it was so embarrassing! And poor Steve! I mean, what could he do? She just swept over him like a tidal wave.

ANNIE: Now, honey—it's only natural he'd like to go out with your mother. He always enjoyed her company. You remember that. (*She hands Susie a glass.*)

SUSIE: But it's different now! All summer long it's been Steve and me. Annie—

575. MS: *Annie lying in bed.*
    SUSIE (*off*): –you know, don't you?
    ANNIE: Know what?
576. MS: *Susie seated in the chair.*
    SUSIE: That I'm in love with Steve. That I've always been in love with
    him—and always will be.
577. MS: *Annie in bed (as in 575).*
    ANNIE (*writhing a bit and looking away, left*): Sure, Susie—but like a
    little girl.
    SUSIE (*off*): No. I don't think it even started like that.
578. MS: *Susie in the chair (as in 576).*
    SUSIE: In a funny way, I always knew. Every time I thought I liked a
    boy, it was because he reminded me of Steve. And then I'd stop liking
    him because—because he wasn't Steve.
    *She looks off left and rises, moving left as the camera pans her. The
    camera tilts down as she finds Annie asleep. She smiles. The camera tilts
    up as she rises again and turns off the bedside lamp. She begins to move
    right (with the camera panning) then pauses and moves left, toward the
    window, the camera following her.*
579. CU: *Susie opening the window curtains as seen through the window from
    the outside.*
Lora's Driveway, exterior, night
580. High MS: *Lora and Steve getting out of his convertible. He closes the car
    door as she starts forward.*
Lora's House, interior, night
581. CU: *Susie in Annie's bedroom looking through the window, as seen from
    outside. She smiles.*
Lora's Driveway, exterior, night
582. High MS: *Lora (facing the camera) and Steve (seen from behind) em-
    bracing and kissing.*
Lora's House, interior, night
583. CU: *Susie (as in 581). She looks upset and shakes her head.*
Lora's Driveway, exterior, night
584. High MS: *Lora and Steve kissing (as in 582).*
Lora's House, interior, night
585. CU: *Susie (seen through window, from the outside, as in 583). She shuts
    her eyes.*
586. MS: *Susie (seen from inside the room) closing the window curtains. She
    moves right and pauses, looking upset; the camera follows her. She moves
    right again and the camera pans, as she turns off a lamp by the chair in
    which she had been seated. She exits frame right.*
587. LS: *Susie exiting Annie's bedroom and entering the hall, as seen from the
    second-floor landing, through the railing. The camera pans left as she*

*comes forward and down a short flight of steps to a small landing. She
continues moving forward and up the next steps toward the camera. She
stops and looks down and off right.*

588. *High* MLS: *front hall, as Lora enters and begins to close the door. She is
wearing a gray-blue, metallic, taffeta evening coat with gray-blue gloves
and a matching purse.*

589. *Low* MS: *Susie, swirling around and exiting left into her room as the
camera pans her. She shuts the door.*

590. *High* MLS: *Lora at the front door, as she closes it and turns around. The
camera pans left and cranes up the stairs as Lora ascends and knocks on
Susie's door, framing Lora in a low shot.*

591. MLS: *Lora at Susie's closed door.*
     LORA: Susie! Are you up, darling?
     SUSIE (*off*): Yes. (*She opens her door and stands in the doorway.*)
     LORA: I just had to tell you. (*She begins to move inside.*)

592. MS: *Susie and Lora as seen from inside the former's room. They are
shadowed. Lora walks in toward the left, as the camera pans her in sil-
houetted profile.*
     LORA: I have the most wonderful news! (*She pauses.*)
     SUSIE (*sarcastically*): You're going to do another picture.
     LORA (*moving into the depth of the frame, seen from behind, the camera
     and Susie following*): No! Not a picture—not a play—(*Turning for-
     ward.*) Never again! (*Turning rear, moving into the frame, the camera
     following.*) Oh, I know you don't believe me. I can't blame you (*Turn-
     ing forward.*) Steve didn't either. He probably won't until our tenth
     anniversary!

593. MS: *Susie, looking upset.*
     SUSIE: Anniversary!

594. MLS: *Lora (facing the camera, in the background) and Susie (her back
to the camera, in the foreground). Lora approaches her and the camera
moves in a bit.*
     LORA (*pausing at Susie's bedpost*): Oh, Steve and I have always been in
     love, but it seems I've never had time for anything but my work. (*The
     camera pans left, eventually framing only Susie.*) So, I just up and pro-
     posed that . . . (*from off-screen*) . . . we get married—Why, Susie,
     what's the matter? Are you all right?
     SUSIE (*leaning, stunned, against the wall*): Yes, I'm fine. I—I hope
     you'll be very happy.

595. MS: *Susie (left) and Lora (right), seen in profile.*
     LORA: We will be. All of us. (*Touching Susie.*) What is it, darling? Tell
     me.
     SUSIE (*moving right into the depth of the frame, toward a mirror, which
     reflects her image*): I'm very tired. Good night, Mother.

LORA: Good night, dear.

Lora turns toward the camera, pauses, then exits behind it. The camera pans left to frame Susie at her dressing table mirror in the background. She walks forward to her bedpost and leans on it, as the camera dollies in.

Dissolve.

Lora's House, interior, day

596. MLS: *Lora (in a bluish-white, lace negligee, with a train) opening the shade of the window in Annie's bedroom. She moves right toward Annie who is resting in bed; the camera pulls back and pans her. She pours coffee.*

LORA: You know, Annie, last night when I told Susie the news—she was like ice. It's strange. I—I thought she would be ecstatic. (*Lora moves left, and the camera pulls back and pans her, as she moves to the foot of the bed, losing Annie.*) She always seemed to—to adore Steve. Something's wrong with her Annie. (*She turns toward Annie and the camera pans right, picking up Annie in the background.*) Do you know what it is?

ANNIE: Miss Lora, you've got to be very careful the way you handle Susie. She's got a real problem.

LORA: Problem?

597. MCU: *Lora.*

LORA: Why don't I know about it? Why didn't she come to me?

598. MCU: *Annie in bed, propped up against the headboard.*

ANNIE: Maybe because you weren't around.

599. MCU: *Lora.*

LORA (*sighing*): You mean I—I haven't been a good mother.

600. MS (*From the foot of the bed*): *Lora (her back to the camera) and Annie (facing the camera).*

ANNIE: I know you meant to be a good mother—the best kind of mother. But look, I meant to be a good one, too—and I failed.

Lora walks off left, the camera tilts up and pans her, losing Annie.

LORA: But you couldn't have been a better mother to Sarah Jane! (*She turns toward Annie.*)

601. MCU: *Annie.*

ANNIE: Then where's my little girl?

602. MS: *Lora. She turns away from Annie and walks left, toward a love seat. The camera tilts down and pans her as she sits.*

LORA: But Annie, that's different! Hers is a very real problem. But what complicated Susie's life? Good heavens, we made a home for her—

603. CU: *Annie.*

LORA (*off*): —prettiest clothes—the best schools—

ANNIE: Susie's in love.

604. LS: *Lora seated on the love seat.*
 LORA: Oh, Annie! Is that all? (*Putting down her coffee.*) Why didn't you say so?
605. MCU: *Annie.*
 LORA (*off*): It's not unusual for a girl Susie's age to be in love.
 ANNIE: It's who she's in love with—that's causin' all the trouble.
606. MCU: *Lora.*
 LORA: Why? Who is it!
607. MCU: *Annie.*
 ANNIE: Mr. Steve.
608. MCU: *Lora (as in 606), stunned.*
 LORA (*beginning to rise*): What?
609. MLS: *Lora rising from the love seat. She moves forward and right, and the camera pans her as she approaches the foot of Annie's bed. She is seen from the rear; Annie faces the camera.*
 LORA: It's impossible! How did it happen? Why did he let it happen?
 ANNIE: I don't think he knows.
 LORA: Annie, it can't be serious!
 ANNIE: It is, Miss Lora—plenty serious.
610. MCU: *Lora.*
 LORA: I'd better have a talk with Susie right now. (*She turns and begins to leave.*)
 ANNIE (*off*): Wait!
611. MS: *Annie leaning forward, as the camera dollies in.*
 ANNIE: Wait!
612. LS: *Susie's bedroom. She is sitting at a desk in the foreground. Lora enters through a door in the background and walks forward to Susie, positioning herself to the left of Susie's desk.*
 LORA: Susie—I've just spoken to Annie.
 SUSIE: Have you?
 LORA: Now I know why you were so upset last night!
 SUSIE: So Annie told you. Well, that's how you usually find things out about me!
 LORA: That's not true!
 SUSIE: Let's face it, Mama! Annie's always been more like a real mother. You never had time for me. By the way . . . (*Handing Lora a piece of paper.*) . . . is this worded correctly?
613. MS: *Lora (on the left) and Susie (on the right).*
 LORA (*reading the paper*): An application to college?
 SUSIE: Uh-hum.
 LORA: But you were going to study in New York! Denver—it's uh— fifteen hundred miles away—
 SUSIE: Sixteen hundred and twenty-eight, to be exact.

LORA: Well, that's quite a distance.

SUSIE: I don't think I'll be missed.

LORA: Oh, don't be unfair, Susie, You know I'd miss you.

SUSIE: I'm sure you'd be too busy to miss anyone . . . (*Rising.*) . . . much too busy! (*The camera tilts up and moves in.*)

LORA: Why, you give me credit for nothing. Yes, I'm ambitious— perhaps too ambitious—but it's been for your sake as well as mine! Isn't this house just a little bit nicer than a cold-water flat? And your new horse—aren't you just crazy about it?

SUSIE: Yes, but I—

LORA (*pointing into the background*): And that closet of yours—

SUSIE (*walking into the background, the camera following*): Has all the dresses fit for the daughter of a famous star.

LORA: Now—just a moment, young lady.

614. CU: *Lora (on the left, facing the camera) and Susie (on the right, her rear to the camera).*

LORA: It's only because of my ambition that you've had the best of everything!

615. CU, *reverse angle of 614: Susie (on the right, facing the camera) and Lora (on the left, her rear to camera).*

LORA: And that's a solid achievement that any mother can be proud of!

SUSIE: And how about a mother's love?

616. CU, *reverse angle of 615.*

LORA: Love?! But you've always had that!

SUSIE (*moving right, toward the bed, the camera panning, and dropping Lora*): Yes—by telephone. By postcard. By magazine interviews. You've given me everything—but yourself! No wonder I went to Annie last night when I told her about Steve. (*She rests her head on the bedpost and sobs.*).

617. MS: *Lora.*

LORA: Oh, Susie. (*She walks right, toward Susie, and the camera pans her, picking up Susie and framing the two in CU.*) If Steve is going to come between us—I'll give him up. I'll never see him again.

SUSIE (*turning right and exiting the frame*): Oh, Mama! (*From off-screen.*) Stop acting!

Lora turns right and the camera pans to frame her and Susie.

SUSIE: Stop trying to shift people around as if they were pawns on a stage!

LORA: But, Susie, I—

SUSIE: Oh, don't worry! I'll get over Steve. But please—don't play the martyr!

Lora sits down, dropping out of frame; Susie runs forward toward her and the camera tilts down to reveal Lora crying. Susie kneels at her feet.

SUSIE: Oh, Mama, I'm sorry. (*Sobbing.*) I didn't want to hurt you. But last night I—I was so unhappy. (*She sobs and rests her head on Lora's lap.*)

LORA: Oh, my darling.

SUSIE (*lifting her head, the camera tilting up*): I don't know—maybe it was all to the good, because—well, this morning I—I—I felt strangely independent and—well, I like the feeling! And—that's why I think I'd—I'd like to go away—at least for a while. Oh, Mama—please try to understand. I'm—I'm very sincere about it.

LORA (*pulling Susie toward her in an embrace and sighing*): Oh, it's funny the way things turn out.

Dissolve.

Lora's House, interior, night

618. MS: *Lora and Steve seated at the dining room table; a maid serves them and exits behind Lora, left. Lora wears a simple gray, street-length sheath with a scoop-neck, adorned by a gold pin.*

STEVE (*to the maid*): Thank you. (*To Lora.*) I still can't get over Susie at the station yesterday. She looked so—grown up when she said good-bye.

LORA: Yes, she did.

STEVE: It does seem awfully quiet here without her.

LORA: Annie and I were talking about that last night.

619. MCU: *Lora (facing the camera, in the center) and Steve (in profile, on the right) at the dinner table.*

LORA: With both the girls gone, we felt so alone in this big house.

STEVE: When did this idea of college come up? Susie never once mentioned it to me.

LORA: She decided suddenly.

STEVE: And why Colorado? It's so far away.

LORA: It's what she wanted.

Kenneth enters from the left and leans over Lora's chair.

KENNETH: Miss Meredith. It's Annie. She's terribly sick.

STEVE: Did you call the doctor?

KENNETH: Yes. He'll be right over.

Lora rises and walks into the background. The camera tilts up and pans left.

KENNETH (*to Lora, who pauses and looks at him*): And she wants the minister, too.

Lora exits in the background, followed by Kenneth and Steve.

Dissolve.

620. MS (*from inside Annie's room*): *the maid opening the door to let the minister in. The camera pans right as he goes to Annie's bed, where we see Lora, Kenneth, and the doctor. Lora nods to the minister. The camera*

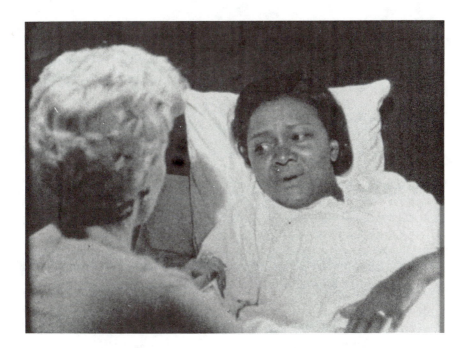

moves in and left as the physician comes forward to Lora, shaking his head.

LORA (*turning away and covering her eyes*): Oh, God—no!

621. MCU: *Annie in bed.*

ANNIE: Hate to dispute you, Miss Lora.

622. MS: *Lora (turning around), Kenneth, and the physician at the foot of Annie's bed.*

LORA: Oh, Annie—don't talk!

ANNIE (*off*): I've got to . . .

Lora moves forward quickly toward Annie as the latter lifts her head. The camera pans right to frame the two of them, with the doctor and Kenneth still seen in the background.

ANNIE: . . . talk

LORA: Oh, please! Please—not now!

ANNIE: You stop cryin'.

LORA: But I—

ANNIE: No—listen to me.

LORA: All right—I'm listening.

623. CU: *Annie (on the right, facing the camera) and Lora (seen from the rear, on the left).*

ANNIE: When my bills are all paid, I want everything that's left to go to—Sarah Jane.

LORA: Of course.

ANNIE (*looking off*): Mr. Steve?

STEVE (*off*): Yes, Annie?

ANNIE (*pulling herself up, the camera panning right*): Find her, Mr. Steve! Find her!

624. *Low* MS: *Steve.*

STEVE: I will. You may be sure.

625. MS: *Lora (facing the camera) and Annie (seen in profile). The doctor is visible in the background, his back to the camera. Kenneth is on the left-hand periphery.*

STEVE (*off*): I will.

ANNIE: Thank you. (*To Lora.*) Miss Lora—just tell her—

626. CU: *Annie.*

ANNIE: —tell her I know I was selfish—and if I loved her too much, I'm sorry—but I didn't mean to cause her any trouble. She was all I had.

627. CU: *Lora (with the doctor, back to the camera, behind her).*

ANNIE (*off*): Tell her, Miss Lora—

LORA: Oh, please, Annie.

ANNIE (*raising her head and becoming visible in the frame*): Promise me! Promise me!

LORA: I promise.

ANNIE (*sighing and lowering her head*): My pearl necklace—

LORA: Yes?

628. CU: *Annie (on the right, facing the camera) and Lora (seen from the rear, on the left).*

ANNIE: I want you to give it to Susie—for her weddin'. Give her a real bridey wedding with all the fixins. Our weddin' day—and the day we die—are the great events of life.

629. CU: *Lora.*

LORA (*sobbing*): Oh, Annie! (*She approaches Annie, as the camera pans, and she puts her head down on the bed. We see Annie again, as well as a photograph of Sarah Jane on Annie's nightstand*). Annie, darling!

ANNIE: There's no cause to cry, honey. (*To the minister.*) Reverend?

630. *Low* MS: *Steve as the minister comes into the frame from the right, Bible in hand.*

MINISTER: Yes, Annie?

631. CU: *Lora (on the left, facing the camera, kneeling by the bed) and Annie (in partial profile, on the right). Sarah Jane's photograph is visible on the nightstand between them.*

ANNIE: I'd like for your wife to have my fur scarf. She always admired that fur. She never believed me when I said it was genuine mink.

632. *Low* MS: *Steve (left, background) and the minister (right, foreground).*
MINISTER: She did, Annie. She did.

633. CU: *Lora and Annie (as in 631).*
LORA (*sobbing*): Oh, please, you don't have to—
ANNIE: And I want Mr. McKinney to have a nice clean fifty-dollar bill.
LORA: M—Mr. McKinney?

634. MCU: *Annie (on the right, facing the camera) and Lora (on the left, kneeling, seen from the rear).*
ANNIE: The milkman at the old cold-water flat. He was so nice and understanding about the bill. I always sent him a little somethin' at Christmastime . . .

635. CU: *Lora and Annie (as in 633).*
ANNIE: . . . in both our names.
LORA (*sobbing*): You've been so good!
ANNIE: Sure hope you're right, Miss Lora. I'd like to be standin' with the lambs and not with the goats—on Judgment Day.

636. MCU: *Annie and Lora (as in 634).*
ANNIE: And my funeral—(*To Steve.*) Mr. Steve, you'll find what I want in the drawer—over there. (*She points toward the right.*)

637. *Low* MS: *Steve and the minister. Steve walks into the background. The camera tilts down as he opens the drawer and takes out an envelope.*
STEVE: I've got it, Annie.

638. MCU: *Annie and Lora (as in 634).*
ANNIE: I wanta go—the way I planned—especially the four white horses, and a band playin'—no mourning—but proud and high—steppin—like I was goin' to glory!

639. CU: *Lora, sobbing.*
LORA: No! I won't listen! There isn't going to be any funeral! Not for a long, long time! You can't leave me! I won't let you!

640. CU: *Annie and Lora (as in 634).*
ANNIE: I'm just tired, Miss Lora. Awfully—tired—(*She seems to drift off.*)

641. CU: *Lora. She studies Annie and looks upset.*
LORA: ANNIE! ANNIE! (*Sobbing.*) No!
She buries her face in the bed and the camera pans right to reveal Annie, dead. The camera holds on the photograph of Sarah Jane on Annie's nightstand.
Dissolve.
Baptist Church, interior, day

642. *Low, canted* MLS: *church's stained-glass window; part of a flower arrangement is visible in the foreground. As we hear the female soloist sing,*

the camera tilts and pans down right, to bring her into view at the pulpit, framed in Low LS, *standing in front of a cross.*

SOLOIST (*singing, off-screen*):   Soon I will be done—
                            Trouble of the world, Lord,
      (*on-screen*):   Trouble of the world,
                            Trouble of the world.

Choir (off) hums.

643. *Low* MS: *Soloist singing behind pulpit, dressed in a black robe with a white collar.*

SOLOIST (*singing*): I soon will be done—
Choir (off) hums.

644. *Low* LS: *Choir loft (above soloist) as the camera cranes down and back over the floral arrangements. As it pans left, it shows Lora, Susie, Steve, and others sitting in the church pews. The women are dressed in black. Lora wears a black feathered hat and Susie a black headband.*

SOLOIST (*singing*):   Trouble of the world,
                        I'm going home to live with God.
                        No more (*off-screen*) weepin' and wailin',
                        No more weepin' and . . .

645. MLS: *side view, Annie's casket (covered in white flowers) before the audience.*

SOLOIST (*singing, off*):   . . . wailin',
                              No more . . .

646. CU: *Soloist singing.*

SOLOIST (*singing*):   . . . weepin' and wailin',
                        I'm going home to live with my Lord—

647. MS: *Lora, Susie, and Steve seated in the first row of church pews, as seen on the diagonal.*

SOLOIST (*singing, off*): —Lord.
Choir (off) hums.

648. *High* MCU: *McKinney (the milkman) sitting in a pew. He bows his head.*

SOLOIST (*singing, off*):   Soon I will be done—
                        My trouble . . .

649. *Low* MS: *Soloist singing behind the pulpit.*

SOLOIST (*singing*):   . . . of this world,
                        Oh, my trouble in this world,

650. MS: *Loomis and Edwards in the church audience. Others sit behind them.*

SOLOIST (*singing, off*): Lord, the trouble in this . . .

651. CU: *Soloist singing.*

SOLOIST (*singing*):   . . . world.
                      Lord, I soon will be done—

652. MLS: *Lora, Susie, and Steve in the first row of pews, as seen from the side of the church. Annie's casket is visible in the background.*
SOLOIST (*singing, off*): The trouble of this world,

653. MLS: *Annie's casket, as seen from the side of the church. A man stands against a wall in the background.*
SOLOIST (*singing, off*): I'm goin . . .

654. CU: *Male church members (wearing red sashes), sitting in the pews, as seen on the diagonal.*
SOLOIST (*singing, off*): . . . home—Ooooohhhh—

655. CU: *Soloist singing.*
SOLOIST (*singing*): Oooooohhhhh—to live . . .

656. MCU: *Lora, Susie and Steve, shot from the side of the church.*
SOLOIST (*singing, off*): . . . with my Lord—

657. *Low* MS: *soloist singing behind pulpit.*
SOLOIST (*singing*): Lord. (*Hums.*)
Choir (off) hums.
Dissolve.
Street (on which church is located), exterior, day

658. MLS: *church entrance (as seen from outside) as the pallbearers carry out Annie's coffin. Church members cluster around.*
MINISTER: (*off*) I will lift up mine eyes unto the hills from whence cometh my help. (*On-screen.*) My help cometh from the Lord which made heaven and earth. He will not suffer thy foot to be moved. He that keepeth thee will not slumber. Behold . . .

659. MS, *reverse angle of 658: pallbearers carrying Annie's coffin, as shot from the church steps, looking into the street. Lora, Susie, and Steve walk behind the coffin along with other guests, toward the hearse.*
MINISTER: . . . he that keepeth Israel shall neither slumber nor sleep. The Lord is thy keeper. The Lord is the shade upon thy right hand.

660. *Low* MCU: *Annie's coffin, followed by Lora, Steve, and Susie.*
MINISTER (*off*): The sun shall not smite thee by day, nor the moon by night.

661. LS: *coffin being loaded into the hearse, as the crowd mills around it (seen from the church doorway)*
MINISTER: The Lord shall preserve thee from all evil. He shall . . .

662. *Low* MCU: *Lora, Susie, Steve, and an older, black woman. Steve steps forward and ushers Lora and Susie off, right.*
MINISTER (*off*): . . . preserve thy soul. The Lord shall preserve thy going out and thy coming in.

663. *High* MS: *crowd on the street. Sarah Jane rushes in and pushes her way through. She wears a simple black coat and hat. The camera cranes in after her, moving left as she crosses the street.*

SARAH JANE: Let me through! Please, let me through!
The camera continues to crane in and slightly to the right as a police officer attempts to stop her.
POLICEMAN: Stand back, Miss!
SARAH JANE: But, it's my mother!
POLICEMAN: Stand back, Miss!
SARAH JANE: I'm telling you—it's my mother! (*She sobs. She breaks away and runs to the hearse, the camera following behind her. A pallbearer tries to stop her.*)
PALLBEARER: Please—please, miss!
Sarah Jane pushes past him and runs toward the hearse, the camera following; she throws open its back doors and leans on the coffin.
SARAH JANE (*sobbing*): Mama!
664. MS: *Lora and Steve, seen over the top of a limousine. They look off, toward Sarah Jane, reacting.*
SARAH JANE (*off-screen, sobbing*): Mama!
665. CU: *Susie in the limousine, looking out.*
666. MS: *Sarah Jane, her head resting on the coffin, sobbing.*
SARAH JANE (*sobbing*): I didn't mean it! I didn't mean it!
667. CU: *Sarah Jane, her head resting on the coffin, sobbing.*
SARAH JANE (*sobbing*): Mama! Do you hear me! I'm sorry! I'm sorry, Mama! Mama, I did love you! (*She sobs.*)

668. MS: *pan left with Lora hurrying left from the limousine to Sarah Jane at the hearse. She pulls Sarah Jane around to face her, as the camera moves in.*

    LORA: Oh, Sarah Jane! Sarah Jane, don't!

    Sarah Jane leans against the coffin and the camera pans a bit left.

    SARAH JANE (*sobbing*): Miss Lora—Miss Lora, I killed my mother! I killed her! I wanted to come home! Now she'll never know how much I wanted to come back home!

    Lora pulls her away and they exit right, the camera panning.

    LORA: Come on. Come with us.

    A pallbearer walks into the frame from the right, and closes the hearse doors.

669. MCU: *Susie, seated inside the limousine, as seen through the side window. Sarah Jane, Lora, and Steve enter and sit down. The car drives off, left.*

670. *High* ELS: *street as a marching band and white horses parade by.*

671. LS: *side of street, with crowds along the curb. Two mounted policemen ride by.*

672. LS: *street, as seen from the inside of a store, through the fogged up windows. A sign on the glass (seen in reverse) says "Costume rentals."*

673. MS: *some women and a young girl on the street crying and looking off, toward the procession.*

674. MS, *dolly: marching band walking left down the street, playing their instruments. Crowds are seen in the background along the street.*

675. *Low* MCU: *a young boy on the street against the background of a bakery window. A hand reaches in from off-screen to remove his hat.*

676. LS: *crowd watching the funeral procession go down the street. A little boy stands above the scene, on the base of a statue, in order to get a view.*

677. *Low* CU: *some women and a man on the street, looking off (at the funeral procession). Some people stand above on fire escapes in order to get a view.*

678. MCU: *white horses passing, with crowds of people on the street in the background. The camera begins to move left with the horses.*

679. MCU: *Lora, Susie, and Sarah Jane in the limousine (as seen through the side window). As it moves left, the camera moves with it.*

680. MS: *band passing on street with crowds of onlookers in the background.*

681. LS: *hearse being pulled by white horses, as seen from inside the fogged up windows of the costume rental store (as in 672).*

682. CU: *side of hearse as it passes. As it reveals the coffin inside (through a glass side panel), the camera dollies along with it.*

683. MCU: *Lora, Susie, and Sarah Jane inside the limousine, as seen through the side window. The camera moves with the limousine. Susie turns to*

> *Sarah Jane and the camera moves in through the window, as Lora puts her arms around Sarah Jane, who leans her head on Lora's shoulder. Lora holds out her hand to Susie (in the foreground) and smiles at her.*

684. CU: *Steve inside the limousine, looking off toward the right (toward the women in the rear of the car). He smiles.*

685. CU: *Lora, Susie, and Sarah Jane, posed as they were at the end of 684.*

686. High LS: *hearse, pulled by horses, making its way down the street as onlookers stand on either sidewalk. Fade out.*

687. *Fade in: "The End" written over the image of glass beads piled up (as they were at the end of the opening credit sequence). The words "A Universal-International Picture" are on the bottom of the screen. The theme music comes in and concludes. Fade out.*

688. *Fade in: cast listing, printed over the image of glass beads. Another musical theme is heard.*

The Players

Lora Meredith	Lana Turner
Steve Archer	John Gavin
Susie (16)	Sandra Dee
Sarah Jane (18)	Susan Kohner
Allen Loomis	Robert Alda
David Edwards	Dan O'Herlihy

689. *Dissolve to a continuation of the cast listing.*

Sarah Jane (8)	Karen Dicker
Susie (6)	Terry Burnham
Receptionist	Sandra Gould

And Presenting

Juanita Moore as Annie Johnson
Mahalia Jackson as Choir Soloist

Fade out.

Contexts

Source

Sirk's *Imitation of Life* was based on a popular novel of the same name written by the American author Fannie Hurst (1889–1968). It was originally published by the Pictorial Review Company in 1932. During Hurst's career (between 1918 and 1961), some twenty-eight films were adapted from her literary works, often with multiple versions of the same property (as was the case with *Imitation*). Among the best known such films are: *Mannequin* (1926), *Back Street* (1932, 1941, and 1961), *Four Daughters* (1938), *Four Wives* (1939), and *Humoresque* (1920 and 1946).[1]

The novel *Imitation of Life* concerns Bea Pullman, a woman who is widowed at an early age, becoming the sole support of a young daughter and an aging father. Residing in Atlantic City, New Jersey, she takes over her deceased husband's business —selling maple syrup to hotels, restaurants, and concessions along the Boardwalk. Bea's working is facilitated by her chance encounter with Delilah, a black woman who mistakenly approaches her for a job as a maid. Though Bea cannot afford Delilah's services, they forge an arrangement whereby Delilah and her daughter, Peola, come to live with the Pullmans in exchange for domestic labor. Delilah is an excellent cook and is known for her maple syrup hearts as well as for her waffles. Bea capitalizes on Delilah's cuisine by launching a line of candies and a chain of eateries (using Delilah as a product trademark)—which eventually bring Bea wealth and success as a restaurateur. As the years

1. The other films (excluding the two versions of *Imitation of Life*) that are based on Hurst's work are: *Her Great Chance* (1918), *The Day She Paid* (1919), *A Petal on the Current* (1919), *Just Around the Corner* (1921), *Star Dust* (1921), *Back Pay* (1922 and 1930), *The Good Provider* (1922), *The Nth Commandment* (1923), *The Untamed Lady* (1926), *Wheel of Chance* (1928), *The Painted Angel* (1929), *The Younger Generation* (1929), *Lummox* (1930), *Five and Ten* (1931), *Symphony of Six Million* (1932), *Hello, Everybody* (1933), *Young at Heart* (1954).

go by, the two women wrestle with problems of motherhood. Peola attempts to pass as white, causing Delilah to die of heartbreak; Bea's daughter, Jessie, falls in love with her mother's suitor. The first film adaptation of *Imitation of Life* appeared in 1934, directed by John Stahl, and starred Claudette Colbert as Bea, Louise Beavers as Delilah, Fredi Washington as Peola, and Rochelle Hudson as Jessie. It followed quite closely the narrative line of the Hurst novel.

Sirk's 1959 version (written by Eleanore Griffin and Allan Scott) substantially alters it. The story is updated to the 1940s and 1950s and casts the heroine as Lora Meredith, an aspiring actress. Clearly, this move extends Hurst's original theme of inautheticity, simultaneously crafting an association between theatricality and motherhood. While in the Hurst and Stahl versions the maid is central to the heroine's professional success, in Sirk's rendition, Annie Johnson resides purely on the domestic front. Despite these changes, the basic issues within the novel and film remain identical: female friendship, mother-daughter strife, race relations, work versus family. For this reason, it is

useful to look at the literary source, and I have chosen three passages that reflect these tensions. The first excerpt (from Chapter XV) recounts the initial meeting of Bea and Delilah. The second (Chapter XXX) concerns Bea's decision to send Jessie away to private school, and enacts a discourse of mother-daughter separation. The third (Chapter XXXII) describes Peola's attempt to *pass* as white at school. The film advertisement included (for the Chicago premiere of *Imitation*) makes clear how, even in 1959, the film was being sold as a Fannie Hurst property.

The Introduction discussed Fannie Hurst's friendship with Zora Neale Hurston, and speculated how this may have influenced Hurst's conception of *Imitation of Life*. Since this relationship has not been previously discussed in the literature on the film, it seemed useful to include in this section the women's published tributes to one another. For Fannie, Zora was "an effervescent companion of . . . dancing perceptions," a woman with "the gift of walking into hearts." For Zora, Fannie was a "great artist" who was "drenched in human gravy," an elegant woman who would "never be jailed for uglying up a town."

Excerpts from *Imitation of Life*

Fannie Hurst

M . . . aple syrup and delivery mattered so terribly. It actually gave one little time, beyond an obsessing concern for its creature well-being, to realize one had a baby. Countless little budding impulses seemed to have been nipped in the frozen garden of her expectations. Babies must live, and so the struggle for, rather than the fact of, its existence became paramount.

It was at the end of about the fifth month that it occurred to [Bea], in the light of the increasing orders, to write and obtain from Hiram T. Prynne, of the Sugar Mart, an additional five-per-cent discount for cash. It was also at the end of these months that her hypothetical forebodings of, "what if," resolved themselves into a happening that potentially, at least, was fraught with tragedy.

She returned home one afternoon to find her father seated rigid and unseeing in his chair, her child, as it had rolled from his unretentive lap, dangling and howling head down over the side wheel, where it hung precariously suspended by the lace hem of its dress, which had providentially caught on the lever by which Mr. Chipley propelled his chair. Except for her return, either the child would ultimately have tumbled to the floor or hung there head downward until its cries attracted the possible attention of Mrs. Tannehill, or ultimately ceased in suffocation.

The state of unconsciousness from which her father then emerged, without having been aware of his lapse, was the forerunner of a series to which he was to become subject. But the first was sufficient to stun Bea into the realization that never again could these two be left there alone in this state of their mutual impotence.

The much-mooted problem of a servant became no longer controversial. The crime had been in daring to makeshift so long.

The boon of the additional discounts in her dealings with Hiram Prynne would go a little way toward meeting the additional eight or ten dollars a month the hiring of a servant would entail, and besides, she was about to be initiated into the technique of raising money by way of the pawnshop.

There was one on Atlantic Avenue with the three balls over the doorway. Unbeknown to Mr. Tannehill, Mrs. Tannehill carried on quite a constant series of negotiations there.

The solid silver nut-bowl on the sideboard was reassuring reminder. Her

From *Imitation of Life* (New York: Collier & Son, 1933). (Originally published in 1932 by Pictorial Review Company.) The excerpts include: pp. 89–92, 206–225, 224–229 of the novel.

mother's dozen sterling-silver knives and forks and spoons. Her own pathetically new bridal outfit of prettily engraved silver fish set, dessert spoons, ramekin-holders, and bonbon dish. Her graduating gift of a blue enamel watch with its fleur-de-lis pin to match. If need be, her mother's gold watch with its chased gold case and long gold chain. If need be, too, yes, if need be, the gold horsehead with a tiny diamond eye which her father wore daily even now in his cravat. She would substitute an imitation one, slyly. What Father did not know would not hurt him. He knew so little. Sometimes she wondered if he knew of the death of Mr. Pullman. But in any event, life must go on. . . .

A visit across the railroad tracks to the shanty district where Selene had dwelt, revealed no one else in that particular house who was available for a position at general housework, "sleeping in."

There was the difficulty. Sleeping in. Most of the female domestic help, wives, sweethearts, or what nots of the thousands of negro waiters, chair-pushers, and miscellaneous helpers about town and the Boardwalk, demanded the freedom to return home evenings.

"No, ma'am, I cain't take no job at sleepin' in. I got a husband waitin' table at de Seaside Hotel, and three chillun needs me to put 'em to bed."

"No'm. I got to sleep home. I's married."

"Sleepin' in? No, *Ma'am!*"

It was on her disgruntled and discouraged way homeward across the railroad tracks, as she was mentally framing an advertisement to insert in the *Press,* that suddenly she emulated something she had seen her mother do. In fact, it had been the method by which she had secured the services of Selene.

"Do you know of anyone who wants a position for general housework, sleeping in?" she inquired of the enormously buxom figure of a woman with a round black moon face that shone above an Alps of bosom, privately hoping that the scrubbed, starchy-looking negress would offer herself.

"I sho does, miss, and dat's me. But I's got a three-month-old chile, honey. You white folks ain't got no truck with a black woman wid a chile. I's learned dat, walking my laigs off this mawnin'."

"You mean you would want to bring your baby, too?"

"Honey chile, I'll work for anything you is willin' to pay, and not take more'n mah share of your time for my young un, ef I kin get her and me a good roof over our heads. Didn' your maw always tell you a nigger woman was mos' reliable when she had chillun taggin' at her aprun strings? I needs a home for us, honey, and ef you wants to know what kind of a worker I is, write down to Richmon' and ask Mrs. Osper Glasgow, wife of Cunnel Glasgow, whar I worked since I was married . . ."

"You have a husband?"

"Died six months ago in the Atlantic City Hospital of a lung misery that brought us here from Richmon'. A white nigger, miss, that you'd never think would've had truck with the likes of me. God rest his soul. It wasn't 'til after de Lawd took him dat I learned it was a bigamist's soul. Ef you doan' believe I kin housekeep, miss, wid a baby under my arms, try me."

Why not! The child would insure this woman's permanence. In a town with nine thousand colored population, reliable houseworkers were nevertheless difficult to obtain. With the wives of waiters themselves veering from general housework and angling for the less confining duties of waitress or chambermaid, domestic help was what it had always been in Atlantic City—a nomadic procession of women with home ties of their own, or of slim young blackbirds with no stability whatsoever.

"Is your little one healthy?"

"The purfectest white nigger baby dat God ever dropped down in de lap of a black woman from Virginie. Her pap didn' leave her nothin' but some blue-white blood a-flowin' in her little veins. 'Twas de ruination of her pap, dat blue-white blood. 'Tain't gonna be hern. We's black, me and mah baby, and we'd lak mighty much to come work for you."

So, Delilah and Peola. . . .

Christmases, Easters, and Thanksgivings, except the last two of them, when she had visited her roommate in Baltimore, Jessie came home.

The summer vacations of her tenth, eleventh, and twelfth years, however, were spent in the Switzerland summer branch of Miss Winch's school, along with about twelve of the boarding girls, who were escorted by Miss Winch herself and a Miss Askenasi, junior member of the highly successful firm known as Miss Winch's Hudson School for Girls.

Admission into Miss Winch's school had been something of an achievement. With no prestige other than a business one, which in the nature of the case might have been a deterrent, the by no means simple circumstance of entrance to Winch's was achieved in a manner that mattered with intensity to Bea, because it seemed to place her under the first tribunal of her young daughter's judgment.

It had long since become evident to everyone concerned that the problem of the day-by-day propinquity of Peola and Jessie was one that would no longer keep laid.

"One of us has got to get t'other away from t'other, Miss Bea. Dem two chillun is turnin' black an' white on us now, in earnest. Your chile cain't go startin' in the same public school, tagged on to by mah nigger child—'tain't no good for both."

No argument to that. The time had come for the parting of two tiny ways which had converged successfully enough up to that point.

"You doan' want no public school for yourn, nohow, Miss Bea. Ain't you affordin' one of them fancy boardin'-schools for her?"

A small neighborhood girl who walked with her nurse in the park and sometimes invited Jessie to tea parties off miniature fine china in her own elaborate nursery, had already inculcated into a pair of laid-back and listening little-girl ears the magic of the name Miss Winch's School.

It was during those days of need of decision and action regarding boarding-school for Jessie, that Bea, rather than risk direct application at Winch's, keyed herself up to a piece of aggressive letter writing not easy for her.

MY DEAR MRS. GRENOBLE:

I read of your activities with much pleasure in the Atlantic City papers.

I wonder if you remember me and my first B. Pullman booth for the First Church Fair of which you were patron many years ago. You recall, we left cards at one another's home.

My little daughter is quite a young lady by now, and I desire to enter her in Miss Winch's Hudson School for Girls. Excellent references are necessary and, knowing yours would be that, I am, for old times' sake, requesting that you indorse my application.

Thanking you in advance, my dear Mrs. Grenoble, for any assistance you may give me in obtaining entrance for my daughter into a school of such fine rating as Miss Winch's, I remain

The reply, which immediately she began to await as something which was to determine so much of her status with her child, came with alacrity and enthusiasm.

So when she was seven, a rather lanky, knob-kneed little girl, whose first blondness had dimmed into a freckled sort of eclipse from which it was to emerge again, was entered as boarding student in a school that was practically to monopolize her, body and spirit, for the next decade of her life.

At the period when the circumstances that Jessie was almost the identical height of her mother was still a shock and a surprise to them both, there was not yet much to indicate the Jessie to come. Gone was that quality of golden childishness which had once made it a delight for Delilah to appear with her showy charge among the nursemaids in the park, leaving only a low glow of pallor over a child almost conspicuously a gawk. For the several years of this transition, Jessie, as Flake once put it, teasing her, hung from the joints, knees and elbows dominating her young weediness. There was not so much length, as looseness, of limb; a predisposition, too, not unlike her mother's, had been toward premature growth, except that there was something slab-like and boyish to her kind of slimness. Tender and tiny were these early maturities of Jessie, only half awake, reluctant there in the lathe-like flatness of her pallid body, with its budding breasts slow to emerge from the dream of sleeping flesh.

Even at fourteen, in her manner was something of the startled unease of a boy in a roomful of strangers—half shy, half rebellious, wholly inarticulate. Her blue eyes with their extraordinarily large black pupils darted, her breathing came short, and always her head was half thrown back as if to give ready momentum to imminent flight. A startled-looking little girl, as if her ears were laid back to sound as slight as the falling of a leaf, her eyes wide apart and unquiet, her expression listening, her attention cocked, like a squirrel's.

Time and time again the thought rolled over her mother: The child looks surprised about something. Perhaps she was born with some of my surprise that anything so different—so—so like a bird, could be her father's daughter. Or, for that matter, mine. We never imagined things together. We didn't know how. Us—to have begot her!

Strange were the feelings she engendered in a mother whose imagination had been unprepared for her. It was like holding a bright foreign bird captive in the hand and feeling it breathe fast of all sorts of fears and uncertainties, and then loving to release it and watch it hop exploringly around the house and sometimes actually come perch upon the shoulder.

And as she grew older, and her visits home from school more and more intermittent, especially when the summers in Switzerland became almost part of her school routine, that quality seemed out over her more and more.

She talked so little; so little that her mother came to have secret awe of her silence.

I am one of those mothers who isn't supposed to understand. There are probably teachers, that Miss Askenasi or Miss Winch, in whom she confides. She is more at ease, no doubt, in the homes of her school chums. She never brings them here. She will some day, though, when I give her the proper background. I wonder if I am educating her away from me. That will be a terrible thing, and yet I will go right on doing it. I wonder what she thinks of me. Or if she thinks of me. After all, in my world I stand for something. Wonder just how she feels about that. She never wants things like other children. Almost as if it embarrasses her to be beholden to me. I want to give her. Those are the things that draw parents and children together. Giving. If only there were something she terribly wanted. The right kind of home to which to bring her chums? She never complains. Only doesn't bring them. If only she were of a temperament to come to me, wanting things. We're so formal. It would even be darling if she would nag. Perhaps I am just one of those tired business men to her, wanting to buy my way into her affections. I'm away from home so much. Must seem terribly preoccupied by outside worries. Why, Delilah is a better mother to her Peola than I am to mine! Next year I am going to start a regular campaign to spend more time with her. Next year——

It was just about this time, though, when Jessie was her stand-offish fourteen, that she did something that amounted to a darling and tremendous trifle.

Home for the Easter holidays, a little strange about the house, noncommunicative, except with Delilah, whom she followed from room to room; or with her grandfather, who, even while a babe herself, she had babied, she suddenly, out of a clear sky, began what to Bea turned out to be the delightful inauguration of addressing her as "B. Pullman."

"Hello, B. Pullman!" she had cried, kissing and greeting Bea the evening that, appalled, overwhelmed, and almost unbearably excited, she had entered the apartment after catching Virginia Eden's proposition on the fly.

A dozen methods of procedure for raising the initial downpayment of good-will moneys, mental maneuverings for collateral for loans, were pressing against the hot and troubled inner surface of her forehead as she turned her latchkey that night, conscious that what she needed was to forage, face down, into a bed Delilah would turn back for her, and confront, in a spangled darkness and concentration created by tightly squeezed eyes, the gorgeous dilemma into which a stubbornness of purpose, over which she seemed to have no particular control, had crowded her.

Fishrow in her lap! Wanting it with all her intensity, she nevertheless felt pinioned, appalled, frightened by it. This dazzling project of Fishrow! As if already the arrival of her child for the Easter holidays had not been relegated to a corner of her mind by circumstances that kept nudging and crowding at her for attention.

On top of her latest determination to open a Pullman in the Wall Street district, with a lease pending for precious footage in the financial district, with Flake in Detroit following up an important location lead there, and the final payment of a twenty-eight-thousand-dollar note to Frazier Bank to be met that week, here an additional something had developed, of her own stubborn volition, it is true, that staggered her.

Partnership acquisition of a good parcel of land, its subsequent subdivision and resale under highly restricted and profitable conditions, was one thing; lone-hand operation another. No two ways about it, whatever of considerable and canny acumen she, Bea, had been able to bring to the immensely difficult task of the purchase of a block of individually owned lots, with prices mounting as suspicion of a promoting project developed, Eden's indispensable contribution had been the important list of the right names she had been able to commandeer as purchasers of building lots in Fishrow.

Twelve lots in all, eight of them, including the double one to Mrs. Kan Casamajor, had sold according to Eden's insatiable lust for names.

Due to certain perceptions in Eden, perceptions entirely lacking in Bea, the quite remarkable balance of at least two of the town's foremost social and professional signatures had been appended to Fishrow deeds.

To swing so growingly important a project alone from this point on!

"You play a lone hand best," Flake had repeatedly told her, after her involvement with Eden had started to show up fissures in their common ground. "It is sex o'clock in the garden of Eden. It is just plain six o'clock in yours. One of you will have to get out."

Well, it had been Eden.

Walking into her home that evening, weighted with this new aspect of an old fear of that perpetual bugaboo, her aloneness, it seemed little short of blessed dispensation to be met by the lovely phenomenon of her young daughter, thawed, of her own sweet will, into the sweet nonsense of: "Hello, B. Pullman! What's the use having a national institution for a mother unless you cry it out loud!"

Jessie's favors, when they came, could be quite lovely. Her over-consideration for her grandfather was one of them. During what was to amount, from this time on, to a practically sustained period of absences at schools in and out of America, not a week was to pass without some token, from a postcard to a package, finding its way to the old gentleman.

"It's so pitiful to me that some poor quirk in Grandfather's brain denies him the happiness of loving you," she told her mother once, a remark which Bea was to keep polished by constantly turning it over in her memory.

It is doubtful if he was ever to place quite definitely in his brain the identity of his granddaughter, except that his eye loved to rove after her, much in the fashion it would follow a mote of sunlight dancing along a wall. Her brightness moved and laughed and danced, like light. There was a male nurse, now, for the old gentleman. John, a taciturn middle-aged Scot, who was to remain with him until Mr. Chipley's demise some sixteen years later in Helsingfors, Finland, of all places, at the age of ninety-two.

Jessie's holidays meant long hours of relief for John, while she wheeled the sack-like figure of her grandfather in the sunny lanes of Central Park, or, with the serious, unamused face of a preoccupied adult, cut rows of paper dolls for him. Alas, they meant these holidays, the most curious exhibition of class consciousness between her and her erstwhile playmate of all hours, Peola, which Jessie now tried to meet with too much show of affability and the dark child with too much sullen reticence. It was for Delilah, however, that she reserved an almost demonstrative adoration; Delilah, who in turn paid her the perfect tribute of reciprocal devotion by emulating in Peola, as far as her sense of propriety dared, Jessie's clothes, hair-dress, and color schemes.

Demonstrativeness toward her mother was sufficiently rare to make the episode of the "hello B. Pullman" memorable. Extraordinary the quality of formal restraint between these two. Always had been. To the mother, who in all her lifetime had almost literally refused her nothing, her requests came timidly, if at all, and then usually by way of Delilah.

"Delilah, you ask the B. Pullman for me, when she comes home tonight, if I may spend Christmas holidays with my roommate, Madelaine Stanhope, at their camp up in the Adirondacks." "Delilah, you ask the B. Pullman for me if I mayn't have one of those fur skating-jackets the girls are wearing." "Delilah, it would help a lot if you would talk up with the B. Pullman the idea of another Switzerland summer for me."

"Law', chile-honey, why doan' you up and warm your mammy's heart by askin' yourself."

She never did. Or rather, she never could. The inhibiting something between these two kept them timid one of the other.

Sometimes it seemed to the mother, thwarted and yet adoring, adored and yet thwarting, that if literally she could hold the yellow head of this girl close to her for as long as she wanted—and that would be days, weeks; hold it as long as she wanted—that something inside her, the something that hungered, would reach out and draw this child of her being back again into the warmth of a body that yearned for it.

"You and your chile is too polite to each other, Miss Bea. What you need to git acquainted is some good old hollering fests, lak me and mine. We yells our lovin'. You two just hurts yourn."

True. It hurt terribly, to be shy of the child you loved. It made seem doubly precious any indication of thaw in her.

"Now is that nice? To address your decrepit old mother that way? What put it into your head, Puss? Where is your respect for the aged? Hello, Bea Pullman! The idea!"

"Well, you are, aren't you, everybody's Bea Pullman. Why not mine? Every time one of the girls or a teacher learns for the first time you're my mother, their eyes turn cartwheels!"

The thought smote her for the moment that their eyes might perform the phenomenon referred to, because of the indefinable snobbery that exists in all school worlds. In her own time, even back in the Atlantic City public school, children of mothers who "worked" were in a subtly relegated class. But none of that here. There was pride in Jessie's voice. Jessie was admiring her.

"I wonder, child, if you wouldn't like to come down one day, while you're home on this vacation, and see our new offices?"

"You bet!"

Actually the child seemed to want it!

If only there were time tomorrow. She would walk her through the offices—not exactly to show off, but for the girls and boys to have a look at her in her natty little velveteen suit, long black-silk legs, blond hair escaping her velveteen cap and flowing over her shoulders.

Tomorrow! Dread of it came surging over her like an engulfing wave. The very dawn of it would be tangled with problems almost too staggering to be faced. Too staggering—yet exciting—yet alluring. "Hurry, Delilah, my dinner. I've heavy going tomorrow."

"Here it is, Miss Honey-Bea, pipin' hot, and I'll turn your bed down."

How well Delilah knew! Hours ahead face down into her pillow, lying there fully dressed, concentration pinioned, the darkness soaring in Katherine wheels before her squeezed eyes, until, finally, exhausted, she rose only in order to go to bed.

Her child had been sweet tonight. Something seemed to have pushed up through the fresh young earth of her. A budding of something that seemed to make her shyly but surely aware of Bea.

One must follow up this something so sweetly and newly begun between them.

But at the moment, so much more so even than usual, there was heavy going ahead.

Meanwhile, Jessie must wait. . . .

Without anyone knowing it, except the strange little crypt herself, Peola, at eight, had "passed."

By one of those feats of circumstance that seem to cerebrate and conspire, one Peola Cilla Johnston, entered into a neighborhood public school one morning by B. Pullman, as she paused long enough in her morning rush to enroll the child, was actually to pursue two years of daily attendance, unsuspected of what she chose not to reveal.

In a public-school system where the northern practice of non-segregation was common, it must have been a simple, if coolly calculated, little procedure, for the eight-year-old Peola to take her place without question among the children, never by word or deed associating herself with the handful of negro pupils in the class.

Only in a city whose density of population could make possible so fanciful an anonymity could this child's small ruse have been possible. Be that as it may, for over a period of twenty-eight months, living within a three-block radius of a public school made up of district children, the fact of Peola Cilla Johnston's race remained unbeknown to schoolmates and teachers alike.

As Delilah, with her face fallen into the pleats of a troubled mastiff, reiterated over and over again: "if I'd 'a' only known all dem months dat my child was a-cheatin' on color! Swear to de good Lawd who is mah Saviour, Miss Bea, I'd 'a' turned in mah grave if I was dead. Cheatin' on color befoh all dem teachers and chillun. Cheatin' on color jes' because de Lawd left out a little drop of black dye in de skin dat covers up her black blood. How kin I git mah baby out of crucifyin' herself over de color of de blood de Lawd seen fit in His wisdom to give her. Lawd, have mercy on mah child's soul, Miss Bea! She cain't pass. Nobody cain't pass. God's watchin'. God's watchin' for to cotch her."

The manner of the upset of Peola's little apple-cart came ultimately by way of an incident treacherously outside calculation.

A sudden freak rainstorm, little short of cloudburst, precipitating itself into the midafternoon of a day that had begun in sunshine, played such havoc in parts of the city that streets were flooded, cellars and subways inundated, and at certain intersections traffic, paralyzed, stood hub-high in water.

Alarmed as she viewed a wind-swept, tree-ravaged section of Central Park, Delilah, in a cape that gave her the appearance of a slightly asthmatic rubber tent, set out for the schoolhouse with galoshes and mackintosh for Peola.

"I starts out for her, hurryin' to git dar before school closin'. Her pap died from bronchitis he cotched in jes' such a storm. When I seen dem trees twistin' and heared water roarin' down de streets like Noah's flood, I started footin' it fast as mah laigs would carry me for mah child, knowin' her pap's weakness in de lungs. . . .

"Miss Bea, all of a sudden, standin' dar in de door of her schoolroom, askin' for mah chile, sweat began to pour on me lak it was rain outdoors. Dat Peola's little face, sittin' down dar in de middle of all dem chillun's faces, was a-stickin' up at me when I asked teacher for mah little girl, lak a little dead Chinaman's. Mah baby turned seventy years old in dat schoolroom. . . . Lawd help her and Lawd help me to save her sinning little soul. . . ."

This was strangely and really quite terribly true. The straight-featured face of this child, Peola, had the look to it of hard opaque wax that might have stiffened in the moment of trance and astonishment following the appearance of Delilah in that schoolroom, into something analogous to a Chinese masque with fear molded into it.

Bea Pullman, walking into the typhoon of hysteria that followed the arrival home after the thunderbolt which had smashed a small universe to smithereens, heard the first commotion while riding up in the elevator.

Facing Delilah in the center of the kitchen, her dark lips edged in a pale little lightening of jade green, was fury let loose sufficient to blast the small body that contained it.

Low-pitched fury, grating along on a voice that was not a child's voice.

"Bad mean old thing. Bad mean old devil. They didn't know. They treated me like white. I won't ever go back. Bad mean old devil. I hate you!"

"O Lawd! O Lawd! saw a brown spider webbin' downward this mornin' and know'd mah chile was a'comin' home brown—O Lawd! . . ."

"Go away—you! Yoo—yoo—yoooooo!"

The words out of Peola's fury became shrill intonations of the impotence of her rage, and finally with her two small frenzied fists she was beating against the bulwark of the body in the rain-glossed rubber cape, beating and beating, until her breath gave out and she fell shuddering and shivering to the kitchen floor.

"May de Lawd," said Delilah, stooping to pick her up as you would a plank, and standing there with her stiff burden outstretched like an offering, the black chinies of her eyes sliding up until they disappeared under her lids, something strangely supplicating in the blind and milk-white balls—"may de Lawd Jehovah, who loves us black and white alike, show mah baby de light, an' help me forget dat mah heart at dis minute lies inside me lak a ole broke teacup."

"Oh, my poor Delilah!——"

"Poor Delilah ain't no matter, Miss Honey-Bea. It's poor Peola."

They wrapped her in warm cloths, with memory of methods used in a previous attack similar to this, and chafed her long, slim, carved-looking hands, and, despite dissuading from Bea, there was a smelling muslin bag, with a rabbit foot attached, that Delilah kept waving before the small quivering nostrils.

"Dar's shameweed in dat bag, and asfidity. Shame, mah baby. Lift de curse from off mah baby. Lawd, git de white horses drove out of her blood. Kill de curse—shame de curse her light-colored pap lef' for his baby. Chase it, rabbit's foot. Chase de wild white horses trampin' on mah chile's happiness. Chase 'em, shameweed. Chase 'em, rabbit's foot. . . ."

"Delilah, that's terrible! That's wild!"

"It's de white horses dat's wild, a-swimmin' in de blood of mah chile. Drive 'em out, Lawd. Drive 'em out, shameweed. If only I had a bit of snail water——"

"Delilah, take away that horrid-smelling bag. Try this brandy—force the spoon between her lips——"

But in the end the services of the physician, with offices on the ground floor of the apartment building, were hastily enlisted.

"This child is in a state of nervous collapse. Has she had a shock?"

"Yes, Doctor. A little upset at school."

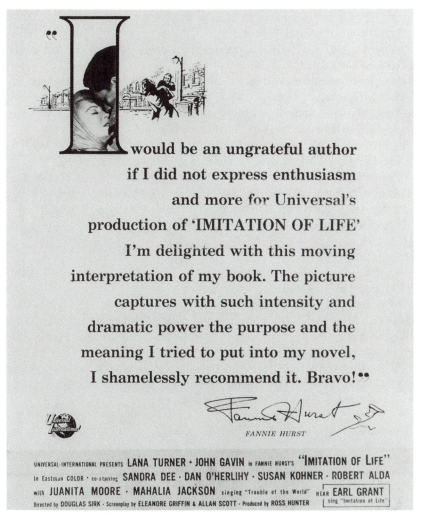

I would be an ungrateful author if I did not express enthusiasm and more for Universal's production of 'IMITATION OF LIFE' I'm delighted with this moving interpretation of my book. The picture captures with such intensity and dramatic power the purpose and the meaning I tried to put into my novel, I shamelessly recommend it. Bravo!

FANNIE HURST

UNIVERSAL-INTERNATIONAL PRESENTS LANA TURNER · JOHN GAVIN in FANNIE HURST'S "IMITATION OF LIFE" In Eastman COLOR · co-starring SANDRA DEE · DAN O'HERLIHY · SUSAN KOHNER · ROBERT ALDA with JUANITA MOORE · MAHALIA JACKSON singing "Trouble of the World" HEAR EARL GRANT sing "Imitation of Life" Directed by DOUGLAS SIRK · Screenplay by ELEANORE GRIFFIN & ALLAN SCOTT · Produced by ROSS HUNTER

This Universal Studio ad copy for *Imitation of Life* makes clear how much the film capitalized on the popularity of Hurst's novel, despite the fact that it had been written twenty-seven years earlier.

"Look at that eye," he said, rolling back the lid. "Rigid."

Poor Peola!

"You have a highly nervous little organism here to deal with, madam. You know that?"

"We do, Doctor."

"Public school?"

"Yes."

"Remove her. Let her have instruction at home or at least where she will receive individual instruction. Get me a bowl of good hot water, Mammy, so I can immerse her feet and get some circulation started."

"Get the one from my room, Delilah."

"Is this your only child, madam?"

"Why, Doctor, this is the daughter of the woman you just sent for the hot water! Peola is colored."

He screwed the top onto his thermometer, slid it into his waistcoat pocket, and reached for his bag.

"I see. My error. Sometimes difficult to detect the light types. Keep her in bed overnight. She'll be all right for school in the morning."

In the doorway he encountered Delilah with the bowl of steaming water.

"Innything else I kin do, Doctor, for to make her free of de spasms?"

"Spank her out of them when you see them coming. Gently, of course. Then dose her with castor oil. She may not be so inclined then to go off into them."

"Ain't you gonna put her into dis heah footbath I brung you, Doctor?"

"A night's rest will fix her up. Good evening."

"Miss Honey-Bea—what—how?"

"Dear, dear Delilah! . . ."

But it was out of the wretchedness of this was born one of the few desires Delilah could ever by inveigled into expressing.

"Miss Bea, I'd love it, when mah chile gets well, for to send her away to school like Miss Jessie. Not no boarding-school, of course, but dar's a colored school teacher in Washington I used to work for could tell me whar I could find a private learnin'-school for mah baby. . . ."

Two weeks later, as boarder and pupil, Peola was installed in the home of Miss Abbie Deacon, daughter of a colored professor of mathematics at Howard University and herself a teacher in the public schools.

Zora Hurston: A Personality Sketch

Fannie Hurst

The late Zora Hurston first swung into my orbit when she was a new graduate of Barnard College. About a decade later she was to swing out of the orbit of so many of us into a mysterious limbo of sustained silence. It required nothing short of her recent death at fifty-five to reveal her whereabouts.

She walked into my study one day by telephone appointment, carelessly, a big-boned, good-boned young woman, handsome and light yellow, with no show of desire for the position of secretary for which she was applying. Her dialect was as deep as the deep south, her voice and laughter the kind I used to hear on the levees of St. Louis when I was growing up in that city. As Zora expressed it, we "took a shine" to one another and I engaged her on the spot as my live-in secretary.

What a quaint gesture that proved to be! Her shorthand was short on legibility, her typing hit-or-miss, mostly the latter, her filing, a game of find-the-thimble. Her mind ran ahead of my thoughts and she would interject with an impatient suggestion or clarification of what I wanted to say. If dictation bored her she would interrupt, stretch wide her arms and yawn: "Let's get out the car, I'll drive you up to the Harlem bad-lands or down to the wharves where men go down to the sea in ships."

Her lust for life and food went hand in hand. She nibbled constantly between meals and consumed dinner off the stove and out of the refrigerator before the meal was served. "Sorry I ate all the casaba melon for tonight's dessert, I was hungry for so many years of my life, I get going nowadays and can't stop."

This was before her first book. Up to this time she had mentioned only vaguely her writing intention and ambitions.

One day after reading the manuscript a strange young man had submitted for my opinion, I dictated a letter to him. When Zora gave it to me to sign, she pointed out that she had added a final paragraph of her own, something to this effect: "I, the secretary, have also read your manuscript. I think better of it than Miss Hurst. Atta-Big-Boy!"

Rebuke bounced off of her. "Get rough with me if you want results. I've been so kicked around most of my life that your kind of scolding is duck soup to me." But after more and more of the same her gay unpredictability got out of hand. "Zora," I exploded one morning after she yawningly announced she was not in the mood to take dictation but felt like driving into the countryside, "consider

From *Yale University Library Gazette* 35 (1961): 17–22.

yourself fired. You are my idea of the world's worst secretary. As a matter of fact, I think I should be your secretary. But you are welcome to live on here until you are settled elsewhere." In the end she remained on for about a year, still in my employ, but now in the capacity of chauffeur. She drove with a sure relaxed skill on the frequent trips north, east, south, and west that we took together.

Uninhibited as a child, she had a subconscious fashion of talking to herself as she drove, expressing thoughts easily audible that ranged from gross vulgarities to florescence, from brash humor to bright flights of fancy and unsuspected erudition. A member of her own race, happening to cross in front of the car, was invariably the occasion for remarks provocative and revealing: "My, what a fine tail my cat's got. But you're not so light as you think. You are yellow, yellow." Next a line from Wordsworth or Millay might come tumbling from her memory.

She once remarked to herself" "I want to put Carl [Van Vechten] in a book. The way he is. The way nobody but me, knows." Then in song: "No one but God and me knows what is in my heart"; then spirituals for one mile, bawdy songs for the next.

An effervescent companion of no great profundities but dancing perceptions, she possessed humor, sense of humor, and what a fund of folklore! Although she seemed to have very little indignation for the imposed status of her race, she knew her people. Probably this insensibility was due to the fact that her awakening powers and subsequent recognition tended to act as a soporific to her early sufferings and neglect.

On one occasion we motored to Eaton, Florida, her birthplace, the first incorporated Negro town in the United States. There we visited her deserted home, a dilapidated two-room shack that indicated what must have been deep squalor, even when its clapboards had been new. "Everybody in this town had the same chance to work themselves out of it that I did," she observed. "But not your talents," I countered. "Then let them use elbow grease for what they are fitted to do. I used it when I had to. I scrubbed and dish-washed. The world will treat you right if you are all right."

It was a vulnerable philosophy at variance with much of her splendor, for splendor she had. It irradiated her work and her personality, or perhaps that is putting the cart before the horse. It is probably because of her vividness, both vulgar and exquisite, that in her girlhood she had never known the pangs of discrimination, which can be even fiercer than those of poverty.

But regardless of race, Zora had the gift of walking into hearts.

Again she once said of her favorite, Carl Van Vechten: "if Carl was a people instead of a person, I could then say, these are my people." Considering her ragged and tattered childhood, this lack of identity with her race was surprising. But in spite of herself her rich heritage cropped out not only in her personality but more importantly in her writings.

Her book of folk tales, *Moses Man of the Mountain,* was written out of race memory, if such a thing there be; her autobiography, *Dust Tracks on a Road,* was the result of experiences conditioned by race. But she herself was a gift both to her race and the human race. That she died in poverty and obscurity was because for a decade at least she had deliberately removed herself from the large group of us who felt puzzlement and still do. Where lurked her ultimate defeat, ending in retreat? Why and how?

Despite her bright accomplishments, her books, including *Tell My Horse* (the result of her explorations into Haiti), *Their Eyes Were Watching God, Dust Tracks on a Road,* are Negro Americana, to the smell of fried chitterlings, which by the way she loved.

Yet the inescapable conclusion persists that Zora remains a figure in bas relief, only partially emerging from her potential into the whole woman. She lived laughingly, raffishly, and at least in the years I knew her, with blazing zest for life. Daughter of a combined carpenter and self-ordained Baptist minister, she sang with the plangency and the tears of her people and then on with equal lustiness to hip-shuddering and finger-snapping jazz.

Illogically, indeed incredibly, irresponsibility was one of Zora's endearing qualities. Zora late, Zora sleeping through an appointment, Zora failing to meet an obligation, were actually part of a charm you dared not douse. One spring, after she was earning with her pen and living in her own little apartment, she importuned me to consent to visit and address one of her classes at Columbia University where she was majoring in anthropology under Dr. Franz Boas. I agreed, and on the appointed day arrived at the University only to find it closed for the Easter holidays and Zora off visiting friends up-state. She was casual about it all and, strangely and uncharacteristically, so was I.

And withal, that recurring and puzzling trait, lack of indignation. On our excursions, we repeatedly encountered the ogre of discrimination. At hotels, Zora was either assigned to servants' quarters or informed that they were full up. When I also refused accommodations, Zora's attitude was swift and adamant: "If you are going to take that stand, it will be impossible for us to travel together. This is the way it is and I can take care of myself as I have all my life. I will find my own lodging and be around with the car in the morning." And that was the way it was, although an ironic incident broke its continuity.

One hot August day returning from Vermont, we drove past a well-known Westchester County hotel. An idea struck me. Zora, in a red head-scarf and one of her bizarre frocks of many colors, looked hot and tired from a full day's driving. At my sudden request we stopped before the Inn. "Do me a favor, Zora. No questions please. Follow me." At the dining-room entrance I pushed ahead. A head-waiter appeared, his expression, when he saw Zora, as if a window shade had been drawn over his face. Before he could come through with the usual, "Sorry, everything reserved," I announced, "The Princess Zora and I wish a table." We were shown to the best in the room.

Following a good meal and some levity, Zora made a remark that revealed for an instant her mental innards: "Who would think," she soliloquized as we resumed driving, "that a good meal could be so bitter." Thus we must rest content with the memory of Zora, a woman half in shadow.

She lived carelessly, at least at the time I knew her, and her zest for life was cruelly at odds with her lonely death.

But death at best, is a lonely act.

But to life, to her people and to people, she left a bequest of good writing and the memory of an iridescent personality of many colors.

Her short shelf of writings deserves to endure. Undoubtedly her memory will in the minds and hearts of her friends. We rejoice that she passed this way so brightly but alas, too briefly.

Two Women in Particular

Zora Neale Hurston

Two women, among the number whom I have known intimately force me to keep them well in mind. Both of them have rare talents, are drenched in human gravy, and both of them have meant a great deal to me in friendship and inward experience. One, Fannie Hurst, because she is so young for her years, and Ethel Waters because she is both so old and so young for hers.

Understand me, their ages have nothing to do with their birthdays. Ethel Waters is still a young woman. Fannie Hurst is far from old.

In my undergraduate days I was secretary to Fannie Hurst. From day to day she amazed me with her moods. Immediately before and after a very serious moment you could just see her playing with her dolls. You never knew where her impishness would break out again.

One day, for instance, I caught her playing at keeping house with company coming to see her. She told me not to leave the office. If the doorbell rang, Clara, her cook, was to answer it. Then she went downstairs and told Clara that I was to answer the doorbell. Then she went on to another part of the house. Presently I heard the bell, and it just happened that I was on my way downstairs to get a drink of water. I wondered why Clara did not go to the door. What was my amazement to see Miss Hurst herself open the door and come in, greet herself graciously and invite herself to have some tea. Which she did. She went into that huge duplex studio and had toasted English muffins and played she had company with her for an hour or more. Then she came on back up to her office and went to work.

I knew that she was an only child. She did not even have cousins to play with. She was born to wealth. With the help of images, I could see that lonely child in a big house making up her own games. Being of artistic bent, I could see her making up characters to play with. Naturally she had to talk for her characters, or they would not say what she wanted them to. Most children play at that at times. I had done that extensively so I knew what she was doing when I saw her with the door half open, ringing her own doorbell and inviting herself to have some tea and muffins. When she was tired of her game, she just quit and was a grown woman again.

She likes for me to drive her, and we have made several tours. Her impishness broke out once on the road. She told me to have the car all serviced and ready for next morning. We were going up to Belgrade Lakes in Maine to pay Elizabeth Marbury a visit.

From *Dust Tracks on a Road* (Philadelphia: J. B. Lippincott, 1942), pp. 238–243.

So soon next day we were on the road. She was Fannie Hurst, the famous author as far as Saratoga Springs. As we drove into the heart of town, she turned to me and said, "Zora, the water here at Saratoga is marvelous. Have you ever had any of it?"

"No, Miss Hurst, I never did."

"Then we must stop and let you have a drink. It would never do for you to miss having a drink of Saratoga water."

We parked near the famous United States Hotel and got out.

"It would be nice to stop over here for the night," she said. "I'll go see about the hotel. There is a fountain over there in the park. Be sure and get yourself a drink! You can take Lummox for a run while you get your water."

I took Lummox out of the car. To say I took Lummox for a run would be merely making a speech-figure. Lummox weighted about three pounds, and with his short legs, when he thought that he was running he was just jumping up and down in the same place. But anyway, I took him along to get the water. It was so-so as far as the taste went.

When I got back to the car, she was waiting for me. It was too early in the season for the hotel to be open. Too bad! She knew I would have enjoyed it so much. Well, I really ought to have some pleasure. Had I ever seen Niagara Falls?

"No, Miss Hurst. I always wanted to see it, but I never had a chance."

"Zora! You mean to tell me that you have never seen Niagara Falls?"

"No." I felt right sheepish about it when she put it that way.

"Oh, you must see the Falls. Get in the car and let's go. You must see those Falls right now." The way she sounded, my whole life was bare up to then and wrecked for the future unless I saw Niagara Falls.

The next afternoon around five o'clock, we were at Niagara Falls. It had been a lovely trip across Northern New York State.

"Here we are, now Zora. Hurry up and take a good look at the Falls. I brought you all the way over here so that you could see them."

She didn't need to urge me. I leaned on the rail and looked and looked. It was worth the trip, all right. It was just like watching the Atlantic Ocean jump off Pike's Peak.

In ten minutes or so, Miss Hurst touched me and I turned around.

"Zora, have you ever been across the International Bridge? I think you ought to see the Falls from the Canadian side. Come on, so you can see it from over there. It would be too bad for you to come all the way over here to see it and not see it from the Bridge."

So we drove across the Bridge. A Canadian Customs Official tackled us immediately. The car had to be registered. How long did we intend to stay?

"You'd better register it for two weeks," Miss Hurst answered and it was done. The sun was almost down.

"Look, Zora, Hamilton is only a short distance. I know you want to see it. Come on, let's drive on, and spend the night at Hamilton."

We drove on. I was surprised to see that everything in Canada looked so much like everything in the United States. It was deep twilight when we got into Hamilton.

"They tell me Kitchener is a most interesting little place, Zora. I know it would be fun to go on there and spend the night." So on to Kitchener we went.

Here was Fannie Hurst, a great artist and globe famous, behaving like a little girl, teasing her nurse to take her to the zoo, and having a fine time at it.

Well, we spent an exciting two weeks motoring over Ontario, seeing the countryside and eating at quaint but well-appointed inns. She was like a child at a circus. She was a run-away, with no responsibilities.

Fannie Hurst, the author, and the wife of Jacques Danielson, was not with us again until we hit Westchester on the way home. Then she replaced Mrs. Hurst's little Fannie and began to discuss her next book with me and got very serious in her manner.

While Fannie Hurst brings a very level head to her dressing, she exults in her new things like any debutante. She knows exactly what goes with her very white skin, black hair and sloe eyes, and she wears it. I doubt if any woman on earth has gotten better effects than she has with black, white and red. Not only that, she knows how to parade it when she gets it on. She will never be jailed for uglying up a town.

The Production/
The Star

ncluded in this section are documents and articles that provide a background for understanding *Imitation of Life* within the discourse of Hollywood circa 1959. The Universal-International "Production Notes" (which function as a press release) make clear how the studio wants to market the film—as a vehicle for the star, Lana Turner. Enormous attention is paid to the cost of her wardrobe and jewels, as well as to the trajectory of her hairstyles within the narrative. While we are told that the film represents "another mother role" for Turner (then thirty-nine and undergoing a transition in her image), we are also assured that "glamor is present in quantities surpassing many of her earlier screen triumphs." Also noteworthy is the discussion of the search (which "stretched two continents") for an actress to play the mulatto, Sarah Jane—and how Universal finds Susan Kohner (a white actress chosen over one hundred black performers) "an ideal choice." (Perhaps, equally "ideal" was the fact that she was a Hollywood insider—the "daughter of film agent Paul Kohner and Mexican film star Lupito Tovar.")[1] Interestingly, in the 1934 film version of *Imitation,* the comparable character (Peola) was played by a light-skinned black actress, Fredi Washington.

The "Production Notes" also make clear how the other players in the film rank in the Hollywood system. John Gavin is seen as the "ideal successor to such stars . . . as Rock Hudson and Tony Curtis" (also in the Universal stable). While it is noted that Gavin's wife, Cicely Evans, plays a bit part in the film, we are assured that (unlike Lora Meredith?) she "has no aspirations to become a full-time actress." Sandra Dee is at the height of her career and is the most "sought-after" teenage actress in Hollywood.

---

1. I do not mean to disparage the performance of Susan Kohner, which I find extraordinary.

Robert Alda is returning to Hollywood after a ten-year hiatus in the theater. Evidently, the "greatest [casting] search of all" pertained to the role of Annie Johnson, eventually filled by Juanita Moore. Ironically, we are told that she once sang at the Paris Moulin Rouge while, in the film, her mulatto daughter must pass for white to perform in Hollywood's "imitation" of the club.

Given Lana Turner's prominence as the premiere star of the film (and her status as archetypal Hollywood movie queen), the rest of the section focuses on her. Two essays contextualize Turner's performance in *Imitation* within the broader framework of her career. Charles Affron's piece focuses on two films in which Turner plays an actress—works that make "a fiction of performance": *Ziegfield Girl* (1941) and *Imitation*. Richard Dyer's article takes a broader viewer, attempting to sketch out Turner's larger screen *persona*. Writing about the films above, as well as *The Bad and the Beautiful* (1952) and *The Postman Always Rings Twice* (1946), Dyer finds Turner a mixture of "sexual" and "ordinary," and a star whose career is marked by "an unusually . . . high degree of interpenetration between her publicly available private life and her films." Furthermore, he finds her image extremely synthetic: "With Turner part of the fascination is with the manufacture itself."

The final piece (taken from the popular press of 1958) reports the "scandal" that preceded the making of *Imitation*—an issue rigorously excised from the Production Notes. (We are, in fact, given no biographical information on Turner at all, in comparison to numerous details about the other performers.) Noteworthy is the manner in which the journalistic discourse merges the levels of life and theater. Entitled *The Bad and the Beautiful,* it opens with a line reminiscent of soap opera and is organized in sections evocative of a scenario: "The Star," "The Crowd," "The Showdown," "The End."

Imitation of Life:
Production Notes

Bridging a span of 25 years without sacrificing a single moment of the dramatic impact of Fannie Hurst's great novel of the 30's, Universal-International has brought to the screen in color a modern-day version of "Imitation of Life" with Lana Turner, John Gavin, Sandra Dee, Susan Kohner, Robert Alda, Dan O'Herlihy and Juanita Moore heading an impressive cast of performers.

Producer Ross Hunter and Director Douglas Sirk—the same team that had made the 1954 film version of "Magnificent Obsession" one of the greatest box-office attractions in Universal-International's history—paired again to apply the same cinematic magic to "Imitation of Life." In its modernized state, the woman who achieved success by packaging pancake flour has become a great Broadway stage star; the ichthyologist who wooed her has been transformed into a photographer who wins fame in the field of advertising. The New York background of the story has been expanded to include Hollywood, too.

But the power of the drama has remained untouched. "Imitation of Life" still tells the same story of a woman whose career dominates her parental responsibilities, the daughter whose formative years are filled with loneliness, the light-skinned Negro teen-ager who battles to "pass" as white, and her broken-hearted mother who injects strength in everyone around her while she gradually loses the most important struggle of all.

"Imitation of Life" affords another mother role for Lana Turner, whose first departure from glamor portrayals to a mother role in "Peyton Place" brought her her first Academy Award nomination in a great film career that has already spanned 20 years of stardom. In this case, however, the glamor is present in quantities surpassing many of her earlier screen triumphs.

The most expensive wardrobe ever to gown a star in U-I history was accorded Miss Turner when Jean Louis, the noted stylist, was borrowed from Columbia to design 34 outfits for Lana, valued at $78,000. U-I stylist Bill Thomas designed outfits worn by Sandra Dee and Susan Kohner. Adding great lustre to this fabulous wardrobe was more than $1,000,000 worth of jewels loaned to the studio by the famous jewelry importing and designing firm, Laykin et Cie. Among the priceless gems worn by Lana are a set of Russian emeralds and diamonds valued at $240,000, a $50,000 star sapphire set, Oriental pearl-shaped diamond earrings worth $9,000, 12-carat multicolored sapphires worth $45,000, a 15-carat diamond set valued at $127,000; and a three-strand necklace of perfectly-matched cultured pearls selling at $4,300. Two armed guards stayed near Lana every minute that the fabulous gem collection was in use.

From the Museum of Modern Art Archives.

"Imitation of Life" actually features two Lana Turners. In the earlier scenes, Lana's hair is shoulder-length, becoming short-cropped and lighter blonde as the story spans a ten-year period. Fans therefore will enjoy the Lana Turner of her early starring days after her well-publicized discovery at the counter of a drug store, as well as the Lana of today, as beautiful as ever but a much finer dramatic artist in her 39th screen appearance.

The casting of John Gavin as the male star of "Imitation of Life" is further proof that Universal-International considers him the ideal successor to such stars developed at U-I as Rock Hudson and Tony Curtis. Launched with great fanfare as the star of Erich Maria Remarque's penetrating story of World War II, "A Time to Love and a Time to Die," Gavin is an ex-Naval officer and Stanford graduate who was lured into a film career by a close family friend, film producer Bryan Foy, and signed by U-I to a long-term contract without a dramatic test. Only three small roles preceded his leap to stardom. Standing 6 feet 4 and weighing 190 pounds, Gavin is married to the former Cicely Evans. In "Imitation of Life" Cicely, a stunning blonde, can be seen as the girl whom John discards to resume his romance with Lana. Mrs. Gavin accepted the role to serve as Director Sirk's good-luck charm (she was an extra in "A Time to Love and a Time to Die") and has no aspirations to become a full-time actress.

A search that stretched to two continents preceded the selection of Susan Kohner to play the light-skinned Negress who pretends she is white. Producer Hunter and Director Sirk interviewed almost 100 Negro actresses and tested five non-Negro thespians before deciding on Susan, the talented daughter of film agent Paul Kohner and Mexican film star Lupita Tovar. Susan, of German-Mexican heritage, is an ideal choice, but it was her superb talent as an actress, coupled with her physical appearance, that won her the role. Miss Kohner, who made her film bow several years ago as Audie Murphy's Italian girl friend in U-I's "To Hell and Back," has since concentrated more on a stage career, appearing on Broadway with Joan Bennett and Donald Cook in "Love Me Little," studying with Sanford Meisner and gaining experience in summer stock in the East. Her last film was opposite Sal Mineo in "Dino."

No other teen-aged actress in Hollywood is as sought-after as is U-I's Sandra Dee, who plays Lana Turner's daughter in "Imitation of Life." The role marked the sixth straight starring part in a ten-month period that included titled roles in MGM's "The Reluctant Debutante" and Columbia's "Gidget," as well as "The Restless Years" with John Saxon, and "Stranger in My Arms" with June Allyson and Jeff Chandler. Now 16 years old, Sandra was the highest-paid teen-age model of all time in New York before U-I brought her to Hollywood and the motion picture screen.

"Imitation of Life" is the second straight about-face in the acting career of former Oscar nominee Dan O'Herlihy. Dan, accustomed to villain roles, is emerging as a screen lover these days, having been paired with Jean Simmons in "Home Before Dark" before coming to U-I to play one of Lana's admirers in this production. Irish-born and trained in the famous Abbey Theater, O'Herlihy was singled out for Academy Award consideration via his powerful portrayal of "Robinson Crusoe." For his new career as a lover, Dan has added a trim mustache in the tradition of Barrymore, Gable, Fairbanks, Flynn and Taylor.

Hollywood spread the welcome mat for one of its favorites when Robert Alda returned to a Hollywood sound stage for the first time in ten years to portray Lana's theatrical agent in "Imitation of Life." As everyone knows, Alda left Hollywood after hitting stardom in the role of George Gershwin in "Rhapsody in Blue." His next success was even greater, as Sky Masterson in the greatest Broadway musical hit of many seasons, "Guys and Dolls." During recent years Alda has spent a great deal of time in Europe, starring in a TV series filmed in Holland, co-starring with Gina Lollobrigida in the Italian production, "Beautiful But Dangerous," becoming the first American ever to star in an original Italian musical comedy, "Moonray's Owner," and making records for Odeon Records of Rome. The big thrill in Alda's life these days is the acting success of his son, Alan, 20, with whom he has appeared in summer theater in the Midwest in "Three Men on a Horse," and who has just won an acting scholarship from the Ford Foundation.

The greatest search of all in the casting of "Imitation of Life" was to locate a Negro actress to play the part immortalized by Louise Beavers in the 1934 version of the film. After interviewing several hundred aspirants, Producer Hunter and Director Sirk settled on Juanita Moore, a former singer who had headlined at Paris' Moulin Rouge and London's Palladium. Miss Moore's career as an actress first blossomed a few years ago when she appeared in Los Angeles for Ebony Showcase in Jean-Paul Sartre's play, "No Exit." Now 36, Juanita played featured roles in such films as "Lydia Bailey" (her screen debut), "A Band of Angels" and "Something of Value." She also appeared on stage in "Take One Giant Step" and "Anna Lucasta."

Also appearing in "Imitation of Life" is the noted gospel singer, Mahalia Jackson, singing "Trouble All the Way" in the deeply emotional funeral sequence.

The famous Moulin Rouge in Hollywood makes a rare appearance in a true-life role for "Imitation of Life" in a sequence in which Susan Kohner earns her living as a showgirl. Featured in the musical sequence is the "Rockin' Chair Blues" number, a featured production number in the Donn Arden revue at the famous night spot, with Miss Kohner joining the regular show members in presenting the number.

In step with the current trend of title songs for movies, tune team Paul Francis Webster and Sammy Fain wrote "Imitation of Life," a ballad that is sung over the film titles by the newest singing sensation Earl Grant, who earned a master's degree in music at the University of Southern California before becoming a headliner performer. Grant has also recorded "Imitation of Life" for Decca Records.

Four Films of Lana Turner

Richard Dyer

Despite the enormous interest in stars, there has been very little study of them, and this (as I found when preparing a study guide for the BFI Education Advisory Service) has predominantly been sociological, concerned with how stars function in general ideological/cultural terms. Such concerns are certainly central to film studies, but we also need to know how stars function within the films themselves, that is, how the films articulate, carry, inflect or subvert the general ideological/cultural functions. This article examines the way a single star image, Lana Turner's, is variously used in films in relation to other elements such as the construction of character, narrative, *mise-en-scène* and so on.

Why Lana Turner? In part, certainly, because I like her; but her work also illustrates certain characteristic features of the star phenomenon. The four films discussed use her in different ways. In *Ziegfeld Girl,* the Turner image sends the film off course and in effect partly cracks open its central mythology, whereas in *The Postman Always Rings Twice* (hereinafter, *Postman*) the image both holds together and also exposes contradictory elements. *The Bad and the Beautiful* elaborates upon and finally celebrates the image, while *Imitation of Life* examines and scrutinises it, holding it up to the light so as to expose it. More generally, Turner illustrates three of the ways that stars function *cinematically* (that is, within the total signifying practice of the cinema industry situated within society as a whole):

1) her career is marked by an unusually, even spectacularly, high degree of interpenetration between her publicly available private life and her films. The star phenomenon depends upon collapsing the distinction between the star-as-person and the star-as-performer. This does not usually mean that the incidents of a film's scenario are taken to be actual incidents in the star's life but rather that they 'reveal' or express the personality or type-of-person of the star. In the case of Turner, however, not only do her vehicles furnish characters and situations in accord with her off-screen image, but frequently incidents in them echo incidents in her life so that by the end of her career films like *Peyton Place, Imitation of Life, Madame X* and *Love Has Many Faces* seem in parts like mere illustrations of her life.

2) In the earlier films, Turner's image exemplifies one of the major forms of relationship between a star and her/his social context, namely the reconciliation of contradiction. Stars frequently speak to dominant contradictions in social life—experienced as conflicting demands, contrary expectations, irreconcilable but equally held values—in such a way as to appear to reconcile them. In part,

From *Movie* (Britain) 25 (Winter 1977–78): 30–52.

by simply being one indivisible entity with an existence in the 'real world,' yet displaying contradictory personality traits, stars can affirm that it is possible to triumph over, transcend, successfully live out contradictions. In the case of Turner, this centres on her being strongly sexual, both for herself and for others (therefore in Hollywood-American terms, extraordinary) but also ordinary. As Jeanine Basinger puts it in 'Lana Turner' (Pyramid Books, 1976), 'She was as much the ice cream parlor as she was the perfumed boudoir.' An interesting feature of Turner's career is that films and publicity seem continually to be condemning or punishing her for this daring combination, yet her survival and growth as an identification figure bespeaks the hold of such a magic reconciliation of opposites on the cinematic imagination.

3) In Turner's later films, the processes of manufacture—the production of the images—are increasingly evident until they become an integral part of the image. With most stars, the point is to disguise the manufacturing so that they simply appear to be what their image proclaims them to be; with Turner, part of the fascination is with the manufacture itself—with her, it is actually beguiling to see the strings being pulled. This is especially true of *The Bad and the Beautiful* and *Imitation of Life,* and also of the Joe Morella and Edward Z. Epstein biography of Turner, 'Lana' (W. H. Allen, 1972), which focuses as much on the fabrication of Lana as on the 'reality' of Judy Turner.

Ziegfeld Girl

Ziegfeld Girl (1941) inherits from Turner's previous career her sexy-ordinary image. In the process of building on it, however, the film gets severely out of joint, turning a production-values-laden musical into quite a serious drama. The Turner parts of the film make explicit what also comes across in the Judy Garland and Hedy Lamarr parts—a fumbling, confused critique of the notion of woman as spectacle at its most glorified, to wit, the Ziegfeld girl.

The sexy-ordinary configuration of the Turner image was crystallised in four moments in her career prior to *Ziegfeld Girl:* her first film role in *They Won't Forget* (1937), her sweater-girl pin-ups, her marriage to Artie Shaw and her starlet roles taken as a whole.

In *They Won't Forget,* she plays a young woman whose every action breathes sexuality—getting her male school-teacher all flustered, telling a soda-jerk to put an egg in her malted milk 'as fresh as you,' and walking down the street with hips swaying and breasts bouncing. She is raped and murdered. The ordinary setting and the ordinary clothes, together with the extraordinary appeal, would be enough to enflame any real man, the film seems to imply (and we never get to know who the rapist and murderer in fact is), and insofar as the film is a message film, it seems to have been a protest against the corruption of the South rather than against rape.

The sweater girl pin-ups date from Turner's appearance in *They Won't Forget,* but they became so widespread in the subsequent buildup that their meaning became rather more generalised. The encapsulate the sexy-ordinary configuration. On the one hand, a sweater is not a glamour garment—it is something cheap, practical, available everywhere. (In none of the portraits does Turner appear to be wearing an extravagantly styled sweater or one made of costly stuff.) On the other hand, worn by Turner, it became blatantly erotic, showing off the breasts, clinging to the waist. The rigid separation of women stars into homely-but-sexless (loose or flattening garments, including sweaters) or sexy-but-exotic (fetishistic fabrics, outlandish designs heightening body features) was collapsed. The girl-next-door was that never-never sex bombshell, plain-knit and voyeur's delight were one.

In February 1940, Turner eloped with Artie Shaw. Four months later, she divorced him. Although sex in a direct form was not mentioned in the coverage of these events, they are still an inflection of the sexy-ordinary configuration. Shaw was a band leader, and the bands were the courtship, dating, heterosexual romance music of the day. Turner's first marriage was at the heart of America's love-and-sex culture. It was also impulsive, although this was not necessarily viewed as a negative quality—it could be considered charmingly youthful, though it had already intimations of immaturity. More important, it was over in four months. Turner's publicly available life was going wrong; something was going sour in the heart of ordinariness.

Certain patterns of the Turner image, then, were beginning to take shape—sexiness perceived in ordinariness, but also associations of this with youth/immaturity and trouble. The starlet roles between *They Won't Forget* and *Ziegfeld Girl* do not appear to have elaborated upon this, but it is clear that the ambiguity of Turner's image was sufficient for MGM to feel equally happy casting her as a good girl (*We Who Are Young*, 1940) or a bad (*Love Finds Andy Hardy*, 1938), a sexpot (*Calling Dr. Kildare*, 1939) or a down-to-earth student (*Dramatic School*, 1938). I think one could argue, as a general rule of the functioning of stars in films, that a star's very physiognomy carries the meanings of her/his image in whatever film she or he makes, in whatever character she or he plays (cf. Lawrence Alloway: 'The Iconography of the Movies' in *Movie 7*, reprinted in 'Movie Reader'). Thus, short of being strenuously performed against the image, it is likely that by 1940 the character played by Turner, just because it was played by her, was already sexy-ordinary, no matter whether the film made something of it or not and virtually regardless of the character as scripted.

Ziegfeld Girl is very conscious of the images of its three main stars, Turner, Garland, and Lamarr. Narrative and treatment are tailored to them. Garland is established as having a vaudeville background and thus all the know-how of the born-in-a-trunk pro; she is dressed in little girl suits and has her requisite wistful follow-up to 'Over the Rainbow' in 'I'm Always Chasing Rainbows' as well as her jazzy, up-tempo spot, 'Minnie from Trinidad.' With Lamarr, everything promotes her remote, exotic beauty—she is foreign, married to a violinist (hence associated with Artistic Beauty), and has no thought of becoming a Ziegfeld girl when the star of the show (Frank Merton/Tony Martin) is stunned by her beauty as he passes her; a glistening close-up shot of her is often inserted into her scenes with other people (whereas it never is of Turner or Garland), which effectively sets her apart from the interaction; in the numbers, she is the statuesque central figure, coming closest to Ziegfeld's prescriptions for his 'girls.' The film's over-all structure can accommodate these two images—they can be used effectively in the numbers, and fit two show businesswomen types (though, as I'll argue below, there are elements of criticism of Ziegfeld girlhood even in Lamarr and Garland). Turner (Sheila) fits less happily.

The film begins by building on the ordinary side of the Turner configuration. She is 'discovered' operating a lift in a department store. Neither a pro nor an exotic beauty, she is just an ordinary working girl rocketed to stardom. This conforms with the publicity surrounding Turner's own 'discovery' at a soda fountain in a Hollywood Boulevard drug store (this is inaccurate, though not drastically so), and meteoric rise to fame (it took rather longer than was publicly known). Her first act on being asked to audition for Ziegfeld is to go and buy an exorbitantly priced leopard-skin coat. This again conforms with her image as a girl who gets a real lift out of possessions. As one fan magazine of the period noted, 'She glitters whether on the beach, in the drawing room, or in the studio restaurant dressed in gingham. She admits she enjoys the luxury that stardom has brought her. And she drives a fire-engine red coupé. Lana is the most spectacular personality to be thrown up by films since Clara Bow.'

Thus far, *Ziegfeld Girl* is simply reproducing a facet of Turner's image. However, as both Basinger and Morella/Epstein state, during the making of the film, MGM and the director, Robert Z. Leonard, were so impressed by Turner that they expanded her role. This affects the film in three ways—building on the elements of the Turner image adds complexity to that image, the impact of her role comes into conflict with the musical's generic requirements, and her increasing centrality also calls into question the film's central motif.

Building on the image of the ordinary girl rocketed to a fame she luxuriates in brings in the complexity of response claimed by the Turner sexy-ordinary image. There is certainly a basic level of delight of the kind the fan magazine evinced. But there is also and equally pathos and condemnation. The impulsive desire to spend, and spend big, is perhaps in itself sympathetic, and is rendered more so in a key scene between Sheila/Turner and her old truck-driver boyfriend Gil (James Stewart). Her desire is located in deprivation, a deprivation the film is careful not to link with her class situation but with her unlucky experience as a child of always being the one who arrived at a party 'after the ice cream ran out.' We are asked to be sorry for her—doubly so when, running after Gil as he leaves in disgust, she trips on the minks she has strewn before him to proclaim her new wealth. We are here being asked to be sorry for her materialism, for what led to it in the first place and what it is doing to her now. Yet in her pursuit of wealth, she goes to the bad. She acquires a sugar daddy, Geoffrey, then, when she snubs him, she takes to drink, is suspended from the Follies, and winds up in a seedy bar with Geoffrey, now himself down and out. It is no longer clear what sort of response is being elicited. She has broken taboos on women's behaviour—losing her man by demanding he adapt to her lifestyle, getting drunk. These demand condemnation (by the conventions of the film's day), and I do not know how far the pathos elements let her off the hook. This ambiguity, the 'bad' woman who suffers for her badness and thus becomes an identification/sympathy figure is the emotional timbre that is caught in all her subsequent films.

As the dramatic-pathetic elements increase with Sheila/Turner's downfall, so they come to occupy the centre of the film. Not only does this mean that the other two star characters' careers are given short shift (as narrative developments in musicals often are), but it also begins to interfere with what is a musical's *raison d'être*, the numbers. Throughout it is clear that the numbers do not quite know what to do with Turner—she has no musical gifts (or none that film has ever developed), and although she would be fine as one of the chorines in Busby Berkeley's Warners depression musicals, the kind of thing Berkeley is staging here, all haughty parading and baroque head-dresses and trains, does not suit her small frame and 'common' face—not yet in her career, anyway. By the time of the last big production number, 'You Gotta Pull Strings,' the Sheila/Turner plot dominates everything and, since the point is that she is not in this number, having been suspended from the Follies, the emotional weight in the cross-cutting between the number and her in the theatre watching is decidedly with her. All the more so when, unable to watch any more, despite having struggled out of her alcohol-induced sick bed to be there, she leaves the auditorium and the film stays with her and not the number. As she hears the finale walk-down music strike up on stage, she holds herself up and begins to walk down the entrance stairs. Thus for the climax of the number (and of all the numbers in the film) we see Turner in the 'surrounding' narrative and not the girls in the 'central' number.

This final walk-down also has a further significance in the film. The walk-down is the defining motif of the Ziegfeld show—it is the moment at which the girls parade themselves and are thus 'glorified' (*sic*). It is used five times in relation to Sheila/Turner. The first is in the first big production number, 'You Stepped out of a Dream.' In this, the camera follows Turner as she walks down the circling ramp. Garland and Lamarr are not similarly treated, although the latter is given a couple of cut-in close-ups of her sculptured face, and she is distinguished from both Garland and Turner by her dress, which is more *haute couture,* less show-girl in style. The effect of the camera sticking with Turner in this number, which for all three characters is their first night as Ziegfeld girls, is to stress her excitement at being a Zeigfeld girl and to associate the walk-down especially with her. The second use of the walk-down motif takes place the next morning at Turner's home (she is still living with her parents): she is trudging down the stairs until her brother says 'Here comes the glamour girl!'—then she straightens up, and descends the stairs as if on stage for the walk-down. Again, in the night-club in Florida, she walks down some stairs as if she and they are in the Follies, only this time it is after quarrelling with Gil, snubbing Geoffrey, and drinking too much champagne. Each walk-down is registering a moment in her career. The next is on stage, in the 'Minnie from Trinidad' number, during which she collapses, drunk, and the last is during 'You Gotta Pull Strings,' as described above.

The walk-down motif in relation to Sheila/Turner links her decline—which the film also, as we've seen, explains in terms of deprivation, materialism and going to the bad—to the core of the Zeigfeld show. In this way, by association, the whole enterprise of Ziegfeld—his girls, woman as spectacle—which the film was clearly set up to celebrate, is called into question. There are intimations of this through the Garland and Lamarr characters. The only one of the three to make it to the top is Garland—but then she has her roots in vaudeville, which is signalled in the film, through the character of her father, as being a more vital and authentic entertainment tradition. (Her father is played by Charles Winniger; in the film he teams up with Al Shean in a recreation of Gallagher and Shean, one of the legendary acts on the vaudeville circuit; this happens just before the enfeebled 'You Gotta Pull Strings' number and 'brings the house down'; effectively, vaudeville has the last say in the film's numbers.) Lamarr, on the other hand, leaves the Follies to join her husband when he gets a job; the very haughty beauty which makes her an epitome of the Zeigfeld girl also makes her 'superior' to show business. Between Garland and Lamarr, Zeigfeld gets it from low and high brows.

What Sheila/Turner adds to this is sex. Clearly, despite the 'Glorifying the American Girl' tag, Ziegfeld was peddling sexuality—but the glorification idea, his use of famous couturiers and chic designers, appeared to elevate his shows above the despised burlesque (which means striptease in American usage). Sheila/Turner drags it down again. Partly, the film takes on Turner's association with sexuality just by having her in it. In addition, some of the dialogue draws attention to it—for instance, when she is worrying about her make-up, Patsy (Eve Arden) wisecracks (as only Eve Arden can) 'Don't worry dear, they won't be looking at your face.' It is on her legs that the camera dwells in this first walk-down, aided by the wide parting in her sequined dress. And, again unlike Garland or Lamarr, it is as a pin-up that she acquires off-stage fame, even winding up on the wall of the garage where Gil works. The crystallisation of all this round Sheila/Turner and her special association with the walk-down motif puts a dent in the hypocrisy of Ziegfeld's glittering sex show. Add to that the emotional weighting given her, her virtually eclipsing the numbers by the end, and one can see how the decision to build on Turner's star image leads the film almost to overturn its own project. The brief scene of reconciliation with Gil (they are going to go to the country to breed ducks) and a perfunctory shot of Garland atop a wedding-cake-style set hardly suffice to set the film properly back on its course.

The Postman Always Rings Twice

Between *Ziegfeld Girl* and *Postman* (1946), Turner's sexy-ordinary image was consolidated. The war proved useful for this. Nothing is more ordinary in the public imagination than the serviceman. Thus the fact that, for instance, the sailors of the S.S. *Idaho* voted her their favourite star, that she married a service-man in life (Stephen Crane) and in a film (*Marriage is a Private Affair,* 1944), and herself joined the WACs in *Keep Your Powder Dry* (1945), all preserved her association with ordinariness. Equally, they preserved the association of that with other things—with plain sexiness in the case of the S.S. *Idaho* men. Indeed, throughout the war Turner was a major pin-up in men's magazines. The marriage to Crane (1942) went wrong—she married on impulse again, knowing next to nothing about him; he was, however, already married, so the marriage had to be annulled; then he got a divorce, but she would not remarry him and he tried to commit suicide twice; she discovered she was pregnant and they remarried; a year later (1944), they divorced, with Turner getting custody of the baby, Cheryl. Following the Shaw fiasco, it was as if Turner and marriage (ordinary marriage to ordinary men) did not go. Not that Shaw or Crane came out of it well, but both marriages set off the central Turner ambiguity—what she touches burns bad, but is that because she is bad or because she is irresistibly attracted to the bad? (And is being attracted to the bad itself badness?) *Marriage Is a Private Affair* similarly dealt with a G.I.'s marriage (after a three-day courtship) going off the rails, through his wife's (Turner's) infidelity, though all ends happily. More generally, Turner's status as sexy leading lady was confirmed by her teamings with Clark Gable in *Honky Tonk* (1941) and *Somewhere I'll Find You* (1942).

These ambiguities, the role of impulse, the play on badness and on the sexy-ordinary configuration all came in useful for the Turner character, Cora, in *Postman*. Without them, the film courts incoherence in its construction of this central character.

I want to consider *Postman* chiefly in terms of the key but neglected question of how a character is constructed in a film. What I want to suggest is that there are here three different methods of character construction, which fit uneasily together. These methods are structural (we understand characters by what they do in the plot or how they function in the narrative), motivational (the reasons provided by dialogue and sometimes other elements such as performance and mise-en-scène as to why a character does such-and-such a thing) and star-based (the star's image already gives the character a certain set of traits). These methods are of course not confined to *Postman*, but I don't want here to get into generalising too hastily from *Postman,* from the methods it uses and the particular way it combines them. One general point, however, is that these methods, like nearly all others, contribute to the construction of an apparently autonomous character (rather than one acknowledged as an aspect of the film's point(s)-of-view)—corresponding, of course, to how we normally talk about characters, ascribing motives and feelings to them as if they are real people independent of us and a narrative's author.

The initial problem with *Postman* is who the film is really about. Structurally, it is a *film noir,* which means that, like nearly all *films noirs,* the narrative is centred on the male protagonist (Frank/John Garfield). His voice-over leads into the film and recurs at various points until we realise he has been telling his story to a priest in prison. Since the film ends there and a priest has been the listener, a certain status is conferred retrospectively on Frank as both the subject of the narrative and its truthful narrator. The film can then be seen as being 'about' the hero's doom. The sense of doom, fate, entrapment is reinforced by the obsessive doubling of events and images in the film, both major narrative incidents (two accidents with a lorry, two attempts to kill Nick, two attempts to leave the cafe, two trials for murder) and minor details of treatment (two lipstick rolls, two vital notes in the cash register, two pushes at the car on the second attempt on Nick's life, the echoes at the lake, the name of the cafe, The Twin Oaks, and the title of the film).

In this context, the woman is a function of the ensnaring structure. The *femme fatale* need not necessarily be evil, but she is the means by which the hero gets drawn into the plot, and hence his doom (whether or not there is a 'happy ending'). Indeed, it is more to the point if she is not simply and utterly evil, for it is precisely the hero's uncertainty on this point, the very unknowability of Woman, that really traps him. (Much of the pleasure of *film noir* resides in the true knowledge of the woman, as good or evil, vouchsafed the hero and hence the [male?] audience at the end—e.g., *The Maltese Falcon, The Lady from Shanghai, Chinatown*).

At one level, Cora in *Postman* is a mere function of the film's structure. She is only there to be the means by which Frank enters the path that leads to his doom, to be the terrible object of his sexuality, terrible because his attraction to her is what leads him to the death cell. Her famous first appearance—the roll of her lipstick along the floor attracting his (and the camera's) attention, followed by a track back along the floor, up her bare legs to her white shorts and halter top—is very directly sexual, and throughout the film her brilliant white clothes are both eye-catching and a sign of the heat of the summer (with all that connotes). The wretchedness of women, in the mind of *film noir,* is that they are such a turn-on for the hero, with disastrous consequences for him (compare the logic of *They Won't Forget*). One can see Cora functioning like this throughout the film's structure.

Yet even in this first scene, it is not as simple as that. On the one hand, Cora as herself a subject is implied—the 'Man Wanted' sign in the opening shots of the film hangs over the scene, we can assume she has rolled the lipstick herself, and the manner in which she does her lips while looking at him suggests a deliberate making of herself into an object of desire. On the other hand, the burning hamburger, so obviously a symbol of lighted passions, and the general atmosphere of heat, suggest a sexual force generated between them both (a sense referred to by almost every reviewer as 'the chemistry' 'sparked' between Garfield and Turner). This sense of Cora as herself a force acting on the narrative derives from the motivational level of character construction in *Postman* being as emphatic as the structural. Cora, and Cora-and-Frank, are provided with reasons for doing things, whereas in other *films noirs* only Frank would be.

Yet as soon as this motivational level comes into play, further problems arise. If one looks at the motives Cora is provided with, they are ambiguous and contradictory almost to the point of incoherence. Why, as indicated by the film, does Cora get Frank to kill Nick? Because, pitiably, she is trapped into a marriage with a dreary older man, largely because she was fed up with other men bothering her ('I was never homey . . . I never met a man since I was fifteen who didn't want to give me an argument about it,' said fiercely/ruefully to Frank but looking straight ahead to camera; the scene where Nick tells her callously that she is to spend the rest of her life looking after his paralysed sister in Canada). And because she is ambitious (her repeated statements to the effect that she wants 'to make something' of herself and the cafe). And because she loves Frank (she leaves the cafe with him; her direct, i.e. 'genuine,' outburst in the kitchen, after she has been contemplating suicide with a kitchen knife, 'If you really love me, you would . . .'), and/or is manipulating him (in an earlier kitchen scene, we get a close-up on 'Can't you see how happy we'd be together?' in which her shifting eyes clearly signal manipulation). And because she is driven by a bad sexuality (the scenes on the beach; her provocative clothes; images of heat). Partly, what is happening here is that the film wants to give Cora motivations, including some that make her a sympathetic figure, but, as her (generic) function in the narrative is to be changeable and unknowable, the film has to keep giving her different, inconsistent motivations. Yet inconsistency on this scale risks being simply incoherent. The film's devices would betray themselves all too quickly without Lana Turner in the part.

Because it is Turner, the contradictions of Cora, and Cora-and-Frank, get an emphasis which amounts to a resolution (more or less—perceptions will differ on this). Cora is sexy-ordinary: her speech about not being 'homey' indicates this clearly enough, as indeed does the extraordinary sexual charge she carries in so suffocatingly dull a setting. The various motivations she is provided with can be loosely organised around the badness syndrome developed in Turner's image. She is attracted to the bad (adultery, murder); this makes her pitiable (she is trapped both by her situation of marriage and by the inexorable repetitions of the plot once she strays from marriage), but it also intimates that she may herself be bad (her sexuality, her manipulation and prompting of Frank to murder). Notions of coherence of character do not permit the coexistence of such traits (except under the rubric of woman the capricious and unknowable, which is not allowable here since, on the contrary, we know too much, and of that much is sympathetic), but notions of the star reconciling or holding in tension key contradictions in the culture (and thus effectively transcending them) do permit them to a certain extent. However, in the process, certain traits are subordinated. Thus Cora's driving ambition, which is granted legitimacy at the motivational level simply in terms of the time allowed it and the straight treatment of it, lacks force since it has no place in the Turner complex. As a result, one either ignores the ambition motive, or denies it legitimacy by regarding it as falsehood or manipulation, or one merely feels that it does not fit.

The motivations of Cora-and-Frank, as a couple and as murderers, are also aided by Turner's presence, though here she is less crucial to the film's coherence. The key to their murderous relationship is impulse. In each of the scenes in which they contemplate murder, a crash of music, where before there was none, signals the thought of murder arising from nowhere rational in their minds. The first of these scenes occurs after Nick, returning drunk from the laundry, nearly crashes into a lorry. Frank blurts out, 'I'd like to see him get plastered like that and drive off a cliff'; music in; they look at each other as Cora says, 'You didn't mean that, you were joking,' and Frank replies 'Course I was'; they kiss. The idea for murder arises spontaneously; music signals its impact; a kiss links it to passion. (In an earlier scene, Frank's suggestion of Cora wanting to make money so as to have some set aside when her husband dies is also met by music and a kiss, though murder as such is not mentioned.) The second such scene takes place in Frank's bedroom. Having elicited from him that he loves her, Cora, fingering the lapel of the dressing gown he is wearing, says 'There's one thing we could do.' Frank replies, 'Pray for something to happen to Nick,' and Cora says, 'Something like that'; music in; Frank exclaims, 'Cora!' Here the link between passion and murder is clearer, but murder is not actually directly referred to. It is clearly in Cora's mind, but she does not have to say the word for Frank to latch on. The music signals its arousal in their 'chemistry.' The third scene takes place in the kitchen, after Frank has discovered Cora with a kitchen knife in her hand. Here there is a more directly expressed impulsive outburst from Cora—'If you really love me, you would . . .' pause; Frank, 'Alright'; music in; Cora, 'No!' This last exclamation suggests that the idea for murder arose in her head without premeditation. Once again, the music suggests the intention to murder is an impulse rather than a rational or cold-blooded plan.

The film, then, does a lot of work on the notion of impulse, even without the input of Turner as Cora. The particular inflection she adds is suffering from one's own impulses. Her impulsive marriages in life had led to suffering of one kind and another, and the film roles reprised this. Consequently the pattern of impulse and entrapment in *Postman* can be read—I would argue, *was* read by Turner's fans—as a source of identification and sympathy. The attraction to bad (often meaning little more than sexual desire) can be seen as an uncontrollable, destroying impulse that anyone can identify with (especially in a sex-negative culture). Yet this means that, at the level of the star image's contribution to character, the film is about Cora at least as much as it is about Frank, even though structurally she is a mere function of his destiny. Thus, if in terms of the relationship between the motivational and star image levels, Turner serves to mask the contradictions of the *femme fatale* type (a type of course that reflects the male construction—and fear of—the female), in terms of the relationship between the structural and star levels, Turner serves to open up the tension between what women are for men and what that means for women as women. (I am not positing here either any brilliance on Turner's part—though I would never wish to denigrate her performing abilities—nor an untutored feminist sensibility on the part of director, writer or whoever; it is rather that in the relationship between her life/films and women audiences, a certain registering and defining of the female experience in this society was possible and that this happens in *Postman* simply because she is in it.) If that accounts for the film's near-incoherence and unsatisfactory feel, it also accounts for the fascination of its elusive play of fate and motivation.

The Bad and the Beautiful

In both *Ziegfeld Girl* and *Postman,* Turner's image contributes to the overall meaning of the film, partially undermining it in the former, largely coming to its rescue in the latter. With *The Bad and the Beautiful* (1953) and *Imitation of Life* (1959), the image becomes itself in part the subject matter of the film. By this time, however, the image's meaning has shifted in certain respects. The sexy-ordinary configuration has become 'glamour' (or, 'Lanallure'), and the badness both more extreme and more pitiable. Both these developments are reproduced, and celebrated, in *The Bad and the Beautiful.*

Glamour and ordinariness are antithetical notions. The ordinary and the everyday are by definition not glamorous. Yet glamour—or the particular inflection of the notion embodied by Turner—is based on manufacture, and can be seen to be the process—the industrial process—by which the ordinary is rendered the glamorous. The glamour industry, in which Hollywood played a decisive part, sold itself on the idea that, given its products, anyone—any woman, anyway—could become beautiful. Turner was living proof of this, and if, later in her career, none of the original material—the ordinary woman—showed through anymore, this was all the more proof that the glamour process worked. . . .

It is this element of manufactured glamour that is emphasised in *The Bad and the Beautiful.* Whenever there is a break in the filming within the film, a hairdresser or make-up artist steps into retouch Georgia/Turner's look. (They are in fact played by Turner's personal hairdresser, Helen Young, and make-up man, Del Armstrong.) The screen test sequence opens with a close-up of her eyebrow being painted in—as any assiduous reader of the fan magazines would have known, Turner had had her eyebrows shaved off for the role of an oriental handmaiden during the filming of *The Adventures of Marco Polo* in 1938, and they never grew again. This shot is (like the casting of hairdresser and make-up man) part in-joke, but also part reinforcing the idea of the manufacture of glamour, not just by heightening beauty that is already there but also by creating artificial beauty where there is nothing.

By emphasising manufacture, the film also emphasises the star image as an illusion. This is evoked in the first shot of Georgia/Turner. A maid answers the phone and says it is Mr. Shields; the camera moves across (is it to another room, or was the maid a reflection in a mirror?), showing us in quick succession first Georgia side-on in a mirror, then her back, then her face full on in a mirror. Already the film is giddy with reflection images, reflections, moreover, of a woman preparing her appearance at a dressing table. How can we, as we watch, pick out the levels of illusion here?—the illusion of reflection, the illusion of make-up, the illusion of the film we are watching . . . Georgia/Turner puts a black lace veil over her head, then turns to listen at the telephone receiver. The camera now finally homes in on her face (rather than the reflection of it), stopping at a perfectly composed glamour framing. The final frame of this brief one-take, then, is both really Georgia (or Turner . . .), not her reflection, and yet is also her at her most 'produced.'

What we have got in the final frame is the *real illusion*. For it is no part of the purpose of *The Bad and the Beautiful* to demystify glamour by foregrounding its manufacture. Rather, the processes of manufacture themselves become fascinating and . . . glamorous. The same holds true for the film's overall depiction of Hollywood. It is rather like a conjuror showing you how a trick is done by quickness of the hand—you are so impressed by the dexterity that you remain as dazzled by how the trick is done as you were before by its magic effect. (This relates to Minnelli's other films; see Jim Cook's remarks on *On a Clear Day You Can See Forever* in *Movie* 24).

Nor is this emphasis on the glamour of illusion-manufacture meant to detract from the notion of the star's special quality or magic. On the contrary, it is the techniques of illusion that stimulate the 'real magic' of the star, the 'truth' of her 'performance'. (The oxymoronic brilliance of *The Bad and the Beautiful* will finally defeat me.) In the dialogue, we have repeated insistences that Georgia is a star. This has nothing to do with talent or acting ability but, as Jonathan (Kirk Douglas) says after her screen test, the fact that, no matter how bad she may be, no-one can take their eyes off her when she is on the screen. Similarly, Jonathan dismisses Lucien's objection that Georgia does not have the poise for a period costume she has designed, observing that Georgia is a star and will therefore be all right. She needs only to be tutored to bring out this innate quality. In the processing of the raw material, the hidden value—star quality—will be revealed. (The film apparently wants to insist that this is not a question of conning the public—nowhere in *The Bad and the Beautiful* is the apparatus of fan magazines, promotion and so on shown directly to have a role in star manufacture, although the press agent, Syd, is seen as a permanent member of the creative studio team.)

In the working out of the narrative, this play on reality and illusion comes to a mesmerising climax. Jonathan cannot get the right effect from Georgia in the marriage scene in the film they are shooting. When they pack up for the day, they have a quiet exchange during which Georgia gazes longingly at him. 'That's the expression I want!' he says. As a result, Georgia pours her feeling for him into the role in the film. It is this that gives 'truth' to her performance. Yet the film has hinted, and is soon to reveal, that he is merely manipulating her. In other words, the truth of her performance rests on a deception.

When Georgia herself realises this, discovering him at home with Lila during the première party, we have the famous car scene, in which, in one long take, she drives into the night, crying hysterically, with headlights glaring into her (and our) eyes, the rain lashing down, the camera twisting around her. What we seem to be getting here is the moment of real reality, assured by the notion that only untrammelled, chaotic, violent emotion is authentic. All the rest is illusion. It is the supreme masterstroke to fabricate this authenticity so completely in a studio mock-up of a car and with the epitome of star artifice, Lana Turner.

Turner's association with badness continued as a defining element of her pub-licly available private life between *Postman* and *The Bad and the Beautiful*. She dated countless men, most of them famous, and hence was widely rumoured to be a nymphomaniac (or, as an MGM executive quoted by Morella and Epstein revealingly put it, 'Lana had the morals and the attitudes of a man. . . . If she saw a muscular stage hand with tight pants and she liked him, she'd invite him into her dressing room'). In 1947, she married Bob Topping, a wealthy heir, three days after his divorce from a previous marriage (in which she was named as co-respondent). The Presbyterian minister who married them was, with much publicity directed against Turner, suspended because Presbyterians are not al-lowed to marry people divorced for less than a year. In 1951, she was separated from Topping; she had an accident in her shower, variously put down to drunken-ness, suicide attempt and pure accident. The films of the period, however—apart from her role as the thoroughly wicked Lady de Winter in *The Three Musketeers* (1948)—do not reflect this emphasis on badness. What does characterise them, apart from their use of Turner as a glamour object, is a tendency to team her with considerably older men, including Spencer Tracy in *Cass Timberlaine* (1947) and a visibly ageing Clark Gable in *Homecoming* (1948, their third film together, but the difference in their ages was more apparent than before).

This teaming is of a piece with the emergence in Turner's publicity, as cru-cially related to her association with badness, of the role of her father. Early in her career, MGM had invented a biography for Turner, giving her a wealthy father ('a mining engineer') who had died in an accident. In fact, she came from a very poor home, her father, who had once been a miner, was a gambler and bootlegger and was murdered by one of his cronies when Turner was ten. The studio had wanted to fabricate Turner as an All American Girl—but when her image was clearly anything but harmed by her turning to the bad, it became useful to let the true story of Turner's past be known via fan magazines, bi-ographies, etc. The inexorable link with badness, and its pitiability, were strengthened by the image of both her sordid origins and her loss of her father—this got her all ways, she was indelibly bad, but could not help it, genetically (who her father was), environmentally (the upbringing he gave her) and psycho-logically (loss of him at a crucial age made the passage to mature heterosexuality problematic). In a culture as drenched, even at the popular level, in naturalising, individuated explanations of personality as America in the 'forties and 'fifties, Turner and her father were a powerful image-complex. In an interview, Turner herself suggested the meaning of her father's death—'Since my life has been wayward and impulsive, always a search for something that is not there, and then disillusionment, I believe I need all the excuses I can make. The shock I suffered then may be a valid excuse for me now. It may explain things I do not myself understand' (quoted by Morella and Epstein).

The idea that Turner's relations with men are somehow related to the early death of her father gives a certain *frisson* to many of her roles—for example, Sheila has a sugar daddy in *Ziegfeld Girl,* Nick in *Postman* is old enough to be Cora's father. But this is all very oblique. With *The Bad and the Beautiful,* it is the key to the relationship between Georgia and Jonathan. (I had better stress before going any further that what follows is not a psychoanalytic reading of *The Bad and the Beautiful,* much less of Georgia and Jonathan; it is rather an analysis of a text that is, rather obviously, informed by popular psycho-analysis, as indeed many films directed by Vincente Minnelli are.) Their fathers bring them together; her dependence upon him depends upon her rejecting her real father and replacing him with Jonathan; the question is whether she can in turn reject this surrogate father.

Their fathers bring them together, although both are dead. Georgia's father, an actor, worked for Jonathan's, a producer, just as Georgia and Jonathan are actor and producer respectively. Georgia's father drew a picture of Jonathan's father, as a demon with a pitchfork, on the (?nursery) wall of his home. It is here that Jonathan and Georgia (legs only visible, dangling from a loft) first meet. Jonathan removes the drawing from the wall, and hangs it in his office. When she goes, an unknown bit player, for an audition there, it is her turning to look at the drawing (together with her lustrous blonde hair seen earlier when she is working as a stand-in) that identifies her to Jonathan. It is moreover her turning, with an identical movement of the head, to look at the drawing in Harry Pebbel's office in the film's framing story that leads into her flash-back of her relationship with Jonathan. This relationship is thus signalled at various important moments by her father's hostile feelings towards his father.

He 'kills' her father. She has 'built a shrine to him' (Jonathan's words) and he breaks it up, smashing the record of her father intoning a 'Macbeth' soliloquy, drawing a moustache on a picture of him. As a result, she is free of her father—

but by substituting Jonathan. In the scene after he has dropped her in the pool (she has gone out and got drunk through fear on the night before shooting begins), Georgia/Turner performs just like a little girl. The accoutrements of glamour are replaced by a head towel and outsize coat (it is his, but it makes her look like the archetypal little girl wearing grown-up's clothes). She sits first on the floor, then on his knee—never in an equal adult position. She speaks, in a little girl voice, such cute lines as 'If we were married, I wouldn't take up much room.' And he tells her 'Love is for the very young.' The naughty little girl, legs dangling over the sides of the loft in the scene of their first meeting, has become the good, meek daughter. She has become his child.

The elision of the sexual and parental relationships in this development is precisely the point—it is the sexuality of daughter-father relationships, and the dangerous sexual consequences of their disruption, that is played on in the Turner image and in the Georgia-Jonathan relationship. In turn, this relates to the theme of her becoming 'authentic.' Just as the car scene signals an explosion of 'real' feeling, so, too, with rather less stops pulled out, does the climax of the scene in her bedroom, where Jonathan smashes her father's 'shrine'. He has sneered at her—'Look at you, you're acting now, playing the doomed daughter of the great man'—and when he smashes the shrine, she attacks him, her hair comes loose and swings in the light. In both cases, the 'real' feeling is signalled by a departure from the static, perfectly groomed look of Georgia/Turner to wild movement with textures (her hair here, her fur in the car scene) that capture and diffuse the light. And in both cases she is being required, forcibly, to reject her father (real or surrogate).

Whether she does succeed, however, in freeing herself from her second father, Jonathan—and hence, like the Turner image, from a father-fixated sexuality—is ambiguous. At the beginning of the film, just before she, together with Fred and James Lee, go into Pebbel's office, she draws a moustache on the shield outside, Jonathan's emblem, exactly the same as the moustache he, Jonathan, draws on her father's portrait (later in the film, though earlier in her 'life'). She laughs with the others. This is clearly an act of defiance, doing to Jonathan what he did to her father. But perhaps it has to be read as only an act, not a real rejection. This is what the film suggests elsewhere. In the framing narrative she is dressed in black (a neat, tight-fitting suit), her hair drawn back. In the flash-backs, she wears light, usually white, clothes, and her hair hangs lustrously. The general contrast, and especially the cut back from the flashing car scene to her immobile, black figure, posed in recall, suggest repression. She is keeping unwanted desire in check, which is not the same thing as being free from it. She tells James Lee that one may grow out of first love, 'but you never get over it.' Directly, this means Jonathan, but, given the pattern of father references in the film, it could also mean her father—or fathers in general. Georgia has grown out of that (the 'mature' repression of desire in adulthood) but not got over it (still hung up on father figures). Of Turner, only the latter was touted as being the case. In the last shot of the film, she, like Fred and James Lee, remains fascinated by Jonathan, unable just to walk out, compelled to pick up the phone to hear what his ideas are. He still exercises his hold on her.

Whether this hold is a father-son one in the case of Fred and James Lee, I'm not sure. What does seem a reasonable supposition is that Jonathan himself is free of his own father. Despite keeping up appearances (paying mourners to attend his father's funeral), he befriends the only man, Fred, who speaks against his father, pronounces his father '*the* heel' and seems to accept Georgia's father's view of him as a demon. He overthrows Pebbel, who is effectively in the position of his father, as head of the studio, and treats him with all the patronising air of the still vigorous son. Jonathan is free of his father, but Georgia really is not. Perhaps this is because psychoanalytic thought (at least of that period) only allows sons to kill fathers. Thus Georgia, like Turner, must remain pitiably locked into her perverse needs and desires.

Imitation of Life

By the time of *Imitation of Life* in 1959, the glamour emphasis in Turner's image had become uppermost. As Jeanine Basinger puts it, '. . . Turner appeared to cut loose her past. For the audience, it ceased to exist. She was their movie goddess—born and raised on film for their pleasure—the product of photogenesis.' The 'bad' elements continued before and after *Imitation of Life,* if anything more scandalous—four more marriages and divorces (Lex Barker 1953–57, Fred May 1960–62, Robert Eaton 1965–69, Ronald Dante 1969–69), accused of breaking up the marriage of Ava Gardner and Frank Sinatra, her daughter's involvement in various scandals (drugs, becoming a stripper, not to mention the Johnny Stompanato affair discussed below), and some film roles: *The Prodigal* (1955) as a wicked priestess, *Portrait in Black* (1960) as an adulterous murderer. However, the effect of all these is more to increase her glamorous otherness and to make her an identification figure, the suffering woman of the woman's film genre. It is these qualities that *Imitation of Life* capitalises upon. More precisely, it uses a quality of 'detachment' characterising Turner's dress and acting styles.

Throughout the films and public appearances of the 'fifties, and on into the 'sixties, Turner became increasingly associated with clothes. The 1965 film *Love Has Many Faces* was sold principally on the strength of its 'Million Dollar Wardrobe,' and the connection between Turner and a certain kind of dress style was essential to the films she made for Ross Hunter (*Imitation of Life, Portrait in Black, Madame X* 1966). Although many different designers worked on her films, notably Edith Head (*Who's Got the Action?* 1962, *Love Has Many Faces*), Jean Louis (*Imitation of Life, Portrait in Black, Madame X*), Helen Rose (*A Life of Her Own* 1950, *The Merry Widow* 1952, *The Bad and the Beautiful, Latin*

Lovers 1953, *Bachelor in Paradise* 1961), and Travilla (*The Rains of Ranchipur* 1955, *The Big Cube* 1969), and although the style very clearly belongs to American 'fifties *haute couture,* there is nonetheless a certain Lana Turner look. This is prominent in *Imitation of Life* and relates to the film's elaboration of what is implied by its title.

The signification of many of the features of the look are those of *haute couture* in general (which has still never been better analysed than by Veblen in his 'Theory of the Leisure Class')—notably expensiveness (especially, with Turner, jewellery, elaborate head-dresses and hairdos) and, distinguishing the wearer from those whose clothes have to permit labour, inconvenience (for Turner, trains, folds in the skirt, off-the-shoulder dresses). Certain others features are more specifically Lana—the use of man-made fibres, so that her high style is associated with glossy, modern artifice rather than 'natural' or 'old-fashioned' values; a quality of hardness in the clear-cut edges of the designs and in the use of colour, which, together with a tendency towards designs that create geometrical patterns around her frame, 'dehumanises' her, plays down qualities of softness, roundness, even warmth; and a certain type of creation that is frankly bizarre and unimaginable outside of movies, even of Turner, such as, in . . . *Imitation in Life,* an outfit consisting of vermilion pants and top, pink necklace, and a piece of pink flower-printed, insubstantial material shaped like an open-fronted dress, cut away at the knees, and trailing out behind in a full spread. The emphasis, then, is on artifice (a feature of the Turner image already dwelt upon), femininity (but one conceived not in the traditional terms of softness, but in terms of elaborateness, ornamentation, plasticity) and sheer impracticality, without connection with ordinary life. The net effect in many of her films is that Turner, in her fabulous costumes is visually detached from her surroundings—India in *The Rains of Ranchipur,* Cornwall in *Another Time Another Place* (1958), a rusty old steam ship, captained by John Wayne, in *The Sea Chase* (1955)—except in those cases where the set-up is itself equally 'unreal': as high priestess of Astarte in *The Prodigal* (revealing clothes that make every movement hazardous), as the richest woman in the world in *Latin Lovers* (in Brazil), and in *Love Has Many Faces* (in Acapulco). In *A Life of Her Own* and *Peyton Place* (1957) she was associated directly with *haute couture* as, respectively, a top model and owner of the town's smartest fashion salon.

The sense that all this gives to many of her film appearances—of her being detached from the events, on show—is central in *Imitation of Life,* for in it she plays a character, Lora, who is, or becomes, a person on show, performing, presenting an image, to be thought of neither as an essence (i.e. an inner human being expressing her self through presentation) nor as interacting with others and circumstances. In the early scenes in the film, she wears ordinary, everyday clothes—blouses and skirts, a suit for interviews—but as she gradually becomes an actor and a star, her wardrobe becomes more and more Lana. If 'life' is essence, interaction, vitality, reality, then Lora/Turner, in her outlandish outfits, is an imitation of it. The problem the film poses (thus bringing in the suffering element in the Turner image) is whether there is, in fact, anything but imitation in life.

The key metaphor for imitation in the film is that of acting. The fact that Lora is an actor, in the professional sense, is only part of this. We never see her on stage, except in rehearsal or taking a bow. Insofar as her profession is relevant to the metaphor of acting, it is in the way that she is set up as 'an actress' quite apart from any ability to act well on a stage. Thus agent Allen Loomis takes her on because he is impressed by her impersonation of an archetypal Hollywood star (this is how she inveigles her way into his office) and he promotes her not by putting her into a play but by taking her to parties *dressed like* an actress (in particular, in mink). Ironically, the only time we get to know anything about a play she is in is when she takes a part as a social worker in a bid for realism. But Lora/Turner acts, puts on a performance, throughout the film. Detached by dress, she is further detached by acting style. Turner has a habit—in her other later films as well—of turning away from the person she is acting with to deliver a line, adopting a posture, head-on to camera although not actually looking into the camera. Even when she does not do this, her acting nonetheless is poised and posed. If one takes as an example someone at the very opposite end of the scale to her, Judy Garland, one can observe how Garland hangs on her acting partner's every word, watching her/his lips or eyes, registering response in minute facial inflections. It is this that gives Garland's performances their characteristically nervy, tense and spontaneous feel. By contrast, Turner's beautifully made-up face moves very little and she does not even always look at her partner. All of this is emphasised time and again in *Imitation of Life,* until the climactic moment when, turning from her sobbing daughter Susie (Sandra Dee), she declares, staring ahead of her, that she will give up Steve (John Gavin) rather than have him come between them. Susie looks at her and says 'Oh mother, stop acting!' The film here draws attention to Turner's posing acting style, making its use of the style to embody 'imitation' explicit.

This use of Turner was given a further emotional charge for contemporary viewers by Turner's involvement in he trial of her daughter Cheryl for the murder of her (Turner's) boyfriend Johnny Stompanato (in 1958). More than one newspaper described her testimony as 'the greatest performance of her life.' Whether or not this was fair of the press, the confusion was compounded by the purely coincidental release of *Peyton Place* around the time of the trial. In it, Turner's big scene has her breaking down in sobs on the witness stand, just as she did at the Stompanato trial. There are of course further overtones of the Stompanato affair in the relationship between Steve and Susie (just as rumour had it that Cheryl had fallen for Johnny), again blurring the distinction between imitation and reality, screen and life.

Acting is only one of the many images for imitation of life used by the film. All of these (for instance, a Nat King Cole substitute to sing the title song; the use of an obviously artificial, stage-set-like backdrop for Lora's home; narrative touches such as having a job writing envelopes to give them a wholly spurious 'personal touch') connect to the central metaphor of acting/performance, but unlike *The Bad and the Beautiful,* with its endless reflections and cross-references which trap everything in the paradoxes of illusionism, *Imitation of Life* does also point, in an ultimately very melancholic fashion, to the possibility, or idea of authenticity.

In fact, nearly all the possibilities pointed to by the film are also pretty well undercut or attenuated by it. Christmas, vividly evoked with bright reds, snow and Xmas trees, is exposed as sham fairly devastatingly by Sarah Jane's material-ist insistence that, since he was real, Christ must have been either black or white and by Annie (Juanita Moore) and Lora's idealist evasion in terms of it being the general idea of Christ that matters. Other possible authenticities are more ambig-uously dealt with. I will look at them primarily as they relate to Lora/Turner.

The possibility of self-affirmation as a source of strength is most explored through the character of Sarah Jane (Susan Kohner) and her imitation of white, but the illusoriness of self-affirmation is underlined in the same way at certain points for both her and Lora. These ways are the use of mirror reflections at moments of affirmation and/or the introduction of the 'Imitation of Life' theme on the sound-track after such declarations. Thus when Lora rings Susie after her triumph in the role of Amy, her sense of fulfilment, achievement, is shown as only in a mirror image of it. (Compare Sarah Jane's fierce 'I'm white!' to probing boy-friend, shown as reflected in a shop-window.)

Another possible source of authenticity is virility, here represented by Steve. Douglas Sirk often has a character like this in his films, embodying promise of virility, to the women and impotent men of the rest of the cast—think of his use of Rock Hudson in *All That Heaven Allows, Written on the Wind* and *The Tar-nished Angels.* The point about these characters—played by actors who are almost exaggeratedly tall, dark and handsome—is that their virility is never put to the test. They may offer the women fulfilment (including, quite clearly, sexual fulfilment), but this remains speculative, to take place well after the end title has appeared. Sirk's films do not even end with the marriage of this male with the female protagonist, only with our assumption that this is the way all heterosexual romances end. Much less is the consummation assured. The ending of *Imitation of Life* is especially ambiguous. In one sense, it is the cobbling together of the nuclear family characteristic of the post-war film melodrama. That is to say that while we end with a nuclear family unit, it is actually made up from bits of other families (Steven is the father of neither girl; neither he nor Lora is Sarah Jane's parent). Moreover, it is shot not as father, mother and children grouped together, but as the women grouped together in the back of the car, with a cut-in shot of Steve looking on benignly from the front seat. In other words, the promise of virility that will set the seal on the family is still only a promise.

The problem with this is what exactly the film thinks of virility. Feminism has correctly exposed the oppressiveness of virility as an idea (as opposed to an idea such as energy or strength that need not be gender-specific), yet it does seem that *Imitation of Life,* and Sirk in his other films, do believe in virility as an idea. What is being critically exposed is the absence or failure of virility. In particular, the association of Steve with a certain view of the countryside (and even more a similar association between Rock Hudson and nature in *All That Heaven Allows*), seems to be presented quite straight, without undercutting, as if Sirk really believes in a natural order of virility and, possibly, the family, at least as ideals.

There is a similar problem with another of the film's alternatives to a life of imitation, namely black culture. The main lines of the Annie-Sarah Jane plot seem to be a repeat of the imitation themes in the Lora plot. The device of the black girl who can pass for white clearly demonstrates the thesis that race is a question of cultural definition, including role-playing, in which biological difference plays no significant part. Annie's investment of her self, her labour, in provision for her spectacular funeral, something which she herself by definition cannot experience, suggests the crippling role of religious mystification in black culture. Yet the film also seems to want to say that black culture *is* more authentic than white, materially and culturally.

The role of Annie and Sarah Jane in the film is to act as the material base to the super-structure of Lora's success, which is mere phenomenal form. Annie almost lives Lora's real, practical life for her. She is the bread-winner (filling in envelopes, doing cleaning jobs, paying the bills) who enables Lora to pursue her career, and she is housewife and mother to Susie. She even at one point controls Lora's relationship with Steve, by gesturing him to go when she thinks Lora should be left alone. In other words, she is the reality, the material existence, that makes Lora's appearance possible. Moreover, it is quite clear that Lora has no conception of what it means to be black; she has no understanding of the reality that makes her life possible. She sees taking the part of the social worker as doing something more 'real' on the stage, yet cheerfully chats about its 'coloured angle' with David (Dan O'Herlihy) in front of Annie, without consulting *her,* without even seeming to register the fact that Annie is serving them drinks. When she upbraids Sarah Jane for her Southern mammy impersonation when bringing in drinks for her (Lora's) guests, she says 'I've never treated you differently'—yet we have just seen Sarah Jane using the back stairs, going to the local school (Susie is at boarding school), expected to help out her black servant mother. Lora has not personally acted differently towards Sarah Jane and yet quite clearly Sarah Jane is getting different treatment. Lora has no conception of the racist structures that underpin her position and Sarah Jane's equally.

In addition to this materialist authenticity granted to blacks, the final funeral set-piece seems to affirm, its narrative significance *vis-à-vis* Annie's life notwithstanding, the cultural authenticity of blacks. Above all, the use of Mahalia Jackson (who really is Mahalia Jackson, not someone imitating her) suggests a core of real feeling in black religion. The fact that Jackson's singing is so 'genuinely' emotional that she cannot lip-synchronise herself with any precision draws attention to the artifice of the film medium which is 'unable' to 'capture' her untrammelled outpouring of emotion. Yet this final affirmation of the authenticity of black culture is also the high point of grief in the film. It is almost as if the film is saying that if there is anything other than imitation it is in suffering.

It is in relation to this that the use of Turner is most interesting, drawing as it does on both her 'artificial' and her 'suffering' image qualities. When Annie dies, Lora/Turner breaks down and cries, and it is as if some authentic feeling has broken through the hard shell of artifice elsewhere promoted by the film. It is worth comparing this with the car scene in *The Bad and the Beautiful*. In both cases, the effect is of Turner shedding her actor's artifices and giving us naked emotion. This may also be how Turner herself experienced it—we cannot know, and I do not wish to detract from her achievement in both cases. However, the effect also derives from the way both these scenes make a formal break from the rest of the film in presentation of Turner. In *The Bad and the Beautiful,* the posed, static nature of her performance is replaced for the car scene by chaotic movement. In *Imitation of Life,* her collapse on Annie's bed makes one realise that as an element of composition everywhere else in the film, she has been used in upright and detached positions, usually still. The actual movement of falling on the bed breaks this, and the break is maintained through the funeral service where she is slumped at an angle in her seat. Whilst of course in both cases this is the art of the film-makers (of whom Turner is one) and whilst the notion of 'naked emotion' does not really have any validity, nonetheless this collapse into suffering, which is also a formal break in the film's compositional patterns *vis-à-vis* Turner, *means* 'authenticity', shedding of artifice, reality not imitation. What is melancholy is that this authenticity is only achieved in an image of collapse, as if the only possible reality behind the imitation of life is grief.

As I have been concerned in this article principally to discuss the star as an aspect of film language, I have tried generally to hold back from spelling out the ideological significance of Turner (and the star phenomenon), but a few words on this may be in order by way of a conclusion.

In this perspective the role of Turner as an agent of coherence (*Postman*) or to reinforce such notions as impulse (her marriages, *Postman*), naked emotion and authenticity (*The Bad and the Beautiful, Imitation of Life*) would not be viewed as progressive. At the same time, the way her image can disrupt a film text (the overall structure of *Ziegfeld Girl,* the centrality of Frank/Garfield to *Postman*) and its foregrounding of the processes of manufacture are suggestive. In a more directly political sense, it seems to me that her combination of sexuality and ordinariness was in itself ideologically explosive (and I have not sufficiently brought out the lower-class elements in this definition of ordinariness), comparable to that later embodied by Marilyn Monroe. To what extent the machinery of glamorisation, punishment and suffering defused this, I'm not sure. I tend always to see ideological struggle within the texts of films, no less in Lana Turner than anywhere else.

Performing Performing:
Irony and Affect

Charles Affron

I f all art is ultimately about itself, self-reflexive art draws the viewer's attention to that fact.[1] Art is made its own subject when its fictional pretexts refer
to its modes of creation, of execution, of performance. "Show biz" configurations in films function the way trompe-l'oeil techniques, virtuosistic lighting, and
other blatant devices of perspective do in painting. It has been argued that these
displays of technique and artifice make it difficult to respond affectively to art
since they create distance between the fiction and the viewer. Can the illusions of
art and performance survive their self-analysis, their *mise en abyme?* Can we be
lost in the illusion if we witness it from backstage? What is affecting about a
movie's movieness, the performance of a performer? The oscillation between the
reality-effect and the fiction-effect in film becomes a source of affect when we see
how performers express their feeling in the service of their performance and as a
reflection of their lives. The fiction-effect then comes to be identified by the
specific expressive activities of performance. The self-reflexive film makes us
more alert to the passage between the two effects than do other sorts of narratives, where the fiction effect is carefully hidden. Indeed, what has been
described as the classic Hollywood style is meant to hide the fiction-effect altogether. But when the characters and the fictions themselves pass from one status
to the other (the actor performing a role within a role in a play/film within a film)
we become conscious of a high level of fictivity. Self-reflexivity then obliges us
to re-examine our response to reality and to art, to discard the too-facile categor-
izations we make, and to grant to art its "real" status. Disoriented by the elisions
of fiction and life, we wonder where performance ends and reality begins. The
film that makes a fiction of performance tests the medium's approximation of
verisimilitude against fictivity; our affect is inflected by our reading activity, our
ability to see performance as performance. Art is *at least* as moving as life when
its expressivity is perceived to be contiguous to that which moves us in life.

This contiguity is clearly displayed in the theatrical narratives of *Les Enfants*

From *Cinema Journal* 20, no. 1 (Fall 1980): 42–52.
1. "Self-reflexive" is perhaps a cumbersome designation, but its utility is demonstrated by Susan
Sontag, *Styles of Radical Will* (New York: Farrar, Straus & Giroux, 1976), p. 139, in her description
of Ingmar Bergman's *Persona*. "In the ways that Bergman made his film self-reflexive, self-
regarding, ultimately self-engorging, we should recognize not a private whim but the expression of a
well-established tendency. For it is precisely the energy for this sort of 'formalist' concern with the
nature and paradoxes of the medium itself which was unleashed when the nineteenth-century formal
structures of plot and characters . . . were demoted." Sontag goes on to define self-reflexivity in
terms of modernism. The designation seems equally applicable to cinematic fictions that have those
"nineteenth-century formal structures of plot and characters."

du paradis, A Double Life and *All About Eve,* in reflections on cinema and photography such as *Funny Face* and *Pretty Baby,* and in the movies' own inside
stories such as *Sunset Boulevard, A Star Is Born,* and *The Bad and the Beautiful.*
The recent Soviet film, Mikhalkov's *A Slave of Love* (1978), recounts the trials of
a group of filmmakers in Yalta during the Russian Revolution. Juxtaposing its
childish characters and the frivolity of the film they are shooting against the harsh
historical reality around them, *A Slave of Love* exposes many cinematic modes:
the documentary, the fiction film, the silent film, the talkie, the black and white
film, the color film. Life is "played" in front of the camera by the movie star
heroine of *A Slave of Love,* who is literally trapped in a tracking shot, pursued by
cavalry as she rides, alone, on a trolley; by Norma Desmond in the final, halated
close-up of *Sunset Boulevard;* by the quasi-amateur theatricals of *Sylvia Scarlett;*
by the passage from high fashion, still photography to the moving camera in
Funny Face, where Fred Astaire's acting lessons turn Audrey Hepburn into a
mobile "Winged Victory" in the Louvre. Photographer and model later dance a
love duet that transcends the stillness of photography through the graceful
camera movements characteristic of Stanley Donen films.

Transcendence of the stage itself is provided by the specifically camera-eye
view of show biz. In Busby Berkeley production numbers, for example, the lens
has the privilege of seeing that to which the theatre audience has no access;
through its constantly variable vantage the camera seems to create patterns from
the mere capacity for shift. In the production numbers of Robert Z. Leonard's
Ziegfeld Girl (staged by Berkeley) the showgirls walking up and down flights of
stairs are seen from angles that challenge our ability to know where we are, and
indeed where they are in relation to the proscenium presumably delimiting their
movements. They are similarly displaced by a narrative apparatus that encloses
them in the double framework of production numbers and verisimilitudinous
fiction. Such challenges to spectatorship are also challenges to performance. In
the remainder of this paper I will focus primarily on Lana Turner in *Ziegfeld Girl*
(1941) and in Douglas Sirk's *Imitation of Life* (1959) as a model for these ambiguities of performance. The Ziegfeld girl is a woman who walks up and down a
flight of stairs because a "creative" man has put her there, and because other men
have bought tickets to see her, to stare at her, to identify her through their gaze.
The woman in film, particularly in elaborate musical production numbers, often
functions as a trope for this specular activity. When a showgirl walks in what we
immediately identify as a space peculiar to cinema, she forces us to recognize
artifice and the objectification of the performer. The showgirl doesn't seem to be
breathing. Her being is a function of her walk, a walk that is supposed to display
sexuality but that is dissociated from sexual walking. Nearly expressionless, the
showgirl is a walking image, subservient to an absurd costume that is not a dress,
that is difficult to wear, that makes her top-heavy and/or bottom-heavy, that
weighs her down and must be carried up. The woman is lost in the metaphoric
value of a costume shot through with stars, awash with sub-acqueous vegetation.

The "American Woman" is "glorified" through fictions that deny essential aspects of her womanness. (A man is rarely desexualized in production numbers; even in mass configurations, he is obviously a man.) In the Warners musicals that bear his stamp, Busby Berkeley often anatomizes women for metaphorical purposes obvious to the most naïve viewer. In the kaleidoscope of arms, legs, faces, and eyes, meaning shifts from the woman as surface to woman as love, as death. The movies make us see the map of the city in the inverted face of Wini Shaw, the ultimate victim of that city in "Lullaby of Broadway" (*Gold Diggers of 1935*).

But if the camera objectifies and metaphorizes the woman it also catches her human presence. Wini Shaw *is* a vibrant singer. The Ziegfeld girl, when seen from the multiplicity of angles in the purview of the camera, is also liberated from the purely approving gaze or the leering eyes of men. She is revealed to have eyes of her own, a life of her own. Cinema does this to image. Its surface generates depth, activity, space. We perceive its images as superficial and then locate those images amidst various spatial, temporal and narrative planes. The very modalities of cinema that relieve objects and performers of their referentiality, their burden of representation, gives them an aura of roundness as they reverberate in the space between the act of performance and that which is being performed.

In *Ziegfeld Girl* the play of flatness and depth is further displayed by the distinctions made among the three protagonists. We immediately perceive Hedy Lamarr and Lana Turner as showgirl types who obviously know how to walk up and down stairs. In many films Lamarr and Turner function primarily as specular objects, bearers of figure and face. We are told that Mr. Ziegfeld got into an elevator, saw "Red" (Turner), the operator, and decided on the spot that she should be in the Follies. "Beautiful" (Lamarr) just happens to be standing on the stage of the theatre, is seen, and signed as well. It is enough to see these women to turn them into showgirls, into images that walk. Susan (Judy Garland) has to perform actively, to exhibit a performing talent not exclusively related to her appearance. At the film's conclusion she is the only surviving performer of the three, singing, dancing, and also revered as image, perched atop a spiral column (a crafty insert from *The Great Ziegfeld,* released five years earlier, in 1936). The film puts her through a series of tests that validates her talent; she becomes an object without losing her status as active performer. (This double nature resonates in Garland's life. Her biographers have commented on the singer's terrible feelings of glamourlessness at that glamour-filled studio, MGM. In *Ziegfeld Girl,* Susan is told, "you're not a showgirl.")

The explicit validation of on-screen performance by the approving glance of an on-screen viewer, a frequent device of cinematic self-reflexivity, becomes a sign of affect when that viewer also has a specifically personal relationship with the performer/image. The first production number of *Ziegfeld Girl* features reaction shots of "Beautiful's" disappointed husband (Philip Dorn), "Red's" enthusiastic brother (Jackie Cooper), slightly nervous boyfriend (James Stewart) and prospective lover (Ian Keith), and Susan's proud father (Charles Winninger). Their attitudes (satisfaction, pride, wounded pride, a leering appraisal of the soon-to-be bought object/woman) reflect back on our own specular activity. The magnification of the viewing process within the film obviously increases our sense of the woman as the viewed object. The three star faces in *Ziegfeld Girl* suggest something of the range of the viewed, from Hedy Lamarr's near-death mask, a figure of stasis (her smile is intrusive to the utter calm of the mask), to Lana Turner, whose American Beauty face actively acknowledges and provokes the admiration of men's eyes, to Judy Garland, whose face is, at this point in her career, a field of constant energy, "pep." To draw our gaze, Hedy simply *is*, Lana *knows*, Judy *performs*. The film's narrative structure will pivot on the malleability and responsiveness of the Turner character, and use the other two stars as polar versions of the performer type. We perceive the woman/object between motion and immobility, it is there that she exposes her own feelings, makes us conscious of spectatorship and invites our passage through various stages of involvement and detachment from the work of art. Self-reflexive art clearly locates us as spectators and engages us in the work of the art.[2] Where are we when we see films from backstage and at whom are we looking when we look at Lana Turner, aware of her need to be seen and desired by men as a movie star, as a Ziegfeld Girl, as a character within the fiction of the film? We are many places at once, looking at the object prismatically, applying particularly cinematic perspectives, long and short, close up and far away, in and out, that connect the manner of our seeing to our thoughts and feelings about what we see, when what we are meant to do, precisely, is to see.

In *Ziegfeld Girl,* among the spectatorial relationships to the showgirl, that of the father is most insistently inscribed. The father is the "author" of the fiction, the generator of the spectacle. He is the authority for what is transpiring before our eyes and the ultimate judge of his own creation. When the creation takes on a life of its own he becomes anguished, disapproving and he threatens to withdraw his gaze, his love. Ziegfeld, the god-like father of the Ziegfeld girls, never appears in the film, but is provided with mediators, high priests who pass on his wisdom and do his bidding. He is the one for whom the girls perform, and for whom they must "behave." Susan's father provides a locus of enactment for the Ziegfeld father configuration. He trains his daughter, constantly expresses his

---

2. Colin MacCabe, in "Principles of Realism and Pleasure," *Screen* 17 (Autumn 1976): 16, defines the viewer's dual situation inside and outside the fiction, in linguistic terms developed by Benveniste. He distinguishes between the *sujet de l'énoncé* and the *sujet de l'énonciation,* "the spectator as viewer, the comforting 'I,' the fixed point, and the spectator as he or she is caught up in the play of events on the screen, as he or she 'utters,' 'enounces,' the film. Hollywood cinema is largely concerned to make these two coincide so that we can ignore what is at risk. But this coincidence can never be perfect because it is exactly in the divorce between the two that the film's existence is possible."

authority and experience (is seen performing with her near the film's beginning as a contemporary, sexual partner), stands in the wings offering encouragement and advice, and threatens rejection if she ignores that advice.

The affective power of this parental authority, eye, gaze almost destroys the daughter's talent. Pop forces Susan to sing a ridiculously "up-beat" rendition of "I'm Always Chasing Rainbows" during an audition. When she betrays his authority, performing the song slowly for the Zeigfeld surrogates, the camera shows her fluctuating relationship to her crestfallen father, seated hunched over at the piano, his back turned to her. She touches his shoulder, drawing strength from his presence, but sings for other men, men who are willing to buy her talent. By dividing the father figure between Pop and the absent Ziegfeld, the film gives the performing act a wide resonance, suggesting that one can care about the performance in very different ways. Its cost is high. A loving hand is placed on the shoulder of the disapproving spectator whose presence validates the performance; it is this spectator who most wants the performance to take place and who fears that when it takes place it will de-identify him. This sequence holds closely together the creation of the performance (what Pop has trained Susan to do) and the loss of a daughter, a loss sounded and seen in the sad song performed for Ziegfeld's men and his girls, charged with the emotion Susan is feeling for her father. And what are the Ziegfeld girls thinking as they watch Susan perform with a talent that we are all meant to esteem more highly than theirs? (Lana Turner, the sweater girl, is told in this film *not* to sing.) The depth of Susan's talent reflects negatively on their superficiality. All they have to do is walk; Susan must prove herself by singing her way to the top of that enormous white pillar. In doing so, she forces us to gauge the distance between her heartfelt singing and the anonymous brunette, balancing half a tree on her head. Our gaze scans the distance between Susan and the showgirl, and then reflects back on itself with some sense of complicity in the ploys that extract performance from acts of emotional display and of self-objectification. If a performer is very lucky, she gets to sing for her supper.

At the climax of *Ziegfeld Girl*, "Red," a victim of the excesses of life and art, leaves the audience before the end of Susan's first night. She is stopped short at the head of the lobby staircase by Tony Martin's rendition of "You Stepped Out of a Dream," a song whose lyrics relate the woman's walking to both her anatomization/objectification (eyes, lips) and her integration into the man's life of fantasy, imagination and affect. This is the song that measured "Red's" showgirl gait the night she herself triumphed on what is now Susan's stage. She "walks" down the stairs and then collapses in an emphatically symbolic death that carries greater weight than the ambiguous (will she indeed die?) final shot of her, moments later, on a dressing room couch. Her act, a fusion of the showgirl's walk and the woman's feelings, is performed in a thrall of memory, illness, and the sense that the only eye upon her, the camera's, is the most important one. It, like ours, sees her through the double optic of photography and fiction, and grants her

her double status as object (showgirl) and as performer (agent of the affect produced by the narrative).

The reflexivity of *Ziegfeld Girl* forces us to examine various modes of the performing self in and out of fiction simultaneously, and read them as a function of ironic transfers—the in-text stage/life juxtapositions with their intricate spatial discordances, the conventional dramatic ironies sustained by our knowledge of the characters, and the extra-fictional reverberations of stage, screen and acting. This is the kind of knowledge exploited by Sirk in *Imitation of Life,* a film that requires us to engage in a textual deconstruction of performance embedded in a narrative that explicitly treats moral issues of race and motherhood. Our emotional response to *Imitation of Life* ultimately depends on the redefinition of conventions of sentimental expression. This recasting of sentimental fiction depends on the resonance Sirk draws from our perception of performance as an act of self-reflexivity, a perception we must have in order to read the film as the director intended.[3]

The first film version of Fannie Hurst's *Imitation of Life,* directed by John Stahl (1934), demonstrates the sufficiency of the sentimental scenario in cinema, and offers a useful point of comparison for the kind of reading that is dictated by Sirk's interventions. Stahl's version exemplifies the near-invisible stylistics of many '30's films. The film's most insistent elements are the clarity of its enactments, the straightforwardness of its stagings and its attitudes about the emotional centers of the film, motherhood and race. Meant to be perceived as a model of clarity, the *persona* of the film's star, Claudette Colbert, is informed with self-possession, intelligence, tact and wit. These are the qualities of Bea, the character who has an unerring sense of where things are, who people are, and who she herself is. The film's title bears no reference to her, but rather to Peola (Fredi Washington), the young black woman who tries to pass for white, the daughter of Bea's black maid, Delilah (Louise Beavers). Bea's resourcefulness, ambition, taste and understanding are successfully exhibited throughout the film in situations that affirm the values she shares with the white, middle-class audience for which the film was intended. Whatever irony there is in this film is so blatant that it does not require the slightest bit of obliquity in order to be read. (Commenting on little Peola's high intelligence, Delilah says, "We all starts out that way. We don' get dumb 'til later on.") The unruffled succession of master-shots and close-ups, of action-reaction shots, the *obviously* codified decor, and the sentimental configurations of mother-love and death conspire to reflect negatively on the imitative life of the black woman who doesn't know her place. Peola refuses to do what is expected of her; everything else in the film illustrates the comfort of the expected.

---

3. Stephen Handzo, in "Intimations of Lifelessness: Sirk's Ironic Tear-Jerker," *Bright Lights* (Winter 1977–1978): 20–22, 32, gives a keen ironic reading of the film. His analysis has helped me illustrate my argument.

Sirk's *Imitation of Life* is a film about race in the late '50's, in an America that has loudly articulated but certainly not resolved the issue of civil rights. What is a viewer to make of a scene in which a black woman embarrasses her white bene-factress with a take-off of a shuffling darky? In terms of the fiction, Sarah Jane (Susan Kohner, a white actress) offends her "good" black mother, Annie (Juanita Moore), but her refusal of the "servant" role and her caricature of traditional race relationships elicits a reading ironic to the in-film reaction of the righteously indignant white woman, Lora (Lana Turner). Yet the ironic reading, the one sanctioned by a society that no longer laughs at Stepin Fetchit, does not com-pletely destroy the sentimental one sustained by the presumed victim of the caricature, the black mother who suffers nobly throughout the film.

For Sirk, the issue of motherhood is just as clouded as that of race. The black and white of motherhood are exposed in clichés of excessive love and excessive egotism; selfless love from a generous heart, love bought with money; the all-too present mother, the eternally absent one; the nurturing ideal, the sex object. Mother has difficulty surviving these caricatures, as well as the caricatures' in-flections. The good black mother neglects her own child and dotes on the white child in her care ("I like taking care of pretty things"). The bad white mother supports the two fatherless families. Yet it is through the bald opposition of negligence and sublimity that the film becomes ironic to motherhood itself. Juanita Moore, the embodiment of a mother's soul, with trembling voice and moist eyes, and Lana Turner, whose inadequate soul is worn as plainly as her highly publicized wardrobe and jewelry (thirty-four costumes!), are displayed in two-shots and in shot/counter-shot rhythms that threaten mother-love itself in their dialectic antagonisms. In Stahl's *Imitation of Life* Claudette Colbert and Louise Beavers enact complementary versions of the good mother. Sirk provides us with a set of discordances, of subversions of our expectations of mother-love fictions.

The black mother who loses her daughter and dies of a broken heart seems to be the film's emotional center, but she is challenged for that distinction by the actress/star/bad mother whose victimization engages the viewer in tensions no less provocative than the racial ones. We perceive Lana Turner to be as inauthen-tic as the "jewels" that cascade behind the credits. The vitality of the Ziegfeld Girl has been codified, reduced to movie-star posturing, "dated," sewn into cos-tumes that are aggressively sexual and often unflattering. If she has forgotten that Ziegfeld Girls shouldn't age, she is brutally reminded by a producer who tells her, "You're no longer a chicken." Much of the characterization is made to reso-nate against our extra-fictional knowledge of Lana Turner, a knowledge not of film buffs but of the vast moviegoing public. We first see the "sweater girl" anxiously looking for her daughter, leaning over a railing and almost out of her bodice. And it is in this pose that she is caught by the photographer who says, "My camera could easily have a love affair with you." The same audience cannot fail to link the in-film rivalry between daughter and mother for the same man with the recent scandal in Turner's life (lightly fictionalized in the novel and film, *Where Love Has Gone*)—Turner's lover stabbed to death by her daughter in the actress's bedroom.

Lora, the clothes-horse movie star, plays a great actress, thereby reviving persistent doubts about the acting ability of Hollywood stars in general, and in particular, a star like Turner whose career was posited upon her appearance. This is not the first time her abilities have been ironized. Even in *Ziegfeld Girl* she plays "merely" a show girl. In Minnelli's *The Bad and the Beautiful,* in the role of a movie star, her screen test is supposed to show the inadequacy of her acting. In spite of this she is engaged by a producer who is struck by her "star quality." When she is giving what is meant to be a great performance in the film within the film (a pastiche of *The Scarlet Empress* and *Queen Christina,* in which the presences of Dietrich and Garbo hover over poor Lana) the camera sweeps back over the visibly moved people on the set and up to a light operator whose tear-filled eyes are ironic for those of us, so many of us, who remember a similar camera movement in *Citizen Kane,* from Susan Alexander's pathetic opera stage to her critics in the flies. But even without such a memory, viewers of *The Bad and the Beautiful* must have difficulty in sorting out Turner's good acting from what is explicitly labelled as bad acting. Even her big scene of hysteria (she loses control of herself while driving a car) is a movie-created effect of editing and lighting. In *Imitation of Life* her acting is constantly and explicitly undercut. The neglected daughter (Sandra Dee) responds to the star's histrionics with "Oh, Mama, stop acting. Please don't play the martyr." The absurd *mise en scène* of her stage triumphs, in front of crudely painted backdrops, is ironic to any notion of what Broadway plays are supposed to look like.

The film's climax, Annie's grandiose funeral, receives a spectacular staging with music, white horses, and a rapt audience, befitting Hollywood's notions of spectacle as well as those of the black woman lying in the flower-strewn coffin. Annie's soulfullness reaches its apogee in the gospel singing of Mahalia Jackson, the voice of black soul acceptable to white America in 1959. Sirk repeatedly intercuts Jackson's singing, the expressionism of which is so thick it is often difficult to distinguish musical sound from weeping and wailing, and the grieving blonds, Lana Turner and Sandra Dee. Somewhere between these comfortable black and white codes lurk disruptive feelings that finally burst forth when Sarah Jane runs to the hearse and pours her sorrow over her mother's casket. Ever conscious of appearances, Lora intervenes to restore order in an imitation of decorous bereavement. Feeling lies between Lora and Sarah Jane, in the play of ironies and ambiguities, not on the surface of the images. The surface belongs to the cascading jewels, the "glamorous" ethos of producer Ross Hunter, the industry that sold Lana Turner as a sweater girl and as an imitation of a great actress, the moviegoers who bought her, and the soceity that identified black and white in terms of caricatures and all-too-easily read fictions.

Imitation of Life is not an easily read fiction. Its obsessively ironic slant tunes us to a disillusionment so great that it inspires compassion for performers and characters. Forced to deconstruct the fiction, we are left floating in the irresolution of the film's pseudo-happy ending. Sirk himself said, "In *Imitation of Life,* you don't believe the happy end, and you're not supposed to."[4] The comic-inspirational mode the director uses for the endings of *Magnificent Obsession* and *All That Heaven Allows,*[5] with their heavily conclusive, posterish iconography (a painted backdrop of a desert, a deer grazing in the forest) would be inappropriate for a fiction as torn within itself as is *Imitation of Life.* Its profusion of ironies leads us not to some stable value, but rather to the value of the ironic processes and their multiple, unresolved readings. The non-values of bad/good, black/white, mother/actress/woman are ironic muddles that catch the muddles of an industry and a society, muddles intolerant of even a patently false resolution. The elements that constitute the muddles remain distinct as they submit to the cruelties of irony. Lora is "five years too late" in starting her career. Lana's career started more than twenty years before, and she, too, is too late. Civil rights are centuries too late. And amidst these mordant ironies, one is reserved for Hollywood itself, feeding on itself in remakes like *Imitation of Life,* trying to hang on to its illusory beauty with the cosmetics of wide screen and Eastmancolor, but as over-the-hill as the film's star. Sirk's irony draws us to this kind of knowledge, to sympathy for blacks in a white society and for stars in Hollywood. We are even brought to feel sympathy for the "Hollywood" film of the late '50's, a product of the studio system's decadence.

The final ironies are reserved for the director himself, who is played out in the ambivalence of this, his final film. Sirk's meticulous art found solutions for the obligatory becolored, cinemascopic manners of the '50's: irreparably faded, their stagings made senseless in the amputated 16 mm. prints we most often see, his films make us wonder if cinematic art is indeed more durable than the transient beauty of a movie star.

---

4. Jon Halliday, *Sirk on Sirk* (New York: Viking, 1972), p. 132.
5. See Jean-Loup Bourget, "God Is Dead, or Through a Glass Darkly," *Bright Lights* (Winter 1977–1978): 23–26, 34, for an interesting analysis of melodrama in *Magnificent Obsession.*

The Bad & the Beautiful

Can a simple girl from a mining town in Idaho find happiness as a glamorous movie queen? To popeyed newspaper readers sated vicariously with this tired story line, the answer struck last week with the finality of a chord of doom: no—in the case of one queen in particular. The chord rumbled for Lana Turner, the Sweater Girl whose feckless pursuit of happiness became men's-room talk from Sunset Boulevard to Fleet Street, and for her shaken, 14-year-old daughter Cheryl, who stabbed Lana's paramour, Johnny Stompanato (*Time*, April 14). Last week a coroner's inquest declared Cheryl's act justifiable homicide, but this decision hardly lessened the sociological impact of a news story that began 22 years ago.

The Star. Julia Jean Mildred Frances Turner was a pressagent's dream ready-made for stardom by Hollywood standards. Her father was killed in a gambling scrape when she was ten; her mother struggled to keep her alive. In Hollywood one day, when she was a well-stacked 16, she was "discovered" as she sat at a drugstore fountain. Hollywood gave her the big buildup. Renamed Lana, she made movies with the biggest of the box-office giants—Gable, Taylor, Cooper—and nobody, least of all the customers, cared if she was not a second Sarah Bernhardt.

As a high-priced commodity, Lana found herself surrounded by people whose paychecks depended on how sincerely they could convince her that she was talented, beautiful and successful. Her enormous salary seemed to be ample proof. Lana scarcely needed to make a decision of her own; the studio did it for her.

The Crowd. Like many other show folk in Hollywood, Lana liked to run with the hoodlum crowd that sprouted into semirespectability in moviedom after World War II. High up in the crowd was a runty gambler named Mickey Cohen. To the movie folk, gum-chomping Mick typified a real-life heavy out of their own films; for the Mick to invite a star to his table in a swank joint seemed as thrilling for the guest as it would be if a rubberneck tourist were asked to drink with Lana Turner. The Mick and his crowd just loved it.

And wanton Lana just loved one of the Mick's boys, olive-skinned, handsome Johnny Stompanato. A small-town boy with big ideas, Johnny was a preening gigolo, brushed his black hair thick and wavy, wore his shiny silk shirts open all the way down to his navel. He was also the fast-buck type, who, police well knew, built his bankroll by making time with thrill-seeking wealthy women, borrowed their money, rarely paid it back. Lana took Johnny in tow, paid his bills, flashed around the town on his muscular arm. When she flew to London

From *Time* 71 (21 April 1958): 17–18.

last September to make a new picture, she and Johnny exchanged impassioned love letters.

> *My beloved love* (she wrote), *just this morning your precious exciting letter arrived. Every line warms me and makes me ache and miss you each tiny moment. It's beautiful—yet terrible . . . I'm your woman and I need you, my man! To love and be loved by—don't ever, ever doubt or forget that! My romance, hah! It's a hell of a lot more than that! That's for sure. I need to touch you, feel your tenderness and your strength. To hold you in my arms, so, so close—to cuddle you sweetly—and then to be completely smothered in your arms, and kisses, oh, so many kisses!*

Johnny-Come-Lately. Back in Hollywood, Johnny cannily saved the letters. His own notes were fourth-grader's work; many of them, laboriously scratched in copy books, were never sent, *e.g.: You know Baby, I'm so lonesome for the touch of you I could die. I try to think back of when you were here and those precious minutes I wasted when my lips were not on yours.*

Johnny wasted no time. One day he turned up in London to keep Lana company. But by then, Lana Turner was wearying of Johnny, and Johnny was too tough to let himself be discarded. They fought. Once he nearly strangled her, grabbed a razor and threatened to cut her face. Lana's studio friends heard about it, got Scotland Yard to get Johnny out of the country.

Lana's fear was clear, and it led to Johnny Stompanato's death a month later. When it happened, all Hollywood broke loose. Newspapers all over the U.S. poured on the black ink and the big type, scrambled wildly for the kind of news that would keep the public buying. They found it. Two-fisted Aggie Underwood, 55, city editor of Hearst's *Herald-Express* (and only woman city editor of a U.S. metropolitan paper), decided that there must have been some love letters. She called Mickey Cohen, who took Johnny Stompanato's death as a personal affront. Cohen's hoods raided Johnny's expensive Los Angeles apartment, found the letters. The Mick turned them over to Aggie. In a few more hours, Lana and Johnny were splashed on the world's front pages for a second performance.

The Showdown. Lana still had one more performance to give. At the Los Angeles Hall of Records, onlookers crowded the corridors to get a glimpse of the drama, ohed and ahed as the principals threaded into the courtroom. Cheryl, detailed in juvenile prison, testified by deposition that the last fight between Johnny and her mother arose after Lana learned that Johnny had lied about his age: he was really 32, not 42, as he had said, Lana, 38 was now determined this time to give him the air.

Taking the stand, in the final scene, Lana told the rest: "He was verbally very violent . . . and I walked into my daughter's room . . . Mr. Stompanato was behind me all the time saying some very bad things . . . I said, 'I told you I don't want to argue in front of the baby.' [Back in my bedroom] Mr. Stompanato grabbed my arm, shook me . . . said, as he told me before, no matter what I did or how I tried to get away he would never let me. If he said 'jump' I would jump, and if he said 'hop' I would hop . . . or he would cut my face or cripple me . . . that he would kill me and my daughter and my mother."

Frightened, Cheryl fled to the kitchen, headed for her mother's room with a knife. "I walked toward the bedroom door," said Lana. "He was right behind me. And I opened it and my daughter came in. I swear it was so fast, I truthfully thought she had hit him in the stomach . . . I never saw a blade."

The End. Lana's desperation rang true, but even a Hollywood scenario might have missed the final touch that came when a man in the courtroom stood and shouted: "This whole thing's a pack of lies. Johnny Stompanato was my friend! The daughter was in love with him and he was killed because of jealousy between mother and daughter!" Then, as an afterthought before he wheeled and stomped out of the room, the man cried: "Johnny Stompanato was a gentleman!"

But Johnny was dead. Lana was still alive; a judge would decide soon whether she would lose custody of her only child. Julia Jean Turner had come a long way in the make-believe wonderland of Hollywood—where moviemen are confident that the Sweater Girl is now bigger box office than ever.

The Director:
Interviews

The following are excerpts from two major interviews with Douglas Sirk conducted in the 1970s (by Jon Halliday and James Harvey). The sections extracted focus specifically on Sirk's association with Universal Studios and on the making of *Imitation of Life*.

Sirkumstantial Evidence

James Harvey

Sirk: I never saw my films after I finished the final cut. I never went to a preview. Universal of course did not favor re-takes. And I can't recall that any of my pictures was affected by the results of a preview. Not long ago Mrs. Sirk and I watched *Has Anybody Seen My Gal* on television. It was in Italian. And I recently saw *A Scandal in Paris*—which I think is an excellent picture. Though it was no success, you know. It just barely got back its money. I saw *Summer Storm* about five years ago. Oh yes—and *All I Desire* too, after Halliday spoke of it.

But you go to Sirk retropectives now and again—you don't watch the films?
No, you don't watch them. No.
Why not?
Because you don't like them. Because you get depressed.
I see.
Because you are dissatisfied with anything once you finish it. But a poet, even a playwright, can re-write. Not a filmmaker. And in the studio days you were tied down beforehand by the script. You can change things but mostly in such a hidden way that the studio won't object.

But as a writer you must know—you are writing a paragraph, you set out in one direction—then you write a sentence or get an idea that changes your whole conception. But if you're making a picture and you shoot scene eighty-four and you find your conception changing, you are just stuck. You can't start over, you can't change those eighty-three other scenes any more. . . .

You described yourself yesterday as a kind of handicraft worker. But surely it's an odd sort of handicraft, when you so often worked to subvert what you were given. You functioned a lot as an ironist and a subverter.
Yes, yes . . .
What you do to the message of Fannie Hurst in Imitation of Life *for example.*
Yes. We played what was between the lines, so to speak.
Were the screenwriters in on that intention? Were they in on the satiric slant?
No. Yes, some of them—yes.
Did Lana Turner or Sandra Dee know that their characters were at all unsympathetic, that the film viewed them ironically?
No. No, actors you shouldn't tell about technical matters. They lose their innocence. If you tell an actor the character is unsympathetic, he'll tell you he's sorry but he can't do that—strange, but he never has been able to do that, and so

From *Film Comment* 14 (July/August 1978): 54–58. (The full interview runs pp. 52–59.)

on. No no, you should never tell an actor such things. In some ways a director is a bit of a doctor—and he must have a helpful manner with his clients.

Turner's costumes are very garish; they often seem to be a joke. Was that intentional?

Yes, of course.

Did she care? Or didn't she notice?

She was very compliant through the whole shooting. She trusted us. And I might add that she wasn't sorry—she was very happy with the picture.

The producer, Ross Hunter, had a great manner with everyone. He was tremendously successful—very charming. "Oh, but it's a crude charm," someone said. Yes, but in Hollywood who will notice if you have a subtle charm? There is one word in the English language, and without this word you couldn't have an American. This word is *wonderful*. Now, this was Ross's word. He used it to everyone, and everyone loved it. He could get anything he wanted.

Some of the sentimental scenes in Imitation of Life *seem very surefire to me, very effective in soap-opera terms. They seem devoid of irony. And so I'm not sure at those points what your attitude is.*

What scenes?

When Annie finds her daughter at the Moulin Rouge night club and then has to pretend not to be her mother in front of the white roommate. It's their final farewell scene. And as pathos, if I may say so, it's extremely adroit.

(*Shrugs.*)

Or the funeral scene.

The funeral itself is an irony. All that pomp.

But surely there is no irony when Mahalia Jackson sings. The emotion is large and simple and straightforward.

It's strange. Before shooting those scenes, I went to hear Mahalia Jackson at UCLA, where she was giving a recital. I knew nothing about her. But here on the stage was this large, homely, ungainly woman—and all these shining, beautiful young faces turned up to her, and absolutely smitten with her. It was strange and funny, and very impressive. I tried to get some of that experience into the picture. We photographed her with a three-inch lens, so that every unevenness in the face stood out.

You don't think the funeral scene is highly emotional?

I know, I know but I was surprised at that effect. When I heard how audiences were reacting to that . . . But that was the reaction of American audiences. When it was dubbed into German, all they got was the Negro angle. It's true the picture wasn't a great success in Germany—far from it. Recently a friend of mine saw it and he said, "But it's such a cold film—and there are no sympathetic people at all in it." So I was surprised at the American reaction. . . . It may be. It may be—I have no talent for sentimentality, so perhaps I simply don't recognize it.

The style of Magnificent Obsession *is ironic then?*

Yes. Overplaying can be underplaying. In *Magnificent Obsession* I often did this. When I have Otto Kruger's face appearing in the glass above Rock Hudson during that operation—that is parody, of course. As I told Halliday about the novel, it's a crazy plot and that saved it for me in a way. But in the film then, there has to be some parody going along with the sincerity. And that was true of a number of pictures of mine. But *Magnificent Obsession* has never been one of my favorite pictures.

A whole picture which I kind of liked was *Written on the Wind.*

Some critics talk about Written on the Wind *as it if were a realistic film.*

No, It's even a kind of surrealism. The people are heightened versions of reality—not realistic characters. (*Laughs.*) A European would say, "Strange people these Americans"—if he took it as naturalism.

Above all in its lighting and colors, it is a non-realistic film. Fassbinder wrote a very perceptive thing about my style—he spoke of the *craziness* of my lighting. He points out that my lighting is never realistic, almost never from where the real light source would be. I was pleased that he saw that.

Remember—*Written on the Wind* is basically one set. By this very fact then, I am investing—I am contriving to paint with a strange brush, so to speak. *Imitation of Life,* on the other hand, is much less compact, much richer in scenes and details. But in fact, with *Written on the Wind,* I had even more opportunity to furnish rooms and interiors lavishly. The studio expected it. But I determined to do the opposite. This material, I decided, is poster material—what you call *placatif.* And the whole picture is in a kind of poster-style, with a flat, simple lighting that concentrates the effects. It's a kind of expressionism, of course, like Wedekind, or the late Strindberg, or the early Brecht. And I avoid what a painter might call the sentimental colors—pale or soft colors. Here I paint in primary colors—like Kirchner or Nolde for example. Or even like Miró. I have the flashing red of a car and I want that to be just as red as possible.

Some people have commented on the blatancy of some of your symbols. In Written on the Wind *the symbolism too is rather poster-like. One critic argues that this blatancy occurs because it is appropriate to the characters—it is they who turn the objects around them into symbols. For example, the boy on the mechanical rockinghorse whom Stack sees just after the doctor has told him that he can never have children.*

That was not a symbol. Some things in this film are meant to be symbols but not that. No no, I remember—the art director had put a horse in front of the drugstore. So I put a boy on top of it, and he was there when Stack came out of the doctor's office. That's all. I never saw any meaning to it at all until Halliday pointed it out to me.

But it gets such emphasis—Stack bugs his eyes at the boy and the music swells.

I don't want to question your statement, for after twenty years I don't remember every detail. It was not intentional. In film you have to learn to use what you find on the set. You can never visualize that situations beforehand because it is always different. Once you have finished working with the writer, with the art director, then you must leave yourself perfectly open and flexible. You may get an idea from the last word or the last gesture of the day's shooting. My first film experience, I worked everything out and nothing worked out. But once I had shed my beginner's ideas, my stage director's notions, I never prepared myself too much. Also I learned to improvise on the set—a method I used to some degree in all my pictures.

On the other hand, you can't get too far away from the story, and you can't change too much of the dialogue, because the front office will tell you that's not the thing. You are tied mostly to a piece of trash. Of course it's quite different for directors now. But sometimes I see these old movies on TV, and they are not so interesting, not so good. Recently I saw an old Bette Davis picture, *All About Eve*. The role of Sanders as the critic was just silly, I thought. So unbelievable, so overdone—there was no sense of humor anywhere in it. But comedy dates very quickly, doesn't it? Though some of Billy Wilder's pictures hold up well, I think. Don't they?

Your favorite screenwriter was George Zuckerman?

Yes. He died not long ago in New York. He was a very gifted man, very flexible. I always encouraged him to write plays. After *Written on the Wind* and *Tarnished Angels*, which he did with me, they wanted to make him a producer. That didn't work out and he went to New York to write for the theatre. That's when I lost touch with him. He was a man of sensitivity—which is almost the rarest thing in Hollywood. Not long ago I was in a bookstore looking through this book on American screenwriters. I was not very interested, and then I saw his name. It was an interview, and he mentioned me. It filled me with nostalgia. Because I have the feeling that I neglected him. He was unhappy in New York, I know. But at that time I was tied up with the Ionesco project.

The dialogue Zuckerman wrote for Written on the Wind *seems rather simplified, rather schematic. Is that right?*

I am not sure what you mean by that. Certainly we wanted to get away from sophisticated dialogue. There is more sophistication in *Imitation of Life*, for example. . . .

Did you make any changes in the midst of shooting during Imitation of Life?

The funeral scene wasn't in the original script. So of course the front office was very nervous about okaying it. "Is it against God?" they said. Ross Hunter told them, "Oh it's wonderful—it's full of religious touches." And as usual, he got what we wanted. It was an expensive scene. For the exteriors, outside the church, we had to go to the Paramount lot to build the set—Universal didn't have the facilities. For the interiors, we found a church in Hollywood.

The Moulin Rouge nightclub scenes are remarkable. Were they done on location?

Partly. We did the nightclub show itself in an old movie theater in Hollywood.

It's all cold and perverse and crazy—and nightmarishly accurate. Especially Susan Kohner's routine with the lounge chair and the champagne, and the girls riding offstage on that conveyor belt—with the overhead shots that make you think of the camps. And it all looks like a real night club act. Was it? Was any part of it?

No, no. It's all invented for the film. We wanted to show that she is not right away with the wonderful world of chorus girls and show business—you know? I wanted something with a certain feeling of cheapness about it.

There's one scene in the movie that puzzles me. I think it works, but still I'm not sure how, or why you made the choice you did. It's the scene where Frankie (Troy Donahue) beats up Susan Kohner after he's found out that she's a black passing for white. It seems very stylized—in a film that is not stylized on the whole. It seems deliberately movie-ish. The set is an obvious fake—you could do a musical number on it. The background music is jazzy and blaring. Frankie's behavior and dialogue seem blaringly exaggerated, and so on.

It's difficult to remember. Mostly you do such things by intuition, by feel-ing . . . as I say, it's hard to remember. But I think I had a slight feeling that the scene could be lacking in cruelty, lacking in drama, because for one things it was so goddam short. It had no build-up to it. Yes I definitely had this feeling. I remember that when I saw the rushes, I was a bit doubtful that the scene would come off as what it should be—a scene of utter degradation of the girl. Let me tell you what I told the writer—I don't remember who it was anymore (there were many writers on this picture). I said we have to get the feeling that this is not just the boy knocking her down, but society. This is another race, this is another power, you have to represent "Whitey" here. Yes, I was only doubtful it wouldn't be extreme enough.

You are right. In a way that scene is like *Written on the Wind*. Expressionistic. It was done with a broad brush and a strong drawing hand. It's not like the rest of the picture—which is impressionistic on the whole. . . .

You said before that the real satisfaction comes from knowing you've suc-ceeded. Do you recall having that satisfaction while you were in Hollywood?

I don't think so. I believe the satisfaction being felt was by Mrs. Sirk mostly. I'm a skeptic—by temperament I'm a pessimist. Of course there are rare mo-ments. Certainly I felt some satisfaction of a kind when the president of Universal told me they were all indebted to me—for giving them the biggest moneymaker in their history. Three months after the release of *Imitation of Life*. But that's a rather passing and silly satisfaction.

That's just the point at which you chose to leave Hollywood.

I couldn't go on making those Ross Hunter pictures. I needed more freedom. The Utrillo picture was my way out—my French bridge to something else, I thought. Then I got ill. Which I took as a sign that I should get out of the picture business. Always, you know, my mind listens to my body, and my body listens to my mind. That's why I've survived so many tyrannies. Even Hollywood.

Sirk on Sirk

Jon Halliday

How did you come to sign up with Universal?
    Back in the Columbia days I got several offers from studios, all of which I had to turn down because Harry Cohn wouldn't release me. I think it was in 1946, after Universal had seen *A Scandal in Paris* they offered me a contract. After my picture with Boyer, I remembered this and went back to see them and ask them if they were still interested. And so they said, 'Yes, but we'd have to sign you for a seven-year contract.' I said, 'OK, I'll sign, on condition you guarantee me one A-picture'—and this was to be *Thunder on the Hill,* which was based on an English play, *Bonaventure.*
And from then on you stayed with Universal?
I did. They were a smaller studio than Columbia. But they were most decent to me. I'd like to go on the record with that.
I became a kind of house director of Universal. Conditions were not perfect, but when I complained about a story, they would say to me, 'If you can get a star, great; you can have more money and pick a better story.' But at least I was allowed to work on the material—so that I restructured to some extent some of the rather impossible scripts of the films I had to direct. Of course, I had to go by the rules, avoid experiments, stick to family fare, have 'happy endings,' and so on.
Universal didn't interfere with either my camerawork or my cutting—which meant a lot to me. In a way, I did see their point of view, running a studio: a film has to make back its money. I think all the best directors would agree with me about that—Ford, Hawks, or Hitchcock certainly would. There has never been a time in show-business, going back to Calderón, Shakespeare, Lope de Vega, Molière, when this hasn't been the case. I think if Shakespeare were alive today he'd shake me by the hand and say, 'My dear boy, I know what it was like in Hollywood. I had to make money, too, and a lot of my stories were lousy'—which they were. Shakespeare put himself into his sonnets, but some of his plays were not so good. . . .
I'm rather perplexed how you came to make something like [Magnificent Obsession], *which is an out-and-out melodrama, to put it mildly.*
Well, first let me tell you how the picture came up, and then I'll try and tell you what I wanted to do with it. Ross Hunter came to me and said, 'I have Jane Wyman.' And I said, 'Oh.' She was still a real star then—and I was terribly interested. He told me: she is interested in a certain story; it's a remake of an old

From *Sirk on Sirk* (New York: Viking, 1972): 85–86, 92–95, 132–135.

Universal picture that did rather well. . . . The point is there was always this actress remembering the picture. Ross Hunter gave me the book and I tried to read it, but I just couldn't. It is the most confused book you can imagine, it is so abstract in many respects that I didn't see a picture in it. Then he showed me an outline he had had done on the old picture by John Stahl—a name which did not mean anything to me. (And, by the way, I did not see the Stahl picture.) I took the treatment home, and I read it. so far as I remember, the outline was quite different from the book. I had the feeling this could make a picture, but I said to Ross, 'Look, we'll be buried under this thing.' And I went home and wandered round the house in a deep depression for a couple of days, and then, thinking it over, I realized that maybe Jane Wyman could be right and this goddam awful story could be a success. And it was; it topped the receipts of the old Stahl picture by more than ten times, it was Universal's most successful enterprise for years.

Your success with the most unlikely material is very striking: do you think that in fact a certain kind of film about modern America, about things that are impor- tant in the society, can only be made in the form of melodrama, if you're working there?

Well, the word 'melodrama' has rather lost its meaning nowadays: people tend to lose the 'melos' in it, the music. I am not an American, indeed I came to this folklore of American melodrama from a world crazily removed from it. But I was always fascinated with the kind of picture which is called a melodrama, in America.

As I told you, at Ufa, I made several pictures which could be called melo- dramas: *Schlussakkord* was one kind of melodrama; and *Zu Neuen Ufern* and *La Habanera* were another kind of melodrama. But all three were melodramas in the sense of music + drama. Melodrama in the American sense is rather the arche- type of a kind of cinema which connects with drama. Most great plays are based on melodrama situations, or have melodramatic endings: *Richard III*, for ex- ample, is practically a melodrama. Aeschylus and Sophocles wrote plenty of melodramas, as well. . . . The *Oresteia* is really a melodrama, I think. But what used to take place in the world of kings and princes has since been transposed into the world of the bourgeoisie. Yet the plots remain profoundly similar. There is melodrama in a novelist like Faulkner, for instance.

I am intrigued by the playfulness, and the insincerity, of men. I think often of the connection between 'play' and 'please.' They are the same thing: a play must please. And, in a way, the American melodrama allowed me to do this.

There is one other thing about *Magnificent Obsession:* I was still working on turning Hudson into a star. Now this meant the first occasion for him to ride into stardom on the name of Jane Wyman. This put him on the map. The picture was an enormous success for both him and Jane Wyman—and that's why the studio wanted to make *All That Heaven Allows* right afterwards.

But how do you set about transforming something like the story of Magnificent Obsession *or, later,* Imitation of Life, *for that matter? Because it is much more extraordinary than your success with stories you like, the Faulkner or the Chekhov. Can you pick out the elements which got you going?*

You have to do your utmost to hate it—and to love it. . . .

Like Imitation of Life?

To some extent.

How was Imitation of Life *put up to you, and did you see the old Stahl picture here?*

As far as I remember, Ross Hunter gave me the book, which I didn't read. After a few pages I had the feeling this kind of American novel would definitely disillusion me. The style, the words, the narrative attitude would be in the way of my getting enthusiastic. But Ross also had an outline done which closely followed the Stahl picture. The picture itself I didn't look at either, not at that time, at any rate. Later on I saw it, after I had finished my own picture. So I was free of any possible influence. I liked it, I thought it was very good, but it belonged to the previous generation. After I had read the outline, I made one change, socially—an important one, I think. In Stahl's treatment of the story the white and the Negro women are co-owners of a thriving pancake business—which took all the social significance out of the Negro mother's situation. Maybe it would have been all right for Stahl's time, but nowadays a Negro woman who got rich *could* buy a house, and wouldn't be dependent to such a degree on the white woman, a fact which makes the Negro woman's daughter less understandable. So I had to change the axis of the film and make the Negro woman just the typical Negro, a servant, without much she could call her own but the friendship, love, and charity of a white mistress. This whole uncertain and kind of oppressive situation accounts much more for the daughter's attitude.

The only interesting thing is the Negro angle: the Negro girl trying to escape her condition, sacrificing to her status in society her bonds of friendship, family, etc., and rather trying to vanish into the imitation world of vaudeville. The imitation of life is not the real life. Lana Turner's life is a very cheap imitation. The girl (Susan Kohner) is choosing the imitation of life instead of being a Negro. The picture is a piece of social criticism—of both white and black. You can't escape what you are. Now the Negroes are waking up to black is beautiful. *Imitation of Life* is a picture about the situation of the blacks before the time of the slogan 'Black is Beautiful.'

I tried to make it into a picture of social consciousness—not only of a white social consciousness, but of a Negro one, too. Both white and black are leading imitated lives. . . . There is a wonderful expression: seeing through a glass darkly. Everything, even life, is inevitably removed from you. You can't reach, or touch, the real. You just see reflections. If you try to grasp happiness itself your fingers only meet glass. It's hopeless.

But Imitation *is somehow like* Magnificent Obsession: *they both come from the same zone of what would be called 'the weepies,' and have the sentimentality that goes with them.*

Exactly. And more or less I had the same tough time fighting this quality in *Imitation of Life* as in *Magnificent Obsession,* knowing also it couldn't be removed from the plot without the whole thing collapsing: that makes it so different from *The Tarnished Angels* or *Written on the Wind.* So you might count all four of them as melodramas.

Now here in *Imitation of Life,* as in the others, I had the contrast of interesting parts and star roles. Lana Turner and Gavin are taking more or less the positions of Bacall and Hudson in *Written on the Wind* or Hudson in *The Tarnished Angels,* while the Malone and Stack characters find their equivalent in the part of Susan Kohner (Sarah Jane Johnson). Again, the same phenomenon occurs—the supporting part is the more interesting and the better acting part. The better part for the director, too; he can make more out of it. Susan Kohner, a complete beginner in pictures, steps forward, putting Turner and Gavin into the shade.

There is another way in which I feel *Imitation of Life* and *Written on the Wind,* though so different, have something in common: it's the underlying element of hopelessness. In *Written on the Wind* the use of the flashback allows me to state the hopelessness right at the start, although the audience doesn't know the end. But it sets the mood. In *Imitation of Life,* you don't believe the happy end, and you're not really supposed to. What remains in your memory is the funeral. The pomp of the dead, anyway the funeral. You sense it's hopeless, even though in a very bare and brief little scene afterwards the happy turn is being indicated. Everything seems to be OK, but you well know it isn't. By just drawing out the characters you certainly could get a story—along the lines of hopelessness, of course. You could just go on. Lana will forget about her daughter again, and go back to the theatre and continue as the kind of actress she has been before. Gavin will go off with some other woman. Susan Kohner will go back to the escape world of vaudeville. Sandra Dee will marry a decent guy. The circle will be closed. But the point is you don't have to do this. And if you did, you would get a picture that the studio would have abhorred.

And this is where Euripides comes to the rescue again. Of course, I know this is a case of calling in the gods to witness in a dwarfish cause. Forgive me for unloading my classical education on you: do you know the last chorus of the *Alcestis?*

The manifestations of Gods happen in many shapes
Bring many matters to happy ends
What we thought would happen does not happen
The impossible is not impossible for the Unknowns
And that is the way it has happened here and today.

You see, there is no real solution of the predicament the people in the play are in, just the *deus ex machina,* which is now called 'the happy end,' and which both Hollywood and Athenians and assorted Greeks were also so keen on. But this is what is being called Euripidean irony. It makes the crowd happy. To the few it makes the aporia more transparent. The theme is basic—I used it in *Magnificent Obsession,* which is in some ways rather like it.

To go back, though, to *Imitation of Life:* I think this picture also shows up one of the big differences between the media of the novel and the movies. The novel has never been subjected to something like Hollywood, to the pressure of time and big money, to sale people, producers, exhibitors—or at least not to such a degree—saying you've got to have a happy end even in the most goddam awful situations. With a novel you are more independent—at least as long as you are working. Until you have finished you are only answerable to your own artistic conscience.

When you made Imitation of Life *did you know you were leaving Hollywood? The funeral looks like a farewell, and the trajectory of the film, too, given the cast of actors, agents, producers, and so on, makes it look like this.*

In my mind I guess I was leaving Hollywood, yes, even before I made the picture. I had had enough. I most likely would have left even if illness hadn't coincided. Even though after *Imitation of Life* I might have been able to write my own ticket, because this was a very big success, certainly the biggest one Universal had ever had—its biggest money-maker of all time.

An indication of this might have been my insisting on the tearing up of the contract I had with Universal, which still had years to run. This was not unlike my leaving Leipzig, when Dr. Goerdeler tried to stop me—though the general situation was very different. Universal tried to hold me too. And to me it was not happy leaving, in a way, because as I told you when talking about my Universal period, they were extremely decent to me. They had become my friends. My agent, like everyone else, considered my move a silly one. They told me, 'You're just reaching the peak of your career and you quit.' It certainly hadn't happened in Hollywood before, where success means everything. So no one understood.

I took a picture with a smaller company, a subject which interested me and which I was supposed to do entirely in France: the life of Utrillo, the painter—or rather of him and his mother, Suzanne Valadon, also a very good painter. I flew to Paris and tried to influence Ionesco to write the script. He consented, and he had interesting and unusual ideas; it would have been a good picture, which would have made it difficult for me to give up the movies entirely. But I fell ill. The doctor told me I would have to take at least a year off, if not more, and this became the definitive break with Hollywood and with picture-making. Later on, having become well again after a couple of years and probably able to go back to Hollywood, I had quite a number of offers: among others, *Madame X*—which is a glaring example. I really toyed with the idea of doing this picture. 'Bending' it again like I had done so often before to something which wasn't quite impossible, because the story—God knows—is. But then I realized all this was a thing of the past. I had outgrown this kind of picture-making which in a way was typical of Hollywood in the fifties and of American society, too, which then tolerated only the play that pleases, not the thing that disturbs the mind. I felt a totally new Hollywood would soon be in the making, a Hollywood open to pictures like *Easy Rider*—at any rate, pictures of a very different brand, and a different style. But I felt I wasn't young enough any more to wait this out, for just going on making pictures would have been ridiculous for me, because I had so many other interests that now had first place in my mind. Though, sometimes I pondered being back there again in Hollywood, experimenting, developing a completely new style, appropriate to a new time which I felt was coming. There is the undeniable lure of this rotten place, Hollywood, the joy of being again on the set, holding the reins of a picture, fighting circumstances and impossible stories, this strange lure of dreams dreamt up by cameras and men. And, in addition to that, as in my Roman days there was the lure of going back and completing a promising career. But I felt I had to stick to my decision to take my illness as more than coincidence. I honestly can't say I was entirely happy about this. I had no roots any more in Europe, and I don't think I wanted to sink new roots into ground that had become foreign to me. In the meanwhile I had become much more at home in America. But I knew that if I went back there I certainly wouldn't be able to resist being drawn into pictures again, so I stayed in Switzerland, where I am not at home either, and sometimes, thinking about myself, it seems to me I am looking at one of those goddam split characters out of my pictures.

Reviews and Commentaries

Reviews

Imitation of Life was not well-received by the press of 1959 (John McCarten of *The New Yorker* deemed it a "Slowly Cooling Clinker"). The film was mocked for its allegedly trite storyline: Bosley Crowther referred to its "basic clichés," and the title of a *Cue* review ("Success Won't Get You Happiness, Bub") travestied the film's banal moral. Also attacked was the movie's sentimental tone: *Time* called it a "potent onion"; the *New York Times* deemed it a "lachrymose tale"; and *Cue* accused it of being "sloppily saturated with sentiment, drenched in tears, bathed in bathos." Finally, it was dismissed for its focus on what Paul Beckley of the *New York Herald Tribune* termed "feminine matters," for its interest in what *Time* called "the career-woman question."

Though recent criticism argues for the ironies of Sirk's presentation, they were largely missed by his contemporaries. Critics sensed the abstract acting style of Sirk's performers, but viewed it as incompetence rather than distanciation. Bosley Crowther charged the actors with giving "an imitation of movie acting," and Paul Beckley found them uninvolved "in what is going on."

All the reviews anthologized here mentioned the film's source, Fannie Hurst's novel, indicating that the author was still a well-known figure at the time. Similarly, most recalled the 1934 Stahl version and made certain comparisons. The *Cue* review invoked the star *persona* of Lana Turner, referring to her as a "glossily artificial clotheshorse." The piece also quoted the Universal production notes (included in a previous section) which cataloged the expense of costumes and jewels for the film. None of the pieces allude to the Stompanato affair.

Counterposed with these negative critiques from the fifties is a campy review and plot summary of *Imitation* by Rainer Werner Fassbinder, who calls it a "great, crazy movie about life and about death. And about America" and for whom the very excesses and extravagances of the narrative (which discredited it with the "serious" press) are evidence of the film's veracity and sublimity. Fassbinder captures the haughtily condescending tone of the movie reviews, pushing the discourse to an extreme: in *Imitation,* he wryly notes: "[characters] are always making plans for happiness, for tenderness, and then the phone rings." As we well know, Fassbinder was highly influenced by Sirk and drew on his *oeuvre* to construct a new blend of melodrama and modernism.

In addition to the contemporary reviews that are included in this section, other national reviews appeared. Among them are:

America 101 (9 May 1959): 314.
Catholic World 189 (May 1959): 154–155.
Commonweal 70 (17 April 1959): 82.
Library Journal 84 (15 March 1959): 843.
Newsweek 53 (13 April 1959): 118.
The New Yorker (25 April 1959): 167–168.
Saturday Review 42 (11 April 1959): 28.

Success Won't Get You Happiness, Bub

Fannie Hurst could always tell a story. And now, no matter how much they garble her 1933 novel—or how they glamorize, revise and "modernize" its simple, sentimental tale until nearly all semblance to honesty and reality is lost—they still can't destroy the solid substance and heart-pull Miss Hurst put into it. "Imitation of Life," soapsuds and all, still basically dramatizes a valid theme: the futility of pursuing "success" outside one's self; and adds the suggestion that no happiness can be found in denying love.

There are half a dozen stories woven through this elaborate, multi-million-dollar production—and several of them are dragged in heavily, and awkwardly. There is the penniless widow who, ambitious to become a "great" Broadway star, denies her love for a young photographer. He in his turn wants to be a "great" artist, but sells his talent to an advertising agency beer account (!). When the busy actress' little girl hungers for love, mama lavishes luxuries on her instead. And mama's best friend, confidante and housekeeper (in the book, her full business partner) is a Negro lady of charm and intelligence, who meets neglect and heartbreak too, when her light-skinned daughter, similarly seeking "success," runs off to the white man's world. Everybody sacrifices that which is most precious, for the tinseled thing they call "success."

All this, and much more, is unfolded against Hollywood's gaudy conception of "Broadway," tenement, penthouse and suburban living. Sections of the film, as noted, are honest; but much of it is sloppily saturated with sentiment, drenched in tears, bathed in bathos.

As the ambitious heroine, Lana Turner is again more concerned with clothes, coiffure and profile than with valid performance. As her suitor, John Gavin is equally shallow in a shallowly written role. Juanita Moore as the actress' Negro friend is far better—but she, too, has been made so insufferably saintly as to destroy any claim to validity. The children are incomparably better than their elders: Karen Dicker and Terry Burnham, and (later) Sandra Dee and the extraordinarily talented Susan Kohner. In one tremendously affecting sequence, Mahalia Jackson sings "Trouble of the World," and of all the picture, this single scene is unforgettable.

The basic flaw in "Imitation" is unwittingly underscored in the film's program note: "This picture affords another 'attractive mother' role for Lana Turner (who wears) the most expensive wardrobe ever to gown a star in Universal history: 34 outfits valued at $78,000 (and) more than $1,000,000 in jewels—including emeralds and diamonds valued at $240,000; a $50,000 star sapphire set; diamond

From *Cue* (18 April 1959).

earrings worth $9,000; 12-carat multi-colored sapphires worth $45,000; a 15-carat diamond set worth $127,000; and a three-strand pearl necklace valued at $4,300."

Pity Lana, the poor working girl! Under the weight of all this phoney diamond-and-sapphire glamor, it was probably inevitable that Miss Turner—insisting upon studio wardrobe O.K.—should revert to the glossily artificial clotheshorse school of acting—which had, I thought, been decently interred years ago. Douglas Sirk ("A Time to Love") directed.

'Imitation of Life'

Paul V. Beckley

"Imitation of Life," based on but not always following in storyline or feeling the Fannie Hurst novel of the same name, focuses mainly on what may be called feminine matters, that is, the conflicts between career and marriage, career and motherhood, the rearing of children, and various kinds of romantic triangles, one between mother and daughter for the love of John Gavin.

The area of its concern has little to do with its generally blurred and slack effect. I should say rather that as a "woman's picture," if there is such a thing, it falls far short of its mark, subsiding into a sudsy formlessness, for which the writing and direction are more responsible than the cast.

It is not so much that Lana Turner's problem, whether to follow a career or relax with Gavin, is one that is not likely to confront me as a man that keeps me from working up any frantic interest in what she'll do. It is rather that the dialogue is usually flaccid and that under the direction of Douglas Sirk neither Miss Turner nor Gavin seems to feel very much involved in what is going on.

The story ambles along from point to point, starting on the Coney Island beach as two mothers, Miss Turner and Juanita Moore, meet and agree to live together in Miss Turner's flat, Miss Moore as her maid and cook. It is here, too, that Gavin, the handsome young man who starred in "A Time to Love and A Time to Die," begins his long and fruitless courtship of Miss Turner.

She prefers a theatrical career and doesn't seem able to manage both career and Gavin, though the reason is obscure. Gavin, getting gradually dusty at the temples but otherwise staying as young as ever, hovers in the foyer of her life, as it were, until Miss Turner's daughter grows into Sandra Dee and falls in love with him.

Interwoven in this situation is what for me seems the real drama in this picture, the struggle of the young actress Susan Kohner to escape from her Negro mother's benign influence and pass into white society. One could wish that the mother's point of view were clearer, but that isn't the fault of Miss Moore's acting, which is both restrained and palpable. Despite an ugly and over-dramatized beating scene when her white boy-friend discovers her racial background, Miss Kohner's plight takes over the picture for me, making the long passages of Turner-Gavin-Dee frustrating.

It may not be that the acting talents of Miss Kohner and Miss Moore alone lift this part of the story so high above the rest of the picture as to leave it in a kind of

From *New York Herald Tribune* (18 April 1959).

shadowy, powdered vacuum. It is more probable that the genuine drama of their conflict stung director and screenplay writers alive.

In any case Miss Kohner's and Miss Moore's are the more impressive performances. Miss Turner's and Gavin's are dulled by lackluster writing, which also leaves Miss Dee little more than a vaguely animated doll in comparison to the vivid, vital young Miss Kohner. If Miss Kohner's faults take the form of a too tempestuous, leg-kicking emotionalism, it looks exciting in contrast to Miss Dee's pretty imperturbability.

Sob Story Back

Bosley Crowther

For positive verification of the old French saying, "The more things change, the more they are the same," consider the new film at the Roxy. It is Universal's "Imitation of Life."

Twenty-five years ago, a picture of the same title, based upon the then popular Fannie Hurst novel, opened at the same theatre. Its star was Claudette Colbert. It was in black-and-white. And the reviewer for this paper tagged it "the most shameless tear-jerker of the fall."

Yesterday's arrival at the Roxy has Lana Turner as its star. It happens to be in vivid color, and a few details in the story have been changed. But otherwise this modernized remake of Miss Hurst's frankly lachrymose tale is much the same as its soggy predecessor. It is the most shameless tear-jerker in a couple of years.

Once more, it circulates a story of the hazards of motherhood at the stage when one's children—in this case daughters—are growing up and preparing to enter the world.

There are two mothers in the situation—and no fathers, by the way; no parents of masculine gender to confuse the rich flow of mother love. One is a lovely young widow who aspires to a theatrical career and somewhat neglects her growing daughter in gaining great success in that field. (In the former film and in the novel, she was a tycoon in pancake flour, but the point was the same: she concentrated on a self-aggrandizing career.)

The other mother is a Negro and is the first mother's loyal maid. She doesn't neglect her daughter, but she has a serious problem on her hands. Her daughter is markedly light-skinned and, as she grows up, she wants to pass for white—so much so that she repudiates her mother and eventually runs away. Thus the poor woman's heart is broken, in the midst of her employer's lush success. The contrast of the mother's compensations from their differing daughters is the story's irony.

As you may sense from this outline, the emotional potentialities are strong, and no reluctance, restraint or artful prudence has been exercised in banging them across. The screen play by Eleanore Griffin and Allan Scott puts the issue positively, and, to make sure there's no vagueness in the dialogue, it is written in basic clichés.

"Tell her I know I was selfish—and if I loved her too much, I'm sorry—but I didn't mean to cause her any trouble. She was all I had." Thus speaks the mother on her death-bed about the daughter who ran away. That is the tenor of the writing—and the simplified feeling—in this film.

As for the Negro mother's funeral, which is the climactic episode, it is a splurge of garish ostentation and sentimentality. Mahalia Jackson is recruited to do a full-voiced wail of "Trouble of the World," while a church is packed with principals and extras who sob noisily and dab at their eyes. And, of course, the wayward daughter who wants to be white shows up at the end and throws herself on the coffin, crying for mama piteously.

Under Douglas Sirk's direction, which is manifested by that episode, Miss Turner and all the others act unreally and elaborately. Miss Turner as the actress, Sandra Dee as her daughter (at 16), Juanita Moore as the Negro mother, Susan Kohner as her daughter (at 18), John Gavin as a suitor of Miss Turner, Robert Alda as her agent in the theatre and Dan O'Herlihy as a doting playwright do not give an imitation of life. They give an imitation of movie acting at its less graceful level twenty-five years ago.

Imitation of Life

Imitation of Life (Universal-International), after a quarter century in Hollywood's root cellar (the first film version of this Fannie Hurst bestseller was released in 1934), is still a potent onion. When passed before the moviegoer's eyes, it may force theater owners to install aisle scuppers to drain off the tears.

"I'm going up and up and up," cries Lana Turner, who plays the Claudette Colbert part in this version, "and nobody's going to pull me down." Sadly her admirer (John Gavin) slouches away, and Lana goes up and up and up until she finds herself in a penthouse with a famous playwright (Dan O'Herlihy), and all of Manhattan at her feet—in Eastman Color. How happy she seems, but how miserable she really is. "Something," the heroine sighs, "is missing." Certainly not one soap-opera cliché is missing.

So much for the career-woman question. But there is another hour to fill—plenty of time to solve the race problem too. So meanwhile, back at the cold-water flat, the Negro maid (Juanita Moore) is having trouble with her light-skinned daughter, who is yearning for the day when she will be old enough to leave home and pass herself off as white. The day comes, the girl does, and the scriptwriters settle down to the point of the picture: an interminable scene in which the poor old Negro maid dies of a broken heart. Excerpts:

Maid: When my bills are all paid (*gasp*), I want what's left to go to [my daughter]. Tell her I know I was selfish (*gasp*), and if I loved her too much, I'm sorry, but I didn't mean to cause her any trouble. She was all I had.

Heroine (*sobbing*): Oh, Annie!

Maid: And my funeral . . . I wanta go (*gasp*) the way I planned. Especially the four white horses and a band playin'. No mournin' . . .

Heroine: No! There isn't going to be any funeral! You can't leave me!

Maid: I'm just (*gasp*) tired, Miss Lora . . . awfully . . . tired . . .

With her last strength she turns to look at a photograph of her daughter. Smiling peacefully, she dies. The funeral takes place in a Hollywood reconstruction of the little old neighborhood Baptist church—an edifice that looks suspiciously like Westminster Abbey on Coronation Day.

From *Time* 73 (11 May 1959): 86.

Imitation of Life

Rainer Werner Fassbinder

Imitation of Life (1959) is Douglas Sirk's last film. A great, crazy movie about life and about death. And about America. The first great moment: Annie tells Lana Turner that Sarah Jane is her daughter. Annie is black and Sarah Jane is almost white. Lana Turner hesitates, then understands, hesitates again and then quickly pretends that it is the most natural thing in the world that a black woman should have a white daughter. But nothing is natural. Ever. Not in the whole film. And yet they are all trying desperately to make their thoughts and desires their own. It's not because white is a prettier colour than black that Sarah Jane wants to pass for white, but because life is better when you're white. Lana Turner doesn't want to be an actress because she enjoys it, but because if you're successful you get a better deal in this world. And Annie doesn't want a spectacular funeral because she'd get anything out of it, she's dead by then, but because she wants to give herself value in the eyes of the world retrospectively, which she was denied during her lifetime. None of the protagonists come to see that everything, thoughts, desires, dreams arise directly from social reality or are manipulated by it. I know of no other film in which this fact is formulated with such precision and with such desperation. At one point, towards the end of the film, Annie tells Lana Turner that she has a lot of friends. Lana is baffled. Annie has friends? The two woman had been living together under one roof for ten years by then, and Lana knows nothing about Annie. No wonder Lana Turner is surprised. Lana Turner is also surprised when her daughter accuses her of always having left her alone, and when Sarah Jane starts being stroppy to the white goddess, when she has problems and wants to be taken seriously, even then Lana Turner can only show surprise. And she's surprised when Annie dies. How could she simply lie down and die? It's not fair, suddenly to find yourself confronted with reality quite out of the blue. All Lana can do is be surprised throughout the second part of the film. The result is that she wants to play dramatic parts in future. Pain, death, tears—one can surely make something out of that. This is where Lana Turner's problem becomes the problem of the film-maker. Lana is an actress, possibly even a good one. We are never quite sure on this point. At first Lana has to earn a living for herself and her daughter. Or is it that she wants to make a career for herself? The death of her husband doesn't seem to have af-

From "Six Films by Douglas Sirk," trans. Thomas Elsaesser, in *Douglas Sirk,* ed. Laura Mulvey and Jon Halliday (Edinburgh: Edinburgh Film Festival, 1972): 104–107. The article was first published in *Fernschen und Film,* February 1971; it was republished as "Fassbinder on Sirk" in *Film Comment* 11 (November–December 1975). It was also published as "Six films de Douglas Sirk" in *Positif,* no. 183–184 (July–August 1976): 71–78.

fected her that much. All she knows about him is that he was a good director. I think Lana wants to carve out a career for herself. Money is of secondary interest to her, success comes first. John Gavin is third in line. John is in love with Lana; for her sake, in order to support her, he has abandoned his artistic ambitions and got a job as a photographer in an advertising agency. Lana cannot understand how someone could give up their ambition for love. John is also rather dumb, he confronts Lana with a choice, either marriage or career. Lana thinks this is fantastic and dramatic and opts for her career.

Things are like this throughout the film. They are always making plans for happiness, for tenderness, and then the phone rings, a new part and Lana revives. The woman is a hopeless case. So is John Gavin. He should have caught on pretty soon that it won't work. But he pins his life on that woman all the same. For all of us it's the things that won't work that keep our interest. Lana Turner's daughter then falls in love with John, she is exactly what John would like Lana to be—but she's not Lana. This is understandable. Only Sandra Dee doesn't understand. It could be that when one is in love one doesn't understand too well. Annie, too, loves her daughter and doesn't understand her at all. Once, when Sarah Jane is still a child, it is raining and Annie takes her an umbrella at school. Sarah Jane has pretended at school that she is white. The truth comes out when her mother shows up at the school with the umbrella. Sarah Jane will never forget. And when Annie, shortly before her death wants to see Sarah Jane for the last time, her love still prevents her from understanding. It seems to her to be a sin that Sarah Jane should want to be taken for white. The most terrible thing about this scene is that the more Sarah Jane is mean and cruel the more her mother is poor and pathetic. But in actual fact, exactly the reverse is true. It is the mother who is brutal, wanting to possess her child because she loves her. And Sarah Jane defends herself against her mother's terrorism, against the terrorism of the world. The cruelty is that we can understand them both, both are right and no one will be able to help them. Unless we change the world. At this point all of us in the cinema cried. Because changing the world is so difficult. Then they all come together again at Annie's funeral, and behave for a few minutes as though everything was all right. It's this 'as though' that lets them carry on with the same old crap, underneath they have an inkling of what they are really after, but they soon forget it again.

Imitation of Life starts as a film about the Lana Turner character and turns quite imperceptibly into a film about Annie, the black woman. The film-maker has turned away from the problem that concerns him, the aspect of the subject which deals with his own work, and has looked for the imitation of life in Annie's fate, where he has found something far more cruel than he would have either in Lana Turner's case or in his own. Even less of a chance. Even more despair.

I have tried to write about six films by Douglas Sirk and I discovered the difficulty of writing about films which are concerned with life and are not literature. I have left out a lot which might have been more important. I haven't said enough about the lighting: how careful it is, how it helps Sirk to change the stories he had to tell. Only Joseph Von Sternberg is a match for him at lighting. And I haven't said enough about the interiors Douglas Sirk had constructed. How incredibly exact they are. And I haven't gone into the importance of flowers and mirrors and what they signify in the stories Sirk tells us. I haven't emphasised enough that Sirk is a director who gets maximum results out of actors. That in Sirk's films even zombies like Marianne Koch and Liselotte Pulver come across as real human beings, in whom we can and want to believe. And then I have seen far too few of Sirk's films. I would like to have seen them all, all thirty-nine of them. Perhaps I would have got further with myself, my life and my friends. I have seen six films by Douglas Sirk. Among them were the most beautiful in the world.

Commentaries

The first three essays in this section (by Fred Camper and Paul Willemen) focus on the broad career of Douglas Sirk and seek to analyze the thematic concerns and cinematic style of his *oeuvre*. They were written in the early 1970s (by American and British critics, respectively), when Sirk began to be championed by Anglo-American theorists as an auteurist Hollywood director who transcended his material to forge a unique and self-reflexive mode.

Fred Camper's essay explores certain motifs in the director's work: blindness, happiness, falseness, impotence, fatalism. Taking a formalistic approach, Camper closely analyzes Sirk's filmic mise-en-scène, noting a direct relationship between that and thematic issues. Notions of falseness are rendered through radical two-dimensionality; a sense of impotence through the "asensuality" of the mise-en-scène; a sense of fatalism through hermetically contained frames. Writing at a moment prior to the influence of deconstructionism (which would valorize multivalence and contradiction), Camper finds Sirk's films "unified," an "unbreakable whole." Though he catalogs their intellectual resonances, he feels that they reflect back on themselves and are "about their own style."

Paul Willemen's article, "Distanciation and Douglas Sirk" appeared in the same 1971 issue of *Screen* as Camper's. Willemen contextualizes Sirk as a "European left-wing intellectual" and attempts to position his work within the frame of twentieth-century art movements (in Germany and Russia) that opposed naturalism: expressionism and symbolism. He finds Sirk's films marked by a stylization that characterized these earlier modes, replete as they are with symbolism, theatricality, parody, choreographed movement, and baroque coloration. In the tradition of auteurism, Willemen sees Sirk as surpassing the "limitations" of his material, introducing "a distance between the film and its narrative pretext." What Willemen finds intriguing is that the gap is "not necessarily perceived by the audience" who is swept away by the emotions of the melodramatic text.

"Towards an Analysis of the Sirkian System" (published in 1972) is a continuation of Willemen's earlier essay. Here he remarks on the burgeoning of Sirk scholarship (and on the publication of several volumes on the director), and goes on to compare Sirk to Bertolt Brecht. Willemen focuses on the myriad "contradictions" in Sirk's dramas: between "distanciation and implication, between fascination and its critique"—paradoxes which he sees mirrored in the social terrain that Sirk represents. He goes on to catalog various formal conundrums within the filmic texts: discontinuities of plot, ambiguities of character, ironies of camera position.

The next set of essays (written in the late 1970s and 1980s) concentrate specifically on *Imitation of Life*. Michael Stern's piece (1979) builds on the work of Camper, attempting to find a match between Sirk's visual style and his dramatic concerns. Stern finds an "optical estrangement" in the image indicative of social "alienation," and a manipulation of space in the film that gives "plastic form" to the notion of psychological "distance." He sees *Imitation* as Sirk's "coldest" film—one marked by "aesthetic inertia" and "emblematic stasis." Stern also prefigures Charles

Affron's concern (see Contexts Section) with theatricality—describing the myriad ways in which the characters in the diegesis can be seen to "act."

Jeremy Butler's essay (1986) seeks to place *Imitation* within its generic framework: domestic melodrama, the "emotional hothouse" of the cinema. Building on structuralist genre criticism of the 1960s and 1970s, he wants to analyze a "feminine" form previously ignored in the literature. After defining domestic melodrama (which focuses on a female, middle-class protagonist caught in a conflict between romantic and familial love), he compares the 1934 and 1959 screen versions of Hurst's novel. Butler's purpose is not only to explicate the thematic and formal dynamics of each text but to demonstrate how the genre has evolved through the decades.

The final two articles exemplify the feminist orientation of writing on *Imitation* published in the late 1980s.[1] In Marina Heung's essay (1987), she seeks to explicate *Imitation* not only as "woman's picture," but as *maternal* melodrama; hence she compares it to *Stella Dallas* (1937) and *Mildred Pierce* (1945). Building on previous feminist criticism, Heung queries the ideological thrust of *Imitation* and explores the possibility that it contains a "feminine point of view." Finding the film a unique "intersection of the issues of race, class, and gender,"

1. Laura Mulvey had initiated this move with her article "Notes on Sirk and Melodrama" (see bibliography). This article discusses issues of genre, ideology, and sexual difference, but concentrates almost entirely on *Written on the Wind*. Hence, it was not included in this volume.

Heung demonstrates how the work conservatively "discredit[s] the maternal type represented in Lora" while elevating Annie as a domestic "ideal." It does so only, however, by masking Annie's status as a working woman (like her employer). Heung sees the film as propagating numerous other deceptions: disguising class conflict as racial strife; displacing the struggle between mistress and servant onto one between mother and daughter. In the figure of Sarah Jane, however, Heung finds a moment of "excess," of "chaos," of "justified rebellion" that facilitates "a subversive reading" of the film. Ultimately, this perspective is not sustained and the "conservative thrust predominat[es]."

Writing in 1989, Sandy Flitterman-Lewis shares Heung's concern with questions of race, as crystallized in the figure of the mulatto daughter. Viewing Sirk as more progressive than does Heung, she finds that he lends a broad, cultural view to his narrative, investing it with a sense of the "irreducible difference of the social realm." For Flitterman-Lewis, Sarah Jane is a figure who is doubly "other"—both black and female—a "signifier of racial and sexual difference." Flitterman-Lewis aims at "connecting the sexual and the social" levels— configuring Sarah Jane as trapped equally by her appropriation of conventional femininity as she is by her acceptance of the dominant race.[2]

2. A number of writers misspelled Sarah Jane's name as "Sara Jane." This has been corrected in the pieces that follow, along with routine typographical errors.

The Films of Douglas Sirk

Fred Camper

Introduction

Sirk is a film-maker whose films do not exist in some metaphysical space which removes them totally from applications to our experience, but who rather in certain respects makes very direct thematic statements about life, happiness, and human knowledge. No critic has been as perceptive as Sirk himself in articulating some of these themes, as in the interview in *Cahiers du Cinéma*. A useful introduction to Sirk might be in terms of these relatively concrete themes.

On the subject of happiness:

> . . . everything, even life, is eventually taken away from you. You cannot feel, cannot touch the expression, you can only reach its reflections. If you try to grasp happiness itself, your fingers only meet a surface of glass, because happiness has no existence of its own, and probably exists only inside yourself. . . . I certainly believe that happiness exists, if only by the simple fact that it can be destroyed.[1]

On blindness:

> I have always been intrigued by the problems of blindness. One of my dearest projects was to make a film which took place in an asylum for the blind. It would only have people constantly groping, trying to grasp things they can't see.[2]

And on aesthetic distance:

> I believe that art must establish distances, and I've been astonished in seeing my films again at the number of times I've used mirrors for they are the symbols of that distance.[3]

The idea of happiness runs through all of Sirk's films like the main theme of a fugue. It is perhaps most explicit in *There's Always Tomorrow*. A familiar soap-opera plot has Clifford Groves, married and with three children, fall in love with

From *Screen* 12, no. 2 (Summer 1971): 44–62. Copyright © 1971 by Fred Camper.

1. 'Entretien avec Douglas Sirk,' *Cahiers du Cinéma,* no. 189 (April 1967): 70.
2. Ibid., p. 23.
3. Ibid., p. 70.

Norma Miller, a woman who he knew when he was much younger, and who in fact had left town because of her undeclared love for him. He falls in love with her, and for a moment is ready to leave his family, telling her that the reality of their love is all that matters, but she answers by saying that the only reality is that of twenty years of Clifford Groves as a husband and father. Their love cannot be, she says, and so she is going back to New York.

Groves' life with his wife and children is shown as a constant series of interruptions. The privacy, the romance he would still like to have with his wife is rendered impossible by the continual intrusion of their children, who are almost as omnipresent as the surrealistically multiplying relatives who crowd the groom out of his own house in *No Room for the Groom*. As Groves himself says, he is 'dead,' a 'walking talking robot.' In this context, his love for Norma develops not as a typical middle-aged promiscuity but as a symbol for the only possible escape, the only possible happiness, the only chance he has to find some real feeling in his life. This is part of the reason why Norma's rejection of the possibility is so devastating: she is consigning him to a living death whose nature he has for the first time realised, and for the first time attempted to escape from. An added irony is the fact that while his 'love' comes so suddenly that rather than love, it might be only an attempt to escape, a part of his 'search for youth,' Norma's love is clearly real, and has endured within her over all these years—and yet it is she who rejects the possibility of its fruition.

Some of Groves' early scenes with Norma have a hypnotic unreality—a little like Ernst's scenes with Elizabeth in *A Time to Love and a Time to Die*. Both are depictions of a momentary happiness which cannot endure; Sirk says of one of the scenes in *A Time to Love:*

> Things which endure may have a certain beauty in themselves, but they don't have that strange fascination which is only manifested at certain moments, like for example in that scene in which Gavin and Pulver realise that it is their duty to be happy since the world around them is falling apart. . . . True happiness never lasts.[4]

The latter statement is true of all Sirk's films. They set up the idea of happiness, and often appear to be showing it for a fleeting instant as a real possibility, but the passage of that instant reveals that the feeling can be perceived only in the form of the entire film, and that in this context it is clearly foredoomed.

It is quite characteristic of Sirk that the narrative forms of his films suggest that any happiness which appears to occur cannot last. The flashback in *Summer Storm* is admirably suited to this purpose. It opens in a drab publishing office; the girl Nadina seems trapped in a maze of wood-and-glass partitions. As she begins to read Fedor's manuscript, describing his life with her and his other friends years ago, we flash back, and the manuscript's story constitutes the bulk of the film.

4. Ibid.

The flashback begins with a shot intended to convey her early happiness with Fedor: the two of them are riding in a brightly lit, idyllic countryside with a rainbow in the background. We know that this happiness is foredoomed for we have seen Nadina as she is years later. But we know it for another, more important reason, one to be found within the shot itself. The countryside is rich, sensual, and like the shots of the pastry in the bakery window which follow, one almost feels its smell and touch. But in no sense is the countryside or anything else about the image 'real.' In fact, it is exactly the opposite; the shot seems to work against our traditional sense of perspective. The parts of the frame are never truly physically independent from one another. While there is a feel to the whole shot, we do not feel that the trees, for instance, have any reality as trees, or in terms of our conceptions of trees. They have no specific independent function or sign, either as symbols or as representatives of 'actual' trees; rather they are inextricably fused into the entire context of the shot. This is not an obvious point which is true of any film; many film images at least on the primary level allow objects to retain their identity as objects. The natural sights and sounds in Rossellini's *India,* for example, are felt first as natural things and only then in terms of their other meanings in the whole film. Sirk allows no such primary associations. To do so would be to permit the viewer to look at the shot and say, 'trees, a rainbow, happiness,' and search for other meanings only insofar as they grow out of the reality of these primary ones. Rather, one looks at the image and says, 'trees, rainbow, supposed to be happiness . . . wait!' for in an instant these elements, in a shot with great apparent spatial depth, are seen as fused into a single surface which allows none of them any independent reality. Thus they suggest happiness not in a primary way but only in the context of that fusion: and so any happiness which they suggest is simultaneously realised to be unreal and impossible. The rainbow, which is supposed in 'nature' to lie in some distant place deep in the sky, looks almost like a painted backdrop. And thus the shot is not so much an expression of even an instant of happiness but rather of the impossibility of happiness. We can see only the 'surface of glass' of which Sirk speaks.

This description applies fairly well to all of Sirk's images. Objects and areas are never allowed to have the primary physical meaning which they have in real life. It is not that Sirk, as would any artist, transforms that primary meaning into something else, an expressive meaning, but rather that in terms of the films the objects can be seen only in terms of their expressive function in the shot. In this sense, the true subject of a Sirk film is not the situation of the film as used by Sirk, or the objects in the frame as transformed by Sirk, but rather the actual subject is the expression of the film itself. More generally, Sirk's films can be said to be *about* aesthetic distances, *about* the mirror images and other reflections he uses so well.

If there is no worldly physical reality to any of the elements of his frames, then his characters can never be said to 'understand' or even see the real world. I am using the word *real* here in a very special way. Of course no formal art ultimately conveys or describes the everyday reality which we are accustomed to experiencing. In the films of Murnau—*Tabu,* for instance—one feels the ships and the sun and moon and ocean mainly as elements of Murnau's vision. But there is a constant sense of transformation. His use of the moon, or of the sea, recalls to our mind various associations we have with the real moon and the real sea. While he is describing the machinations of a cosmic kind of fatalism which is ultimately only of his own imagination, he roots that fatalism and its visual description in the physical world. Thus his films have a sense of reality insofar as they seem to be calling upon, and then transforming, real physical things. His images work in terms of this single transformation: that of the photographed object being transformed into an element of his vision. In a sense, it is this transformation, the arrival at his vision, that along with the vision itself is the deepest subject of his films. *Arrival* rather than vision arrived at, so our attention is fixed on his imaginative ordering and conversion of the things, the objects—ultimately, the light—which we have already come to know in everyday life. His films consequently have a certain feeling of total conclusiveness, a sense that the imaginative construction they effect is a kind of real truth or final reality, for the process by which that construction is reached from everyday objects is clearly shown. And so, since the active process of transformation rather than the passive state of an already-arrived-at vision is the subject of his films, we are permitted to view the things in the films both in their 'real' everyday sense, with the collective associations we bring to them (and which Murnau—and other filmmakers like his—used), and in their place in the film. This double association that objects retain makes their use as elements in the film all the more convincing: for it appears that the film's vision is built on some type of real, physical reality. By allowing us to see the transformation, by making it a part of the film, Murnau permits his art to retain some sense of primacy, some feeling that it is about one way of looking at the real world.

Sirk, on the other hand, works in exactly the opposite sense. It is the sense of a vision already arrived at, a transformation already effected, a surface which has already been reached that dominates his films. The objects in his films have a kind of fixity of meaning, and any additional implications and resonances generally come not from associations with the objects themselves as much as from the more formal qualities of the image, which in turn assign the objects and people fixed positions in the frame. Happiness is something which in the deepest sense is never shown in Sirk, can never be shown, because the happiness he conceives of implies a kind of reality of experience which the very qualities of his images deny. His films are not about some physically real subject which is being transformed, but about the passive qualities of the images themselves. The complete unreality can be described as a kind of falseness, an anti-sensuality. The colours in *Written on the Wind* are far from realistic; rather they seem 'false' on any possible level. The red 'sunlight' on Kyle's face in the plane is neither psycho-logically symbolic nor realistic even on the level of imagination—as are, say, Minnelli's colours—but rather seems to call attention to its own falseness. Paradoxically, it is this very falseness which holds the extraordinary expressive force that can make Sirk's films so powerful.

In a sense, then, all characters in Sirk are totally blind, surrounded as they are, not by real things but only by falseness. There is no question of seeing 'reality' on any level or attaining any genuine understanding since such concepts are completely excluded by the formal qualities of Sirk's images.

Falseness

The notion of falseness, and of the characters' relationship to that falseness, is one that bears further exploring. 'False' is of course used here not to indicate a flaw, or that the film does not measure up to some arbitrary standard of realism, but rather to indicate the nature of a feeling that seems to be created within the context of the films themselves. In this regard, the question might well be asked 'false with respect to what?' because falseness is not a common emotion like fear which can be created alike in every member of an audience. To say that the look of a film feels false in terms of the film's own expression implies that the film itself suggests some other standard of reality. While Sirk can never show an experience more real than the primary feelings his films generate, he is able to use the films themselves to suggest that some reality higher than the films does in fact exist. It is important to understand that this suggestion is made entirely within the formal context of the films, rather than being imposed from without by some visual equivalent of an opening title 'the story you are about to see' or formal correlate of the dream-plot.

What Sirk does is to develop relationships in his films between characters and surrounding objects, between characters and their feelings, between object and object, which by their very nature are suggestive of their own unreality or incompleteness. In Sirk's idea for a film about blind people, the audience would know that the characters were blind, and they themselves would know it, and so while the film would presumably develop the idea that a certain fullness of reality can never be experienced, we, as observers rather than participants in the blind person-to-object relationship, would know that the real object in fact existed, and that it was simply that the people could not see it. More importantly, the blind people themselves would be aware of their blindness, aware that they cannot see—i.e., fully understand and experience—the objects they are touching. This method of using one kind of seeing to suggest the existence of a reality far beyond it is no more of a paradox than suggested by writers on Earth who describe the Infinite, or God, or by the characters in Plato's cave learning of the existence of the sun. When Naomi Murdoch in *All I Desire* returns to her family, and stands outside on the lawn looking through the window at a presumably happy dinner table, the shots of the family seen through the window from her point of view are not meant to convey the reality of a happiness which she is outside of. Rather, the effect of her seeing them through the window conveys only the sense of *outsideness* itself. The family is reduced to shadows behind a pane of glass. There is no question of happiness in such a context. But what is important is the glass itself: for here is a concrete sign of the unreality of which I have been speaking. We *know* that the family is unreal to Naomi; she can only see their shadows, so to speak, and from a distance. We *see* the things which is the concrete representation of that distance: the pane of glass, the frame of the window. It is by thus crystallising the unreality itself, by making that unreality, that frozen, static position, his subject, that Sirk makes us aware of it. His continual shooting of action in mirrors is another example of this.

It is not only the pane of glass that makes us aware of the unreality, but the nature of the entire relationship between Naomi and her family. Even though invited inside her house, she remains emotionally an outsider for much of the film. Sirk makes systematic use of narrative situations which place an individual outside an action which he would like to be a part of. Sirk is then able to explore the relationship between, really the distance between, the character and the action. Particularly clear examples of this occur in *Has Anybody Seen My Gal* and *The Tarnished Angels*. Here are narrative representations of the impossibility of reaching, or merging with, idealised real experience. All that matters to Fulton in *Has Anybody Seen My Gal* is the family to which he cannot reveal himself; thus he is separated from the only thing he seems to care about. He must relate to them through the mask of the identity he has assumed. Again we have a relationship whose nature is made clear by the internal structure of the film.

In *The Lady Pays Off*, Diana, playing a young 'match-maker,' arranges that her father eat dinner with Evelyn Warren. We see this dinner from Diana's position on a stairway above them. Sirk's assumption of her point of view here, like Naomi's in *All I Desire*, does not have the effect of making us identify with this character. In order to do so, it would be necessary for us to assume the character's point of view almost unconsciously, seeing what she sees as if it were a primary reality. Instead, Sirk in both situations constantly makes us aware that we are merely taking one possible point of view, the one that the character takes; further, that we are separated observers, not active participants, in the action. Our active knowledge of the point of view we are taking also keeps us aware of the possibility of other points of view, such as those of the characters we are watching, even if at the moment we are powerless to assume them. Separated by the pane of glass or the height of a stairway we view an action in which the characters whose place we occupy has a vital interest. But our conscious awareness of the distance makes us realise that the pane of glass, or the height, also separates *them* from *us*, and consequently reality or happiness is not to be found in the hoped-for ability to assume their positions; for then, looking at our former place from the other side of the real or metaphorical pane of glass, we would be just as separated from it, and from the rest of our surroundings. This is a crucial point in Sirk. There are many points of view that the camera, or a character, can take; but rather than contributing by simple addition to a total picture each remains separated from the others; and it is their very multiplicity that renders hopeless the possibility of real seeing. The more possible points of view there are, each equally valid but each inevitably separated, the more hopeless the situation appears, because the only thing that is increased is the multiplicity of possible separations.

It is thus that Sirk makes us aware of the unreality of everything that we, and his characters, see. He is able to use frames that are 'false' to make us aware of that very falseness, by setting up internal relationships such as those already described between different ways of seeing the same thing. As the viewer of character becomes aware of the distance and separation as a conscious element, so he also feels the implication that somewhere, in some other space, there is a physical reality. This is something which his characters also speak of and long for: for instance, Father Fulton in *The First Legion* with his desire to return to the 'real world out there'; or to the memories of his childhood. But no more real existence is ever shown in Sirk; this is precisely what he wishes to deny, and awareness of it occurs only to the extent that it is needed as a reference back to the flatness of the frames.

Flatness is perhaps a better word than unreality or falseness, both of which have negative connotations which should be avoided, and it also suggests another method by which Sirk creates his style. On the deepest expressive level, his frames never possess anything remotely resembling three-dimensional perspective, but rather they all operate in a kind of pre-Renaissance flatness. This is true even of the shots which would appear to the casual viewer to possess spatial depth, such as the deep-focus shots taken inside the houses in *Take Me to Town* or *There's Always Tomorrow*. The camera, in wide angle, shows a deep and apparently 'realistic' room. But simultaneous with this perception we feel that the back of the room, the background, seems to have as much force, power, or presence as the foreground. The shot often places the foreground objects to the sides of the frame, leaving large spaces at the centre for the background. This background seems to impinge, come forward, make itself felt with a rare and mysterious force. Finally, we feel that all parts of the frame are fused into a single level of depth, a single surface. This can be said to apply to all of Sirk's shots; it is more obviously true of a film like *Written on the Wind,* which specifically works with colours and flat textures.

Ultimately this works toward the same end as the internalised relationships and endistancing effects. What do we mean by physical reality, sensual presence, if not a kind of three-dimensional full-bloodedness which Sirk's frames would so obviously exclude? His characters, all living things, are forced into a kind of living death, or life only as shadows. Indeed, the world of a Sirk film is not unlike a Platonic shadow-play.

One might read the foregoing and wonder what the purpose of a Sirk film is at all, when a 'higher' reality is available to our everyday senses. This would be to misunderstand the relationship between life and art. The whole point of Sirk is not to lead us to some more physical experiencing of things, but to show us the beauty of his anti-physical, two-dimensional perspective. The references to some unseen higher existence in his films only serve to lead us back to the film's own world; to add that much more force to the crystallisation of his vision. Ultimately, as an artist, Sirk does not deal in despair but in aesthetic beauty.

Two-Dimensionality

The flatness of Sirk is not one of complete equality or balance. Indeed, one of the things that gives his films so much force is the individual power that can be imparted to specific objects and events. At times, this seems to take on an almost causal form, as if certain events occurring within this flatness were in fact the cause of that flatness. One example can be found in *Shockproof,* in the scene in the oil-camp. Griff and Jenny, the hunted lovers, live in a hut whose 'walls' are of wire mesh; trying to hide their faces to avoid discovery, they are in constant view of their prying neighbours. Sirk makes the neighbours particularly crude; their constant presence in the frame seems to render impossible and even ridiculous the tenderness of Griff and Jenny's love. The images themselves, with Griff and Jenny in the foreground and the characters seen through wire screen in the background, have the effect of making the other couple seem intrusive, ever-present. One might think that the screen, the separation, would keep them apart. On one level it does; it prevents any real physical contact or full-blooded relationship. But it also reduces the other couple to more nameless, terrifying presences; visible through the screen, they become it; fusing into the surface with Griff and Jenny, their presence there has a kind of perverse, nameless voyeurism which actually mocks their desire to be alone.

The use of individual objects or characters to similar ends occurs throughout Sirk. Mirror shots are the most common example. The mirror image clearly exists on a different physical level from that of the characters, and is hence separated. But—in the scene between Annie and Sarah Jane in her dressing room toward the end of *Imitation of Life*—the presence of both the reflection and the character in the same frame tends to unite them into a single surface. Ultimately, the presence of the reflection and its fusion with the character reduces the character herself to the status of a mere reflection, just as the presence of the other couple in *Shockproof* debased and mocked the idea of any feeling between Jenny and Griff. More generally, the presence of a reflection merely in the same context or sequence, as in the pan to Fedor's mirror image in the restaurant in *Summer Storm,* has the same effect. In fact, just as we have described all Sirk's frames as shadow-plays, so we might just as well describe them as mirror images or reflections.

I have not made clear enough the chilling, starkly terrifying effect that many of these images can have. When Helen, thinking she is alone in a room in Toni's house in *Interlude,* first sees the reflection of his wife in the piano cover, the shot of that reflection has a kind of ghost-like presence which devastates any sense of security that the passive staticism of Sirk's style might have led us to feel. The appearance of the evil doctor in a room in Allison's house in *Sleep, My Love* has a similar unsettling effect. While these objects ultimately work toward keeping the other characters frozen into the surface, their apparent emergence from that surface in order to effect this is precisely what is so striking. Sirk's staticism is not a passively postulated style but one which is crystallised actively and with considerable force.

Related to the terrifying events is the more general power which can be imparted to objects in Sirk. This has been explored in more detail elsewhere with respect to *The First Legion,*[5] and I will return to it in discussing *The Tarnished Angels.* The main point is that quite often objects which have no apparent symbolic meaning can take on force within the frame similar to that of Mrs. Fischer's piano-reflection. They have a similar effect; partially emerged from the staticism, they help return all other things to it, and are ultimately themselves a part of it. In fact, the shot of Mrs. Fischer is itself a reflection; it can be said to 'emerge from staticism' only insofar as it upsets the kind of complacent balance which the film's style might have led one to feel up to this point.

The unusual force that can be attained by a Sirkian reflection or object implies that his frames are not balanced with any kind of equality. It could not be said that each part of the frame is the equal of every other. The same is true of Sirk's use of the narrative structure as a whole.

Narrative

Sirk has stated that he realised after making *A Scandal in Paris* that American audiences were not receptive to 'nuances that have a double meaning and make us smile.' The implication is that soon after coming to America, he found it necessary to tone down his tendency toward this type of irony. Indeed, a German film like *Zu Neuen Ufern* or one of his first American films, *Summer Storm,* has a density of occurrences, a rich level of ironies, which form a good deal of the basis for the film's structure. By contrast, *All That Heaven Allows* or *Magnificent Obsession* would appear to be far less dense and intense. But beyond these superficial details one can find a similarity in the use of narrative form among all four films, one which reflects on Sirk's style and method as a whole.

Many films, for instance those of Hawks, build their effect through a cumulative process of addition of scenes. The narrative line of the film does not have a

5. See Dave Grosz *"The First Legion:* Vision and Perception in Sirk," *Screen* 12, no. 2 (Summer 1971): 99.

classic or fatalist determined form, but rather progresses with a kind of natural, improvised rhythm. Each scene builds on the previous one, so that the film is no more than the sum of all the scenes seen in order. No single scene either dominates the film or gives the feeling of having determined any part of its action larger than the relative length of the scene in the film. All the scenes exist in a kind of equal balance. Sirk's narrative structures are the exact opposite of this. No scene can be viewed in isolation from the whole. The sections do not combine by addition, but like pieces of a puzzle—the overall narrative form of the film—whose total picture has been determined in advance. The order in which the pieces are put together—the order of the film's scenes—is not of paramount importance. But each scene is meaningless without referring to the whole—both the scenes that preceded it and the scenes to follow. Most important, each piece of the puzzle, each scene, is not necessarily of equal importance. Indeed, some scenes can be so crucial as to exert a determining effect on the meaning of the surrounding scenes. It is only in the most general visual sense that an individual shot or sequence in Sirk may be said to contain all his meanings. Insofar as the meaning of the individual incidents and of the story as a whole is concerned, single events, even single objects, can exert a pivotal influence.

A good example occurs in *All That Heaven Allows*. The film is full of flat surface textures and bright 'false' colours. Like many of Sirk's films, it seems to largely forsake the power of individual objects for the simpler beauty of surfaces, areas of colour and texture. While this type of style has transcendent complexity in a film like *A Time to Love and a Time to Die,* in *All That Heaven Allows* one imagines it might simply be Sirk's response to the relatively simple story that was assigned to him. The plot concerns a middle-aged widow who would like to find happiness with her gardener, Ron Kirby, but whose friends try to force her into a more conventional pattern which involves marrying a smooth sweet 'respected citizen' older, rather than younger, than herself. Things seem to progress along fairly predictable lines, and while watching the film we may guess that it will be relatively sparse in ironies or object-power, and is perhaps more a question of Sirk responding to his material rather than a total expressive integration of form and content. This misconception might lead us to see the film as a relatively impersonal project filmed by Sirk with his characteristic eye for beautiful colours and surfaces.

Midway through the film, the widow's son comes home from Princeton University for Christmas. Her son and daughter have raised particularly strong objections to her interest in her gardener. Earlier, someone had suggested to her that, as a widow, she should get something 'suitable' to occupy her time—like a television. Now, a man wheels in her Christmas present from her children—a TV. He unwraps it and holds it before her, and the camera dollies in on the TV screen itself, in which her face can be seen reflected as she gazes at it, ghost-like isolated, alone, as he says that in this box she can find 'drama . . . comedy . . . life's parade at your fingertips.' In an instant, in one of the most chilling moments in any film, we have a complete representation of the movement of the film as a whole, the attempt of the other characters to reduce the apparently more real feelings she has for Ron Kirby to 'drama . . . comedy . . .life's parade at your fingertips.' The film, taken as a whole, can almost be said to pivot around this single shot. The expressive force of every image, the meaning of every surface, is to some extent informed by its presence and implications.

Similarly, *Magnificent Obsession* pivots to some extent around a single shot. Randolph throughout the film gives his religious philosophy, about how you can accomplish almost anything if you are in touch with the source of infinite power.' This phrase has a special irony for Sirk, since on the one hand everything is trapped and there are no sources of power strong enough to transcend the surface, while on the other the objects that partially emerge from that surface do seem to have a power which is almost limitless—limitless, at least, in terms of being able to exert causal influence on the world of the film. The shooting is somewhat like that of *All That Heaven Allows,* although there is more contrast in the frames and the surfaces are not as smooth. At the end of the film, Bob Merrick is about to perform an operation on the woman he loves, with very slim chances of success. Even if he can save her life, she will remain hopelessly blind. He doesn't want to perform it, saying that he is not qualified and it will not succeed. Randolph urges him to. In the operating room, he hesitates before beginning, and then sees Randolph's face, standing and watching from outside, reflected in a mirror above his head. This has enormous causal force, partly as another powerful reflection and because of Randolph's claim to represent the 'source of infinite power.' In the context of the film, it is this shot of his reflection that is the true source of infinite power: it is what causes Merrick to operate, the woman to live and miraculously see again, an apparently impossible conclusion which is a tribute to the power of reflections over all logic much as the end of *The First Legion* imparts a similar power to objects. Finally, the entire religious philosophy of the script has meaning only in the context of that one shot of Randolph: it seems to sum up the entire mechanism of the film, and yet it is also a reflection.

On the other hand, a film like *Zu Neuen Ufern* is extremely rich in similarly ironic events. Because of their multiplicity, the film does not pivot around any one of them, but has rather many points which serve almost as signposts or references for the movement and meaning of the rest of the film. The characteristic form in both cases is one of a story filmed with a general style which is its deepest meaning, but containing specific shots or events or objects which seem to be concrete—even verbally representable—crystallisations of the meanings of that style. Sirk uses the narrative not as an excuse for scenes, or for the creation of some other form, but as a pre-determined pattern which imposes itself like a matrix over the entire film. As the film progresses, events crystallise the meaning of that pattern, to the point where the thrust of the earlier scenes is often clearest only after the film has ended.

The mocking nature of many of these crystallising events should be clear.

Sirk's films are full of bitter, mocking ironies, which is perhaps what Sarris meant when he spoke of Sirk's 'dark humour.'[6] One of the earliest examples occurs in *Zu Neuen Ufern*. Gloria Vane is in love with Sir Albert, and goes to prison for him; getting out, she finds him engaged to another; broken-hearted, she takes a job singing in a sleazy casino. Sir Albert comes in; she spots him while she is singing, breaks down and cannot continue. Here is an instance of real feeling appearing to break through: but it forces her off the stage and ultimately out of the frame. Immediately following her break-down, a dancing girl comes out in a ridiculous clown-like costume and struts up and down on the stage, mocking and ultimately reducing any feeling Gloria might have had. This absurd clowning is what the world requires of her, not any real feeling, or even singing which reflects such feeling; the casino audience regards this as false, and the clown-girl as 'real' entertainment. The entire context of the film excludes such feeling; the clown girl is Sirk's comment on people who think they have attained it.

In many of his other films, Sirk chooses to make his last shot not one of the characters but rather some animal or object which seems to comment absurdly on the characters' plight. The stuffed fish at the end of *No Room for the Groom* emphasises the static nature of animals, and ultimately of the characters. The monkey at the end of *A Scandal in Paris,* on the other hand, appears animate, but uses its motion simply to mock or mimic the earlier motions of the people. Perhaps the greatest 'mocking' ending is that of *Summer Storm.* The flashback has ended, the cold present returned; despite Nadina's hope, all chance of love between her and Fedor has passed. Trying to get back his manuscript, Fedor is shot; before falling, he drops a dance card which he had given Nadina years ago, on which he had written 'I love you.' The last shots show the trash being swept off the floor; the dance card is dropped into the waste basket, open and with the words 'I love you' plainly visible, and another heap of soot is dumped on top of it and the words. Such is the reduction of the film: real love to the written word, and the words then to just another surface layer in the layers of garbage in the trash basket.

The relationship between the individual and the object which is mocking him has similarities to the relationship between individuals and things they are looking at as described in *All I Desire* and *The Lady Pays Off.* The mirror reflection or other mocking object is no more (or less) real than the characters' actual state. In *Written on the Wind,* Kyle speaks to a doctor who implies that he might be sterile, which brings out his neurotic fears of impotence. He leaves the drugstore where they talk, a broken man, to be suddenly confronted with a little boy bouncing up and down on a wooden horse. The hideous grotesqueness of this image, the unashamed physicality of the child appearing to remind Kyle even more of his own state, is indescribable. But the image of the boy does not reveal some

6. Andrew Sarris, *The American Cinema* (New York: Dutton, 1968).

hidden truth of which we were not aware; it does not serve to delineate Kyle's character any more clearly. In terms of the factual structure of the character and the story it is thoroughly superfluous: and this is precisely the point. It is its apparent gratuitousness, coming after Kyle has already been told in effect that his sperm count is low, that makes the shot so powerful: it is like an exaggerated reflection of Kyle's own view of himself, coming at him with an illogically sadistic force merely for the purpose of being there, of mocking him. Sirk's art is constructed out of such reflections; rather than being superfluous, they are the very substance of his films.

Consequently, the animals, or the end of *Summer Storm,* which do in a sense represent an absurd view of existence, should not be taken as prime examples of mocking relationships in Sirk. Such relationships have their greatest meaning and impact to the degree that the 'mocking' image appears to be simply another view or reflection of the object mocked. Sirk's mirror images gain some of their power from the inexplicable feeling that one's own reflection holds—or reveals—another side of oneself, terrible truths one wishes to avoid—the ultimate truth that a mirror can reveal that oneself, everything, is only a reflection. But before reaching this stage of frozen feelings, Sirk's reflections can have unlimited and terrifying suggestive powers. All his other 'mockeries' have similar effects—they appear to be only mirror images, other versions or perceptions, of things within the central objects or characters. This process reaches a complexity so great that one can almost say that all the objects in Sirk are only masks or reflections cast of all the other objects.

The use of reflections or mockery is never meant to convey a sense of complete surrealist or absurd disconnection. Rather than being strictly absurd, the last shot of *Summer Storm* gains much of its power from being such a devastatingly clear representation of the process of the entire film. The mocking object is not something stuck in the film by Sirk to give it a sense of ridiculousness, but rather is in fact the *same thing* as the object mocked. If it seems absurd this is only to make clear to us the absurdity of our normal view—that the primary objects we see—as the characters' bodies in *A Scandal in Paris*—are in some sense the 'real thing.' The use of a monkey as a character finally conveys the feeling that the characters were similarly ridiculous throughout the film—and that both monkeys and people are only two-dimensional reflections of a presumed three-dimensional world outside of our vision and beyond the frames. The characters and the monkey are two poles of the same class of objects—as red and cyan may be opposites, but they are both colours—which relate to each other as does Kyle to the boy on the toy horse in *Written on the Wind*. The initial appearance of one as the falsification of the other gives way to a perception—forced on us by the unity of Sirk's surfaces—of both as falsifications, falsifications only in the sense that one might use the endlessly recurring reflections to infer by their recurrence the existence of some other world. Such a world is outside Sirk's vision and not otherwise relevant to his films. Reflections and mockeries are like the relationships between 'outsiders' and the worlds they idealise. The frame places all things in a single context which makes separate objects all seem reflections of each other.

This is the final and clearest meaning I can describe in Sirk. The sense of frames as unified wholes, containing separate areas, pieces of the puzzle, which draw meaning only from the total picture gives way to a sense of the interdependence of every object coming from the fact that ultimately all the objects are views of the same thing. Not that they have all emerged from some primary object or shape, a sense that some of Brakhage's films give, but rather that they are all views of some general space which by its very nature is two-dimensional. As one can say that while red and cyan are opposites they are both colours, and that while reflections of different objects in a mirror are all reflections, so Sirk's objects[7] are limited to their own class or state of being. As Sirk's films are 'about themselves,' one finally has a feeling that his real meaning is in the actual style or general space or state of being of which all his objects are a part. The difference between different objects is finally only a localised one, simply a specific materialisation, one possible way of seeing, the general space. Beyond this general beauty the interest in Sirk comes from the wonderfully imaginative multiplicity of different materialisations in his films.

In a sense, then, any general truth that can be found in Sirk has relevance to the entire film in which it occurs and to all his work. The pivotal events have special relevance because, invested with special power, they ultimately seem to be closer, or stronger, materialisations. Every general intellectual point that we can make about Sirk, every category into which we can place his events, is ultimately equally true of *every* event in his films. Kyle's impotence in *Written on the Wind* may be a metaphor for the film's entire state, and impotence is a theme, like blindness, which recurs explicitly in several Sirk films. But like blindness, it has its greatest meaning when understood as a metaphor for all of Sirk's *oeuvre,* for the state of every character. The flatness of all Sirk's frames, their lack of flesh-and-blood physicality, would seem to be a description of such impotence. The only objects which have force in Sirk are completely asensual, like the mysteriously powerful objects which ultimately exact a kind of vengeance in *The First Legion,* or the more direct and voyeurist couple in the adjoining cabin in the oil-camp in *Shockproof.* In this context, the unnaturally red sunlight on Kyle's face in *Written on the Wind* can be seen as another metaphor for his impotence; the colour is as rich as any in the film, but by its falseness conveys the sense that the greatest possible richness is ultimately asensual. By making us directly aware of its falseness, it calls attention to itself, away from Kyle, rendering him even more distant and powerless.

In discussing impotence, Sirk has said 'if you think too much about the sexual

---

7. *Object* is used throughout to connote not simply an inanimate object or 'thing' but every separate area in a Sirk frame—an inanimate object, a person, an animal, or even an area of texture. It is in this general sense that I now speak of Sirk's whole world as consisting of objects.

act you lose your sexual power.'[8] In a sense, this statement holds a key to the
nature and cause of the theme of impotence in Sirk. His films do not show
primary physical reality but objects filtered through endistancing perception, a
constructed reality whose only subject finally is itself. This kind of endless self-
reflection can be seen to lead to falseness—if all one's thoughts derive from self-
contemplation, they form a kind of endless loop of reflections which cannot be
real—and the 'thinking too much' that causes this is a kind of generalisation of
Sirk's remark 'thinking too much about the sexual act.' Thinking too much on
something finally transforms one's attention from the thing itself—an object or a
sexual act—to one's own thoughts *about* that thing. This is the deepest implication of the red sunlight in the plane cockpit in *Written on the Wind*. Its unreality
seems its own subject in such a final way as to exclude any other kind of reality.
This creates the feeling of Kyle being trapped in this grotesqueness of self-
contemplation and mockery; a feeling of total powerlessness, of despair.

One should never mistake such despair for a hopelessness without beauty. This
is made clearest by the end of *Imitation of Life*. Sarah Jane breaks into her
mother's funeral procession. Having rejected her mother and her values through
the years, and broken her mother's heart, she now, and too late, is sorry. She
breaks open the hearse, screaming, 'Mama, I did love you,' and clutches at the
coffin. But the coffin is covered with a huge bouquet of flowers, and she can
reach only at those flowers. Once again, trying to find real feeling, one reaches
only surfaces.

But the funeral procession of *Imitation of Life* is one of the most transcen-
dently beautiful sequences of any film. Its despair is transcended by the very
beauty of the surfaces which the sequence itself celebrates. While certain kinds
of real feeling are excluded, the flowers, the shots of the procession through
frosted glass, the final high shot, have the beauty of a kind of triumph—the
triumph of surfaces over reality perhaps, but just as well, the triumph of art over
life. If Sirk's films are about their own style, then this sequence is ultimately
celebrating its own beauty. But Sirk seems to have gone beyond the almost impotent flatness of some of his earlier films to a kind of sensual celebration of the
very flowers, the colours, that had previously had mocking connotations. When
Sarah Jane clutches at the flowers, she has reached the only kind of beauty that is
possible to man in Sirk's films—and her blindness is not in her earlier refusal to
recognise the reality of her mother's love, but rather in her refusal now to
recognise—as do the other characters—the beauty of those surfaces.

Melodrama

Perhaps one of the reasons why Sirk has not attained any great degree of 'serious'
recognition is that so many of his films were made in the genre of the soap-opera,

8. 'Entretien avec Douglas Sirk,' p. 69.

which is probably the type of film most reviled by anti-film intellectuals and aesthetes. To be sure, there are valid objections that can be made to soap-operas, at least on social grounds. To paraphrase Polonsky's very perceptive remarks about popular fiction, the soap-opera is generally based on a series of 'if onlys.' 'If only I was twenty years younger'; 'if only his phone hadn't been engaged then'; 'if only he had known about the baby.' These correspond to a series of invented choices which, were they made at some time in the past, would have made everything fine in the present: 'then I would have married her,' 'then she wouldn't have committed suicide,' 'then he would have taken care of her.' This entire process is a kind of false, cheating romanticism which sets up situations which in fact never existed, which seeks to attribute all our present troubles to an unfortunate past mistake or chance occurrence. The romanticism comes from the attempt to play on the viewer's fantasies, allowing him to rewrite the past without reference to human failings in order to fantasise about a wished-for present that in fact can never be. It is a cheap kind of manipulation of audience wishes; Polonsky is quite correct when he calls it 'the pornography of feeling.'[9]

The very first set of these 'if onlys' and invented choices is in fact, along with another 'if only she had told me that she loved me,' the basis of Sirk's *There's Always Tomorrow*. But here Sirk parts company with romanticism, real or false; here the resemblence ends. For to understand the film on all its levels is to know that no true happiness is ever possible. Every frame's tight static unity specifically excludes any romantic imaginings outside of the context of the film. And the final meaning of the script itself is precisely that you can never go back; that any such feelings (about the possibility of real love) that might exist are entirely outside of the context of the film, and thus, outside of the context of what is allowed to the characters.

I bring this up not to answer a possible objection to Sirk but to re-state the unity of all the different elements in his films. Everything in the frame crystallises into an unbreakable whole which suggests nothing but itself. A Murnau or a Rossellini frame suggests that it is only a part of some half-unseen larger order, which in Murnau represents a kind of unfathomable fate. But if Murnau's fate is unfathomable because it is unseen, Sirk's fatalism and sense of despair is inexplicable precisely because it is so clearly visible, visible on the same level of expression as the other elements of the film. This is to say, there are no successively deeper levels of meaning suggested by a Sirk film. The meaning of his frames reflects back only on themselves, which is to repeat that Sirk's films are about their own style. Every element in a Sirk film is on some level a reflection or mockery only of some other element of that same film. The revelations—the moments which seem to take on special power—lead us only to more reflections of those revelations, until we realise that the only real revelation is that everything is a reflection.

9. *The Director's Event,* ed. Eric Sherman and Martin Rubin (New York: Atheneum, 1969).

Thus Sirk's films are remarkably unified and self-contained. One could almost take the succession of points I have already made, and construct a giant chart with arrows connecting each aspect of Sirk to every other to show that they are all inter-related. Object power creates flatness of surface; flatness of surface allows objects properly placed amidst the flatness to attain power; mockeries are reflections of the only possible reality in Sirk; the greatest knowledge possible to a Sirk character is the awareness of his own blindness. This is why it is generally those characters that attempt to reach out beyond the blindness, attempt to see, or actually believe that they can see, that are the ones that are doomed. A list of the characters killed or otherwise devastated in Sirk's films reads like a list of all the characters who attempted to reach some real understanding and control of their surroundings; who thought they had such understanding; who tried to use it to find happiness. From *Summer Storm* to *Imitation of Life* this pattern is repeated, the exceptions invariably being the relatively unconvincing 'happy' endings of *All I Desire* or *All That Heaven Allows,* or the clearly ambiguous ones like *Magnificent Obsession.*

One qualification should be made to the notion that all events in Sirk are self-contained. It is true that they do not actively create meanings or further ideas outside of the context of the film. But the most powerful events occur with a kind of irrational or at least inexplicable power, and are placed in a position which is strictly speaking illogical but whose very surprise helps to generate that power. In most of the films, the impossibility of understanding seems entirely attributable to the surfaces of the frames themselves. But there are a few—*The First Legion, The Tarnished Angels, A Time to Love and a Time to Die*—which also seem haunted by a kind of unseen fatalism or foredooming, not unlike the feeling of hopelessness created by the flashback form of *Summer Storm.* To an extent this feeling is attributable to the narrative forms that these films take. But as is made clear by *A Time to Love and a Time to Die* there are instances where an irrational power seems to strike at the characters almost as if from outside the context of the film. This power never materialises in any sense, nor are its properties even hinted at as they are in Murnau. It is not so much something unseen as it is something which is beyond seeing. This sense of fate occurs to a smaller degree in all of Sirk's films, though it is generally difficult to separate it from the more internal causes. But finally it seems to me to be the opposite correlate of the equally-unseeable sense of 'reality' or 'happiness' in Sirk; fate is the negative side of this, a kind of unspeakably sadistic evil.

Distanciation and Douglas Sirk

Paul Willemen

The imitation of nature is a means but not an end in art. Theatre that simply aims at accurate rendering of reality is meant for people with little imagination. Art is inevitably determined by a set of conditions and patterns.

Valery Bryusov

I would have made Imitation of Life *anyway, for the title alone. There is a marvellous saying in English, which I think expresses the essence of art, or at least, of its language, 'seeing through a glass darkly.'*

Douglas Sirk

his radically different interpretation of the word 'imitation' given by Bryusov and Sirk pinpoints quite clearly the main question raised by Sirk's films: how should art relate to reality? Bryusov's statement, appearing in the fourth issue of *The World of Art* (1906), the Russian symbolist magazine, has to be placed in the context of the symbolist reaction against naturalism. In this article, Bryusov attacks the Moscow Art Theatre for the 'unnecessary faithfulness to life' of its productions. Such efforts to imitate 'reality' on the stage had been the most dominant characteristic of the bourgeois theatre between *c.*1750 and 1910. This type of theatre, described by Siegfried Melchinger as 'illusionist,'[1] constituted an attempt to create the illusion that the events which were taking place on the stage were, in fact, 'real,' and the intention was to make the spectator forget that he was watching a performance in the theatre.

The cinematic equivalent to illusionism can be found in the theories of André Bazin, where the cinema is viewed as a means of duplicating or reproducing reality. When Bazin applies this bias to filmed plays, he came to the logical conclusion that film had to reproduce the theatrical experience by explicitly emphasising the stage conventions, stressing the point that the essence of theatre is the representation of a literary text. As this text has been specifically designed to function within the four walls of the stage (the three physical walls together with the footlights), Bazin argues that the filmed play has to recreate this theatrical echo-chamber, or else the text has to be drastically altered in order to adapt it to the new, open situation of the cinema. Bazin's model for the ideal theatrical film is *Henry V* because Olivier successfully succeeded in depicting the 'reality' of a

From *Douglas Sirk,* ed. Laura Mulvey and Jon Halliday (Edinburgh: Edinburgh Film Festival, 1972): 23–29. First published in *Screen* 12, no. 2 (Summer 1971): 63–67.
1. Siegfried Melchinger, *Drama zwischen Shaw and Brecht* (Bremen, 1957).

theatrical performance, making use of the camera simply as a recording instrument. Here we are faced with a kind of second-degree realism, a faithful reproduction of a stylised event. Bazin's concept of a theatrical film is, in fact, a documentary of a stage-play; such a theory is useless when discussing any genuine influence the theatre might have had on the cinema, or indeed, for discussing theatrical influences detectable in Sirk's work.

On reading Sirk's essays and interviews, it is possible to deduce that Sirk is familiar with all the major theories of representation formulated in the first two decades of the century in Russia and Germany. Although Sirk's aesthetic position can in no way be confused with either expressionism or symbolism, it is quite evident that he shares the complete rejection of the conventions of illusionism which characterises these movements. Without fully subscribing to any single movement, Sirk was undoubtedly greatly influenced by the theatrical revolution which immediately preceded his career as a stage director. When analysing his American films it becomes apparent that many stylistic features which had been rehabilitated by expressionism together with the symbolist concept of *correspondances* were adapted by Sirk to suit his own purposes. In his American melodramas in particular, it is possible to discern the echoes of such expressionist prescriptions as:

> *'The melody of a great gesture says more than the highest consummation of what is called naturalness.'* (Paul Kornfeld)
> *'The dullness and stupidity of men are so enormous that only enormities can counteract them. Let the new drama be enormous.'* (Yvan Goll)
> *'Man and things will be shown as naked as possible, and always through a magnifying glass for better effect.'* (Yvan Goll)

However, for Sirk, such prescriptions represent a source of inspiration and become no more than echoes, detectable in his magnification of emotionality, his use of pathos, choreography and music, reverberating within the mirror-ridden walls of a Sirkian decor. The meaning of this kind of stylisation does not become clear on the first viewing of a Sirk film. In order to grasp its full significance it is necessary to take into account the circumstances under which Sirk was required to work—the big Hollywood studio. Subject matter as well as general narrative outline were imposed upon him, as was the necessity of pleasing a very large audience for the maximum possible profits. This meant that he had to make films for the 'average American' audience, of which Sirk has said, 'Irony doesn't go down well with the American public. This is not meant as a reproach, but merely that in general this public is too simple and too naïve—in the best sense of these terms—to be susceptible to irony. It requires clearly delineated positions, for and against.'

As a European left-wing intellectual, Sirk, surprisingly enough, found these new circumstances very stimulating, and he wholeheartedly embraced the rules of the American genres, especially those of the melodrama. He drew on his theatrical experience not to break the rules of these genres, but to intensity them. This intensification is brought about in a number of ways:

(i) by the deliberate use of symbols as emotional stimuli, the most striking feature of these symbols being their total unequivocalness (e.g., the association of Kirby in *All That Heaven Allows* with a Christmas tree and a deer; Sarah Jane's mud-stained white dress in *Imitation of Life*);

(ii) by setting the action in an echo-chamber reminiscent of a stage (e.g., *Imitation of Life* is made almost entirely in long shot, which emphasises both the spaciousness and the confinement of the decor);

(iii) through the use of choreography as a direct expression of character (e.g., Sarah Jane's dance in *Imitation of Life* and Mary Lee's dance in *Written on the Wind*);

(iv) through the use of baroque colour-schemes (e.g., in *Written on the Wind*).

The subject matter of these melodramas differs in no way from run-of-the-mill products; in fact, Sirk made quite a lot of re-makes. However, by stylising his treatment of a given narrative, he succeeded in introducing in a quite unique manner, a distance between the film and its narrative pretext. The most striking example of this 'through a glass darkly' technique can be found in the credit sequence of *Imitation of Life*. As the titles begin to appear on the screen, a large number of 'glass' diamonds slowly drift down across the screen, as if poured by an invisible hand, until they finally fill the screen by the time the director's credit appears. In an interview he gave to *Cahiers du Cinéma*,[2] Sirk explains in some detail the importance he attaches to stylisation, and stresses the importance he attaches to establishing a distance between the audience and the depicted action. However, such statements can be misleading. In general in his melodramas Sirk does not employ techniques to distanciate his audience. On the contrary, he mercilessly implicates the audience in the action. (Ample proof of this can be found in the audience's near hysterical reactions to his films involving abundant tears and/or self-protective laughter.) Such reactions seem to indicate that the distance Sirk is referring to is not necessarily perceived by the audience. However, this does not mean that distance does not exist within the film itself; merely that there appears to be a discrepancy between the audience Sirk is aiming at and the audience which he knows will come to see his films. We can even assume that Sirk is well aware of this discrepancy; in fact in some of his films he takes great care to ensure that the audience does experience a sense of distanciation, for instance, by making use of an epilogue in *Tarnished Angels*. In such cases as these where, in general, he had more directorial control, the techniques he employs differ in kind from those he employs in the melodramas.

When we compare Sirk's films with other melodramas, such as the films of Frank Borzage, Leo McCarey and Vincente Minnelli, it becomes evident that

---

2. *Cahiers du Cinéma*, no. 189 (April 1967).

Sirk's rhetoric does not refer to the idealist dichotomy of reality/fantasy which characterises their work. Instead Sirk informs the surface reality of the plot and characterisation with a secondary reality. This reality can consist of:

(i) a different story, as is the case with *Sign of the Pagan,* where Sirk grafted undercurrents of *Tamburlaine* on to the main narrative;

(ii) a criticism of the surface reality (*Written on the Wind, All I Desire, Imitation of Life*) which Sirk achieves by relying on techniques of stylisation which refer the viewer to aesthetic concepts developed in the theatre (e.g., intensification of the rules of the genre) which result in a totally anti-illustionist mode of representation.

Yuri Tynyanov[3] in a study of Dostoyevsky and Gogol points out that stylisation and parody are, in fact, closely linked to each other: 'Both live a double life: beyond the work, there is a second level, stylised or prosodised. When stylisation is strongly marked, it becomes parody.' To avoid any confusion, it must be stated that the term 'parody' as used by Tynyanov, does not necessarily imply 'comic.'[4] He defines parody as 'the mechanisation of a particular procedure, a mechanisation which, of course, will only be noticeable where the procedure to which it is applied is known. Hence, if the parody's style is not sufficiently familiar to the audience, they will be unaware that something is being parodied.' Although the notion of parody cannot be applied to the entire *oeuvre* of Sirk, some of the films have strong parodic elements in them. This becomes most evident in Sirk's use of cliché. What was referred to earlier as the deliberate use of symbols for emotional effect could, in Sirk's case, also be read as the deliberate use of cliché. Sirk's melodramas abound with cliché-images[5] (e.g., a deer and a Christmas tree are symbols for nature; a mink coat stands for success; a red-lit cabaret stands for depravity; a red dress and fast cars stand for irresponsibility and loose-living). Here we are confronted with a deliberate and systematic use (i.e., a mechanisation) of a stylistic procedure which characterises the stories in women's weeklies. It is extremely difficult to make any clear-cut and precise distinction between stylisation and parody, but Tynyanov's remark about Dostoyevsky could easily be applied to Sirk: 'It may very well be that this delicate interweaving of stylisation and parody, covering the development of a tragic subject, constitutes the originality of the sense of the grotesque in Dostoyevsky.'

From these somewhat brief observations, we can conclude that Sirk makes his films on two levels by superimposing on to the cinematic mode of representation (i.e. the duplication of the pre-filmic world) a rhetoric informed by the theatrical

3. Youri Tynyanov, 'Destruction, Parodie' (1921) in *Change,* no. 2 (1969).
4. Tynyanov points out that 'the comic is a *colour* which usually accompanies parody, but it is in no way the *colour* of parody itself. If the parody of a tragedy will be a comedy, the parody of a comedy can be a tragedy.'
5. 'Cliché-images' as opposed to 'cliché-situations' the latter being part of the script, not of the treatment.

concepts and theories developed at the beginning of this century in Russia and Germany. This second level constitutes an extra link in the usual chain of representation (whether it is perceived by the audience or not), producing a distanciation effect originating in the first place in a distance between the director and the action. This level, produced through stylisation, can also be used to parody the stylistic procedures which traditionally convey an extremely smug, self-righteous and *petit bourgeois* world view paramount in the American melodrama. If we apply the categories outlined by J-L. Comolli and J. Narboni in their editorial in *Cahiers*,[6] we would have to place Sirk's films in category E: 'films which seem at first sight to belong firmly within the ideology and to be completely under its sway, but which turn out to be so in an ambiguous manner.'[7] As Roland Barthes pointed out, a rhetoric functions as the signifier of an ideology;[8] and by altering the rhetoric of the bourgeois melodrama, through stylisation and parody, Sirk's films distanciate themselves from the bourgeois ideology.

In order to discover what ideology Sirk's films do convey, it might be fruitful to examine the relationship between Sirk's work and the authors whose influence he admits to, such as the seventeenth-century Spanish dramatists. The similarities between the work of Pedro Calderón de la Barca and that of Sirk[9] offer invaluable clues for such an investigation. Both artists share an interest in schematised moral and religious conflicts, a belief in fatality, a scepticism towards 'appearances' in life, a belief in the reality of innocence, beauty and love; both favour tragedy and operetta as dramatic forms. The title to a play by Calderón could, in fact, be used to summarise Sirk's attitude towards reality: '*En esta vida todo es verdad y todo es mentira*' (In this life all is truth and all is lies).

6. *Cahiers du Cinéma,* no. 216, translated in *Screen* (Spring 1971).
7. The ideology in question is the twentieth-century French bourgeois ideology. Obviously the ideology Sirk seems to convey is its American counterpart.
8. Roland Barthes, 'Rhétorique de l'image,' in *Communications,* no. 4 (1964).
9. It is also relevant to note that in 1911, theatre director Nikolai Evreinov restaged works by Calderón Lope de Vega and Tirso de Molina in St. Petersburg. Spanish drama of the seventeenth century exercised a greater influence on the theatrical revolution of 1910 than is usually acknowledged.

Towards an Analysis of the Sirkian System

Paul Willemen

S ince the *Screen* issue of Summer 1971, a great deal has been written on Sirk's work; the interview book, *Sirk on Sirk*[1] by Jon Halliday was pub- lished and a book of essays compiled by the Edinburgh Film Festival and edited by Jon Halliday and Laura Mulvey, *Douglas Sirk*[2] was published recently. In addition, the magazine *Monogram* devoted a special issue to the melodrama with special emphasis on Sirk's work and *Positif* reviewed the *Screen* issue, adding new material, some of which was translated into English and included in the Edinburgh book. In conjunction with the book, the Edinburgh Film Festival mounted an extensive retrospective of Sirk's work which was subsequently taken over en bloc by the National Film Theatre. Douglas Sirk himself spent a great deal of time and energy answering questions and helping critics and students in the arduous but rewarding task they had set themselves: to try and understand how a Sirk film works.

As Jon Halliday points out in *Douglas Sirk* (p. 60), Sirk has been praised either for his stylistic qualities or else for being a master of the weepie. With the excep- tion of the two articles by Halliday and J.-L. Bourget, the essays in *Douglas Sirk* reflect these two apparently irreconcilable approaches. Sirk is either praised for making extraordinary films in spite of the exigencies of the weepie as a genre, or else it is the weepie-genre itself which is validated, and Sirk is brought forward as its most accomplished practitioner. Indeed it is these genuine contradictions within the work of Douglas Sirk which to some extent invite both approaches.

In order to understand this contradiction and to assess the function of such contradictions in the Sirkian system, one must again turn to Sirk's theatrical experience in Germany in the twenties. In 1929 Sirk staged Brecht's *Threepenny Opera* with immense success. As left-wing intellectuals in the German theatrical world, both artists reacted against expressionism, although it is quite clear that both were equally influenced by the movement. Brecht's early plays bear witness to this, as do some of Sirk's Hollywood films; *The Tarnished Angels* in particular. In fact, Sirk makes a direct allusion to expressionist ideas in the phantasmagoria speech in *Captain Lightfoot*. Although it is not clear whether Brecht approved of Sirk's production of the *Threepenny Opera* (*Sirk on Sirk,* p. 23), during his career in Hollywood Sirk made frequent use of techniques Brecht had pioneered in the

From *Screen* 13, no. 4 (1972–73): 128–134. Copyright © 1972 by Paul Willemen.
1. Jon Halliday, *Sirk on Sirk,* Cinema One Series (London: Secker & Warburg, 1971).
2. Jon Halliday and Laura Mulvey, eds., *Douglas Sirk* (Edinburgh: Edinburgh Film Festival, 1972).

play and achieved very similar results. In his study *Lecture De Brecht*[3] Bernard Dort describes Brecht's pre-epic technique as that of the 'boomerang image.' Brecht presented the theatre public with the image of life that it wanted to see on the stage, but in order to denounce the unreality of such an image, to denounce its ideological character (p. 189) Brecht himself explained that the *Threepenny Opera* attacks bourgeois conceptions not only by choosing them as a content, by the mere fact of presenting them on the stage, but also by the manner of presentation itself. The play shows a way of life which the spectator wishes to see portrayed in the theatre. At the same time, however, he is forced to confront aspects of this life with which he would rather not be confronted: he not only sees his wishes fulfilled, but he sees them criticised and is thus forced to perceive himself as object, rather than subject. Bernard Dort continues:

> The picturesque robbers of the *Threepenny Opera* are not bandits: they are robbers only as the bourgeoisie dreams them. In the final analysis we realise that they are in fact members of the bourgeoisie. Or, more precisely, it is through the disguise of the robbers that the spectators will come to recognise themselves as being bourgeois. A subtly engineered set of displacements and discontinuities facilitates such a self-recognition. In this way Brecht has attempted to sabotage the notion of the theatre as a mirror (for our fantasies). . . . Brecht puts on the stage what seems to be the image of the kind of exotic society that the spectator wants to see. In fact what the spectator discovers in the very unreality of such an image, is himself. The mirror of the stage does not reflect the world of the audience any more, but the ideological disguises of the audience itself. Suddenly, at that point, the mirror refers us back to our own reality. It bounces the images of the spectacle back to us—like a boomerang. (pp. 190–191)

Sirk's films operate in a similar way. It has been shown how Sirk takes distance from the spectacle he presents, but that there is no distance between the audience and the film (*Douglas Sirk*, p. 23). In fact, Sirk mercilessly implicates the audience by the use of techniques deliberately designed to involve the spectator emotionally (*Sirk on Sirk*, p. 70). In contradistinction to social-comment-melodramas such as *A Tree Grows in Brooklyn*, *Gentleman's Agreement* (both by Elia Kazan), *Peyton Place* (by Mark Robson), *No Down Payment* (by Martin Ritt) etc. Sirk's films short circuit the so-called channel of communication between director and audience. Instead of inscribing the director's personal view or message into the film and thus by extension denying that any 'personal' statement must to a very large extent be dictated by both the society and the industry within which the director works, Sirk inscribes his distance from the spectacle into the film. In this way, the diegesis ceases to appear transparent: it becomes the point beyond which the spectator cannot go. It is this sense of an absence

3. Bernard Dort, *Lecture De Brecht* (Paris: Eds du Seuil, 1960).

behind the diegesis, so to speak, which Fred Camper (*Douglas Sirk,* p. 79 ff) quite mistakenly describes as a two-dimensionality within Sirk's films.

Sirk's films could be described as the opposite of a distorting mirror: the world the audience wants to see (an exotic world of crime, wealth, corruption, passion, etc.) is a distorted projection of the audience's own fantasies to which Sirk applies a correcting device, mirroring these very distortions. This conjunction of, or rather contradiction between distantiation and implication, between fascination and its critique, allows Sirk to thematise[4] a great many contradictions inherent in the society in which he worked and the world he depicted. It equally gives us the means to read Sirk's own contradictory position within that society and vis-à-vis that world.

Jon Halliday has indicated (*Douglas Sirk,* p. 59 ff) and has been supported on this point by Sirk himself (*Sirk on Sirk,* p. 89) that the society depicted in most of the films is characterised by a smugness and complacency masking decay and disintegration from within, just beneath the surface. Sirk also indicates his own contradictory position within the society in which he found himself (*Sirk on Sirk,* p. 86). He was attempting to make a critique of a society which: (a) provided him with the money and the tools to make his films, but (b) would not be offended to the extent that it would withdraw its support in the form of box-office receipts. These primary contradictions generated further, secondary contradictions in Sirk's work:

1. Although the films were products of, for and about Eisenhower-America, they were misunderstood at that time. Sirk explained this in terms of the American audience's failure to recognise irony (*Sirk on Sirk,* p. 73) and the lack of a genuine film culture based on a theory of aesthetics (*Sirk on Sirk,* p. 72).
2. Now that these films are beginning to be understood, even in English-speaking countries, American society has undergone a process of social change and now produces quite different films. This change contributes to some extent to the contemporary critic's tendency to misread Sirk's films: critics tend to judge Sirk's presentation of Eisenhower-America by the standards of contemporary critiques of ideology, thus committing the mistake of neglecting the true relevance and meaning of the films at the time they were produced. One of the major contributions of Jon Halliday's writing on Sirk is precisely that he situates Sirk's films in their own historical context, a fact the critic has to grasp before he can comment on the relevance of Sirk's films in our own historical context. Within the films themselves, these

---

4. This term is used in the sense of transforming the conditions of production into a theme through a process of internalisation. American capitalism can be internalised into a theme by a systematic refusal to use, or alternatively by a systematic use of extremely expensive camera movements, such as crane-shots or tracking-shots.

externally determined contradictions are mirrored in a wide variety of ways, often differing from film to film:

1. Displacements and discontinuities in plot construction: 'The supporting part in the picture is your hidden leading man' (*Sirk on Sirk,* p. 98). Examples of this can be found in *Sign of the Pagan, Written on the Wind, Thunder on the Hill,* etc. A creative use of discontinuity can be seen in Sirk's comments on his happy-endings: 'It makes the crowd happy. To the few it makes the aporia more transparent' (*Sirk on Sirk,* p. 132).

2. Contradictions in characterisation: '(Taza is) a symbolic in-between man: he is an Indian, but there has seeped into the character this element of civilisation' (*Sirk on Sirk,* p. 82). Also Kyle Hadley's invitation to Lucy (in *Written on the Wind*) to come and 'meet an entirely different character' which manifests itself only when he's 'up in the blue' but is present in the background throughout the film. In fact, all Sirk's best films contain such split-characters.

3. Ironic use of camera-positioning and framing: in *The Tarnished Angels,* the identification with the solid character, Burke Devlin, is undermined by the camera which shoots him in low angles, so that he appears to hover over the Shumanns as a bird of prey. As we 'see' through Devlin's eyes, this is a classic example of the camera-style achieving a boomerang-image. In *All That Heaven Allows,* such irony is achieved in the first scenes within the close-knit Scott family by framing Cary Scott in such a way that she always remains separated from her two children. In this context, Tim Hunter's comments on *Summer Storm* (*Douglas Sirk,* p. 31 sq) and Mike Prokosh's essay on *Imitation of Life* (*Douglas Sirk,* p. 89 sq) abound with examples of such inner contradictions.

4. Formal negations of ideological notions inherent in the script: *Magnificent Obsession* contains many such elements of parody: the 'true source of spiritual life' is compared to electricity supplying the current for a nondescript sort of table-lamp; the camera movement revealing the god-like purveyor of worldly wisdom benignly nodding to Bob Merrick when the latter is about to perform a tricky operation. Other examples of such elements of parody and of the ironic use of cliché are given in the essay *Distantiation and Douglas Sirk* (*Douglas Sirk,* p. 23 ff).

5. Irony in the function of camera-movement: Sirk's camera, as a rule, remains at some distance from the actors. The space in the diegesis, although rigorously circumscribed, is vast and solidly established. Longshots and mid-shots predominate. The camera, however, is almost continuously in motion. This mobility of the camera is designed to implicate the viewer on an emotional level (*Sirk on Sirk,* p. 43), while the distance from the characters suggests detachment.

This last type of contradiction, that between mobility (i.e. insecurity, emotional involvement) and distance (i.e. detachment, solidly establishing a locus for the diegesis) refers to a dialectic which is perhaps the most dynamic aspect of the Sirkian system, because it underpins the very notion of the Sirkian spectacle: people put themselves on show in order to protect themselves. Mirrors are nearly always there, in the background, to remind them of the fact that they live in a world where privacy is virtually non-existent. The characters are aware of being under scrutiny, so their best protection is to try and take command of the situation by determining their own appearance, if necessary even by deliberately putting on an act. However, the *persona* developed in this way functions as a trap: it is the *persona,* the pretence which comes to dominate, causing conflicts against which there is no further defence. Thus the persona in fact is shown to reveal them in a far more naked and vulnerable way. At the same time, the audience is presented with what it would like to see—such as people suffering the extremes of anxiety, titilating sexual images—while the criticism of such voyeurism is inscribed in the film itself. We are not just looking into a world which is unaware of our watchful presence (the mirrors amongst other things convey this lack of privacy within the film), nor are the characters in the diegesis mere puppets in the hands of the Great-Manipulator-Behind-The-Scenes. We watch them, they are aware of being watched and perform accordingly, attempting to protect them-selves by controlling what they allow us—and their fellow characters—to see. The effect is that the audience sees nothing more than the distortions and constraints which it forced upon the spectacle in the first place. In other words, the audience's ideology is unmasked and is made to rebound back upon itself. Awareness of its own reality is forced upon it, against its wishes. This dialectic also finds its representation within the film: although the characters are aware of being under scrutiny (a form of surveillance manifested as pressures to conform to standards of behaviour imposed on them by their environment), they refuse to recognise the mirror-image of themselves, or better still, they refuse to look into the mirror. This is amply illustrated by Cary Scott's fear of the TV-set in *All That Heaven Allows.* Blindness can be another such refusal to see, as in *Magnificent Obsession.* Helen Phillips has lost her sense of security (security being a husband whose life depended on the immediate availability of a resuscitator!) and refuses to see the man who wants to restore that security. A Sirk film sets out to do for the audience what the TV-set does for Cary Scott or surgery for Helen Phillips. This dialectic between self-protection and exhibitionism, sensationalism and puritan-ism is particularly relevant for the whole of the Hollywood cinema, even today (see Charles Barr's analysis of Sam Peckinpah's rape-scene in *Straw Dogs,* in *Screen* 13, no. 2, 1972).

Only now, after Jon Halliday's interview book and the preliminary explora-tions published in the Edinburgh Film Festival's book of essays, has the ground been cleared for a more accurate and comprehensive study of the work of Doug-las Sirk. Such a study would have to examine in some detail this extremely complex web of contradictions, the interaction of which forms the Sirkian system.

Both the views of Sirk as a Marxist critic of Eisenhower-America or of Sirk as the greatest exponent of the bourgeois weepie are equally misguided. In fact, Sirk's position in the history of the American cinema closely parallels Tolstoy's position in the history of Soviet literature. Lenin considered Tolstoy to be a unique and extremely valuable artist because he dramatised and presented, the contradictions within Russian society at the turn of the century, a time when Tsarism wasn't strong enough to prevent a revolution while the revolution did not yet have enough strength to defeat Tsarism. Sirk performed a similar function in the American cinema in the fifties: he depicted a society which appeared to be strong and healthy, but which in fact was exhausted and torn apart by collective neuroses.

In this context, it becomes possible to understand and explain the enormous success of many of Sirk's best films at the time of their release, and the subsequent neglect and/or rejection of his work by the 'intelligentsia' for many years. The reason for this is analogous to the reason why Brecht's *Threepenny Opera* was, and still is, such a huge public success. As Bernard Dort points out, the technique of the boomerang-image carries with it some ominous pitfalls. Either the sophistication of the process is ignored, thus allowing the bourgeois audience to operate a recovery-manoeuvre: the audience indeed recognises its own image as bourgeois, but enhanced with the exotic prestige of robbers (or corrupt millionaires, actresses or stunt fliers). Or alternatively, if the audience is more knowledgeable about aesthetic processes, they have to reject such a representation, as their ideology does not allow them to recognise themselves in that mirror-image. Hence the rejection or willful misreading (by turning it into camp) of Sirk's films by the reviewers and nostalgia-freaks.

In spite of these pitfalls, the fact remains that, taking into account the historical and economic context within which he worked, Sirk developed the most refined and complex possible system to convey his critique under the circumstances. Even if they did not allow him to make this critique as explicit as he might have wanted to (except perhaps in films such as *Written on the Wind* and *The Tarnished Angels,*) the Sirkian system at least manifested and thematised the contradictions within that society in a way which, throughout American film history, has perhaps only been equalled by Ernst Lubitsch.

Imitation of Life
Michael Stern

I n his review of *A Time to Love and a Time to Die* Jean-Luc Godard wrote, "I love ostriches. They are realists. They believe only what they see. When everything is going wrong and the world gets too ugly, they need only close their eyes very firmly to blot out the exterior world."[1] As Ernst and Elizabeth blotted out the death around them to allow for the momentary belief that it did not exist, so all of Sirk's heroes close their eyes in order to live an imitation of life. The Sirkian theme of blindness suggests that nothing else is possible. The look of the films themselves intimates an artificial world. The melodramatic structures describe events distilled from an illogical—and therefore unknowable—reality. There are in fact few directors who are as centrally concerned with the very nature of the medium—film as an imitation of life—as Douglas Sirk.

This is a film about distances—between people, between perception and the world, between form and feeling and, implicitly, between art and life. It is a mammoth work, Sirk's last film, and his last project before he left America for good. There is a sense in which it is a summary work. As *A Time to Love and a Time to Die pared down* Sirk's methods to the clearest strategies of form and purity of theme, *Imitation of Life* seems to be a grand, diffuse, and elaborate receptacle for everything that composed the body of his previous work in America. "I would have made *Imitation of Life*," Sirk told *Cahiers du Cinéma* in 1967, "in any case, for the title."[2]

Like *Magnificent Obsession, Imitation of Life* was a remake of a successful John Stahl tear-jerker from the 1930s. Stahl's film is a fascinating example of the earlier melodramatist's commitment to the material and, as such, it provides a foil for Sirk's interpretation. The earlier version is in many ways an expression of the directness and conviction that characterize so many American films from the early 1930s. Andrew Sarris has described Stahl's characteristic image as a frieze. Characters are depicted in a clear and noble perspective, without either directorial ambiguity or an implied self-doubt. Dialogue rendered in medium two-shots reinforces the film's directness and its concrete sense of time and place.

In fact, for all of the artifice with which the genre is naturally encumbered, Stahl's film today appears to be a painfully head-on approach to a real social

From *Douglas Sirk* (Boston: Twayne, 1979), pp. 183–197.

1. Jean-Luc Godard, "A Time to Love and A Time to Die," in Tom Milne and Jean Narboni, eds., *Godard on Godard* (New York: Viking, 1972) pp. 134–35.
2. Jean-Louis Comolli, "Entretien avec Douglas Sirk," *Cahiers du Cinéma*, no. 189 (April 1967): 70.

problem. The staircase in his film (which in Sirk's films is so often the scene of cataclysmic eruptions of the plot: cf. *Written on the Wind,* or Laura Meredith's brush-off of Steve Archer in *Imitation of Life*), serves as a quiet but unavoidable reminder of the social stratification at the root of the film. One of the most powerful moments of the film is the subdued scene in which Stahl's camera gazes implacably at the staircase as the whites move up and the Negro girl hesitates, then descends to her place.

Mention should also be made of the significant fact that in Stahl's film the girl who passes for white is played by Fredi Washington, a light-skinned Negro. This gives the film an obvious "documentary" strength that Sirk's *Imitation of Life* lacks. Steve Handzo accurately made the point when he wrote that Fredi Washington "brought her own anxieties to the role seemingly aware that there was no future for an attractive, intelligent black woman in the Hollywood of the 1930s."[3]

Stahl's film is an accurate rendering of Fannie Hurst's sense that struggle and conviction provide material success and spiritual reward. Certainly there are obstacles to overcome, problems (like racism) to solve, but both book and film suggest that, in the melting pot that is America, all things are possible if we work hard enough to achieve them. Sirk, on the other hand, reverses this attitude. "Success doesn't interest me," he said. "I am empassioned only by failure."[4] Fannie Hurst's book ends with a reconciliation. "Opportunity was at hand," she wrote. "New life, as if waiting for the signal to raise the curtain, was about to begin."[5] Stahl's film ends with a funeral, but it is a warm and majestic moment. It is followed by a light scene that shows Bea and Steve happily together, their carefreeness signified by the "quack quack" of her toy ducks in the bathtub.

How different is Douglas Sirk's version! From the beginning, coincidence rather than hard work determines events in Sirk's film. Lora Meredith (Lana Turner) and her daughter Susie meet Annie Johnson (Juanita Moore) and her daughter Sarah Jane by accident on the beach. Lora takes the Negro woman and her daughter into her home "temporarily," but after a few chance phone calls and fateful twists of plot, their lives are intertwined.

One of the subtle changes in Sirk's version is that Annie's role as servant is never clearly defined. When brought into Lora's home with her daughter, she serves as maid and friend equally, whereas in Stahl's film she is a maid who happens also to be friendly with her mistress. Annie's uncertain role intensifies her daughter's confusion about her own position within white society.

The most significant change in plot from the first version of the film is that Sirk's heroine is an actress. In Stahl's film her success rises out of an Aunt Jemima-like pancake business, a role that Steven Handzo has pointed out "is a commercial adaptation of women's domestic role and, to an audience presum-

3. "Intimations of Lifelessness," *Bright Lights,* no. 6 (Winter 1977–78): 22.
4. Comolli, p. 69.
5. Fannie Hurst, *Imitation of Life* (New York, 1959), p. 279.

ably weighted with middle-class housewives, an option they could plausibly identify with for a woman suddenly forced to support herself."[6] Lora Meredith's ambition to be an actress, on the other hand, is a starry-eyed fantasy, reflecting not only the most impossible kind of success, but the very material of which Sirk's film is fashioned—acting, scripts, make-believe. Her role in Sirk's film requires her to act constantly. Even when she is not on stage, the character Lora Meredith seems to be performing—for her children, boyfriend, herself. Sirk depicts her success in the film as a parabolic burlesque of success fantasies, complete with swirling covers of *Time* and *Newsweek,* boundless applause, and bright lights. Interestingly, her career is not unlike Douglas Sirk's American experience. Beginning down and out, Lora first makes a reputation as a come-dienne. Like Sirk, her first serious project is called *Stopover* (the original title for Sirk's first American melodrama, *All I Desire*). She then turns to idealistic projects—at which point the parallel to her director's career becomes unworkable—unless we see her global recognition as Sirk's ironic reverse mirror image of his own status as a virtual nonentity behind the grand success of his films.

Lora's career is an imitation, as much as is Sarah Jane's passing for white. Sirk's interpretation of the title broadens the issues of the film beyond race. Like the war in *A Time to Love and a Time to Die,* race provides the opportunity for Sirk to explore the full signification of the title. It can be said that this film is a meditation on the imitations of life that define the bounds of Sirk's aesthetic and philosophical attitudes. It is this principal of dislocation that provides the key to a complex film.

Each of the characters of the film remains unsatisfied in their struggles because each has closed her eyes too tightly and has come to accept the appearances of her life as its reality. Interestingly, men are peripheral to the film's concerns, and the one possible male/female relationship indicates why. Steve Archer exists for Lora only to remind her (and the audience) of the falseness of her success. He is positioned in the film as a concrete principle signifying the potentially normal relationship that Lora, blind as she is, denies herself. She seems at first to be the film's least sympathetic character partly because (in theory) she does have a chance to find happiness, and she consistently turns away. The situation of the other women is without hope. There is no Steve Archer waiting in the wings for them.

Lora Meredith's coldness derives also from the qualities brought to the role by Lana Turner. Her reputation as an ambitious and self-serving starlet had only recently come to a violent head in the highly publicized Johnny Stompanato murder (in which daughter Cheryl stabbed Lana's playboy-paramour—an im-plied rivalry upon which the film also preys in its "imitations" of real life). Thus, when Sirk asks his audience at the beginning of the film to accept her as a

6. *Bright Lights,* no. 6, p. 20. Subsequent brief quotations are from the same source.

struggling ingenue, there is a built-in doubt. Further, the character's age in the film, as Steve Handzo noted, makes her aspiration "somewhat impractical and self-indulgent."

The falseness one senses at the center of the character must also be attributed to a startling performance. That is not to say that suddenly Lana Turner became an emotive thespian, but, rather, that Sirk drew from her a reflective conscious-ness about her own limited screen *persona*. Sirk told me, "After *Imitation of Life*, Lana Turner said, 'Douglas, for the first time you have made me feel like an actress. It is not just being beautiful.'—which, of course, is all she has ever been required to do. A sophisticated actress in this part would not have been any good. This character is supposed to be a lousy actress. She got to where she was by luck, or bullshit, or what-do-I-know, by dumb audiences. But she really grasped that part." Sirk capitalizes on the correspondence of Lana Turner and Lora Mer-edith, using it to remind us not only of Lora Meredith's limitations as an actress, but of the character's limitations as a representation of real life.

Sirk's direction of Turner has her constantly glancing out of the frame, dis-tracting her attention from the business in which Lora Meredith is involved, emphasizing again the distance between the actor and the role. In a more general sense, Lora Meredith is motivated throughout the film by invisible forces, out of the frame. The telephone calls that interrupt her, the casting calls, knocks on the door, and intangible visions of success all draw her attention from what is visible in the film toward something outside the character's purview.

Lana Turner's color in the film is pink, extending from her clothes to her bedroom and even to her car. It is a livery that, like her miraculous montage of success, functions in its excess to mock that which it seems to signify. For Lora is anything but the soft, pastel-shaded person that pink implies. Her self-involvement and lack of passion make her, in Steve Handzo's words, "one of the coldest and strangest protagonists for a Hollywood film."

Annie, the maid, leads a different kind of imitation of life. Her skin is brown, and the sobriety of her character is expressed in a scheme of solid, weighty colors. She appears as the sturdy, reliable, content servant and yet, as the film shows, she is the most fragile of its characters. But unlike Lora Meredith's appearance/reality conflict, which manifests itself as a constant during the film, Annie's character is developed temporally. This functions in the peculiar evolu-tion of the film's focus, which tends more and more toward Annie as her character is revealed. When she tells Lora Meredith about her friends at church and about the milkman from the old cold-water flat to whom she has been send-ing Christmas gifts over the years, the audience is as surprised as Lora.

There is a psychological irony about Annie's character that balances the emo-tional gravitation of the film toward her funeral. As she becomes the focus of attention, not only is the fragility of her character revealed, but so are her strengths. The more she seems to be the victim of her daughter's callousness, the more Sirk shows that callousness as a reaction to Annie's need to possess the daughter. For, in a way, Annie is like Marion Groves of *There's Always Tomorrow*—living through her child, oppressing Sarah Jane with her mother love. Annie will not let her go. She follows her to Harry's Club in New York and causes her to lose her job. She follows her to Hollywood and lurks there, too, around the edges of her daughter's life. Finally, when she has become the receptacle for all the film's emotions, the ultimate victim, she also attains an implacable strength. In the last scene of the film, she has been transformed into an object—the flower-draped coffin—like so many objects in Sirk's films, unassailable by the characters. Sarah Jane returns to try to touch her mother, but she has become unreachable—at once the most pitiful and powerful of Sirkian signs.

The psychological irony of Annie's character is compounded by the social dimension of her situation. When she first comes to live with Lora Meredith, she *pretends* she is a servant, and everyone—including Lora and Annie herself—seems to believe it. In fact, her role throughout the film as servant, confidante, companion, and friend is purposely ambiguous. Her color relegates her to the menial position. Yet the film shows that far greater demands are made on her from all sides. And of course the structure of the film leads to her as the leading character. It is her coffin at the end before which all other characters supplicate. What all of this means is that Annie is a character whose life takes the form of many imitations. She and Sarah Jane are the quintessence of the basic rootlessness that plagues so many of Sirk's troubled heroes.

The race problem is crystallized in the character of Sarah Jane. On the social level, she is guilty of seeing her mother only as we and Lora have—as a passive object to be conveniently used. Growing up in the household of the four women, Sarah Jane *sees* her mother being a servant. And yet Sarah Jane is treated not like a servant, but as some kind of quasi-daughter. The point is viciously made when Lora unthinkingly (and thoughtlessly) asks her to carry some hors d'oeuvres into the living room to entertain an Italian producer. Disgusted by the demeaning role in which she has seen her mother, Sarah Jane can interpret this request in only one way—as a demand that she, too, "imitate" (and thereby become) a servant. She does so, in an aggressive burlesque of demeaned servitude.

In an effort to escape the humiliation that she sees as inevitable, Sarah Jane runs off to lead yet another imitation of life. Although her mother thinks she is working in a library, Sarah Jane is actually performing in a garish underground dive. The merriment here is like that of *The Tarnished Angels*—forced, mechanical, leering. Sarah Jane sings a song called "Empty Arms," the lyrics of which invite the lecherous men in the audience to fill up her empty arms. It is a completely demeaning role, ironically so, inasmuch as this represents Sarah Jane's attempt at liberation. The irony is made concrete in the masks of comedy and tragedy that hang on the wall of the club. Sarah Jane has turned herself into a sex object, the masks recalling Carey Scott's objectification on the TV screen in *All That Heaven Allows*, described as "comedy, drama, life's parade. . . ."

The next stop in Sarah Jane's search for a new identity is Hollywood—

symbolic source of imitations of life, actual source of this *Imitation of Life*. We see her performing in a night-club act that is a surreal burlesque of the fun and carefree life she wants. But again, like the party in *The Tarnished Angels*, the movement in the act is joyless. Sarah Jane is one of dozens of regimented show girls wielding giant champagne bottles and miming the gestures that signify having a good time. "I wanted something with a certain feeling of cheapness about it," Sirk said.[7]

After the act we see Sarah Jane in a motel. Her roommate speaks of "the guys" who are coming to pick them up—a suggestion that Sarah Jane's role as a party girl extends beyond the stage. Again, Annie intrudes on her, and after a wrenchingly emotional expression of Annie's masochism and Sarah Jane's crumbling resolve to resist it, the roommate intrudes on their farewell. Annie voluntarily gives the impression that she is Sarah Jane's maid, come to pay a call. "I never knew you had a mammy," the girl says. "All my life," Sarah Jane replies, after silently mouthing the word "mama" as she waves good-bye. It is a cathartic point in the film, for the imitations of life that both women have been leading have crystallized into an opaque barrier between them. The silence of Sarah Jane's farewell to her mother is rendered as if the daughter were helplessly watching her recede into an unreachable, impenetrable space. In fact she *is*, for this last time Sarah Jane will see her mother. This scene and the funeral that follows are a kinetic restatement of the last shot of *A Time to Love and a Time to Die*, a visualization of the meaning of death in Sirk's films—stillness, opacity, a reflection of a life (Annie's) that can no longer touch or be touched.

Sarah Jane's career is also an imitation of Lora Meredith's show-business success. But Sarah Jane's world is only an imitation of the imitation, a distorted reflection of the parties and champagne that characterize the white woman's life. Whereas Lora Meredith's success incarnates the falseness of society's values, Sarah Jane's degradation is an expression of her hopeless alienation, even from a dubious culture. This leaves her no place to go. In a racial sense, she does not, and can never, know her place.

"*Imitation of Life*," Sirk said, "is about the situation of the blacks before the slogan 'Black is beautiful.'"[8] Sarah Jane's passing for white is the original "imitation of life" that defined the title, but Sirk does not seem as interested in direct social analysis of the race issue as he does in the problem of personal identity. Like many of Sirk's heroes, Sarah Jane is trapped by what she is, and so she assumes a different role—or tries to. There is a multiple irony here. Sarah Jane *is* a Negro; but she is *not* black. She declares into the mirror, "I am white," and as we in the audience see her, she is correct. The fact that the role is played by a white woman reinforces Sirk's insistence on Sarah Jane's problem being internal, a matter of self-perception. Of course, in Sirk's world, as we have seen in count-

7. James Harvey, "Sirkumstantial Evidence," *Film Comment* 14, no. 4 (July-August 1978): 57.
8. *Sirk on Sirk*, p. 130.

less cases, the internal traps are ironclad. In her own eyes—if not those of the world—Sarah Jane will always be a Negro. Like Kyle Hadley's sense of impotence, or the spiritual vacancy of Bob Merrick's life, Sarah Jane's feeling of subordination cannot be escaped. Being both internal and socially conditioned, it is impossible to eradicate by even the most elaborate imitation of white life. Sarah Jane is doomed by the discrepancy between what she is and the way she insists on seeing herself.

The profound despair Sirk generates out of Sarah Jane's inevitable doom is played off against the petty problems of the fourth woman, Lora's daughter Susie. As he did with Lana Turner, Sirk reinforces the screen persona of Sandra Dee (formerly *The Reluctant Debutante* [1958] and, in 1959, *Gidget*) and makes of the character a vacant personification of the dominant culture's bankruptcy. In perfectly coiffed hair and costumes that seem to echo her mother's, Susie appears rather like a Lora Meredith Doll. Her imitation of Lora is suggested by her crush on Steve Archer (the mother's boyfriend), which, pitifully, neither Steve nor Lora takes seriously. In fact, Lora is unaware of Susie's designs on Steve until Annie tells her, "You've got a real problem with that girl." What Annie reveals to Lora is the stuff of soap opera—that Susie is in love with Steve. And at this point the revelation and the soap opera seem unimportant to the audience. Annie is on her deathbed, and gradually the mother-daughter rivalry has been drained of dramatic significance in what has become *Annie* and *Sarah Jane's* film. As Annie lies dying, revealing the private life that none knew she had, and none thought to ask about, we begin to see the problems of Lora and Susie as directorial camouflage—used to bring us into what looks like a basic mother-daughter melodrama (cf. *Mildred Pierce,* 1945), but which is at last revealed to be about much graver problems.

"The irony is," Steve Handzo wrote, "that Turner's 'real problems' are the concerns of the comfortable, recycled from the imitation-of-life movie melodramas of the 1940s. The problems of soap opera are individual, personal, and capable of resolution by individual moral choice. . . . The problems of Moore and Kohner are those of survival and identity; they are collective, racial, social, and open-ended—incapable of resolution within the conventions of the women's picture." It is a stunning strategy, one that reflects not only the director's sensitivity to the limits of genre convention, but more importantly to the way that genre reflects the limits of our own perception of social problems. Sirk does not take us in through the "servants' entrance" to study the problems of racism with the high-minded concern of a liberal do-gooder (cf. Kazan's *Pinky,* 1949, or Lora Meredith's "serious" play about the social worker), an approach that makes it all too easy to tsk-tsk the problem, then walk away. *Imitation of Life* ushers us into the comfortable and generically reassuring parlor of the women's film, reveals the shallowness of its concerns and characters, all the while asserting the real—and very uncomfortable—problems that normally do not show themselves in the essentially soothing context of the women's film.

In this sense, it is not Sarah Jane who is leading the imitation of life, but Lora. With her million dollars' worth of jewels and Jean Louis wardrobe, the heroine of *Imitation of Life* pales next to the dark and moving story that appears first in the film's shadows, then emerges as its motive force.

Jeanine Basinger has described Sirkian irony as forcing "an audience to re-evaluate conventional expectations."[9] Molly Haskell called his melodramas "subversive."[10] Sirk's relationship to the stuff of which his movies were made is one of the most complex and elusive directorial postures in the cinema. The issues of distancing or subversion become especially problematic when one considers that Sirk's films enjoyed the widest popular acclaim—from audiences who, it is safe to say, felt neither distanced nor subverted by his emotionally charged work. The concept of reevaluation comes perhaps closest to the mark. Certainly, it describes the aesthetic strategy of *Imitation of Life*.

To emphasize the reevaluation that characterizes this film more clearly than any other, Sirk modified his style considerably. After the kinetic paroxysms of *Written on the Wind* and *The Tarnished Angels* and the fluid purity of *A Time to Love and a Time to Die,* Sirk's last film appears at first to be strangely static, more descriptive than dialectical. The montage suggests not process and change, but accumulation of images. The mise-en-scène is more mannered than in any other Sirk film—almost as if each camera set-up were a distorted imitation of a classical melodramatic scene or portrait.

The color scheme of *Imitation of Life* is a vivid example of Sirk's turning toward a heraldic mode of signification. The baroque patterns of intense, enameled color that characterized *Written on the Wind* are formalized in this film into a procession of specific tonal emblems. One can hardly speak of "orchestration" of color in *Imitation of Life,* as one *must* speak of it in Sirk's earlier melodramas, because color here has been reduced to a series of individual notes: the blue of the cold-water flat, the screaming red fire hydrant that dominates the foreground as Sarah Jane first runs away from school, the dominant black of the funeral. A cross-reference here would be the color films of Kenji Mizoguchi (*Empress Yang Kwei Fei,* 1955; *Shin Heike Monogatari,* 1955) about which Mizoguchi's cinematographer Miyagawa Kazuo said, "He always used color as an element in the overall design. For example, Kiyomori, before leaving for battle, is very angry; at this time the gate behind him is a ferocious red. Red was the color for anger. Blue, for sadness, just as much as black."[11] Sirk rings similar color tones, with the ironic undercurrent that the dominant funereal black into which all other colors have fed at the end of the film is Annie's color and represents not merely the black of mourning but the racial issue as well. Only once does Sirk abandon the single-toned palette on which colors are heraldically mounted. That is in the

9. "The Lure of the Gilded Cage," *Bright Lights,* no. 6 (Winter 1977–78): 17.
10. *From Reverence to Rape* (New York, 1974), p. 271.
11. Peter Morris, *Mizoguchi Kenji* (Ottawa, Canada, 1967), p. 45.

Hollywood night club, during Sarah Jane's dance. Steve Handzo reminds us that "in further contrast to the subdued colors of Turner's world, the night clubs are a garish wonderland of reds and purples and all of the gaudiness stereotypically associated with blacks merchandised to sensation-seeking whites." Furthermore, the sudden eruption of chaotic color into the relatively schematized design of the film suggests the frenzy of Sarah Jane's flight. By virtue of its colors, the night club appears to be another world (a gaudy imitation), far from what we have seen as the reality of Sarah Jane's life. The colors become a sign of the extreme desperation and rootlessness that characterize her attempts to escape her blackness.

Like the film's color design, its optical qualities suggest Sirk's attempt to create a specific iconography with which he can imitate the film's emotional patterns. We have seen him do so via montage and kinesis in earlier films, but here individual shots are made to carry the film's kinetic charge. One of the most distinguishing optical features of this film is Sirk's use of extreme wide-angle lenses. The lenses exaggerate space between people and they also distort features in a manner that reminds one of mannerist painting. When, for instance, Annie says good-bye to Sarah Jane in the Hollywood motel room, the wide angle lens visually stretches the characters and the space between them—as if Sirk were wringing from the scene an exaggerated emotionality. The movement of Annie's coffin from its bier in the chapel into the hearse is also done with an extreme wide angle lens, expanding the sign the way a primitive painter might paint an object twice as large to give it proper emphasis. What the primitivist and modernist share is a disregard for naturalism. Both modern and primitive art speak as a system of signs given meaning by specific manipulation of a formal pattern.

The depth of space created by Sirk's use of wide angle lenses also establishes a sense of receding boundaries in the world the characters inhabit. All of the characters in *Imitation of Life* are metaphorically lost—a spiritual condition rendered by a filmic space that lacks any sense of wholeness. Not a single shot in the film shows us Lora Meredith's house as a specific, bounded space. The lack of exterior establishing shots is compounded by typically Sirkian angles that tend to confuse, rather than establish, the interior space. The effect of this strategy is to make each scene in the Meredith home appear as though it is happening in a strange and unfamiliar place, thereby reinforcing the bafflement and lack of grasp on life that all the characters share.

Sirk's spatial manipulation in *Imitation of Life* gives plastic form to what has been the determining principle of the film—the creation of distances. The optical estrangement of Sirk's characters from a receding environment is an expression in kinetic terms of the alienation that defines the psychology of each of them.

The spatial and psychological distances are expressions of the film's purposeful pulling away from any kind of subjectivity or sense of directorial commitment to one element of the film over another. *Imitation of Life* tends toward a state of aesthetic inertia. Elements such as success and failure (thematic), plot and subplot (dramatic), angle and reverse (cinematographic), or length of shots within a montage (kinetic) all approach a balance as the film seems to accumulate toward its conclusion. The quiescence of Sirk's final formal pattern is rendered as the dominant black of the funeral, black being the color in which all other colors exist, subsumed without any character or visual force of their own. It is ironic—and yet entirely logical as an extension of this pattern—that this most emotionally cathartic of films is also Sirk's coldest, in which all of the formal patterns that compose the film resolve into an emblematic stasis and in which the director's presence finally recedes into a passive and distant gaze upon the emotions he has generated.

The climactic nature of this resolution signals an end not only to the film's aggregation of deliberate emotional notes, but to the elaborate aesthetic orchestration of Douglas Sirk's directorial career. Annie's funeral begins with the extreme emotionality of interior wide angle shots, then moves outside, where Sarah Jane's return is filmed in distanced high-angle long shot. The intense confrontation of Sarah Jane with her mother's coffin is followed by a series of measured long shots as the hearse and funeral band proceed down a cavernous street. The characters are invisible now, inside a black limousine. The hearse, drawn by horses, is a ghostly vehicle, moving like a vampire's coach, driven by a faceless driver along an unfamiliar, rainswept pavement. The images are a visualization of the final distance, death, that is *Imitation of Life*'s last note.

As Annie emerges from the narrative of this genre picture to become the object around whom all the emotions of the film gravitate centripetally, so her funeral becomes Sirk's dirge for all the unrealized dreams out of which his films are formulated. The accumulative style of *Imitation of Life,* sounding notes singly in a grand procession, building a detailed summary of all the mistaken perceptions, lost chances, beautiful moments, and unfulfilled desires that characterize his world, resolves here into static long shots that convey a stilled image of death's final reign.

The last shot of the film appears to be filmed from inside an antique shop, showing the passing hearse framed in the shop window. It is a beautiful image of death, seemingly preserved as if a precious painting on a canvas, an impenetrable surface, rather than through a window looking out on the world. This last imitation—a mournful sign of irrevocable loss and timeless beauty—is the concluding image of Sirk's film career.

Imitation of Life (1934 and 1959): Style and the Domestic Melodrama

Jeremy G. Butler

> *What is love without the giving?*
> *Without love you're only living*
> *An imitation, an imitation of life.*
>
> Title song, *Imitation of Life* (1959)

The scene opens on a middle-class, urban classroom filled with elementary school children—all white. The teacher, also white, reads to the children in order to pass the time while a rainstorm rages outside. They select their favorite book, *Little Women,* and the teacher begins reading: "Jo was very busy in the garret, for the October days began to grow chilly, and the afternoons were short. For two or three hours the sun lay warmly in the high window . . ." A matronly black woman (Louise Beavers) interrupts, appearing at the door. Seeing her, one of the students (Dorothy Howard) visibly stiffens and hides behind her book. The black woman, Delilah, enters and says, in noticeable dialect, "It's raining so hard I brought rubbers and coat to fetch my little girl home." At first it appears there has been some mistake, but then Delilah sights her white-appearing daughter, Peola, half-concealed behind a book: "My poor baby, Teacher, has she been passing?" Delilah's nurturing impulse has quickly become Peola's uncovering. The child runs from the classroom shouting angrily at her mother, "I hate you. I hate you. I hate you!"

For both mother and daughter, emotional restraint has given way. Moreover, if this sequence from *Imitation of Life* (John Stahl, 1934) succeeds with the viewer, then his/her emotional defenses ought to be crumbling also. Further, this scene typifies one of the few film genres that can stare unblinkingly at emotional upheaval: the American domestic melodrama. We have seen films in which daughters deny mothers, mothers humiliate daughters, women sacrifice quietly for lovers/husbands/children, and, more rarely, families smother *men.* Domestic equilibrium is threatened repeatedly by forces both internal and external—be they World War II (*A Time to Love and a Time to Die*), juvenile delinquency (*Rebel Without a Cause*), cortisone (*Bigger Than Life*), racial controversy (*Imitation of Life*), fatal disease (*No Sad Songs for Me*), or the protagonist's repressed desires (*Peyton Place*). Domestic melodrama's status as emotional hothouse is undeniable; it addresses itself directly and boldly to that arena of internecine emotional combat, the family.

From *Jump Cut,* no. 32 (April 1986): 25–28.

Until quite recently, though, this celebration of pathos has discouraged serious consideration of the genre. The feelings it generates seemed somehow too "easy," somehow "unearned"—*bathetic* rather than truly pathetic. Or the films were said to be manipulative, just pulling the right strings to get a desired emotional response from the ticket-buyer. Early popular culture critics encouraged this disdain by concentrating on genres which conventionally attract a male audience and deal with "masculine" themes (e.g., Robert Warshow on the gangster and Westerner, and André Bazin on 1930s genres).[1] Even today fewer monographs on the domestic melodrama match the still growing volume of literature on the seemingly moribund Western. At least the melodrama is alive and well—making appearances in movie theatres (e.g., *Whose Life Is It Anyway?*) and dominating daytime television.

One of the Women's Movement's direct effects on film culture has been a heightened interest in how our culture represents romance and the family. This interest has led to an increased understanding of the domestic melodrama's thematic motifs, narrative structure and presentational style—rescuing melodrama from the Woman's Picture ghetto.[2] Still, much work remains to be done. What I am dealing with in this essay is how the genre has evolved over the years, particularly from the 1930s to the 1950s. I can best illustrate this change by analyzing two films that share a common narrative base: Fannie Hurst's *Imitation of Life*. Universal Studios initially released a film based on this story in 1934, under the direction of melodramatist John M. Stahl, and then remade it in 1959, with Douglas Sirk as director. The scene which begins the present paper will anchor my analysis. As that one scene evolved, I believe, so evolved the domestic melodrama.

As in any genre study, the critic must construct the genre's parameters. For lack of space, I here put aside thorny methodological questions (the "empiricist dilemma"—see Andrew Tudor and Edward Buscombe)[3] and rely on an empirically derived, somewhat common-sensical notion of the genre. I have found this definition of melodrama useful, and readers will judge its utility for themselves.

1. Robert Warshow, *The Immediate Experience: Movies, Comics, Theatre and Other Aspects of Popular Culture*, with an introduction by Lionel Trilling (New York: Atheneum, 1974); André Bazin, *What Is Cinema?*, ed. and trans. Hugh Gray (Berkeley: University of California Press, 1967), pp. 28–29.

2. Molly Haskell, "The Woman's Film," in *From Reverence to Rape: The Treatment of Women in the Movies* (New York: Penguin, 1974) pp. 153–188; Laura Mulvey, "Notes on Sirk and Melodrama," *Movie* 25 (Winter 1977–78): 53–57; and Griselda Pollock, "Report on the Weekend School," *Screen* (Summer 1977): 105–119.

3. Andrew Tudor, *Theories of Film* (New York: Viking, 1973), pp. 135–144. Or, as Edward Buscombe, after Wellek and Warren, describes it: ". . . if we want to know what a Western is we must look at certain kinds of films. But how do we know which films to look at until we know what a Western is?" Edward Buscombe, "The Idea of Genre in the American Cinema," *Screen* (March/April 1970): 35.

First of all, the domestic melodrama exists basically within the realm of Hollywood classicism, but it differs from most mainstream cinema (1915–1960) in several respects. Most importantly, it features a *woman* protagonist. The strongest female actresses of the so-called "Golden Era" starred in melodrama—and not as the hero's pet, buddy, antagonist or object of desire. Bette Davis, Greta Garbo, Joan Crawford, Irene Dunne, Margaret Sullavan occupy the emotional center of their domestic melodrama films. Whereas most classical films follow men in their worldly exploits, the domestic melodrama represents the women and families "left behind." For example, rather than watch the decline of a concert pianist, we follow the woman with whom he thoughtlessly flirted and then deserted (*Letter From an Unknown Woman*). Or, rather than following the soldier's adventures on the battlefield, we learn about the trauma on the homefront (*Since You Went Away*). It seems as if the domestic melodrama has chronicled the "lives" of mainstream cinema's supporting cast—providing us with sentiments that were mostly left unspoken in violent genres such as the Western, the gangster film, and the war movie. In these latter genres, love merely enters as an inconvenience; in melodrama it remains the central concern.

What we need to specify, then, is melodrama's particular conception of love. The films usually allow women two types of love: (1) romantic love of lover/husband, or (2) domestic love of children. (On rare occasions—e.g., *Marked Woman*—sisterly affection does arise, but it is the exception that proves the rule.) Romantic love seems the ideal state of happiness and women pursue it obsessively. If achieved it remains constant (few screen characters fall *out* of love) and transcends all earthly troubles. In some films romantic love may even transcend death. (At the conclusion of *Seventh Heaven* the viewer is not quite certain if Chico—Charles Farrell—has returned *from the grave* to his lover, or if everyone just thought he was dead.) Romantic love, however, often confronts domestic love. In U.S. cinema marriage initiates domestic love—and usually signals the end of romance. This may be why most romantic films' characters *approach* marital union but do not achieve it until literally seconds before the end credits roll.

In contrast, domestic melodrama dwells on daily life after the couple join together. At the altar, life ceases to consist of the couple's adventure in romance and becomes the family's struggle for survival. This brings us to melodrama's principal theme: the glory of self-sacrifice. As Molly Haskell has noted, "The domestic and the romantic are entwined, one redeeming the other, in the theme of *self-sacrifice* which is the mainstay and oceanic force, high tide and low ebb, of the woman's film."[4]

The 1934 *Imitation of Life* interweaves stories of domestic love with those of romantic love, eventually bringing the two kinds of love into conflict. The film pairs a white woman, Bea Pullman (Claudette Colbert), and her child, Jessie (as

---

4. Haskell, "The Woman's Film," p. 157.

a baby, Baby Jane; as a young woman, Rochelle Hudson), with a black woman and hers (see the above scene). Delilah's nurturing releases Bea from her maternal duties and thus frees her for romantic intrigue with Steve Archer (Warren William). Delilah fits comfortably into the "mammy" type: large framed, self-effacing, religious to the point of superstition, uneducated but "wise" in matters of the heart, and above all else totally committed to nurturing not just her own daughter but Bea's daughter and Bea herself. Donald Bogle would place Delilah within the "aunt jemima" subtype: "Often aunt jemimas are toms blessed with religion or mammies who wedge themselves into the dominant white culture."[5] In fact the film makes Delilah so typical that she becomes reified into an image or symbol of what she is—or rather, of what she is to white culture. In an ideologically blunt sequence, the white mother and now pancake entrepreneur, Bea, coaxes Delilah into an aunt jemima posture to exemplify for the painter what Bea wants for her pancake shop's sign. Delilah's image then appears in the shop window and finally develops into an immense neon sign: "32 million packages sold last year," it declared, as a huge "aunt" Delilah maneuvers a flapjack.

The mammy/aunt jemima character type stands first and foremost for nurturing—raising and caring for children and adults. Indeed, in the cinema and other popular culture media the black matron's nurturing abilities assume superhuman characteristics. Her powers extend beyond that of white women. As Delilah protests when her daughter threatens to leave, "I'm your *mammy*. I ain't no white mother!" White women, she implies, do not have as strong a bond to their children—a notion supported by *Imitation of Life,* where Delilah's grief over her daughter's departure will eventually bring her to death. The mammy fits well within melodrama's bounds, for indeed she is the apotheosis of the film's protagonist, since she is devoted, beyond rational thought, to her children. Within *Imitation of Life,* Delilah functions to remind Bea of motherhood's responsibilities—which Delilah exemplifies through martyrdom. Delilah's position within the narrative serves to bring the protagonist's dilemma into sharp relief.

In recent years, since perhaps World War II, the mammy/aunt jemima type has been criticized as offering a negative image of black women. Writers on blacks in white culture have commented on this character-type's exploitative nature. Specifically, a mammy character does not just represent nurturing; she also promotes black women's exploitation as nurturers of white characters who hire and use her. Films present characters like Delilah as satisfied, even pleased, with this inequitable arrangement. When Bea tries to incorporate Delilah into the business, one founded on *Delilah's* secret recipe, Delilah sees it only as Bea's rejecting her and her mothering abilities. Furthermore, the film ridicules Delilah's inability to grasp financial matters. This scene ends with Bea's business manager, Elmer (Ned Sparks), grumbling about Delilah, "Once a pancake, always a pancake.'

---

5. Donald Bogle, *Toms, Coons, Mullattoes, Mammies and Bucks: An Interpretive History of Blacks in American Film* (New York: Viking, 1973), p. 9.

Of course, the more significant arena for Delilah's nurturing powers lies in her relationship with her defiant daughter, Peola. Delilah pleads with Peola to stop the girl's rebellious ways and make her accept things as they are—to accept their inferior economic status and seek only an elevated spiritual position. The aunt jemima resigns herself to her earthly oppression, secure in the knowledge of heavenly reward. Religion becomes one of white culture's principal means of pacifying blacks, and characters like Delilah, with her demand for a massive funeral, endorse it. Peola rejects her mother's acquiescence, however—as evidenced by the sequence beginning the present paper. She demands the material, worldly rewards that white men and women enjoy.

She thus exemplifies *Imitation of Life*'s theme of racial identity. As a black woman who appears white, she may select her race. Will it be black culture (Delilah) or white (the classroom and, later, a job in an all-white restaurant)? Significantly, Delilah's death brings Peola back to "her place" within black culture. As we learn in the film's final scene between Bea and her daughter, after Delilah's martyr's death, Peola has elected to return to the "teacher's" college and supposedly has quieted her desires for first-class citizenship. The film's narrative, therefore, signifies the correctness of Peola's actions and endorses black submission to the white status quo.

In the 1934 *Imitation of Life,* the words and actions of a black working-class woman, Delilah, validate the rights and values of white middle-class culture. In this way the film exemplifies one of domestic melodrama's main tenets: "Central to the woman's film is the notion of middle-class-ness, not just as an economic status, but as a state of mind and a relatively rigid moral code" (Haskell).[6] This code is illustrated in the domestic melodrama by its representation of the family and work. Sounding remarkably like Frederick Engels,[7] Haskell writes,

The circumscribed world of the housewife corresponds to the state of woman in general, confronted by a range of options so limited she might as well inhabit a cell. The persistent irony is that she is dependent for her well-being and "fulfillment" on institutions—marriage, motherhood—that by translating the word "woman" into "wife" and "mother," end her independent identity. She then feels bound to adhere to a morality which demands that she stifle her own "illicit" creative or sexual urges in support of a social code that tolerates considerably more deviation on the part of her husband. She is encouraged to follow the lead of her romantic dreams, but when they expire she is stuck.[8]

Haskell's comments clearly describe plot developments in *Imitation of Life.* As Delilah's labor releases Bea from mothering duties, Bea can begin a social life. We know Bea had married her first husband for economic reasons, but he

6. Haskell, "The Woman's Film," p. 159.
7. Frederick Engels, *The Origin of the Family, Private Property and the State,* with an introduction by Evelyn Reed (New York: Pathfinder, 1972).
8. Haskell, "The Woman's Film," pp. 159–160.

died, leaving her the child and little financial support. Now established as the
"Pancake Queen," Bea has the freedom to pursue a man for the mere pleasure of
it. However, anyone familiar with the genre's conventions knows that such hedo-
nism can't last long.

In short order, Delilah dies of a broken heart and Bea's daughter, Jessie, falls
in love with the man Bea herself had planned to marry. 1930s films seldom
tolerate a single, older woman's independence, especially not domestic melodrama. Delilah's death seems to teach Bea a lesson. Soon after, she sends her
lover on a sea voyage (he's an ichthyologist) so that her daughter won't be disturbed by their marriage. Domestic love of daughter has triumphed over romantic
love of fiancé. The film ends as it begins, with mother and daughter alone together. Bea speaks of the film's first scene in which Jessie called out for her
rubber duck. "I want my quack-quack," quotes Bea teasingly as the music rises,
"I want my quack-quack." Fade to black.

Marxist feminists argue that woman's consignment to limited wife and mother
roles serves the interests of the bourgeoisie and its (dominant) ideology. Women
are charged with the wifely duty of maintaining the worker (providing food and
sex, maintaining the home as a site of re-creation and recreation, washing, re-
pairing clothes, and so on) and the motherly duty of producing, nurturing, and
socializing new workers (children). Deviations from these roles—such as the
independent, sexually active, but not reproductive, woman—disrupt this
scheme. It is not surprising, therefore, that a major ideological apparatus such as
the cinema does not condone sexually active, single, female characters. This can
be seen easily in a broad range of films from all over the world: the perils of Anna
Moore (Lillian Gish) in *Way Down East* (1920), Marguerite's (Camilla Horn)
burning at the stake in F. W. Murnau's silent *Faust* (1926), Mildred Pierce's
(Joan Crawford) murderous daughter in the film of the same name (1945), the
murder of Nana (Anna Karina) in *Vivre Sa Vie* (1962), Bree Daniels' (Jane
Fonda) persecution in *Klute* (1971), and the butchering of countless sexually
active teenage women in today's horror films (e.g., *Halloween,* 1979). True,
some of these films do present the victimized woman sympathetically, but female
viewers easily get the central message: express your sexuality outside of marriage
and you will be punished. (Instances of film misogyny of this sort may possibly
correlate with the times that the greatest male fear of women exists in the work-
place: e.g., the post–World War II years and the current recession.) Although
Bea does not suffer as intense punishment as the above women, she becomes
restricted to her reproductive role and forced to repress her non-reproductive
desires.

The 1934 *Imitation of Life*'s representation of work is somewhat less conventional than the way it inhibits the independent woman. Unlike the legions of films
that coerce women into choosing between career and marriage (as recently as
Girlfriends, 1978), *Imitation of Life* elides the difference between the two by
basing Bea's career on Delilah's nurturing, i.e., the latter's pancake recipe. Fur-

ther, even though Bea works, she remains close to her daughter. The real threat to this happy bourgeois structure becomes Steve, the object of Bea's sexual desire. Bea does not have to choose between family and business, but between lover and family/business. Thus, through a strange, unconventional twist, Bea's return to daughter Jessie also signifies a return to her business, Aunt Delilah's Pancakes. Nowhere does the film present work as exploitative or alienating; indeed, the film valorizes Bea's rise from proletariat to bourgeoisie—a Horatio Alger for women. The book jacket for the paperback edition of *Imitation of Life* sums up the novel as a "penetrating portrait of a woman who dreamed of success, achieved it, and then had to ask herself the question, 'Is success enough?'"[9] I think Bea would answer that question: "No. It is not enough, but it will do for economically depressed 1934."

The rigidity of the socioeconomic code governing *Imitation of Life* finds metaphoric expression in its visual style. Stahl's filming of the novel relies heavily on static, rectangular compositions. One may see this illustrated in the classroom sequence which I began with. Frames-within-the-frame structure many of the shots.

Additionally, the interior shots of the classroom seem dominated by rectangular shapes: the classroom windows and the blackboard and map. These compositions create a conventional stasis or equilibrium. One may posit an equivalence between the static, calcified compositions of Stahl's visual style and the rigid moral structures of white society that limit black people's options. Just as Peola becomes entrapped within a culture that categorizes her as a second-class citizen, so too the *image* of Peola gets caught in a web of strongly drawn horizontal and vertical lines. Delilah also remains snared within constrictive societal rules, and her figure's soft rounded bulk contrasts with the classroom's hard angles.

My interpretation is supported by similar rectangular compositions occurring throughout the course of the film—in particular, the aforementioned scene involving Delilah, Bea, and Elmer, the business manager, in which they attempt to incorporate Delilah. Just as Delilah does not understand the financial papers and the benefits they may accrue her, and just as she remains symbolically "other" from the world of economics (representing, as she does, the spiritual world and extreme domestic love), so she persists as an anomaly in the tidily constructed home of the white mother. Furthermore, white culture exploits not only her physical labor but also her appearance. Her image becomes reified into a corporate trademark—without her ever comprehending the financial world. Similarly, the white mother, Bea, also remains constrained within this economic and moral structure, but the film offers her an avenue for escape: Steve Archer. Even the film's mise-en-scène marks Steve as a man outside of conventional society's influence; he has most significant scenes in the garden rather than the house that

9. Fannie Hurst, *Imitation of Life* (New York: Permabooks, 1959).

pancakes built. Thus *metaphoric* meanings can be constructed from the film's visual style: closed, rectangular compositions suggest socioeconomic entrapment; open compositions suggest potential liberation.

Having discussed some of the domestic melodrama conventions operating in *Imitation of Life* (1934), we may now summarize a working definition of the genre:

1. A woman protagonist—or a man in a woman's conventional position (see *There's Always Tomorrow*).
2. A middle-class economic *and moral* code governing work and the family: labor as ennobling, woman as wife or mother.
    (A) Romantic love as the ideal state, transcending material needs.
    (B) Domestic love as the overriding concern of women with children— often leading to the mother's superhuman sacrifices. Prevails over romantic love in most cases.
3. A basically daytime mise-en-scène (cf. 1930s Westerns): balanced, closed compositions; "three-point" lighting; aesthetically "conservative."

Imitation of Life (1934) well represents each of these tenets and illustrates how a topical theme (racial inequality) becomes shaped to fit the genre's demands: Peola's *mother* becomes the target of her anger as the anger remains displaced from its true target, white societal structures. Melodrama is equipped to deal with mother/daughter strife, but not with racial inequality. Consequently, the latter remains repressed, "unspoken," a "structuring absence."

Armed with this tentative definition of 1930s melodrama, we may now proceed to the next step—to understand how the genre has changed over the years. I can best illustrate this by looking closely at the 1959 film version of Hurst's novel, produced by Universal once again and directed by Douglas Sirk. Indeed, most contemporary criticism of melodrama has focused on the 1950s and the ways in which stylists such as Sirk, Vincente Minnelli, Nicholas Ray, and others have changed the genre. I do not wish to turn the present genre study into yet another auteur analysis (see Jim Kitses on the Western and Colin McArthur on the gangster film),[10] however, and shall confine myself to ways in which *Imitation of Life* (1959) exemplifies general principles of 1950s melodrama.

The later *Imitation of Life* calls into question many of the values the earlier version affirmed. Bourgeois life no longer seems as comfortably attractive as it did in 1934—or so films of that time tell us. Much of 1950s cinema satirizes or openly attacks the various ideological apparatuses of the capitalist, middle-class state (see *Will Success Spoil Rock Hunter?, No Down Payment,* and *Sweet Smell of Success*—all from 1957). Sirk's *Imitation of Life* has as its theme not the importance of success and the validity of maternal sacrifice, but the corrupting

10. Jim Kitses, *Horizons West: Anthony Mann, Budd Boetticher, Sam Peckinpah: Studies of Authorship Within the Western* (Bloomington: Indiana University Press, 1969); Colin McArthur, *Underworld U.S.A.* (New York: Viking, 1972).

influence of ambition and the incompatibility of romance and prosperity. This later film version considerably alters Hurst's novel. First, all but one of the names have been changed: Bea becomes Lora Meredith (Lana Turner); the white daughter, Jessie, becomes Susie (as a child, Terry Burnham; as a young woman, Sandra Dee); Delilah becomes Annie Johnson (Juanita Moore); the black daughter, Peola, becomes Sarah Jane (as a child, Karen Dicker; as a young woman, Susan Kohner); and Steve Archer remains the same (John Gavin). Second, the avenue the white mother chooses to pursue success becomes shifted to show business—represented by the decadent agent Allen Loomis (Robert Alda). He lectures Lora, "Me, I'm a man of very few principles and they're all open to revision." Unlike Stahl's film version where Bea sets up a business as a family venture, based on Delilah's pancake formula, Sirk's narrative equates Lora's profession with ugly, cheap sexuality. Lora claims she'll make it "her way," but to do that she endures a seemingly loveless romance with her playwright, David Edwards (Dan O'Herlihy). She herself admits at one point, "Funny, isn't it? When you make it, then you find it doesn't seem worth it. Something's missing." What is missing is her daughter, Susie, and her lover, Steve. Her pursuit of a career and denial of both Steve (who proposes, saying, "I want to give you a *home.*") and Susie signify her rejection of love, both romantic and domestic—a rejection, however, the film cannot endorse.

The crisis point arrives when Lora tells Susie of her plans to wed Steve, whom, at this point, Susie also loves. The film's unspoken tensions finally become articulated when Susie charges, "*Annie*'s always been more like a real mother to me." Recognizing that her theatrical career has distracted her from her responsibilities as a nurturer, Lora vows to return to Susie. This is complicated, however, by the two women's competition for one man, Steve. The 1930s solution to this problem is mother gives up lover. That solution is rooted in the ideology of the suffering woman and it's outdated. It no longer satisfies the fissured social structures of the late 1950s. In 1959 the mother may actually choose the lover over the daughter, but she cannot do so without first exorcising her guilt by *offering* to reject him. In any event, *Imitation of Life* (1959) *does not resolve this problem.* It remains an enigma because Annie's death halts all development of the narrative and there is no post-funeral sequence, as in the 1934 film. The fact that Susie denies her mother's offer of self-sacrifice ("Stop acting. *Please* don't play the martyr!") indicates that Bea's sacrifice would be a parody, only a "role," in 1959. So it is that the film, in the final analysis, makes the choice for Lora—and that choice does *not* entail surrendering the lover.

By 1959 the cinema's attitude toward blacks had shifted considerably, but Annie is still recognizable as a mammy/aunt jemima figure. She is much less conventionally "black" than Delilah (gone is the dialect, for example), but she has essentially the same function in the narrative as did her earlier counterpart. She remains the woman who must sell her special nurturing talents in order to survive. However, much of Sirk's version becomes eaten from within by irony.

Even though the black mother as mammy continues, her figure provokes tension within the fictional world. Once again the key to understanding the film's theme resides in the black daughter's actions. Following the farewell scene between Annie and Sarah Jane in Sarah Jane's hotel room (the last time the young woman will see her mother alive), a dancer friend of hers remarks facetiously, "So honey-chil', you had a *mammy!*" Sarah Jane responds, "Yes, all my life." The dancer's snide use of the term indicates its fall from favor since the 1930s. Sarah Jane disregards the intended irony, however, in her reply. The viewer also disregards the dancer's tongue-in-cheek attitude when he/she accepts Annie as the true mammy; just as in 1934, she cannot bear to "unborn" (Delilah's term) her own child. Sarah Jane's repentance at the end ratifies the sacrifice of the mammy figure ("Momma [still not 'mammy'], I did love you," she screams), but all the tensions are not ameliorated as in the 1934 rendition. Peola (1934) has been forgiven her rebellious travesties and, we are told, will return to her white-culture delimited role. The adult Sarah Jane (1959), although griefstricken at the funeral, may give up her show business career (as a white dancer), or she may just as plausibly continue it. The *funeral* concludes the 1959 film and thus some doubt remains as to Sarah Jane's future activities—just as doubt remains about the resolution of the Lora/Steve/Susie dilemma.

In both films the black mother equals "mammy" and stands in contrast to the white mother. Their contrast generates the theme of domestic love and its impediments. At the denouement the film endorses Delilah/Annie's ultimate sacrifice and implicitly challenges Bea/Lora to match it. Bea does; Lora may or may not. Thematically, these events suggest that a certain amount of the 1934 moral code's stability has been disturbed by 1959. Women are now, as Brandon French has observed, "on the verge of revolt."[11] Haskell characterizes a major ideological shift between 1934 and 1959; she discusses the unresolved discord in 1950s American society (as represented in the cinema) which results in "the paradox— the energy, the vulgarity, the poverty of values, the gleaming surfaces and soulless lives, the sickness of delusion, the occasional healthy burst of desire—of America, of the fifties, of the cinema itself."[12]

As I have posited a metaphoric meaning for the style of the 1930s *Imitation of Life,* so can one interpret melodrama's 1950s style by looking at the sequence from 1959 that compares with the one beginning the present paper. In work conducted elsewhere[13] I perform a detailed, shot-by-shot comparison of these two sequences. Space does not permit but a summarized account of that analysis here.

11. Brandon French, *On the Verge of Revolt: Women in American Films of the Fifties* (New York: Frederick Ungar, 1978).
12. Haskell, "The Woman's Film," pp. 171–172.
13. Jeremy G. Butler, "Toward a Theory of Cinematic Style: The Remake" (Ph.D. dissertation, Northwestern University, 1982).

The most obvious differences between 1934 and 1959 are visual ones—though significant audio changes might also be mentioned (e.g., the use of music in 1959 and its absence in 1934). In terms of visual style, then, the 1959 version constructs a world of dynamic disequilibrium, when compared to 1934's equilibrium and stasis. To choose one example among many: In 1934 the black daughter is framed by many rectangles within the frame as she exits the school. In 1959 the camera is placed at a lower, oblique angle, with the coats forming a large bulk in the right foreground; the background is lit so that strange, almost expressionist shadows are cast on a peculiarly nondescript segment of grade-school architecture. This composition draws one's eye into the background where it will meet with the fleeing daughter; significantly, she comes aggressively *toward* the camera, in contrast to the daughter's receding movement in the earlier version.

Metaphorically, we may interpret the later film's visual style as expressing Haskell's paradox. The 1959 version's off-kilter angles, unnaturalistic lighting, character (and camera) movement and dynamic set design (featuring Sirk's trademark, the mirror) provide visual equivalents of the repressed cultural tensions of the 1950s. Just as social values are no longer concrete, so is the narrative action "threatened" by style.[14] Further, just as the black daughter provides the most disruptive thematic and narrative element, so she becomes represented in the most violently dynamic compositions over the course of the entire film. Thematically, the most interesting of these is the already mentioned sequence in which Sarah Jane denounces Annie just before the mother dies. Sarah Jane has ostensibly left her mother in order to enjoy the advantages of white culture, but this scene illustrates just how illusory white bourgeois values are. The connotation strongly indicts the disrepute of her places of employment (e.g., Harry's Club). Style echoes this sense of the illusory in the unconventional shot of Sarah Jane and Annie in the hotel room. Sarah Jane's image becomes doubled as if to signal her duplicity (looks white though actually black) and the superficiality of white values. After all, if the film incarnates white-culture success in the ultra-white characters Lora and Susie, themselves living an "imitation of life," the viewer can only wonder about the worth of such success. Thus the 1959 version of *Imitation of Life* may be read as a critical, disrupted vision of a world that 1930s Hollywood usually took for granted. Just as conventional thematics have come slightly untethered in the film, so have conventional stylistics.

One may properly wonder, however, if this stylistic evolution characterizes the genre or comes as the result of an inspired-genius auteur's reaction against generic conventions of the time. Several writers on Sirk have been drawn to him

---

14. Some of these instances approach Geoffrey Nowell-Smith's concept of "conversion hysteria" in melodrama. See Geoffrey Nowell-Smith, "Minelli and Melodrama," *Screen* (Summer 1977): 117–118.

specifically because of the ideological rupture they see embodied in his mise-en-scène. David Grosz typifies this approach:

> The films of Douglas Sirk, some of the most sublime and deeply felt in American cinema, are rooted in a self-analytic visual style. This must be at the center of any discussion of Sirk's work.[15]

Further, Paul Willemen invokes the *Cahiers du Cinéma* editorial delineating a taxonomy of film and ideology; he asserts that Sirk's films fit into the category of films which initially appear to be fully and unquestionably within bourgeois ideology but which, upon closer examination, reveal cracks and fissures within it.[16] Willemen expands,

> As Roland Barthes pointed out, a rhetoric functions as the signifier of an ideology; and by altering the rhetoric of the bourgeois melodrama, through stylisation and parody, Sirk's films distanciate themselves from the bourgeois ideology.[17]

Jon Halliday's comments on *Imitation of Life* support the same position, but without Willemen's ideological perspective: "Sirk has used his command over 'style' to transform the awful story [*Imitation of Life*] more by light, composition, camerawork, and music than anything else."[18]

André Bazin's admonitions against a "cult of personality" ring in my ears when reading Grosz, Willemen, Halliday, and others.[19] Was Sirk really alone in his critique of both bourgeois ideology and the conventions of 1930s melodrama? It's my belief that the elements of Sirk's visual style which these writers extoll are more a function of the genre than of the solitary genius. Thomas Elsaesser has traced similar ideological strategies in "tales of sound and fury" by Vincent Minnelli and Nicholas Ray, as well as Sirk.[20] Intriguing claims have been made for these films' style, but the claims remain clouded by auteurist notions and

15. Dave Grosz, "THE FIRST LEGION: Vision and Perception in Sirk," *Screen* (Summer 1971): 99. This issue of *Screen* is devoted entirely to Douglas Sirk. Several articles from it have been reprinted in Laura Mulvey and Jon Halliday, eds., *Douglas Sirk* (Edinburgh: Edinburgh Film Festival, 1972).

16. Jean-Luc Comolli and Jean Narboni, "Cinema/Ideology/Criticism," trans. Susan Bennett, *Screen* (Spring 1971): 27–36. It originally appeared in *Cahiers du Cinéma*, no. 216 (October/November 1969): 217. This translation has been reprinted in several places, including Bill Nichols, ed., *Movies and Methods: An Anthology* (Berkeley: University of California Press, 1976), pp. 22–30.

17. Paul Willemen, "Distanciation and Douglas Sirk," *Screen* (Summer 1971), p. 67. Reprinted in Mulvey and Halliday, *Douglas Sirk*, pp. 23–30.

18. Jon Halliday, *Sirk on Sirk: Interviews with Jon Halliday* (New York: Viking, 1972), p. 10.

19. André Bazin, "La Politique des Auteurs," in Peter Graham, ed., *The New Wave* (Garden City, N.Y.: Doubleday, 1968), pp. 137–155.

20. Thomas Elsaesser, "Tales of Sound and Fury: Observations on the Family Melodrama," *Monogram*, no. 4 (1972): 2–15.

obscured by a lack of system. Moreover, even work by non-auteurs such as David Miller (*Back Street,* 1961), Michael Gordon (*Portrait in Black,* 1960), and David Lowell Rich (*Madame X,* 1966) evidence the genre's stylistic disequilibrium so valorized by Sirkphiles. Here I cannot go much further than posing such questions, however, for we still sorely need a systematic analysis of the domestic melodrama's stylistic evolution.

"What's the Matter with Sarah Jane?": Daughters and Mothers in Douglas Sirk's *Imitation of Life*

Marina Heung

Even at casual glance, Douglas Sirk's *Imitation of Life* (1959) has considerable importance in the history of the Hollywood film. Fannie Hurst's novel[1]
had already been adapted into film in 1934 by John Stahl, but Sirk's version
achieved far greater commercial success than did its predecessor, earning it status
as one of Universal's highest grossing films in history.[2] Also, as Sirk's last work
before his voluntary retirement, the film represents the culminating achievement
of an important career. And, with the waning of the woman's film genre in the
late fifties (to await its revival, with new inflections, in the early seventies), the
release of *Imitation* in 1959 and its subsequent phenomenal success seem in
retrospect to be a fitting summation of the genre, or, as Molly Haskell has said,
one of its "glorious—and subversive—last gasps."[3] Yet, beyond its immediate
historical context, *Imitation* has unique relevance to film criticism and feminist
scholarship in the mid-eighties.

Recent writings about the woman's film have drawn on the notion that, given
the inherently patriarchal outlook of the typical Hollywood product, this particular genre represents a body of work that at least purports to assume a feminine
point of view and to address the conflicts and aspirations of a predominantly
female audience. As a sub-genre of the woman's film, the maternal melodrama,
in particular, has received much attention. Finding in it a treatment of a topic
often ignored in other genres (namely, the relationship between mothers and
daughters), critics have been seeking further insight into the way the patriarchal
code typically positions women in relation to the institution of the family. In light
of its concern with mother-daughter relationships, and with woman's work and
woman's place, *Imitation* is obviously a pertinent example. Its unique story
structure is a rarity, even within the context of the woman's film, in that it ex-

From *Cinema Journal* 26, no. 3 (Spring 1987): 21–43. Copyright © 1987 by the Board of Trustees of
the University of Illinois.

1. Fannie Hurst, *Imitation of Life* (New York: P. F. Collier and Son, 1933).
2. Sirk claims that the film was Universal's "biggest money-maker of all time." *Sirk on Sirk: Interviews with Jon Halliday* (New York: Viking Press, 1972), 133. Similarly, the short biography of Sirk
in *Douglas Sirk*, ed. Laura Mulvey and Jon Halliday, states that the film was "Universal's largest ever
box-office success" (Edinburgh: Edinburgh Film Festival, 1972), 109.
3. Molly Haskell, *From Reverence to Rape: The Treatment of Women in the Movies* (New York:
Penguin Books, 1974), 271.

plicitly develops a parallel between its two female protagonists, one white and one black. As a result, a discourse on race becomes a crucial complication of the prototypical themes of the woman's film. By juxtaposing Lora Meredith (Lana Turner), a white actress, with Annie Johnson (Juanita Moore), her black maid, and by counterposing the two women's relationships with their daughters, the film offers an opportunity to observe an unusual and revealing intersection of the issues of race, class, and gender. Ultimately, an analysis of the film in these terms yields an understanding of how the woman's film expresses ideologies about issues as diverse as woman's work and woman's suffering, mother-daughter relationships, bonding between black and white women, and the possibility of women's resistance to the social order.

In her essay "When Women Wept," Jeanine Basinger suggests that, as the "core of women's films," the sub-genre of the "rise-to-power" film has a plot which "usually reflected the conventional wisdom that the woman who rose to power, either economic or sexual, was going to be an unhappy woman."[4] In this mode, the subtext of films such as *Blonde Venus* and *Mildred Pierce* is a discourse on the "woman's sphere"; in them, worldly success for women usually necessitates failure as wives and mothers. In the balance between domestic happiness and career success, then, the issue is usually decided in favor of the former, since each film typically ends by reinscribing women within the home and family. Thus, Douglas Sirk's avowed aversion for the American cliché of success (as in his saying, "Success is not interesting to me"[5]) aptly converges with the overt theme of his version of *Imitation of Life,* in which Lora Meredith's hunger for theatrical fame is shown to be a hollow dream. The title of the film comments on Lora's aspirations, and its point is reiterated early in the film just before her discovery by David Edwards, a well-known director, when her beau Steve Archer (John Gavin), pleads with her, saying, "Most of the time you're out there fighting to get somewhere—breaking your heart trying to do for yourself and Susie and I want to do for you. . . . I want to give you a home, take care of you. . . . What you're after isn't real. . ." This pivotal scene ends on a note of doom as Lora, having rejected Steve's offer after a phone call from her agent, runs out alone into the snowy night. This foreboding is soon confirmed when, a Broadway star at last, Lora wistfully tells her maid Annie about her director's disappointment with success and, in so doing, implicitly voices her own disillusionment: "He can't stop [his frenetic activities]—if he did, he'd be sure to find out how sad he really is. And I know that feeling. Funny—isn't it? After all this time, struggling, and heartache, you find out it doesn't seem worth it—something is missing."

Lora's wistful admission proves Steve right about the hollowness of her ambitions; more importantly, it is part of her punishment for choosing success and

4. Jeanine Basinger, "When Women Wept," *American Film* 2 (Sept. 1977): 54–55.
5. *Sirk on Sirk,* 119.

renown over a happy home. Peter Biskind has noted (paraphrasing Betty Friedan): "The career woman had replaced the vamp as the *femme fatale* of the fifties; the scarlet letter stood for ambition, not adultery."[6] In *Imitation,* Lora's transgression exacts a punishment that explicitly highlights her violations of her maternal role; here, the theme of the "rise-to-power" film converges with that of the maternal melodrama, in which, as suggested by Linda Williams, the themes of idealization and punishment coincide as a result of the "device of devaluing and debasing the actual figure of the mother while sanctifying the institution of motherhood. . . ."[7] Lora's punishment, like that of so many mothers in the maternal melodrama, is the loss of her daughter's love and respect. Yet, unlike Mildred Pierce and Stella Dallas, both of whom illustrate how "good maternal love incurs humiliation and rejection when it becomes fanatical, Lora exemplifies the opposite type of the "bad" mother, implicitly winning for herself the scarlet letter "A" for ambition.

Lora's fate as a mother is foreshadowed in the opening shot of the film, which shows her on the boardwalk on Coney Island frantically looking for her missing daughter. Steve Archer takes a picture of her plight and later dubs the photograph "mother in distress." Throughout the film, Lora's neglect of her daughter, for which she attempts compensation by giving her "everything [she herself] missed," leads irrevocably to their confrontation near the end of the film, when, in answer to Lora's defense that "It's only because of my ambition that you've had the best of everything—and that's a solid achievement that any mother can be proud of," Susie (Sandra Dee) retorts by asking, "And what about a mother's love?" She adds that Lora has never given her love except "by telephone, by postcard, by magazine interview—you've given me everything but yourself!" As in *Mildred Pierce,* Susie's indictment of her mother takes the form of sexual rivalry; just as Veda finally marries Mildred's lover, so Susie falls in love with Steve.* The perversity of her choice of a love object implies that Lora's emotional abandonment of her has created this monstrous inversion of roles and affections.

The ideological project of Sirk's film, to discredit the maternal type represented in Lora, comes into even sharper relief when we compare it to the original novel and to the first adaptation. In both the novel and earlier film, the Lora Meredith character is Bea Pullman (Claudette Colbert in the film), a widow of a maple syrup salesman in Atlantic City. To support herself and her young daughter, Bea takes over her late husband's business and builds it into a multi-million dollar enterprise with the help of Delilah, her black maid (Louise Beavers in the

6. Peter Biskind, *Seeing Is Believing: How Hollywood Taught Us to Stop Worrying and Love the Fifties* (New York: Pantheon Books, 1983), 263.

7. Linda Williams, "'Something Else Besides a Mother': *Stella Dallas* and the Maternal Melodrama," *Cinema Journal* 24 (Fall 1984): 3.

* Veda (Ann Blyth) never marries Monte Beragon (Zachary Scott). She marries Ted Forrester (John Compton).—Ed.

film), who also has a daughter. Both earlier versions highlight a typical theme of the maternal melodrama, succinctly described by Christian Viviani as "an apologia for total renunciation, total sacrifice, total self-abnegation."[8]

In the novel, Bea's rise to wealth and fame makes her an emblem of women who are succeeding in business for the first time. Indeed, the novel is meant as a cautionary tale on the price of success, a notion condensed in the headline of a magazine article that Bea writes, entitled "What Price Business Career to a Woman?"[9] Delilah echos this point by admonishing her mistress: "Outta all dem men down dar in Wall Street, supportin' and lovin' deir wimmin, you ain't one of 'em . . . I want some lovin' for you, honey—some man-lovin'. . . . You ain't nevah had your share."[10] Eventually, Bea falls in love with her business manager, Flake, but on the last page of the novel, she discovers her fiancé in an embrace with her daughter and thus realizes that he is going to become her son-in-law instead. Unlike Susie's infatuation with Steven in the Sirk film, however, this denouement in the novel is not depicted as a daughter's retaliation against a negligent mother. In fact, the surprise ending follows the daughter's return from school to declare that her mother is the "darlingest person in the world."[11] Thus, Bea loses her lover and her hopes for a traditional home and romantic bliss, but she does not lose her daughter's love. As the narrator comments near the end of the film, "She had built a colossus, when all she had ever wanted was a home-life behind Swiss curtains of her own hemming, with a man who had awakened her as Flake had."[12]

The novel is about the price of success; the 1934 film is about the price of motherhood. Stahl's film sympathetically depicts Bea's determination and shrewdness in building a pancake empire, and success is shown to have laudable rewards—affluence, renown, social position, and domestic happiness. Furthermore, far from jeopardizing her maternal role, we see that Bea's business actually enables her to be a more attentive mother: once she sets up her pancake shop on the boardwalk, Bea integrates her spheres of work and family by putting the family quarters in the back of the restaurant, so that she simply has to use a connecting door to gain access to either. At the same time, departing from the novel, success is shown not to preclude romance; indeed, the appearance of the dashing and worldly Stephen Archer (Warren Williams) at Bea's evening party is like the crowning touch of Bea's achievements. When her daughter develops a teenage crush on Stephen, however, Bea resolves to send her lover away, realizing that only his absence will enable her daughter to outgrow her infatuation. Thus, while the novel emphasizes the incompatibility of personal happiness and

8. Christian Viviani, "Who Is Without Sin? The Maternal Melodrama in American Film, 1930–39," *Wide Angle* 4 (Summer 1984): 16.
9. Hurst, *Imitation,* 277.
10. Ibid., 220.
11. Ibid., 346.
12. Ibid., 318.

material success, the Stahl film defines renunciation as concomitant to noble motherhood, choosing to valorize Bea for her willingness to give up her devoted lover for her daughter's sake.[13] As Linda Williams has noted, the dominant emotion in the woman's film is "joy in pain, pleasure in sacrifice."[14] The ideology of such a film is fundamentally patriarchal, validating (again to quote Williams) "what patriarchy has claimed to know all along: that it is not possible to combine womanly desire with motherly duty."[15] The film opens to show Bea bathing her infant daughter. Its closing line of dialogue alludes to a toy rubber duck in the opening scene. But when Bea repeats the childish prattle, "I want my quack-quack! I want my quack-quack!" this rather absurd refrain nevertheless speaks to a "good mother's awareness of inevitable deprivation and unfulfilled desire as her accepted lot.

In Sirk's *Imitation*, it is Annie, Lora's black maid, who exemplifies the prototype of the sacrificial mother ennobled through suffering and self-denial. When, from her sick bed, Annie tells Lora that Susie is in love with Steve, the ensuing exchange between them is Annie's implicit indictment of Lora as a "bad" mother:

Lora: Why don't I know about it [Susie's problem]? Why didn't she come to
    me?
Annie: Maybe because you weren't around. . . .
Lora: You mean . . . I . . . haven't been a good mother.
Annie: I know you meant to be a good mother—the best kind of mother. But
    look—I meant to be a good one too, but I failed.

Annie's suggestion that she, too, failed as a good mother is not meant to be taken seriously, for her lack of personal ambition, stoical devotion to her daughter, and unquestioning acceptance of her social status all make her a corrective to Lora's maternal failures. Through Annie, the film celebrates a specific maternal ideal while denigrating the type Lora represents. To underscore this point, Annie effectively becomes a surrogate mother for Susie, reading her and her own daughter Christmas stories while Lora is rehearsing stage lines, and acting as confidante and advisor to the teenaged Susie. Aptly enough, in the first scene of the film, Lora, the "mother in distress," runs down the boardwalk steps and encounters Annie (whom she has yet to meet) coming up the same steps with two hot-dogs in

13. It is interesting to note that Lora makes an identical offer to Susie, only to have this scornful response from her daughter: "Oh, mama, *stop acting* . . . stop trying to shift people around as if they were pawns on a stage. Oh, don't worry, I'll get over Steve, but *please*, don't play the martyr. . ." There is also a difference (between the two films) in why the two daughters fall in love with their mothers' lovers; in the earlier film, it is because Bea goes off with Delilah to look for Delilah's daughter, who has run away to work as a cashier in a restaurant; in Sirk's version, it is because Lora is too involved with her career.
14. Williams, "Something Else Besides a Mother," 2.
15. Ibid., 15.

hand, one for her daughter, and one for Lora's. The transference of maternal roles prefigured here is directly stated in Susie's later accusation of Lora: "Let's face it, mother: Annie's always been more like a real mother to me—you never had time for me."

In explaining why Annie's portrayal in his film departs so drastically from her earlier incarnations, Sirk stated: "Maybe it would have been all right for Stahl's time, but nowadays a Negro woman who got rich *could* buy a house, and wouldn't be dependent to such a degree on the white woman. . . . So I had to change the axis of the film and make the Negro woman just the typical Negro, a servant, without much she could call her own but the friendship, love, and charity of a white mistress."[16] However, despite Sirk's seemingly neutral appeal to historical plausibility, the differences in Annie's portrayal have wide-ranging ideological implications. In the two earlier versions, Delilah is an indispensable collaborator in Bea's business. It is her pancake recipe that Bea markets so successfully. In the novel, since the business is named after Delilah ("Delilah Delights"), Delilah herself becomes a well-known public icon, and she also plays an active role in training "corps of Negro women" to staff the various restaurants around the country."[17] In the Stahl film, Delilah has similar importance in the business venture, her prominence expressed visually in the gigantic billboard (seen twice in the film) showing her likeness above the slogan, "32 million packages sold last year"; Bea also acknowledges her contribution by offering her a 20 percent share in the company. In this film, the underlying theme of the two women's lives is that sacrifice and suffering are a mother's lot regardless of her achievements in the public sphere. Indeed, in learning this lesson, Bea is a direct beneficiary of Delilah's example, so that after she sees the heartbroken and dying Delilah, she says to her daughter, "I've seen such a tragedy. . . . Poor Delilah. . . . Darling, if anything should ever come between us, it would kill me. . . ." And so, Bea concludes that she, too, must sacrifice her own happiness to avoid Delilah's fate.

Actually, all three versions of *Imitation of Life* support the basic polemics of the rise-to-power film, while ringing individual changes on specific themes. Distinctive in the 1959 version is the depiction of Annie as a maid with no direct involvement in Lora's career, through which Sirk sharpens the contrast between the two spheres of work that the two women occupy, effectively validating one while discrediting the other. As a result, this portrayal of Annie as a black domestic seen in contrast to Lora, a white career woman, touches on the issues of gender, class, and race in ways that the other two versions do not. However, while this difference makes Sirk's version the most interesting of the three, a scrutiny of his film also reveals a systematic suppression and displacement of these issues through recourse to the ready-made ideology of the maternal melo-

16. *Sirk on Sirk,* 129.
17. Hurst, *Imitation,* 176.

drama. This is to say that Sirk has Annie function as a foil to Lora in order to reinforce the polemics of the maternal melodrama and of the woman's film, and, conversely, the generic framework used in his film makes possible a masking and distortion of the issues of race, class, and gender that are raised by Annie's portrayal as a black domestic.

Actually, Annie's role in Sirk's film is based on an inescapable irony, which is that Annie is, herself, a working woman. Yet, remarkably, Annie's working status is constructed so as to allow her to function as Lora's foil without calling this fundamental contradiction into question. This fact inevitably raises the issue of Annie's ideological significance in the Sirk film, especially because of her greater prominence in this film as compared to the two earlier versions of the story. In fact, Rainer Werner Fassbinder has remarked on how *Imitation* "starts as a film about the Lana Turner character and turns imperceptibly into a film about Annie. . . ."[18] As Fassbinder recognizes, the emotional weight of the film falls heavily on Annie's relationship with Sarah Jane (Susan Kohner). Thus, Annie's heightened importance and the contradictions embedded in her characterization conspire, as we shall see, to introduce a series of disturbances in the film that exceed its basic polemical operations. We therefore must agree with Geoffrey Nowell-Smith's conclusion that the "importance of the melodrama . . . lies in its ideological failures."[19]

The depiction of Annie cannot be an ideologically neutral one, since, as black domestic, she occupies the sphere of work that has become identified in this century with black women as a group; as sociologists have shown, black domestic service is an exemplary case for demonstrating the intersection of class, race, and patriarchy.[20] At the same time, the use of the parallel story structure in *Imitation* potentially offers a promising instance of a fictional treatment of a black domestic's relationship to her white mistress, a subject that has also concerned some researchers recently.[21] However, as I intend to show, the film seeks

18. Rainer Werner Fassbinder, "Fassbinder on Sirk," *Film Comment* 11 (Nov. 1975): 24.

19. Geoffrey Nowell-Smith, "Minnelli and Melodrama," *Screen* 18 (Summer 1977): 118.

20. Judith Rollins, for example, has suggested that "examining the relationship between black female domestics and their white female employers does, indeed, afford an extraordinary opportunity: the exploration of a situation in which the three structures of power in the United States today—that is, the capitalist class structure, the patriarchal sex hierarchy, and the racial division of labor—interact." Judith Rollins, *Between Women: Domestics and Their Employers* (Philadelphia: Temple University Press, 1985), 7. See also Bonnie Thornton Dill's observations based on her study of black domestic workers, in "Race, Class, and Gender: Prospects for an All-Inclusive Sisterhood," *Feminist Studies* 9 (Spring 1983): 140–145.

21. See Rollins, *Between Women*. The subject is also treated extensively in David M. Katzman, *Seven Days a Week: Women and Domestic Service in Industrializing America* (New York: Oxford University Press, 1978), 184–222. Interesting first-person accounts of this relationship from the domestic's point of view can also be found in Robert Hamburger, *A Stranger in the House* (New York: Macmillan Publishing, 1978) and Robert Coles and Jane Hallowell Coles, *Women of Crises: Lives of Struggle and Hope* (New York: Delacorte Press, 1978), 229–273.

to mask the nature of the employer/employee relationship between Lora and Annie, and also to displace the potential conflict between mistress/maid and black/white onto the framework of a mother/child conflict, the prototypical theme of the maternal melodrama.

To start, Annie's status as Lora's maid is clearly established in the film. Annie addresses Lora as "Mis' Meredith" or "Mis' Lora," and she often appears in a black uniform and a white apron. When during their first meeting, Lora wistfully expresses the wish for "someone to look after Susie," Annie eagerly chimes in: "A maid to live in? Someone to take care of your little girl? A strong, healthy, settled-down woman who eats like a bird and doesn't care if she gets no time off and will work real cheap?" Here, Annie is clearly offering herself as Lora's maid. Yet, contrast this episode with Delilah's arrival at Bea's house in the Stahl film, in which Delilah has found the wrong house in answer to an ad for a maid. When Delilah stays on, we understand that she has managed to persuade Bea to hire her.[22] As Sirk shows it, however, Lora invites Annie to stay overnight at her apartment, but there is no hint of any agreement between them, only a display of benevolence freely given and gratefully received. The next morning, seeing her underwear hung up to dry, Lora tells Annie with embarrassment, "You shouldn't have done my laundry." Then, as both women sit and address pay envelopes, Annie talks about putting their earnings into "our kitty," to which Lora wryly responds, "'*Our*' kitty? Seems like you intend to stay. . . ." A similar impression, that Annie chooses to stay on strictly out of her own initiative, is conveyed about Annie's performance of her chores: when Lora admonishes her for doing her laundry, Annie's reply is, "I like to take care of pretty things." And, when Lora moves everyone into a country mansion, she gently reminds Annie, "You know you can have anyone you want in here to help you"—an odd suggestion indeed, implying that, as a servant, Annie would be in a position to bring in help for herself. This scene is altogether a strange one, for it has Annie asking Lora, as the movers unload elaborate furnishings, "Do you think we can really afford all this?" This remark suggests, if only for comic effect, her co-ownership of the new habitat. To sum up, Annie's ambiguous depiction as a servant is reflected in the placement of her bedroom. In the Stahl film, Delilah sleeps downstairs and Bea upstairs; in this film, however, Sarah Jane emphatically lives upstairs with Lora and Susie, and, as we gather from the scene in which Susie looks down from Annie's room to see her mother kissing Steve in front of the house, so does Annie.

Two incidents in particular illustrate how the film obfuscates Annie's working status. In the first, Annie's success in getting a delivery out of the milkman prompts Lora to muse ironically, "He thought you were my maid. Now he thinks

22. Elsewhere in Stahl's film, there are reminders of Delilah's status. At one point, Delilah says that her dream is to be in a situation where she "wouldn't have to do housework for anyone." Later, when Bea offers her a 20 percent interest in the company. Delilah recoils from the offer, protesting, "I want to stay your maid."

I'm rich." In the second example, Lora bluffs her way in to see Allen Loomis, her agent, by pretending to be a Hollywood star. When Loomis dials her home number, Annie unwittingly protracts Lora's deception by answering, "Mis' Meredith's residence. . . ." Half embarrassed, half triumphant, Lora reaches for the phone, saying smugly, "That'll be Annie, my maid—I'll talk to her." In explicitly addressing the issue of Annie's relationship to Lora, these two incidents are anomalies in the film. However, they also vehemently deny Annie's servant status even while invoking it, for both play on the implicit premise that the milkman and Loomis are wrong in assuming Annie to be Lora's maid. Thus, while neither scene clarifies *what* Annie's true status is, both lead the audience to conclude that seeing Annie as a maid would be an error.

To examine the black female domestic as she exists in historical fact and cultural myth helps to highlight the strategies used in *Imitation* to construct Annie along specific ideological lines. On one level, Annie fulfills the archetypal image of the southern mammy. Indeed, Annie has almost all of these qualities listed by Jessie W. Parkhurst in her essay, "The Black Mammy in the Plantation Household": "She was considered self-respecting, independent, loyal, forward, gentle, captious, affectionate, true, strong, just, warm-hearted, compassionate, fearless, popular, brave, good, pious, quick-witted, capable, thrifty, proud, regal, courageous, superior, skillful, tender, queenly, dignified, neat, quick, competent, possessed with a temper, trustworthy, faithful, patient, tyrannical, sensible, discreet, efficient, careful, harsh, devoted, truthful, neither apish nor servile."[23] By portraying Annie in this fashion, the film essentially reaches back to an image of domestic servitude derived on one hand, from the southern plantation, and on the other, from an outdated model. So, when Lora tells Annie that she can bring in extra help if she needs it, her reference to "help" is based on an archaic view of domestic service that is earlier echoed by Annie's offer to her: "You wouldn't have to pay no wages. Just let me come and do for you." The notion of "help" defines domestic service as a quasi-familial, fluidly defined relationship between employer and employee, established through casual recruitment, bound by a loose verbal agreement to exchange labor for a home, and sustained through personal loyalty.[24] This personalized view of domestic service has prompted David Katzman and Judith Rollins to isolate it as a crucial factor in promoting the exploitation of the domestic.[25] In the same vein, Faye E. Dudden suggests that the nostalgia for "help" is often a longing harking back to the early-

23. Jessie W. Parkhurst, "The Black Mammy in the Plantation Household," *Journal of Negro History* 23 (July 1938): 353.
24. See, for a detailed discussion, Faye E. Dudden, *Serving Women: Household Service in Nineteenth-Century America* (Middletown, Conn.: Wesleyan University Press, 1983), 13–43.
25. Judith Rollins has declared, "What makes domestic service as an occupation more profoundly exploitive than other comparable occupations grows out of the precise element that makes it unique, the personal relationship between employer and employee." Rollins, *Between Women*, 156. See also Katzman, *Seven Days a Week*, viii.

nineteenth-century desire for a "'perfectly good understanding and good feeling' between master and servant."[26] Thus, although the figuration of domestic service as "help" could only have existed as just such a nostalgic memory in the late fifties, *Imitation* renders it as an unremarkable contemporary phenomenon. Furthermore, historically speaking, the black woman was instrumental in shifting the trend of domestic service from live-in to live-out status,[27] her quintessential struggle always being to choose between her taking care of her employer's family or her own.[28] Sirk's film, however, creates a fantasy situation in which Annie's adoption into Lora's home as a live-in maid, far from separating her from her daughter, actually makes it possible for Sarah Jane to be properly "mothered" while gaining access to a luxurious life-style.

To pursue the issue of how the film constructs the idea of work, there is yet another curiosity, noted by Fassbinder, which is our uncertainty over whether or not Lora is a good actress.[29] In answering Fassbinder, one concludes that the film is actually indifferent to the question of Lora's talent. Rather, Lora's work is treated as an abstraction, first because Lora is condemned simply for choosing to work outside the home, and second, she does the kind of work that brings her affluence, celebrity, and independence (fatally associated with impersonation or "imitation"). Fassbinder, however, might just as well have noted the film's representation of Annie's work: its status as work for pay is systematically denied, and it is depicted throughout as voluntary help done out of devotion and choice. As Dudden notes, "help" denotes "less an occupation than an activity,"[30] and as such, Annie's full-time commitment to labor is presented as unproblematic and invisible. Thus, the ease with which the audience accepts this impression only testifies to the prevalent cultural prejudices concerning white women's and black women's work. For white women, work is viewed as a problem, a matter of weighing crucial alternatives, while for black women, it is a natural signifier of their assumed status in white society.

In studying the black household worker, Bonnie Thornton Dill concludes that "class origins, racial discrimination, and social conceptions of women and women's work came together during the first half of the twentieth century to limit work options and affect family roles and the self-perceptions of one group of Afro-American women born between 1896 and 1915."[31] The release of *Imitation* in 1959, therefore, coincided with the time when this generation of women would have been in their maturity as working women. However, failing to recognize the multiplicity of factors converging to dictate Annie's social status, the

26. Dudden, *Serving Women,* 12.
27. See Dudden, *Serving Women,* 224; Katzman, *Seven Days a Week,* 199.
28. See Jacqueline Jones, *Labor of Love, Labor of Sorrow: Black Women, Work, and the Family from Slavery to the Present* (New York: Basic Books, 1985), 128–130.
29. Fassbinder, "Fassbinder on Sirk," 24.
30. Dudden, *Serving Women,* 6.
31. Dill, "Race, Class, and Gender," 140.

film chooses rather to isolate, as a central dynamic in her characterization, only her race. For Annie, this theme is primarily realized through her conflict with her daughter, Sarah Jane. Sirk describes Sarah Jane's thematic function in the film, as "the Negro girl trying to escape her condition, sacrificing to her status in society her bonds of friendship, family, etc., and trying to vanish into the imitation world of vaudeville. The imitation of life is not the real life. Lana Turner's life is a very cheap imitation. The girl . . . is choosing the imitation of life instead of being a Negro. The picture is a piece of social criticism—of both white and black."[32] In her way, Annie becomes Sirk's spokesman in the film by telling Sarah Jane, "It's a sin to be ashamed of what you are—and it's even worse to pretend, to lie." A "bad" daughter to Lora's "bad" mother, Sarah Jane's refusal to accept her racial identity leads her to reject her mother and, indirectly, to cause her mother's death. The prominence of the theme of race, however, also turns out to be one operation by which the film dilutes or disguises the issue of class; namely, by transposing situations with a class component into racial terms. Thus, while Sarah Jane's extreme behavior could easily signify her objections to her mother's working status, the dramaturgy of particular episodes guides us toward a racially weighted interpretation of her actions. For instance, when she and her mother are shown their room in Lora's apartment, she protests, "I don't want to live in the back—why do we always have to live in the back?" On face value, her objections potentially reflect a class awareness, but meanwhile the camera chooses to dwell, with obvious implications, on a shot of the black doll she discards on the floor as the scene ends. Later, the teen-aged Sarah Jane is outraged at Lora's suggestions that she is dating Hawkins, the son of a chauffeur, and she is further incensed immediately afterward when Annie suggests that she attend a church party, where all she'll meet are "busboys, cooks, chauffeurs—like Hawkins. . . !" But here, too, the meaning of Sarah Jane's ire is slanted by the way she chooses to exact her revenge against Lora and Annie, by walking in on Lora's guests with swaying hips, a tray on her head, and a southern drawl—all in imitation of a plantation slave.

Such strategies in *Imitation* illustrate D. N. Rodowick's point about the "'eloquent silences' of the domestic melodrama which map out the network of resistances in which its narratives fail."[33] What is at stake in this film, I would argue, is the need to suppress the true location of potential conflict: that between white mistress and black servant. The purpose is, in fact, to render invisible Annie's working status and to make her relationship to Lora seem simply personal, and consequently unproblematic. Where the issue of race is concerned, the basic strategy is to transpose the issue onto the framework of the maternal melodrama, so that the site of conflict is between a black woman and her

32. *Sirk on Sirk,* 130.
33. D. N. Rodowick, "Madness, Authority and Ideology in the Domestic Melodrama of the 1950's," *The Velvet Light Trap,* no. 19 (1982): 44.

white-skinned daughter, rather than between a black domestic and her white mistress. Seizing on the built-in theme of mother/daughter conflict in the maternal melodrama, the film is able, by a sleight of hand, to formulate the issue of race as familial rather than social. As a result, it is mother and daughter who are each other's antagonists, not two black women and a racist society. Annie dies, more or less because of her daughter's treatment of her, not because of the innumerable hardships typically suffered by domestics.[34] Throughout the film, Sarah Jane's revulsion at her own blackness is directed almost exclusively against her mother. For instance, after Annie inadvertently exposes Sarah Jane's color to her classmates at school, Sarah Jane turns on her mother to demand, "Why did you have to be my mother? Why?" Other characters, too, focus on Sarah Jane's blackness as a maternal issue, so that when Frankie, Sarah Jane's white boyfriend, discovers her color, his fury takes the form of this demand: "Just tell me one thing—is it true? Is your mother a nigger?" After arriving home from Frankie's assault, Sarah Jane's rage is predictably vented against her mother: "[Frankie] found out I'm not white—'cos you keep telling the world I'm your daughter." In all of this, Annie, as Sarah Jane's mother, becomes a symbol of the blackness that Sarah Jane considers her curse. At the same time, one notes that the strategy of framing the racial issue as a maternal conflict depends on the expedient of making Sarah Jane a black woman who looks white, rather than a black woman who will not accept the consequences of being (and looking) black. In the latter instance, Sarah Jane's rebelliousness would constitute a statement about racial injustice. As depicted in the film, however, Sarah Jane's whiteness is crucial in dictating our view of her as having a problem, that is to say, a neurosis compounded of identity confusion, a daughter's unreasonable rejection of her mother, and an opportunistic exploitation of an accident of nature to defraud society.

In discussing *Imitation,* Michael Stern argues that the film reflects Sirk's awareness of how his use of melodrama limits his treatment of larger social problems.[35] Actually, I would argue the opposite point—that the film is symptomatic of this limitation, for, as we have seen, easier explanations are arrived at by drawing upon the ideologies embedded in generic conventions. Indeed, Annie's question—"How do you tell your daughter that she was born to be hurt?"— seems to acknowledge the central proposition of the maternal melodrama, that women, especially mothers, are "born to be hurt." By appealing to this belief, the film lends credence to Annie's resignation to her suffering, while demanding that the audience assent to its inevitability. By the same logic, we can see that one of Lora's sins is her sustained refusal to suffer. Her theatrical triumphs have fitting titles like "Happiness," "Always Laughter," and "Born to Laugh." It is her decision to star in a film called "No More Laughter" that precipitates the events

34. These are listed in chapter 1 of Katzman's *Seven Days a Week;* see 3–43.
35. Michael Stern, *Douglas Sirk* (Boston: Twayne Publishers, 1979), 192.

leading to her realization of guilt. For Annie, however, who is only too prepared to suffer, any questions about the rationale for her victimization are dissolved into the general propositions about women's suffering embedded in the genre. In this way, the conundrum made of her fate exemplifies what Thomas Elsaesser has identified as the failings of melodrama, its refusal "to understand social change in other than private contexts and emotional terms [and] a lamentable ignorance of the properly social and political dimensions of these changes and their causality [which have] encouraged increasingly escapist forms of mass entertainment."[36]

The preceding discussion has shown the strategies in *Imitation of Life* operating to promote certain ideologies about woman's place in relation to gender, class, and race. Yet the film might be less worthy of this lengthy analysis if it did not offer the possibility of a subversive reading that provides a corrective to, although it may not undermine, the dominant ideologies of the film. This alternative reading reveals Sarah Jane, rather than Lora or Annie, to be the center of disturbance in this film. In Sarah Jane, the dominant discourses in the film converge: like Lora, she resists confinement within the home, and unlike Annie, she transgresses the limitations placed on her by class and race structures. More important, she has the ability to activate the themes suppressed in the film and is thus the vehicle for what Tania Modleski has termed (in another context) "an outlet for the repressed feminine voice."[37] So, while the film falls short of consciously commenting on its own limitations, it does, through Sarah Jane, allow for a reading that goes against the grain of its basic ideological formulations. Indeed, Sirk himself seems to have intimated Sarah Jane's unexpected importance in the film by saying that "the supporting part is the more interesting and the better acting part. The better part for the director, too; he can make more out of it. Susan Kohner, a complete beginner in pictures, steps forward, putting Turner and Gavin in the shade."[38]

Pamela Cook notes that in *Mildred Pierce*, Mildred's daughter Veda is "the threat of chaos, the excess of which Mildred's discourse calls into being and which it cannot resolve."[39] In *Imitation*, Sarah Jane likewise presents the threat of chaos because she has the catalytic ability to activate the themes that are otherwise suppressed in the film. Ironically, this power in Sarah Jane often derives from her willingness to role-play and mimic—in other words, to "imitate." For instance, she parades in front of Lora's guests in an exaggerated parody of a slave, drawling in a mock-servile accent: "Fetch y'awl a mess of crawdaddies, Mis' Lora, fo' y'awl and yo' friends." When Lora comments

36. Thomas Elsaesser, "Tales of Sound and Fury," *Monogram,* no. 4 (1973): 4.
37. Tania Modleski, "Time and Desire in the Woman's Film," *Cinema Journal* 23 (Spring 1984): 21.
38. *Sirk on Sirk,* 130.
39. Pamela Cook, "Duplicity in *Mildred Pierce,*" in *Women in Film Noir,* ed. E. Ann Kaplan (London: British Film Institute, 1978), 78.

coldly on her "trick," she continues, "Ah learned it from mah mammy, 'nd she learned it from her ol' mastah 'fo she 'longed to you." The shock value of Sarah Jane's performance here comes from the exact targeting of her resentment while she acts it out. It is directed at Annie for her servility and at Lora, whom she now exposes not as Annie's benefactress, but as an owner of servants. Near the end of the film, there is another instance in which Sarah Jane's role-playing indirectly illuminates the true positioning of herself and others. When the dying Annie goes to see Sarah Jane in a motel, their encounter is interrupted by the appearance of one of Sarah Jane's girlfriends. Mother and daughter then act out the pretense that Annie is simply Sarah Jane's childhood mammy, with Annie explaining to the friend, "I used to take care of her." When, after Annie's departure, the friend says to Sarah Jane in mock glee, "So—honey chile, you had a mammy," Sarah Jane, stricken with guilt, pretends to agree, sobbing, "Yes—all my life!" The pathos of this scene makes it one of the emotional highpoints of the film. Its ironic power, however, derives from its exposure of a dynamic suppressed in the film, which is that Annie has indeed played the role of mammy for Lora and Susie. Thus, through a particularly cruel transference, it now seems appropriate for her to agree to enact a similar role for her own daughter. In this scene, the substitution of "mammy" for "mother," a degrading insult to Annie, makes explicit the mislabeling of roles that has persisted throughout, whereby Annie's working role as servant has been systematically disguised as a personal and familial one instead.

Even in her misguided self-destructiveness, Sarah Jane's refusal to accept socially imposed strictures helps to illuminate her social positioning in ways that her mother's acquiescence does not. By performing in a tawdry nightclub, she displays herself as a sexual object for her clientele, and by trying to pass for white, she incurs physical assault from Frankie, her white boyfriend. Yet, the fact that Sarah Jane's nightclub act is obviously a pathetic imitation of Lora's theatrical success impels us to understand, if not to condone, her smoldering frustration with the constraints relegating her to such demeaning means for satisfying her aspirations. Similarly, although Frankie's attack on her seems an inevitable punishment for her masquerading as white, his violence nevertheless gives credence to Sarah Jane's fear and rejection of a social system that renders her victim of such chastisement.

A subversive reading of the film, therefore, sees Sarah Jane in a posture of justified rebellion against her mother's powerlessness and servility. Judith Rollins (speaking, aptly enough, of why domestics might identify with their mistresses) has said that identification is "a mode of coping with a situation of powerlessness that precludes overt attack against those with power."[40] In this light, Sarah Jane's view of her connection to Annie as her curse, and her resulting refusal to identify with her mother, signify her unspoken recognition of the root of Annie's

40. Rollins, *Between Women*, 222.

powerlessness. As Geoffrey Nowell-Smith has concluded, the cause of women's "suffering and impotence" in melodrama is "the failure to be male"[41]—only here in Annie's case, hers is the failure to be both male and white. Sarah Jane's problem of identity is, as D. N. Rodowick suggests, typical of how the domestic melodrama portrays social conflict as "cris[es] of identification": "The forward thrust of narrative is not accomplished through external conflict and the accumulation of significant actions, but rather through the internalization of conflict in a crisis of identification: the difficulty which individual characters find in their attempts to accept or conform to the set of symbolic positions around which the network of social relations adhere and where they can both be "'themselves' and 'at home'."[42] In *Imitation,* daughters punish mothers by exhibiting neuroses that exemplify such crises. Thus, Susie punishes Lora essentially by committing an error in sexual identification that leads her to fall in love with her mother's lover. Lora's career success supplies Sarah Jane with a model of behavior defined in professional terms (but one that also has overt sexual connotations, as Sarah Jane's lascivious nightclub act makes clear). In this context, Lora, as an object of false identification, is again the culprit, and her functioning in this respect gives the mirror motif, for which Sirk is renowned, further significance: as the falsely seductive mirror in which Susie and Sarah Jane see themselves, Lora becomes the site on which the "normal" and "healthy" identification processes between mothers and daughters are played out according to a sinister and perverted scenario.

Geoffrey Nowell-Smith has argued that the melodrama differs from tragedy in that in the former the "locus of power is the family and individual power" rather than social power, so that "the question of law or legitimacy, so central to tragedy, is turned inward from 'Has this man a right to rule (over us)?' to 'Has this man a right to rule a family (like ours)?'" This question, Nowell-Smith continues, can be expressed in terms of the underlying question in the family romance, which asks, "Whose child am I?"[43] Accordingly, Sarah Jane's rejection of Annie and her implicit modeling of herself after Lora addresses the issue of parentage, and so illustrates E. Ann Kaplan's point that "feminism was in part a reaction against our mothers, who had tried to inculcate the patriarchal 'feminine' in us, much to our anger."[44] Identifying with Lora, Sarah Jane allies herself with a woman who, in her own way, has risked transgression; at the same time, her choice of symbolic parentage leads her to commit not only a fundamental violation of familial relationships—disownment of her mother—but also, by implication, perhaps the most heinous of familial crimes, matricide, as suggested by Sarah Jane's public admission over Annie's coffin, "I killed my mother!"

41. Nowell-Smith, "Minnelli and Melodrama," 116.
42. Rodowick, "Madness, Authority and Ideology," 42.
43. Nowell-Smith, "Minnelli and Melodrama," 115, 116.
44. E. Ann Kaplan, "The Case of the Missing Mother: Maternal Issues in Vidor's *Stella Dallas,*" *Heresies* 16 (1983): 81.

On a more subtle, but no less significant, level, Sarah Jane's selective identification with parental figures is taken one step further—through her identification with her father. Sarah Jane's father (briefly mentioned only once and never seen in the film) is, empirically speaking, entirely peripheral to the dramatic plot. However, as the sole father and husband in the film, and also as the patriarchal ideal to whom Sarah Jane traces her lineage, he has a significant place in the family plot crystallized in the film's question, "Whose child am I?" Throughout the film, by insisting on her own whiteness, Sarah Jane repeatedly invokes her bond to her father who, in Annie's words, was "practically white." By defining herself in terms of her patrimony, Sarah Jane instinctively casts her allegiance with a figure that to her represents power, both as a male and as a black man who can pass for white. (In the same vein, it might also be significant that Sarah Jane as child claims affinity to Jesus Christ, haughtily saying, "He was white—like me," and thereby proclaims her identification with one of the archetypal patriarchal figures in the Christian pantheon.)

Sarah Jane's father is a contradictory figure in this film, and not only in his appearance as a black man who looks white. On one hand, he can be seen to exemplify the absent father who, as D. N. Rodowick has noted, "in the 1950s [melodrama] . . . functioned solely to throw the system into turmoil by his absences through death or desertion, his weaknesses, his neglects, etc."[45] On the other hand, Sarah Jane's father has a distinguishing attribute placing him in a posture of resistance to the patriarchal system that his absence could otherwise be seen to validate. The exact racial identity of Sarah Jane's father is in doubt. Annie's explanation that "he was practically white" could mean that his ancestry was predominantly white, or that he was a black man with very light skin.[46] It is this fundamental ambiguity in his racial identity that gives Sarah Jane's father his symbolic power in the film. Portrayed as an individual with no name, no history, and no fixed racial identity, he can be seen as a man who passes a tragic flaw down to his daughter, or alternately, as a man who can resist social categorization and therefore social control. In his ambiguity, he has access to the "different kind of representation [escaping] rigidity of fixed identity" that Linda Williams imagines might offer the promise of transcending the "dialectic between the maternal unrepresentable and the paternal already-represented."[47] *Imitation,* however, reverses Williams's dialectic (adapted from Jane Gallop and Julia Kristeva): in the film, it is the maternal figure, Annie, who represents the already represented, and the father figure, Annie's husband, who is the unrepresentable. As that which is

---

45. Rodowick, "Madness, Authority and Ideology," 44.
46. In the novel, Delilah makes it clear that her husband was black, describing him as "a white nigger" who "didn't leave [his daughter] nothin' but some blue-white blood a-flowin' in her little veins. . . ." She also states that he was born of two "Virginia darkies," with a strong suggestion that both he and his daughter look white only through an accident of nature. In the Stahl film, Delilah says of her husband: "[He] was a very light-colored man."
47. Williams, "Something Else Besides a Mother," 11–12.

unrepresentable, Sarah Jane's father has the power to resist the strictures of social and racial stratification, and this freedom is what Sarah Jane chooses to exploit in identifying with him. She tells Susie at one point, "[My mother] can't help her color, but I can—and I will." Argued this way, Sarah Jane's father can be seen as an approximation of the end product of the project, described by Marianne Hirsch, of "dismantling the sameness and unity of the symbolic order that has excluded woman, of creating a discourse of plurality [which] depends on a re-definition of the individual subject. . . ."[48]

As a catalytic force in the film, Sarah Jane dismantles the film's basic strategy of displacement and obfuscation by opening up the site where the issues of social hegemony converge. Through her identification with a symbolic figure who is paternal, male, and white, Sarah Jane provides a recognition of the alignment of forces in society that act to oppress her and to relegate her and her mother to a subordinate position. While the ingrained ideology of the maternal melodrama solicits our consent to seeing Sarah Jane's defiance as structured around her conflict with her mother, the insertion of the theme of the father nevertheless offers the possibility of locating the conflict properly within the realm of the family and of society as institutions of power. Thus, although the overriding structure of the maternal melodrama would couch the question of woman's suffering in terms of a dialectic between good mothers and bad mothers, Sarah Jane ruptures this reading by illuminating the issues of authority and social control and thus calls into question the closure of the melodramatic framework. In the final analysis, of course, Sarah Jane's declaration of allegiance to her father is self-defeating, for this figure who offers hopes of resistance can do so, within the terms of the narrative, only by operating as a negative force and by remaining an imaginary and ill-defined entity.

Sirk's work has always had a special place in the debate over whether melodrama is an inherently conservative or subversive form. For instance, Paul Willemen has proposed that "Sirk's position in the history of the American cinema closely parallels Tolstoy's position in the history of Soviet literature, . . . [because like Tolstoy] he depicted a society which appeared to be strong and healthy, but which in fact was exhausted and torn apart by collective neuroses."[49] Or, as Laura Mulvey suggests in her essay on Sirk while the "view of melodrama as a safety valve for ideological contradictions centered on sex and the family seems to deprive it of possible redemption as progressive, it also places it in the context of

48. Marianne Hirsch, "Mothers and Daughters," *Signs* 7 (Autumn 1981): 211.
49. Paul Willeman, "Towards an Analysis of the Sirkian System," *Screen* 13 (Winter 1972): 133. This debate is more or less implicit in most recent writings about the woman's film. The essays cited above by Cook, Elsaesser, Modleski, and Williams provide useful perspectives. A valuable contribution to the discussion can also be found in E. Ann Kaplan's "Theories of Melodrama: A Feminist Perspective," *Women and Performance: A Journal of Feminist Theory* 1 (Spring/Summer 1983): 40–48.

wider problems."[50] At the same time, the issue of "narrative rupture," particularly that which results from the imposition of an arbitrarily neat and happy ending, has further occasioned the claim made by various critics for the inherent conservatism of the genre. Thus, E. Ann Kaplan describes the "need [in melodrama] to re-inscribe the feminine in its location as defined by patriarchy [so that even though] the narrative may allow brief expressions of female resistance to that positioning, and glimpses of other possibilities for women . . . the 'correct' family order must be re-established by the end of the film."[51] With a different emphasis, while recognizing the inevitable tension between contradictions in ideological content and their forced resolution, Mulvey nevertheless argues that "the strength of the melodramatic form lies in the amount of dust the story raises along the road, a cloud of over-determined irreconcilables which put up a resistance to being neatly settled in the last five minutes."[52] Here again, Sirk's own well-documented uneasiness with the requirement of the happy ending makes him both an exemplary case and a thoughtful commentator.[53] In fact, he has specifically addressed this issue in relation to *Imitation,* saying:

> you don't believe the happy end, and you're not really supposed to. . . . By just drawing out the characters you certainly could get a story—along the lines of hopelessness, of course. You could just go on. Lana will forget about her daughter again, and go back to the theatre and continue as the kind of actress she has been before. Gavin will go off with some other woman. Susan Kohner will go back to the escape world of vaudeville. Sandra Dee will marry a decent guy. The circle will be closed. But the point is you don't have to do this. And if you did, you would get a picture that the studio would have abhorred.[54]

However, although Sirk's deliberate use of irony may be typical of his other work, *Imitation* stands out among his films in that the conservative thrust of its ending predominates over whatever ironic subtext Sirk might have intended. Thus, while it remains to be seen whether, in the context of Sirk's *oeuvre, Imitation* is the exception that proves the rule, and while it might be no more than speculative to relate this aspect of the film to its tremendous commercial success, the film would seem to demand a qualification of Laura Mulvey's point that the strength of melodrama lies in its ability to resist the blandishments of the happy ending. In this, Sirk's last film, the sheer emotional power of its final scene,

50. Laura Mulvey, "Notes on Sirk and Melodrama," *Movie,* no. 25 (Winter 1977–78): 53.

51. Kaplan, "Theories of Melodrama," 45.

52. Mulvey, "Notes on Sirk and Melodrama," 54.

53. See Sirk's own remarks on happy endings in *Sirk on Sirk,* 119. As one of the many discussions of Sirk's problematic endings, see Jon Halliday's discussion of *All That Heaven Allows,* in *Douglas Sirk,* ed. Mulvey and Halliday, 65.

54. *Sirk on Sirk,* 132; see also p. 52. Sirk's comments on his ironic intentions in this ending are quoted by James Harvey in "Sirkumstantial Evidence," *Film Comment* 14 (July–Aug. 1978): 55–57.

along with the symbolic weight of its *mise-en-scène,* finally operates to lay to rest the subversive energy of Sarah Jane and to reinstate Annie, in her death, as the emotional and ideological center of the film.

Throughout the film, as a foil for Lora, Annie is notably devoid of ambition and accepting of her servile status. Apparently, though, Annie's desire for an elaborate funeral is one ambition she has. Before her death, she tells Lora, "I'm getting on, and [a big funeral is] the one thing I've always wanted to splurge on. I really want it elegant . . . ," adding that she wants "four white horses, and a band playing, no mourning, but proud, and high-steppin' horses like I was going to glory." In requesting the staging for her "going to glory," Annie seems to be visualizing it as an occasion for a public spectacle rivaling one of Lora's theatrical triumphs, at which "all the friends" she has will be in attendance. At her funeral, it seems, Annie can enjoy the glory denied her in life. Accordingly, her funeral symbolically reverses the conditions of her working life: where she labored in anonymity and isolation, she is now honored in public by a community of friends (and, it appears, of total strangers as well); where her life-style was humble and her work seemingly without monetary value, the sheer ostentation of the occasion testifies to the tangible recompense for such a life; and where she served whites without complaint, now she is among her own—the scene is designed to be pervaded with black, Annie's color, so that even Lora's blondness and habitual white attire are doused by the color of mourning.

The pageantry of the scene suggest Annie's unspoken craving for recognition. Its climactic moment comes when Sarah Jane, in full view of a gathering of blacks and whites, finally "recognizes" her mother by declaring, "It's my mother!" Given Annie's contentment with living and working in oblivion, the inscription of recognition as a central motif in the scene of her funeral must be significant. The fundamental irony, though, lies in the suggestion that for Annie, her annihilation is the prerequisite for recognition, and that only in death can she declare publicly that she has a family, a community, and deserved compensation for her life of servitude. Without directly addressing its ironic implications, Michael Stern notes how, during her funeral, Annie "has been transformed into an object—the flower-draped coffin—like so many objects in Sirk's films, unassailable by the characters."[55] In the same vein, we can make sense of a detail in the scene that has puzzled some critics: two long shots, intercut with the exterior shots of the funeral procession, taken from inside a store to frame the cortege within the storefront window. The radical shift in physical distance and vantage point effected by these two seemingly unmotivated shots signifies that, as an icon, Annie has entered the realm of public and communal consciousness, here represented by a removed and anonymous point of view like that of a stranger looking on.

In discussing the ending of *Stella Dallas,* Linda Williams has noted how the

---

55. Stern, *Douglas Sirk,* 189.

"final scene functions to efface Stella even as it glorifies her sacrificial act of motherly love [because] Stella loses both her daughter and [herself] to become an abstract (and absent) ideal of motherly sacrifice."[56] Just such a simultaneous eradication and glorification of Annie occurs in the last scene of *Imitation*. Yet a comparison of this ending with those in Sirk's other films suggests a departure from Sirk's usual strategy. Christopher Orr, for instance, comments on the ironic happy endings in films like *Magnificent Obsession* and *All That Heaven Allows*, saying that in them "Sirk's mise-en-scène undermines [their] sentimental and complicit content. . . ."[57] In *Imitation*, however, while the irony is not far beneath the surface, the primary drive of its ending is toward closure and ideological containment, rather than open-ended and subversive interrogation. In discussing the conclusion of *Written on the Wind*, Orr further suggests that its "epilogue calls attention to contradictions within the film's ideological project [because an epilogue is] something added on, a site for information not integrated by the narrative. . . ."[58] If, ideologically speaking, the ending of *Written* is a "mistake" (Orr's characterization), then, in contrast, *Imitation* represents Sirk's much more successful attempt to avoid concluding his film on such an overt note of contradiction and disjunction.

Appropriately enough, the success of *Imitation* in its drive toward closure hinges on the clustering of its *mise-en-scène* and symbolism around the central metaphor of the film, that of imitation. As already noted, Annie's funeral as a public spectacle parallels the various performances by Lora and Sarah Jane seen throughout the film. However, unlike the anonymous audiences at Lora's stage appearances and the shadowed male caricatures at Sarah Jane's cabaret acts, Annie's audience is seen more frontally and at closer range. Not only are members of the congregation during the funeral service individually identified (including, for example, Annie's minister; Lora's agent, Loomis; the director, David Edwards; and even the milkman from the old cold-water flat, Mr. McKenny), but this entire audience also collectively assumes a distinct identity as Annie's community, and even more specifically, as Annie's black community. Thus, the various bystanders who salute Annie's passing cortège have a concrete dimension lacking in the other audiences seen in the film. Also, in a film in which most of the scenes take place indoors, the opening out of the final scene into the outdoors, combined with the use of objective extreme long shots and panoramic high camera angles, contributes to its pseudo-documentary effect. The use of an exterior location has even further significance: throughout the film, the characters are continually seen through narrow doorways and corridors, or framed within windows and mirror frames, so the progression of Annie's cortège through an unconfined exterior terrain provides a retrospective commentary on

56. Williams, "Something Else Besides a Mother," 16.
57. Christopher Orr, "*Written on the Wind* and the Ideology of Adaptation," *Film Criticism* 10 (Spring 1985): 2.
58. Ibid., 1–2.

the "unreal" and confined existence of the other characters while suggesting Annie's own liberation into a more authentic space. In this light, the two shots taken from inside a store, discussed above, take on more meaning. In contrast to the rest of the film, in which the characters are portrayed as surrogates or mirror reflections of each other and in which the visual motif of the mirror recurs, these two shots allow a view of the world through glass rather than as a mirrored reflection. Finally, even the appearance of Mahalia Jackson plays a role in marking this scene off as something other than an "imitation." The lack of explanation of Jackson's relationship to any of the characters in the film gives her singing at Annie's funeral the semblance of a documentary performance within a fictional film.[59] Annie has been represented as the only main character who does not fall victim to false identification and role-playing. Therefore, Jackson's appearance at Annie's funeral in her own guise as a professional singer both duplicates and authenticates the meaning of Annie's life, so that her unmediated performance and Annie's unassuming stance collaborate to lend the lie to the inauthentic work performed by Lora and Sarah Jane.

As we might expect, Sarah Jane's function in this scene is illuminating. At Annie's funeral, Sarah Jane makes her most public and her most humiliating appearance, but with a significant twist. When she weeps over her mother's coffin, we are all convinced that at least this time she is not performing. The public spectacle that she makes of herself, then, is paradoxically, the one that both redeems her and implicitly repudiates her previous performances in the film, as when she humiliates Lora in front of her guests or when she forces Annie to pretend to be her mammy. After Sarah Jane's tearful recognition of her mother, she, with Lora and Susie, are ushered into a waiting limousine. In this concrete image, we see the remaining protagonists removed from the public gaze just when Annie becomes the cynosure of the same gathered audience. Here, too, we observe the process by which the three women are reconstituted into the semblance of a nuclear family, complete with a father-figure, Steve Archer, who occupies the front seat of the limousine. As Steve turns to look back at the women, his look is ambiguous in its import, bespeaking reassurance, protectiveness, or punitive satisfaction. This aspect of the ending, in fact, echoes that in *Mildred Pierce,* when, after Mildred has been cleared of the murder of Monty, she walks off with Bert, her estranged husband who has been absent for much of the film. As Pamela Cook comments, "Mildred's take-over of the place of the father has brought about the collapse of all social and moral order in her world. . . . In the face of impending chaos and confusion the patriarchal order is called upon to reassert itself and take the Law back into its own hands, divesting women completely of any power they may have gained while the patriarchal order was temporarily impaired."[60]

59. The closing credits of the film state that Mahalia Jackson appears as a "choir soloist." However, the credits included in *Sirk on Sirk* indicate that Jackson appears in the film as "herself"; see p. 171.
60. Cook, "Duplicity in Mildred Pierce," 75.

Finally, perhaps the uniquely insidious aspect of *Imitation* is suggested visually by the elongating distance between Annie's hearse, carrying her off into glorious oblivion, and the limousine containing Lora. This image makes concrete yet another area of silence in the film. Whereas several critics have seen the depiction of close mother-daughter relationship in the maternal melodrama as a subversive gesture in itself,[61] *Imitation* potentially explores another dimension still by explicitly addressing the issue of bonding between black and white women. Unfortunately, in actual practice, this promise is, as we have seen, negated through the film's refusal to recognize potential conflict between Lora and Annie or subsumed to the polarization of Lora and Annie as "good" and "bad" mothers. Nowhere is there an attempt to establish a basis for seeing these two women as the product of individual histories and social conditions. But without this, there can be no insightful revelation of what may ultimately bind them. As Bonnie Thornton Dill reminds us, "The structures of race and class generate important economic, ideological, and experimental cleavages among women. These lead to differences in perception of self and their place in society. . . . Thus, I would argue for the abandonment of the concept of sisterhood as a global construct based on examined assumptions about similarities, and I would substitute a more pluralistic approach that recognizes and accepts the objective differences between women."[62] Reinforcing Dill's argument, Gloria I. Joseph and Jill Lewis titled their study of shared issues between black and white women *Common Differences* to signal their commitment "to actually examine side by side, dynamically, those very differences and conflicting visions" that must form the groundwork of true dialogue.[63] Underlying the work of Dill and of Joseph and Lewis is the belief that the first step toward true bonding is the acknowledgment of unique differences, and perhaps potential conflict, between individuals. Thus, although the possibility of cooperation between black and white women is a powerful fantasy in *Imitation,* the film tellingly ends with the image of final separation between its two protagonists, whose relationship with each other remains the deepest level of silence in the film.

And so it seems that Sirk's *Imitation of Life* is fantasy, although perhaps bogus fantasy, on many levels. However, it is perhaps also fantasy with an even more serious agenda than we have recognized thus far. In his essay on John Ford's *The Searchers* (1956), Brian Henderson suggests a reading of the film that considers its historical context, specifically, of its release two years after the U.S. Supreme Court ruling (*Brown v. Board of Education of Topeka,* 1954) that sought to end public school desegregation in America. Initially wondering why this film has

61. Janet Walker writes, "Solidarity among women (represented by Mildred and Veda [in *Mildred Pierce*]) represents the greatest threat to patriarchy. Female collectivity provides a vision of a world without men." See Janet Walker, "Feminist Critical Practice: Female Discourse in *Mildred Pierce,*" *Film Reader* 5 (1982): 170.
62. Dill, "Race, Class, and Gender," 138, 146.
63. Gloria I. Joseph and Jill Lewis, *Common Differences: Conflicts in Black and White Feminist Perspectives* (Garden City, N.Y.: Anchor Books, 1981), 13.

continued to exert so much power over its audience through the years, Henderson notes the treatment of "the questions of kinship, race, marriage, and the relations between tribes [Indian and white]," and, by seeing the idea of adoption as a metaphor for racial desegregation, he concludes that the film is "a myth about non-whites by and for whites . . . and a manual for non-whites adopted by white society, telling them what they may expect and what is expected of them."[64] Taking inspiration from Henderson, we see that Sirk's film, released five years after *Brown,* coincided with a period when the issue of desegregation was still controversial. It too deals with issues of kinship and adoption; in fact, it foregrounds the themes of interracial relationships, miscegenation, and the adoption of blacks into white families. Quite obviously, unlike *The Searchers,* the treatment of race is overt, not disguised. Interestingly, Henderson's analysis is based on a "de-centering" of the character of Ethan (John Wayne) in order to promote the centrality of Martin (Jeffrey Hunter), a half-breed. In discussing *Imitation,* we too have seen how Sarah Jane, a black woman who looks white, is the catalytic character whose presence in the film convulses many of its unspoken themes.

In this perspective, *Imitation of Life* can be read not only as an incipient attempt to offer a convincing picture of black-white bonding, but also a film that programmatically propounds the conditions for the assimilation of blacks into the American "family." In this light, Sarah Jane's crisis of identification must be understood as a struggle to test the limits of her power both in her adopted family and, by extension, in the larger social scheme. In the melodrama, Geoffrey Nowell-Smith has said, 'what is at stake . . . is the survival of the family unit and the possibility for individuals of acquiring an identity which is also a place within the system, a place in which they can both be 'themselves' and 'at home,' in which they can simultaneously enter, without contradiction, the symbolic order and bourgeois society."[65] In analyzing *The Searchers,* Henderson argues that the film teaches non-whites that they must agree to act according to white man's laws if they are to be accepted in white society. The message of *Imitation of Life* is no less sobering and peremptory. Indeed, the lesson that Sarah Jane learns is clear: although her appearance and her upbringing may give her the desire and the ability to pass for white, she must not forget who and what she is. In the final analysis, Sarah Jane's mistake is to insist that adoption means assimilation; her transgression is to resist her own contingent status. Here, the theme of racial integration intersects with that of domestic service, for the vigilant but invisible presence of the servant within the sanctified privacy of her employer's home is an analogue in miniature of the contradictory terms by which blacks like Annie and Sarah Jane can remain as adopted members of the American family: invited, even appreciated, but intrinsically alien.

64. Brian Henderson, "The Searchers: An American Dilemma," *Film Quarterly* 34 (Winter 1980–81): 12, 22.
65. Nowell-Smith, "Minnelli and Melodrama," 116.

Imitation(s) of Life: The Black Woman's Double Determination as Troubling "Other"

Sandy Flitterman-Lewis

There are many ways to trace the distance between the two film versions of Fannie Hurst's 1933 novel, *Imitation of Life*—a space marked chronologically by the dates 1934 (John Stahl) and 1959 (Douglas Sirk).[1] There is the contrast between the melodrama of Stahl (with its highly emotional effects and its emphasis on familial conflicts) and the social consciousness of Sirk (with its representation of irreconcilable racial and class contradictions). Or there is the New Deal economic optimism of the mid-30s which is contradicted by the post-Civil Rights acknowledgment of the determining social fact of race characteristic of the early 60s. And from a psychoanalytic standpoint, there is the contrast between the utopian dual realm of maternal reciprocity in Stahl's film, and the recognition, in Sirk, of irreducible difference, an acknowledgment that all social organization is constituted in and by division. (Thus Stahl's and Sirk's films, from this perspective, can be seen to correspond, respectively, to the Imaginary and Symbolic psychic registers elaborated in Lacanian theory.) And nowhere is the transforming contrast between the two films more profoundly seen than in the representation of the black woman, her textual figuration as sexual and racial signifier. In the 25-year distance between the two texts, the emotive focus shifts from the maternal world of the nurturing mammy to the milieu of the sexually scandalous and resisting mulatto.

Yet in each film's representation of the transgressive woman—the black daughter who looks white, and who, because of the contradition between being and seeming which defines her, can fit comfortably into *neither* culture—there is a correspondence between feminine sexuality and alterity which results in a sexualization of the radical "otherness" of the black woman. Therefore, in terms of a reading which sees *both* films, in fact, as parables of feminine identity (for the textual disturbance in each film involves transgressions of both racial and sexual categories as the young woman asserts a female identity of her own construction, independent of social definitions and contraints) there is a continuity which serves to strongly unify the two texts across their apparent differences in focus.

From *Literature and Psychology* 35, no. 4 (1988): 44–57.

1. Another version of this article was originally presented as a paper on a panel entitled "Images of Black Women in American Film," at the Society for Cinema Studies Annual Conference, held at New York University, June 18–15, 1985. My thanks to Kathryn Kalinak, Joan Dagle, and Miriam Hansen for suggestions and support.

Both films tell the same story of two single women, one black, the other white, who join together to create both a home and respectable upbringing for their two daughters. Two parallel dramas develop: the white woman's romantic involvement becomes a source of conflict, as her daughter becomes a rival for the affections of her lover; and the black woman's maternal desire is challenged by her light-skinned daughter's violent refusal of her mother's culture, her drive to "pass" for white in the dominant society. Stahl's version has Bea Pullman (Claudette Colbert) becoming a financial success by parlaying Delilah's (Louise Beavers) family pancake recipe into a fortune as a packaged mix; her daughter Jessie (Rochelle Hudson) falls in love with her fiancé, ichthyologist Steven Archer (Warren William) while Peola (Fredi Washington) attempts to escape into the world of commerce by becoming a cashier in a white establishment. Sirk recasts these conflicts in his characteristic self-reflexive terms—the iconography of performance, spectacle, and visual display. Lora Meredith (Lana Turner) becomes a successful stage (and eventually film) actress while Susie (Sandra Dee) reacts to her neglect by falling in love with her mother's boyfriend, advertising photographer Steve Archer (John Gavin). Annie Johnson (Juanita Moore) assumes the role of domestic servant (increasingly so, as Lora's career develops) and Susie's confidante, while Sarah Jane (Susan Kohner) degrades herself by pursuing a career as a performer in sleazy nightclubs. Both versions end with the spectacular and tragic funeral of the benevolent mammy character (whose heart has been broken by the separation from her daughter), as the grief-stricken daughter rushes, too late, to publicly sob her guilt and sorrow—a scene, in both versions, impossible to view without tears.

Even this brief summary attests to *Imitation of Life*'s status as a classic maternal melodrama: In each film the articulating conflict is one in which the agonies of separation, for mother *and* for daughter, provide the trauma and the tears, the very core of melodrama in the maternal realm. However, from the standpoint of the radical alterity evoked by the mulatto—the irrefutable "otherness" which characterizes the light-skinned black woman, that living contradiction—it is the daughter's story. She is, in her very existence, the simultaneous signifier of racial and sexual difference alike. The term "mulatto," the ultimate other, immediately suggests miscegenation, which itself evokes both forbidden sexual relations and the impossible mixing of races. "Half-breed," "half-caste": Even in its synonyms, the sexual and racial allusions are unavoidable. Beyond the instant signification with the mulatto bears, Peola and Sarah Jane resist prescribed categories; they defy what is considered proper behavior for both their race and for their sex. (This is slightly more complicated for Peola, where the question of sexual propriety has more to do with what is considered correct class behavior for black women specifically—but I will discuss this more fully in a moment.) In the case of Peola and Sarah Jane, then, it is the transgression both of racial and of sexual boundaries—the assertion of difference itself—which provides each text with its traumatic matrix.

Variety was perspicacious in its contemporary review of the Stahl film:

The most arresting part of the picture and overshadowing the conventional romance . . . is the tragedy of Aunt Delilah's girl born to a white skin and Negro blood . . . Girl is miserable being unable to adjust herself to the lot of her race and unable to take her place among the whites. This is, of course, very grim and harsh stuff.[2]

Yet, in the terms I am proposing, it is not the individual *conflict* of either Peola or Sarah Jane which is "very grim and harsh stuff," but the women themselves, subversive sisters at odds with a culture's definition of them. Both women struggle for identity, an identity born of difference that makes them part of neither the culture of the mother (Delilah pleads, "The Lord made you black; accept it for yo' mammy, your mother dear.") nor the dominant one. But this conflict is also one of feminine self-definition, for to remain with the mother (that is, to be black, and to be like the mother) means to accept a notion of an "essential" self and to assume the position of daughter, child, and servant. On the other hand, to assert difference from the mother (which, paradoxically, means masquerading similarity with the dominant culture by passing for white) involves the assertion of a conventional sexuality, of adult femaleness, in a movement which thrusts the daughter into a world of symbolic relations and circuits of exchange. (From this perspective, Peola's job as cashier is not so far removed from Sarah Jane's work as nightclub performer; the latter is merely on a continuum in which the manipulation of familiar definitions of the sexual explicitly foregrounds the woman's function within a symbolic relay.)

Thus both Peola and Sarah Jane attempt to enter into a cultural realm (a world of sociality, of discursive relations) by resisting prescribed categories of behavior, yet this resistance leads them to accept other prescriptions, other demands—for these are the only alternatives available. In both cases this resistance can only be articulated, then, as a refusal of socially dictated positions on either side, a transgression of culturally determined racial and feminine boundaries. Peola's assertion of self involves the crossing over into social territory forbidden to "black ladies"; Sarah Jane's involves exaggeration and excess as she "plays out" the cultural definition of female sexuality to its extreme. And as each woman appeals for autonomous life, her attempt to independently define a position within the social system involves sacrifice and death, for the price of this entry into the realm of symbolic relations is a separation from the mother which ultimately kills her. The "very grim and harsh stuff," then, is, in fact, the mulatto daughter herself, the sexual and racial "other" who can be neither black nor white, mother nor wife (the socially sanctioned positions of the adult female), who, as each film tells us, must perpetually be her mammy's daughter.

Yet in spite of this crucial thematic which is shared by both films, there are

2. *Variety,* November 27, 1934.

important divergences that mark the separate texts. It is clear, from the outset, that Sirk's version differs considerably from Stahl's in the representation of social contradictions, and this leads his film far beyond the individual focus of the melodramatic mode. For Sirk, social forces achieve a kind of prominence which makes the drama the result of irreducible social consequences rather than the function of individual problems.[3] For, in fact, there are two discourses which traverse each film—the mother-daughter discourse and the racial discourse. Where Stahl chooses to deemphasize the racial drama, making the Delilah-Peola conflict a subset (and thus an elaboration) of the structuring *maternal* crisis (Bea's renunciation of Steven in the name of her daughter's happiness), Sirk foregrounds the inextricability, the absolute interdependence, of the racial and maternal discourses, and this implies a broader, more comprehensive social view. He does this by making Sarah Jane the textual focus of the film, the locus of the articulating contradictions and the site of dynamic energy. Whereas, in the Stahl version, in the words of Donald Bogle, "Peola [is] a character in search of a movie . . . ,"[4] in the Sirk version Sarah Jane *becomes* the movie, her disruptive sexuality a sign of her inability to resolve the contradictions of the two discourses, and her psyche a battlefield where social forces collide.

A comparison of the way in which each film begins and ends should illustrate the contrasting approaches—Stahl's utopian vision of maternal reciprocity and Sirk's confirmation of the irreducible difference of the social realm. So concerned is Stahl with the recuperation of difference into an idealized maternal unity, that by the close of his version of the film, race as an issue has disappeared entirely. The circularity of the film's structure implies that the happy resolution— the return to the maternal scene of the film's beginning—involves the evocation of a tender duality between mother and daughter, one based on the exclusion and non-recognition of disruptive alterity (be it racial or paternal/social). The film opens on a scene of familial harmony, as Bea gives her toddler a bath (the child gleefully splashes the water, calling for her bath toy, "I want my quack quack!"), and closes with an evocation of this primordial moment. As the film ends, Bea, having renounced Steven for the sake of her daughter's happiness, recalls to Jessie how she first came to know Delilah: "I was giving you a bath, and you kept calling for your duck." And then, arm around her daughter, she wistfully repeats, "I want my quack quack." Her nostalgic tone indicates a yearning for that untroubled unity, the simplicity of mother-daughter sharing which she has attempted to recapture through her sacrifice of romance. This circularity signifies

3. "The picture is a piece of social criticism—of both white and black. You can't escape what you are. Now the Negroes are waking up to black is beautiful. *Imitation of Life* is a picture about the situation of the blacks before the time of the slogan, 'Black is Beautiful.' I tried to make it into a picture of social consciousness—not only of a white social consciousness, but of a Negro one, too. Both white and black are leading imitated lives. . ." Douglas Sirk, *Sirk on Sirk: Interviews with Jon Halliday* (New York: Viking Press, 1972), p. 130.
4. Donald Bogle, *Toms, Coons, Mulattoes, Mammies, and Bucks* (New York: Bantam, 1974), p. 82.

a reassertion of the utopian maternal which in fact structures the entire film; the atavistic reference to an originary moment of dual reciprocity implies an isolation from all social context, from all difference and disturbance. And it is not accidental that the film's resolution, from which all question of race and class has been excluded as well,[5] implies a renunciation of sexual and symbolic relations in the name of a reciprocity between females.

On the other hand, the question of race is unavoidable in Sirk. The most striking evidence of this is, first of all, in the *mise en scène*. Sirk designs a color system in the film which articulates this social fact in a subtle yet pervasive way. For, while the film enjoys a wide and vibrant spectrum throughout—from the pastel reds, whites, and blues of familial ideology, to the scandalous yellows, peaches, and aquas of sexual transgression—this is all utterly reduced by the film's end to the irreconcilable blacks and whites of Annie's funeral, spectacular in their silent testimony to the real tragedy of Annie. A second way in which race is inscribed in the film involves characterization. It is in the closing moments of the film, as Sarah Jane enters the mourners' car, that she assumes the functional position of maid in a family newly-constituted by Steve, Lora, and Susie. This visual configuration, in which Sarah Jane effectively substitute for her mother, implies the absolute impossibility of repudiating the social questions of race and class: Sarah Jane has come "home." Thirdly, Sirk's version of the film opens immediately within a social realm—the contrast with Stahl is unavoidable. From the intimate space of the child's bath another "bathing" scene unfolds: We are in the middle of Coney Island. A sequence of four long shots (from extreme to general), teeming with vibrant activity, situates what will eventually become the focus on individuals within an inescapable social context. Even before the Lana Turner character is visible, we see her ankles, among other anonymous pairs of legs, behind the rails of the boardwalk. We are already located within a register of loss, for absence hovers over the text from the outset—Lora can't find her child. It is thus within a fully-populated milieu of social activity that the main characters are introduced—Annie has found Susie and takes care of both of the children, while Steve, an itinerant photographer, snaps random shots on the beach.

The ending of Sirk's film is equally marked by loss and the social construction it implies. For, it is within the context of the spectacular extravagance of Annie's funeral (a full band, white horses, uniformed pallbearers with plumes, a Harlem crowded with mourners) that Sarah Jane returns. As noted, the last shots of the film place her in the limousine with the surrogate family (by implication, her employers), and, as such, reinforce her acceptance of the symbolic position of the black woman. No longer willing to struggle to "be" as she "seems," Sarah

5. Sirk commented on this as well, recognizing that while he liked Stahl's film very much, and thought it "very good," "it belonged to the previous generation," for it portrayed the characters in a way "which took all the social significance out of the Negro mother's situation." Sirk, *Sirk on Sirk*, p. 129.

Jane becomes fully black by taking her mother's place, and in so doing, she accepts her black identity with resignation. The terms of her revolt and its consequences—sexual display and humiliation—having been dictated by the possibilities available to women in the dominant culture, her refusal to conform to "blackness" has meant only that, ironically, she must assume the dominant definition of "whiteness." Yet, this is an effort that results, tragically, in parody. At odds with either position, Sarah Jane must finally acquiesce to that from which she had tried to escape.

Because of this, the unavoidability of racial difference—the impossibility of ignoring the profound effects of class and gender on all social relationships—is stamped irrevocably on the film's conclusion. There is no way to elide the racial and sexual discourses, to exist somehow outside of those imperatives: There is no possibility of "passing." Sirk has commented on the hopelessness of this closed circle, on the lie of the happy ending.[6] In contrast to Stahl's bittersweet lament for a narcissistic ideal (and its suggestion of a utopian maternal realm), Sirk posits a dialectical discourse in which everything is mediated by social contradictions. His critical vision is one that foregrounds the irreducible racial and sexual realities of a social system which segregates races and dictates specific roles for women: The drama of the individual is never separate from its social inscriptions.

And yet when we consider *both* films from the standpoint of the resisting daughter, the figure of refusal in whose transgressive position the discourses of sexuality and racial otherness coalesce, it becomes clear that Sirk's film, in fact, only makes explicit the racial and sexual subtext which was already present in the Stahl film, but suppressed. A close look at several sequences form each film will demonstrate the extent to which the contradictions inherent in the character of the mulatto woman are expressive of pervasive social facts, and the extent to which *each* film (explicitly or not) is able to dramatize these contradictions within the melodramatic form.

The first sequence involves a confrontation between Peola and her mother. In keeping with the thematic of business and finance which structures the Stahl version (Bea becomes a pancake magnate, Delilah's image as a nurturing mammy is commodified to sell the product, the first masculine presence in the film is a property-owner from whom Bea rents store-space, and so forth), Peola attempts to prove her whiteness by establishing herself in a circuit of commerce—she becomes a cashier in a white restaurant. As Delilah goes to retrieve her, forcing herself into Peola's new life like the forbidden and repressed past that she represents, she instigates a conflict for her daughter between the desire for the social realm and the pull of the maternal. This is depicted with impressive economy in a visual dynamic which involves the interplay between a centrally-framed character and the edges of the frame, edges which alternately signify

6. See Sirk, *Sirk on Sirk,* p. 132.

forces of repression and desire for Peola and Delilah. Firstly, the opening shot of the sequence—a train speeding through the night—seems to evoke a sort of mythical descent to an unknown place as Delilah seeks the truth of Peola's disappearance, and in so doing, it marks the sequence as a privileged moment of exchange. As Peola stands at the register, a couple (one of the few anonymous representatives of the social world in the film) enters the restaurant, and as they leave the frame left, they designate the space that will signify Peola's desire to pass for white in the social milieu of commerce and exchange '("I want to be white. Like I look," she says earlier to her mother). At the precise moment that the couple leaves the frame, the camera begins to move forward, past Peola and out the window, simultaneously disclosing Bea and Delilah and introducing the repressive pole of the dialectic. After several shots alternating the searching mothers with the defiant daughter, Peola is shown in a camera movement that parallels and reverses the original track. She takes money from a man in a straw hat—a small financial transaction which mimics Bea's capability in the world of commerce. They exchange pleasantries, he purchases a cigar, and in this significant shot, as the camera moves laterally to re-center Peola in the frame, the horrified recognition of her mother's presence is matched with silence on the soundtrack. It is at the precise moment when the man disappears from the frame that Peola, isolated and alone, expresses surprise and anger at the sight of her mother offscreen. This is a crucial shot, for what is *off* screen, and hence "unseen," is the "unrepresentable" repressed background of Peola; invisible to the viewer at this precise time, her conflict is understood by what is represented on her face.

This initiates a figural system in which the right edge of the frame, the mother's space, signifies repression (Peola's denial of her color) while the left edge of the frame signifies legitimation in the masculine world (Peola's desire for acceptance). A silent exchange of looks between mother and daughter creates the core of the sequence; the rest of the sequence has either music, dialogue, or ambient noise to attenuate the power of the image. Here the emphatic silence underscores the interplay of desire and repression which forms the central conflict of the film. The following shot maintains the association of desire with the left frame edge, repression with the right, as Delilah looks offscreen left, toward the object of maternal desire, her daughter. In the final shot of the sequence, the parallel between the right edge and repression is maintained, as the restaurant owner (observing Bea comforting Delilah) represents the social world of legitimate authority, that order which does not sanction the violation involved in trying to "pass" for white. It is thus by means of a powerful visual exchange that Stahl affords Peola the prominence denied her by the narrative text.

The second sequence reformulates Peola's conflict in other terms. Here Peola's desire for autonomy in the white world is viewed as unnatural, against the essential order of things. When Delilah pleads eloquently (in what must be the most quotable moment in the film)—"I can't give up my baby. . . . You can't ask your mammy to do this. I ain't no white mother. It's too much to ask. I ain't got the spiritual strength to beat it. I can't hang on no cross. You can't ask me to unborn my own child!"—she is evoking the perennial association of woman with the forces and processes of the physical world (and aligning it to the spiritual one as well). It is the culmination of a series of statements in the film which associate Delilah, motherhood, and acceptance of blackness, with nature, essence, and femininity ("Cookin's natural with me." "It ain't romantic to want a man, just natural." And to Peola, "He made you black. Don't be tellin' Him what to do."). It is in this sense that Peola's struggle for her own definition of herself—her own definition of herself as female—is at the same time a refutation of established dictates which traditionally associate woman with an essential naturalness. This equation of femininity, naturalness, and maternity is reinforced in another way throughout the film. In what recurs as an almost hypnotizing refrain, Delilah repeats, "I'm your *Mammy,*" at three crucial points in the film—at her daughter's first adult expression of rejection of her race, in the sequence just noted, and finally on her deathbed. This poetic reiteration, like a litany that weaves itself through the moments of narrative crisis in the film, seals the compact between psyche and culture that gives the film its articulating conflict.

Sirk brings the *sexual* nature of the mulatto woman's transgression to the fore, and this is my point. For, concomitant with the explicit social consciousness of the Sirk text is a recognition of sexual difference as the founding fact of all cultural processes, and this is elaborated in the emphatically sexual content of Sarah Jane's revolt. Three sequences demonstrate the way in which Sarah Jane's resistance is figured in terms of a highly codified definition of female sexuality, a definition associated with performance, spectacle, and visual display. They form a continuum from adolescent sexuality to an excessive manifestation of sexual objectification in its most blatant expression, as Sarah Jane performs in a sleazy nightclub. As such, the three sequences serve to reinforce the correspondence between femininity and racial otherness which, I have maintained, is at the center of each film's problematic, when this is understood as the mulatto woman's story.

The first sequence takes place in the teenage Susie's bedroom, as Sarah Jane tells Susie about her boyfriend. In what can be read as a juvenile parodic striptease, borrowing iconography from *Gilda* (Hayworth's astonishing first appearance in the film, beaming as she shakes her mane of hair, "Me, decent?"), Sarah Jane undresses, dances, slinks, reclines in her slip. A showgirl-in-training, she performs for an imaginary audience, as the only viewer to her "dance" is her teenage confidante, Susie. This is prelude to a conversation in which she reveals that her rebellion against her blackness has been initiated by her sexuality.

Sarah Jane:　"He's white, and if he ever finds out about me—I'll kill myself. And if I have to be colored, then I want to die."

Susie: We've always talked things over, but you've never told me this before."

Sarah Jane: Because I've never had a boyfriend before."

Here the sin of "passing" is linked intimately (and explicitly) with sexuality; racial awareness emerges with new force because of the desire to be loved by a man. Sarah Jane reflects about her mother: "She can't help her color, but I can and I will . . ." And then with determination, about her boyfriend, she says, "I'm going to be everything he thinks I am!" This implies that for Sarah Jane, acceptance of adult female sexuality is based on denial of race, on deception, and conversely, that racial self-hatred emerges with sexuality. Finally, a horrified Susie says, "If my mama ever found out, she'd never stand for it." To which Sarah Jane replies, "I don't care. Your mother doesn't own me." Here, importantly, and finally, the maternal relationship is converted to one based on class; Sarah Jane's racial awareness, as well as her sexual awareness, become a form of class-consciousness, determined out of a situation of oppression. In this way the association of maternity and ethnicity first expressed in those sequences of Stahl's film here become politicized and sexualized in a manner corresponding to the social vision of Sirk.

The second sequence under discussion depicts Sarah Jane serving canapes to Lora and her guests, balancing the tray on her head and drawling in an exaggerated Southern accent, "Here's a mess of crawfish fo' yo', Miz Lora," and responding to Lora's outraged question ("Where did you learn that little trick?") with "I l'arned it from my Mammy, who l'arned it from her Massah, 'fore she belonged to you!" Sarah Jane's grotesque parody of blackness, servitude, and femininity falls into the articulating framework of the film which has established an equivalence between woman and spectacle. The instances of inscription of the visual are too numerous to fully acknowledge here, but briefly they include Lora Meredith's career (which goes from advertizing icon to the more sanctioned forms of sexual objectification as star of stage and screen); Sarah Jane's career as a night-club performer (an ironic and perverse version of this); Steve's work as a photographer ("My camera could have a love affair with you") which becomes established through his first photo of Lora ("Mother in Distress"); a world populated by agents, writers, publicists, and others who trade in the performance of the female star. Here, with the hors d'oeuvres, Sarah Jane's spectacle of degradation is prompted by a desire to manipulate the codes of race ("You and my mother are so anxious for me to be colored, I was going to show you I could be"). And as she adopts a strategy of posing, of self-conscious mimicry, exaggeratedly performing the social dictates for a woman of her color, the text itself uses this parody to foreground the fact that race is, above all, a matter of social construction. What makes Sarah Jane black or white is in fact socially defined, and in this sense, race is seen to be an effect of discourse. By the end of the film, however,

Sarah Jane no longer resists her determined social position; rather, she assumes her black identity by fitting into the "family" in her designated place. And as a servant, her mother's successor, she is no longer capable of the rebellion of parodic performance, nor is it necessary. She has accepted the definition of blackness which, in the sequence of the canapes, had been crucially hers to resist.

Finally, the sequence in which Sarah Jane performs in a sleazy night-club is one of the most memorable and compelling parodies in film history. As Annie goes in search of her daughter and finds her performing in an unsavory dive, she becomes a forced witness to Sarah Jane's soft-core spectacle, a shadowy figure of despair among the bloated faces of leering men. For although Sarah Jane desires legitimation as a white woman, her only currency in this transaction is her sexuality. She becomes the ultimate mimic, manipulating the codes of sexual behavior in an attempt to dictate her own social position, an impossible task. This manipulation is doomed to failure, for Sarah Jane can only conceive of assimilation as "acting a part" (in this sense the night-club performance is on a continuum with that in the bedroom and the one at cocktail hour). Because she has so fervently resisted the terms of "propriety" for black females, she is incapable of understanding those terms for whites. Thus her assertion of identity becomes a mere parody of a highly conventional notion of female sexuality already existing in the dominant culture. As such it can provide no true liberation, but only the imitation of revolt. This leads to the first confrontation between mother and daughter, and the latter's adult denial of race (and thus it recalls the sequence in which Delilah intrudes on Peola's job as cashier). Each daughter is concerned with "passing" not only as a white person, but as an adult female in a world of men. Here in the night club (as in the restaurant of Stahl's film) rejection of the mother bespeaks a desire for the self.

The lyrics to Sarah Jane's song clearly evoke the symbolic register of the psyche, a fact which reinforces the psychoanalytic interpretation connecting the sexual and the social: "Empty is the saddest, loneliest word . . ." "An empty purse can make a good girl bad, so fill me up with what I formerly had." It is possible to see this as a Song of the Symbolic, in which the castrated woman is seen as lacking, always partial, never whole. This adds another dimension to the parody of Sarah Jane's performance: It is almost as if, in a repetition of her statement about color to Lora after the hors d'oeuvres, she is saying "I am so anxious to be a woman, I wanted to show that I could be . . ." From the moment she sings this song, we know that her revolt has failed. For just as Sarah Jane cannot escape her blackness, she is equally prevented from escaping her symbolic positioning as a woman. Her options are the options of the culture—wife, mother, daughter—and these are circumscribed and defined by her race.

The foregoing analyses have demonstrated a parallel between racial and sexual otherness, a radical alterity which is expressed textually in the figure of the mulatto in the two versions of *Imitation of Life*. Peola and Sarah Jane deny their race, and in so doing they deny their sex as well. For it is in the figure of the mammy that blackness becomes associated with femininity, the matrilineal heritage of the female, regardless of her race. In each version, when this mammy goes to reclaim her daughter, this "return of the repressed" becomes inscribed as a resurgence of the feminine. For as Peola cries, "It's because of you, you *made* me black! I won't be black!" she is expressing both the racial self-hatred of the mulatto and the sexual self-hatred of the female in patriarchal culture. Race and sex forever doom these characters to alien status in patriarchal society. Doubly determined by an existence as cultural other, the black woman's social marginality is nevertheless textually pre-eminent in *Imitation of Life,* a disturbing force which engenders, in each of its versions, the very soul of both films' tragic core.

Filmography and Bibliography

Sirk Filmography, 1934–1959

The films included in this filmography are works that Sirk directed, completed, and for which he was credited. The dates given for each film represent *release* dates. (If a British release date for Sirk's American films preceded the American release date, the film was dated to reflect the earliest release. The dates of the German films are based on Berlin releases.) For more detailed credits on these films and for information concerning unfinished projects, see Jon Halliday's *Sirk on Sirk* (New York: Viking, 1972), 141–172 ("Biofilmography").

European Period

1934   *Der Eingebildete Kranke* [*The Imaginary Invalid*]
Based on Molière's *Le Malade imaginaire*.

Dreimal Liebe [*Three Times Love*]

[*Third short film*, title unknown]

1935   *April, April*
Screenplay by H. W. Litschke and Rudo Ritter.

'T was één April [*It Was in April*]
(Dutch-language version of *April, April*).
Codirected by Jacques van Pol.

Das Mädchen vom Moorhof [*The Girl from the Marsh Croft*]
Screenplay by Lothar M. Mayring, from the novel by Selma Lagerlöf.

Stützen der Gesellschaft [*Pillars of Society*]
Screenplay by Dr. Georg C. Klaren and Peter Gillman, from the play *Pillars of Society* by Henrik Ibsen.

1936   *Schlussakkord* [*Final Accord*]
Screenplay by Kurt Heuser, Detlef Sierck (Douglas Sirk)

Das Hofkonzert [*The Court Concert*]
Screenplay by Franz Wallner-Basté and Detlef Sierck, from the play *Das Kleine Hofkonzert* by Paul Verhoeven and Toni Impekoven.

La Chanson de Souvenir [*Song of Remembrance*]
(French-language version of *Das Hofkonzert*).

1937   *Zu Neuen Ufern [Life Begins Anew/To New Shores]*
Screenplay by Detlef Sierck and Kurt Heuser, adapted from the novel by Lovis H. Lorenz.

La Habanera
Screenplay by Gerhard Menzel.

1939   *Accord Final*
Screenplay by I. R. Bay, based on his own story.

Boefje
Screenplay by Detlef Sierck and Carl Zuckmayer, from the novel by M. J. Brusse.

American Period

1943   *Hitler's Madam*
Screenplay by Peretz Hirshbein, Melvin Levy, and Doris Malloy, from a story by Emil Ludwig and Albrecht Joseph and *Hangman's Village* by Bart Lytton.

1944   *Summer Storm*
Screenplay by Rowland Leigh and Douglas Sirk, from the adaptation by Douglas Sirk and Michael O'Hara [Douglas Sirk] of *The Shooting Party* by Anton Chekhov.

1946   *A Scandal in Paris*
Screenplay by Ellis St. Joseph, based on *Memoirs* of François Eugène Vidocq.

1947   *Lured [Personal Column-G.B.]*
Screenplay by Leo Rosten, from a story by Jacques Campaneez, Ernest Neuville, and Simon Gantillon.

1948   *Sleep, My Love*
Screenplay by St. Clair McKelway

and Leo Rosten, from a story by Leo Rosten.

Slightly French
Screenplay by Karen de Wolf, from a story by Herbert Fields.

1949   *Shockproof*
Screenplay by Helen Deutsch and Samuel Fuller.

1950   *Mystery Submarine*
Screenplay by Ralph Dietrich and George W. George, from a story by George W. George and George F. Slavin.

1951   *The First Legion*
Screenplay by Emmet Lavery, from his play.

Thunder on the Hill [Bonaventure-G.B.]
Screenplay by Oscar Saul and Andrew Solt, from the play *Bonaventure* by Charlotte Hastins.

The Lady Pays Off
Screenplay by Frank Gill, Jr., and Albert J. Cohen.

Weekend with Father
Screenplay by Joseph Hoffman, from a story by George F. Slavin and George W. George.

1952   *Has Anybody Seen My Gal?*
Screenplay by Joseph Hoffman, based on a story by Eleanor H. Porter.

No Room for the Groom
Screenplay by Joseph Hoffman, based on the novel *My True Love* by Darwin L. Teilhet.

1953   *Meet Me at the Fair*
Screenplay by Irving Wallace, from the adaptation by Martin Berkeley of

The Great Companions by Gene Markey.

Take Me to Town
Screenplay by Richard Morris, from his story *Flame of Timberline*.

All I Desire
Screenplay by James Gunn and Robert Blees, from the novel *Stopover* by Carol Brink, adapted by Gina Kaus.

1954 *Taza, Son of Cochise*
Screenplay by George Zuckerman, adapted by Gerald Drayson Adams from his own story.

Magnificent Obsession
Screenplay by Robert Blees, from the novel by Lloyd C. Douglas and the script by Sarah Y. Mason and Victor Heerman, adapted by Wells Root.

Sign of the Pagan
Screenplay by Oscar Brodney and Barre Lyndon.

1955 *Captain Lightfoot*
Screenplay by W. R. Burnett and Oscar Brodney, adapted from his own novel by W. R. Burnett.

All That Heaven Allows
Screenplay by Peg Fenwick, from a story by Edna Lee and Harry Lee.

1956 *There's Always Tomorrow*
Screenplay by Bernard C. Schoenfeld, based on a story by Ursula Parrott.

Written on the Wind
Screenplay by George Zuckerman, from the novel by Robert Wilder.

1957 *Battle Hymn*
Screenplay by Charles Grayson and Vincent B. Evans, based on the true story of Colonel Dean Hess, later written into a book entitled *Battle Hymn*.

Interlude
Screenplay by Daniel Fuchs and Franklin Coon, adapted by Inez Cocke from the scenario by Dwight Taylor, loosely derived from the novel *Serenade* by James Cain.

The Tarnished Angels
Screenplay by George Zuckerman, from the novel *Pylon* by William Faulkner.

1958 *A Time to Love and a Time to Die*
Screenplay by Orin Jannings, from the novel by Erich Maria Remarque.

1959 *Imitation of Life*
Screenplay by Eleanore Griffin and Allan Scott, from the novel by Fannie Hurst.

Selected Bibliography

Note: This bibliography concentrates on the criticism in the English and French languages.

Affron, Charles. "Performing Performing: Irony and Affect." *Cinema Journal* 20, no. 1 (Fall 1980): 42–52.

Almendarez, Valentin. "*Imitation of Life*." *Cinema Texas Program Notes* 9, no. 4 (26 November 1975). [Published by the University of Texas, Austin.]

Amiel, V. "Quelques leçons à faire pleurer (sur *Mirage de la vie*)." *Positif*, no. 259 (September 1982): 19–20.

Beylie, C. "Frank, Douglas, Orson, et les autres." *Cahiers du Cinéma*, no. 319 (January 1981): 40–43.

Biette, Jean-Claude. "Les noms de l'auteur." *Cahiers du Cinéma*, no. 293 (October 1978): 23–30.

———. and Dominique Rabourdin. "Entretien avec Douglas Sirk." *Cinéma* [Paris], no. 238 (October 1978): 10–31.

Bleys, J. P. "Quand Douglas Sirk s'appelait Detlef Sierck." *Cahiers Cinématheque,* no. 32 (Spring 1981): 79–85.

Bourget, Eithne. "Une surface de verre." *Positif,* no. 229 (April 1980): 54–55.

———. and Jean-Loup Bourget. "Note sur Sirk et le theatre." *Positif,* no. 142 (September 1972): 63–67.

Bourget, Jean-Loup. "L'apocalypse selon Douglas Sirk." *Positif,* no. 142 (September 1972): 55–62.

———. *Douglas Sirk*. Paris: Edilig, 1984.

———. "Situation de Sirk." *Positif,* no. 137 (April 1972): 35–46.

———. "Vers de nouveaux rivages: Les débuts americains de Douglas Sirk." *Positif,* no. 281–282 (July–August 1984): 57–69.

Bright Lights 2, no. 2 (Winter 1977–78) [Special issue on Sirk]. Includes: Andrew Sarris, "Sarris on Sirk" (p. 5); Jane Stern, "Two Weeks in Another Town," pp. 28–29. Michael Stern, "Interview," pp. 29–34.

Brunner, Mathias and Kathryn Bigelow. "Douglas Sirk." *Interview* (July 1982).

Butler, Jeremy. *"Imitation of Life:* Style and the Domestic Melodrama." *Jump Cut,* no. 32 (April 1986): 25–28.

———. "Toward a Theory of Cinematic Style: The Remake." Ph.D. dissertation, Northwestern University, 1982.

Byars, Jackie Louise. "Gender Representation in American Family Melodramas of the Nineteen-Fifties." Ph.D. dissertation, University of Texas, Austin, 1983.

Camper, Fred. "The Films of Douglas Sirk." *Screen* 12, no. 2 (Summer 1971): 44–62.

Camper, Fred. *"The Tarnished Angels." Screen* 12, no. 2 (Summer 1971): 68–94.

Carcassone, P. and J. Fieschi. "Les exiles." *Cinématographe,* no. 65 (February 1981): 15–19.

Comolli, Jean-Louis. "Entretien avec Douglas Sirk." *Cahiers du Cinéma,* no. 189 (April 1967): 17–70.

"Courts métrages de Douglas Sirk." *Positif,* no. 227 (February 1980): 53.

Decaux, E. and B. Villien. "Douglas Sirk." *Cinématographe,* no. 80 (July–August 1982): 24–30. (Interview.)

DelGaudio, S. "The Mammy in Hollywood Film: I'd Walk a Million Miles for One o' Her Smiles." *Jump Cut,* no. 28 (April 1983): 23–25.

"Documents on Sirk: with a Postscript by Thomas Elsaessar." *Screen* 12, no. 2 (Summer 1971): 15–28.

"Douglas Sirk." *Positif,* no. 259 (September 1982): 12–31. (Dossier, review articles, and interview with Sirk.)

Douglas Sirk: The Complete American Period. (Catalogue of the University of Connecticut Film Society/ September 11–December 12, 1974).

"Douglas Sirk at 79 in Return to U.S." *Variety* 197 (14 November 1979): 5.

Duval, B. "Douglas Sirk: Le voyant lumineux." *Image et Son* 337 (March 1979): 10–11.

Dyer, Richard. "Four Films of Lana Turner." *Movie* [Britain] 25 (Winter 1977–78): 30–52.

Fassbinder, Rainer Werner. "Six Films by Douglas Sirk." Trans. Thomas Elsaessar. In *Douglas Sirk,* ed. Laura Mulvey and Jon Halliday. Edinburgh: Edinburgh Film Festival, 1972: 95–107. [The article was first published in *Fernschen und Film,* February 1971; it was republished as "Fassbinder on Sirk" in *Film Comment* 11 (November-December 1975). It was also published as "Six films de Douglas Sirk" in *Positif,* no. 183–184 (July-August 1976): 71–78.]

Feuer, Jane. "Melodrama, serial form and television today." *Screen* 25, no. 1 (January-February 1984): 4–16.

Flitterman-Lewis, Sandy. "Imitation(s) of Life: The Black Woman's Double Determination as Troubling 'Other.'" *Literature and Psychology* 35, no. 4 (1988): 44–57.

French, Warren, ed. *Douglas Sirk.* Boston: Twayne, 1979.

Godard, Jean-Luc. "Tears and Speed—Jean-Luc Godard on *A Time to Love and a Time to Die.*" *Screen* 12, no. 2 (Summer 1971): 95–98.

Greenspun, Roger. "Phantom of Liberty: Thoughts on Fassbinder's *Fist-Right of Freedom.*" *Film Comment* 11, no. 6 (November-December 1975): 8–10.

Grosz, Dave. *"The First Legion:* Vision and Perception in Sirk." *Screen* 12, no. 2 (Summer 1971): 99–120.

Halliday, Jon. "Notes on Sirk's German Films." *Screen* 12, no. 2 (Summer 1971): 8–14.

———. *Sirk on Sirk.* New York: Viking, 1972.

Handzo, Stekphen. "Imitation of Lifelessness: Sirk's Ironic Tear-jerker." *Bright Lights* 2, no. 2 (Winter 1977–78): 20–22.

Harvey, James. "Sirkumstantial Evidence." *Film Comment,* no. 14 (July-August 1978): 52–59.

Henry, M. and Y. Tobin. "Entretien avec Douglas Sirk." *Positif,* no. 259 (September 1982): 23–31.

Heung, Marina. "What's the Matter with Sarah Jane?" *Cinema Journal* 26, no. 3 (Spring 1987): 21–43.

"Hommage" [and filmography]. *Cinéma* [Paris], no. 384 (January 1987): 8.

Horrigan, James. "An Analysis of the Construction of an Author: The Example of Douglas Sirk." Ph.D. dissertation, Northwestern University, 1980.

Hurst, Fannie. *Imitation of Life.* New York: Collier & Son, 1933. (Originally published in 1932 by Pictorial Review Company.)

Klinger, Barbara Gail. "Cinema and Social Process: A Contextual Theory of the Cinema and Its Spectators." Ph.D. dissertation, University of Iowa, 1986. (The final chapter focuses on *Written on the Wind.*)

Lehman, Peter. "Thinking with the Heart: An Interview with Douglas Sirk." *Wide Angle* 3, no. 4 (1989): 42–47.

McCourt, James. "Douglas Sirk: Melo Maestro." *Film Comment* 11, no. 6 (November-December 1975): 18–21.

———. "Journals: James McCourt in New York." *Film Comment* 16, no. 2 (March-April 1980): 2, 4.

McKegney, Michael. "Film Favorites: *Imitation of Life.*" *Film Comment* 8, no. 2 (Summer 1972): 71–73.

McNiven, R. D. "The Middle-Class American Home of the Fifties . . . Use of Architecture in Sirk's *All That Heaven Allows.*" *Cinema Journal* 22, no. 4 (1983): 38–57.

Magny, Joel. "Miroir de la vie: la mort de Douglas Sirk." *Cahiers du Cinéma,* no. 392 (February 1987): 42–47.

Masson, A. "Un triste et profond murmure d'applaudissements." *Positif,* no. 259 (September 1982): 12–15.

Menil, A. "L'imitation." *Cinéma-tographe,* no. 80 (July-August 1982): 31–33.

Morrison, S. "Sirk, Scorsese, and Hysteria: A Double(d) Reading." *Cine Action,* no. 6 (Summer/Fall 1986): 17–25.

Mulvey, Laura. "Notes on Sirk and Melodrama." In *Home Is Where the Heart Is: Studies in Melodrama and the Woman's Film,* ed. Christine Gledhill. London: British Film Institute, 1987. [Originally published in *Movie* 25 (Winter 1977/78): 53–57.]

——— and Jon Halliday, eds. *Douglas Sirk.* Edinburgh: Edinburgh Film Festival, 1972.

Nacache, Jacqueline. "Le mirage de la vie." *Cinéma* [Paris], no. 282 (June 1982): 96–97.

Neale, Steve. "Douglas Sirk." *Framework,* no. 5 (Winter 1977): 16–18.

Prokosh, Mike. "*Imitation of Life.*" In Mulvey and Halliday, pp. 89–93.

Pulleine, T. "*Imitation of Life.*" *Monthly Film Bulletin* 48, no. 574 (November 1981): 229.

———. "Stahl into Sirk." *Monthly Film Bulletin* 48, no. 574 (November 1981): 236.

Ruedi, Peter. "*Imitation of Life.*" *Theater Heute* (June 1983); 2–7.

Sarris, Andrew. "Films in Focus: Star Drek." *Village Voice* 25 (17 December 1979): 55.

———. "Sarris on Sirk." *Bright Lights* 2, no. 2 (Winter 1977–78): 5.

Saxton, Christine. "The Collective Voice as Cultural Voice." *Cinema Journal* 26, no. 1 (Fall 1986): 19–30.

Sconce, Jeffrey. "*Imitation of Life.*" *Cinema Texas Program Notes* 27, no. 2 (1 November 1984).

Screen 12, no. 2 (Summer 1971) [Special issue on Sirk].

Selig, Michael. "Contradiction and Reading: Social Class and Sex Class in *Imitation of Life.*" *Wide Angle* 10, no. 4 (1988): 13–23.

Sirk, Douglas. "Journal occulte." *Positif,* no. 281–282 (July-August 1984): 66ff.

———. "Obituary for Rainer Werner Fassbinder." *Framework,* no. 20 (1983): 4–5.

Stern, Jane. "Two Weeks in Another Town." *Bright Lights* 2, no. 2 (Winter 1977–78): 28–29.

Stern, Michael. *Douglas Sirk.* Boston: Twayne, 1979.

———. "Interview." *Bright Lights* 2, no. 2 (Winter 1977–78): 29–34.

———. "Patterns of Power and Potency, Repression and Violence: An Introduction to the Study of Douglas Sirk's Films of the 1950s," *Velvet Light Trap,* no. 16 (Fall 1976).

Tobin, Yann. "Une sequence pour l'éternité." *Positif,* no. 281–282 (July-August 1984): 62–65.

Valot, Jacques. "Mirage de la vie." *La Revue du Cinéma,* no. 373 (June 1982): 63–64.

Willemen, Paul. "Distanciation and Douglas Sirk." In *Douglas Sirk,* ed. Laura Mulvey and Jon Halliday, Edinburgh: Edinburgh Film Festival, 1972. First published in *Screen* 12, no. 2 (Summer 1971): 63–67.

———. "Towards an Analysis of the Sirkian System," *Screen* 13, no. 4 (1972–73): 128–134.